Verse by Verse Commentary on

PROVERBS

Enduring Word Commentary Series

By David Guzik

The grass withers, the flower fades,
but the word of our God stands forever.
Isaiah 40:8

Commentary on Proverbs

Copyright ©2020 by David Guzik

Printed in the United States of America
or in the United Kingdom

Print Edition ISBN: 978-1-939466-56-3

Enduring Word

5662 Calle Real #184

Goleta, CA 93117

Electronic Mail: ewm@enduringword.com

Internet Home Page: www.enduringword.com

Contents

Proverbs 1 – Wisdom's Beginning and Call 7

Proverbs 2 – The Protective Power of Wisdom 19

Proverbs 3 – Wisdom from Trusting God 27

Proverbs 4 – The Path of the Just & the Way of the Wicked 41

Proverbs 5 – Warning Against Adultery 50

Proverbs 6 – Wisdom on Debts & Work, Sin & Seduction 62

Proverbs 7 – The Story of Seduction 73

Proverbs 8 – In Praise of Wisdom 84

Proverbs 9 – Wisdom's Feast and Folly's Funeral 92

Proverbs 10 – Contrasting Lives, Contrasting Destinies 100

Proverbs 11 – Blessings to the Righteous and Upright 113

Proverbs 12 –Words, Deeds, and Destiny 127

Proverbs 13 – The Value of Correction 138

Proverbs 14 – The Contrast Between Wisdom and Folly 152

Proverbs 15 – The Words of the Wise 167

Proverbs 16 – Of Righteousness and Kings 182

Proverbs 17 – Wisdom, Justice, and Family 198

Proverbs 18 – Wisdom in Getting Along with Others 211

Proverbs 19 – Fools and Family Life 226

Proverbs 20 – Wisdom, Weights, and Wickedness 239

Proverbs 21 – Peace, Prosperity, Preparation 255

Proverbs 22 – Rich and Poor, Raising Children 269

Proverbs 23 – Words of the Wise.....283

Proverbs 24 – Wisdom, Love, and Respect.....295

Proverbs 25 – Hezekiah's Collection of Solomon's Proverbs.....307

Proverbs 26 – The Nature of the Fool and the Lazy Man.....320

Proverbs 27 – Planning for the Future, Receiving Honor.....331

Proverbs 28 – The Blessings and the Courage of Wisdom.....344

Proverbs 29 – Rulers, Servants, and the Fear of Man.....363

Proverbs 30 – The Wisdom of Agur.....378

Proverbs 31 – The Wisdom of King Lemuel.....393

Bibliography – Page 411
Author's Remarks – Page 413

Proverbs 1 – Wisdom's Beginning and Call

A. Wisdom's beginning.

1. (1) The proverbs of Solomon.

The proverbs of Solomon the son of David, king of Israel:

a. **The proverbs of Solomon**: The Book of Proverbs is a collection of practical life wisdom given mostly in short, memorable statements. Though part of a larger body of wisdom literature that includes Job, Psalms, Ecclesiastes, and the Song of Solomon, the Book of Proverbs is unique.

i. It is unique in its structure, being mostly a collection of individual statements without much context or organization by topic.

ii. It is unique in its theology, being concerned with practical life wisdom more than ideas about God and His work of salvation.

iii. Proverbs is also unique in its connection with the secular literature of its time. Neighboring kingdoms had their own collections of wisdom literature, and in some places, there are significant similarities to these writings.

iv. As Ross notes, "The genre of wisdom literature was common in the ancient world, and a copious amount of material comes from ancient Egypt." Some of the Egyptian works are titled:

- *Instruction of Ptah-hotep.*
- *Teaching of Amenemope.*
- *Instruction of Ani.*

Some of the Babylonian works are titled:

- *Instruction of Shuruppak.*
- *Counsels of Wisdom.*
- *Words of Ahiqar.*

v. There are several sections of Proverbs (22:17-23:14, 22:23, 22:26-27 are examples) that seem to be borrowed from *The Teaching of Amenemope*, an ancient Egyptian writing. There is debate as to who borrowed whom, but most scholars believe *Amenemope* is earlier.

vi. "If Proverbs is the borrower here, the borrowing is not slavish but free and creative. Egyptian jewels, as at the Exodus, have been re-set to their advantage by Israelite workmen and put to finer use." (Kidner)

b. **The proverbs**: Proverbs teach wisdom through short points and principles but should not be regarded as "laws" or even universal promises.

i. "Proverbs are wonderfully successful at being what they are: *proverbs.* They are not failed prophecies or systematic theologies. Proverbs by design lays out pointed observations, meant to be memorized and pondered, not always intended to be applied 'across the board' to every situation without qualification." (Phillips)

ii. "Naturally [proverbs] generalize, as a proverb must, and may therefore be charged with making life too tidy to be true. But nobody objects to this in secular sayings, for the very form demands a sweeping statement and looks for a hearer with his wits about him. We need no telling that a maxim like 'Many hands make light work' is not the last word on the subject, since 'Too many cooks spoil the broth.'" (Kidner)

iii. "Proverbs itself makes this clear. A proverb is not a magical formula, bringing wisdom and blessing by incantation: 'Like a lame man's legs, which hang useless, is a proverb in the mouth of fools' (Prov. 26:7)." (Phillips)

iv. Proverbs rarely quotes other parts of the Hebrew Scriptures, such as the *torah* or law. "An analogy to this is American folk wisdom which, although often dominated by Christian morality and presuppositions, contains few allusions to the Bible or Christian theology." (Garrett)

c. **The proverbs of Solomon**: Solomon was the king of Israel famous for his wisdom. In 1 Kings 3:3-13 Solomon asked God for wisdom to lead God's people and God answered that prayer. 1 Kings then presents a remarkable demonstration of Solomon's wisdom, seen in his response to the problem of the two women and the deceased son (1 Kings 3:16-28).

i. There is also this description of Solomon's wisdom: *He spoke three thousand proverbs, and his songs were one thousand and five. Also he spoke of trees, from the cedar tree of Lebanon even to the hyssop that springs out of the wall; he spoke also of animals, of birds, of creeping things, and of fish. And men of all nations, from all the kings of the earth who had heard of his wisdom, came to hear the wisdom of Solomon.* (1 Kings 4:32-34)

ii. The opening, **the proverbs of Solomon** should not be taken to mean that Solomon was the author of all these proverbs. There are a few other authors specifically mentioned. Yet, it may well be that Solomon collected all these other proverbs and set them in his book. Whether Solomon was the collector or some unnamed later person, we can't know for certain.

iii. "The book tells us that it is the work of several authors. Three of these are named (Solomon, Agur and Lemuel), others are mentioned collectively as 'Wise Men', and at least one section of the book (the last) is anonymous." (Kidner)

iv. Yet, the prominence of **Solomon** in these wonderful statements of wisdom gives the reader pause. We know that this remarkably wise man did not finish his life in wisdom.

2. (2-6) The purpose of the Book of Proverbs.

To know wisdom and instruction,
To perceive the words of understanding,
To receive the instruction of wisdom,
Justice, judgment, and equity;
To give prudence to the simple,
To the young man knowledge and discretion—
A wise *man* will hear and increase learning,
And a man of understanding will attain wise counsel,
To understand a proverb and an enigma,
The words of the wise and their riddles.

a. **To know wisdom and instruction**: In the opening of his collection of proverbs, Solomon explained the purpose of these sayings of wisdom. They are intended to give the attentive reader **wisdom**, **instruction**, perception, and **understanding**.

i. **To know wisdom**: "We're living in the 'information age,' but we certainly aren't living in the 'age of wisdom.' Many people who are wizards with their computers seem to be amateurs when it comes to making a success out of their lives." (Wiersbe)

b. **To perceive the words of understanding**: The reference to *sight* (as also in Proverbs 3:21) implies that these words of wisdom could be *read* and were in fact read.

i. "In Sumer and in ancient Egypt, schoolboys wrote down the instruction literature, and in ancient Israel most children were literate (Deut. 6:9; 11:20; Judg. 8:14). With the invention of the alphabet in the first half of the second millennium, any person of average intelligence could learn to read and probably to write within a few weeks. The earliest extant text in Hebrew (ca. 900 B.C.) is a child's text recounting the agricultural calendar. A. Millard says that ancient Hebrew written documents demonstrate that readers and writers were not rare and that few Israelites would have been unaware of writing." (Waltke)

c. **To know wisdom**: It is helpful to remember the difference between **wisdom** and *knowledge*. One may have knowledge without wisdom. Knowledge is the collection of facts; **wisdom** is the right use of what we know for daily living. Knowledge can tell one how financial systems work; **wisdom** manages a budget properly.

> i. "It is probably a safe bet to say that most people today are not much interested in wisdom. They are interested in making money and in having a good time. Some are interested in knowing something, in getting an education. Almost everyone wants to be well liked. But wisdom? The pursuit of wisdom is not a popular ideal." (Boice on Psalm 111)

d. **To receive the instruction of wisdom**: Proverbs is something of a school of wisdom. We come to it with open hearts and minds, receiving its teaching. If we do, it will show as **justice, judgment, and equity** flow from our lives.

> i. "And herein, as one well observeth, the poorest idiot being a sound Christian, goeth beyond the profoundest clerks that are not sanctified, that he hath his own heart instead of a commentary to help him to understand even the most needful points of the Scripture." (Trapp)

e. **To give prudence to the simple**: The **simple** one is uneducated and needs instruction. The wisdom of this book will make the young, inexperienced one know what to do and how to do it in life. It will give **the young man knowledge and discretion**.

> i. One characteristic of the **simple** man is that he is gullible. *The simple believes every word, but the prudent considers well his steps.* (Proverbs 14:15)

> ii. **Simple**: "The word indicates the person whose mind is dangerously open. He is gullible, he is naïve. He may have opinions, but he lacks deeply thought-through and field-tested convictions." (Phillips)

> iii. "The son and the gullible (1:4 and 5) stand on the threshold of full adulthood. The time is at hand when the son and the gullible (vv. 4-5) must make a decisive stand for the godly parents' and sages' world-and-life views and values. Two conflicting worldviews make

their appeal, 'of Wisdom/Folly, Good/Pseudo-Good, Life/Death,' and one must choose between them, for there is no third way." (Waltke)

f. **A wise man will hear and increase learning**: The Book of Proverbs is not only for the simple and inexperienced. Even a **wise man** will find much to help and guide him, if he will only **hear**. Even a **man of understanding** can **attain wise counsel** from Proverbs.

i. "Proverbs is not simply for the naive and the gullible; everyone can grow by its teachings. Discerning people can obtain guidance from this book so that they might continue in the right way." (Ross)

g. **To understand a proverb and an enigma**: The wisdom of the Book of Proverbs can also help us to solve difficult problems and some of the **riddles** of life.

3. (7) The foundation of all wisdom.

The fear of the LORD is the beginning of knowledge,
***But* fools despise wisdom and instruction.**

a. **The fear of the LORD is the beginning of knowledge**: The Book of Proverbs focuses on practical life wisdom more than theological ideas. Yet it is founded on a vital theological principle – that true **knowledge** and wisdom flow from **the fear of the LORD**.

i. This **fear of the LORD** is not a cowering, begging fear. It is the proper reverence that the creature owes to the Creator and that the redeemed owes to the Redeemer. It is the proper respect and honoring of God. Several writers give their definition of **the fear of the LORD**:

- "But what is **the fear of the LORD**? It is that affectionate reverence by which the child of God bends himself humbly and carefully to his Father's law." (Bridges)

- "A worshipping submission to the God of the covenant." (Kidner)

- "'The fear of the Lord' ultimately expresses reverential submission to the Lord's will and thus characterizes a true worshiper." (Ross)

- "*The fear of the Lord* signifies that *religious reverence* which every intelligent being owes to his Creator." (Clarke)

ii. God should be regarded with respect, reverence, and awe. This proper attitude of the creature toward the Creator is **the beginning of knowledge** and wisdom. Wisdom cannot advance further until this starting point is established.

iii. If true wisdom can be simply gained by human effort, energy, and ingenuity (like the rare and precious metals of the earth), then the **fear of the LORD** is not essential to obtaining wisdom. But if it comes from God's revelation, then right relationship with Him is the key to wisdom.

iv. "What the alphabet is to reading, notes to reading music, and numerals to mathematics, the fear of the LORD is to attaining the revealed knowledge of this book." (Waltke)

b. **The beginning of knowledge**: Solomon probably meant **knowledge** here mostly in the sense of *wisdom*. The idea that the fear of the LORD is the beginning of wisdom is also found at Job 28:28, Psalm 111:10, Proverbs 9:10, and Ecclesiastes 12:13.

i. **Beginning** has the sense of "the first and controlling principle, rather than a stage which one leaves behind; cf. Eccl. 12:13." (Kidner)

ii. "The fundamental fact, then, is that in all knowledge, all understanding of life, all interpretation thereof, the fear of Jehovah is the principal thing, the chief part, the central light, apart from which the mind of man gropes in darkness, and misses the way." (Morgan)

iii. "The fall of man was a choosing of what bid fair 'to make one wise' (Gen. 3:6) but flouted the first principle of wisdom, the fear of the Lord." (Kidner)

B. Instruction to a son.

1. (8-9) Appeal to hear and receive the wisdom of parents.

My son, hear the instruction of your father,
And do not forsake the law of your mother;
For they *will be* a graceful ornament on your head,
And chains about your neck.

a. **My son, hear the instruction of your father**: This is a warm and appropriate scene. A **father** speaks to his **son**, encouraging him to receive the wisdom of his parents. It is often the nature of the young to be slow to receive the wisdom of their older generation.

i. The mention of a **son** reminds us of another tragedy or irony regarding the life of Solomon. The man who had 700 wives and 300 concubines left record of only one son, Rehoboam – and he was a fool.

ii. Because both the **father** and the **mother** are mentioned, we know that teaching the children wisdom is the responsibility of both parents.

iii. The mention of **instruction** shows that Solomon understood that children are not to be taught only, or even primarily, through bodily punishment (such as a spanking). Children are regarded as capable of thought, learning, and obedience beyond blind submission.

b. **They will be a graceful ornament on your head**: The idea is that the **instruction** and **law** given from parent to child will adorn the life of their children, if they will only receive it. Like a crown **on your head** or **chains about the neck**, such wisdom will be a reward to a younger generation.

2. (10-14) The enticement of sinners.

My son, if sinners entice you,
Do not consent.
If they say, "Come with us,
Let us lie in wait to *shed* blood;
Let us lurk secretly for the innocent without cause;
Let us swallow them alive like Sheol,
And whole, like those who go down to the Pit;
We shall find all *kinds* of precious possessions,
We shall fill our houses with spoil;
Cast in your lot among us,
Let us all have one purse"—

a. **My son, if sinners entice you**: Solomon first warned his son about the danger of bad company. The actions of some people clearly reveal them to be **sinners**, more than in the general sense in which we are all sinners. The young must resist the enticements of these men.

i. Significantly, this *first* instruction and warning in the book of Proverbs speaks to the company we keep and the friendships we make. There are few more powerful forces and influences upon our life than the friends we choose. It has been said, *show me your friends and I can see your future*. It speaks to the great need for God's people to be more careful and wiser in their choice of friends.

ii. **Do not consent**: "They can do thee no harm unless thy will join in with them…. Not even the devil himself can lead a man into sin till he *consents*. Were it not so, how could God judge the world?" (Clarke)

b. **Come with us, let us lie in wait to shed blood**: When the wicked plot their evil actions, the wise son will not **consent**. He will distance himself from them, no matter what the promised or potential gain may be (**we shall fill our houses with spoil**).

i. Part of their enticement was simply the sense of belonging: **come with us**. "Apparently in ancient Israel, no less than in the modern world, the comradeship, easy money, and feeling of empowerment offered by gangs was a strong temptation to the young man who felt overwhelmed by the difficulties of the life he confronted every day." (Garrett)

ii. Solomon described the words of **sinners** in terms of their real meaning and effect, and not what they actually said. Surely such sinners would appeal to riches and quick gain, and not merely invite this one to **shed blood**. Solomon tells us to hear what people *mean* with such promises of quick and easy riches, not only what they *say*.

3. (15-19) The end that will come upon the plotters of violence.

My son, do not walk in the way with them,
Keep your foot from their path;
For their feet run to evil,
And they make haste to shed blood.
Surely, in vain the net is spread
In the sight of any bird;
But they lie in wait for their *own* blood,
They lurk secretly for their *own* lives.
So *are* the ways of everyone who is greedy for gain;
It takes away the life of its owners.

a. **Do not walk in the way with them**: The guidance from father to son was simple and clear. Stay away from the wicked and all their plotting, **for their feet run to evil**.

i. **In vain the net is spread in the sight of the bird**: "The bird does not see any connection between the net and what is scattered on it; he just sees food that is free for the taking. In the process he is trapped and killed. In the same way, the gang cannot see the connection between their acts of robbery and the fate that entraps them." (Garrett)

ii. Tragically, Solomon's company with sinners – in the form of his wives who were given to idolatry – became a trap he himself was caught in.

b. **They lie in wait for their own blood**: Ultimately, the gain promised by the wicked can never be fulfilled. They say, *let us lie in wait to shed blood* (Proverbs 1:11), but in fact they are the hunted. They seek to take the life and livelihood of others, but their greed **takes away the life of its owners**.

C. Wisdom calls to the simple ones.

1. (20-21) Wisdom's public call.

Wisdom calls aloud outside;
She raises her voice in the open squares.
She cries out in the chief concourses,

At the openings of the gates in the city
She speaks her words:

a. **Wisdom calls aloud outside**: Solomon presents wisdom as a person, a woman who offers her guidance and help to the world. Her cry is **aloud** but often ignored.

i. "And this wisdom is said to cry with a loud voice, to intimate both God's earnestness in inviting sinners to repentance, and their inexcusableness if they do not hear such loud cries." (Poole)

ii. "The greatest tragedy is that there's so much noise that *people can't hear the things they really need to hear*. God is trying to get through to them with the voice of wisdom, but all they hear are the confused communications clutter, foolish voices that lead them farther away from the truth." (Wiersbe)

b. **Outside…in the open squares…. the chief concourses…the gates in the city**: Wisdom presents herself to everyone in every place. She offers her help to anyone who will give attention to **her words**.

i. "Here the open proclamation…to make it clear that the offer of wisdom is to the man in the street, and for the business of living, not to an élite for the pursuit of scholarship." (Kidner)

2. (22-27) An appeal to the simple ones.

"How long, you simple ones, will you love simplicity?
For scorners delight in their scorning,
And fools hate knowledge.
Turn at my rebuke;
Surely I will pour out my spirit on you;
I will make my words known to you.
Because I have called and you refused,
I have stretched out my hand and no one regarded,
Because you disdained all my counsel,
And would have none of my rebuke,
I also will laugh at your calamity;
I will mock when your terror comes,
When your terror comes like a storm,
And your destruction comes like a whirlwind,
When distress and anguish come upon you.

a. **How long, you simple ones, will you love simplicity?** Wisdom begins her appeal by addressing those who most need her help – the **simple ones**, those who are untrained in the ways of wisdom.

i. She challenged those without wisdom to give account for their lack, asking "**How long?**" How many more weeks, months, or years will the **simple ones** reject or neglect wisdom's help?

ii. "If the call has been extended for some time—'How long?' (v. 22; see also Isaiah 65:2)—then this warning is given for a prolonged refusal. Because wisdom has been continually rejected, wisdom will laugh at the calamity of those who have rejected it." (Ross)

iii. The problem with these **simple ones** was that they *loved* their **simplicity**. They preferred their foolish ignorance than the effort and correction required by the love and pursuit of wisdom.

b. **For scorners delight in their scorning, and fools hate knowledge**: This *scorn* describes those who boastfully reject and despise God's wisdom. They **love** their simplicity and scorn, and they **hate knowledge**.

i. "*Scorners* think they know everything (Proverbs 21:24) and laugh at the things that are really important. While the simple one has a blank look on his face, the scorner wears a sneer." (Wiersbe)

ii. "*Fools* are people who are ignorant of truth because they're dull and stubborn. Their problem isn't a low IQ or poor education; their problem is a lack of spiritual desire to seek and find God's wisdom." (Wiersbe)

iii. We can see a downward progression. You started gullible, then became a fool, and ended up a scorner (mocker).

c. **Turn at my rebuke; surely I will pour out my spirit on you**: The embrace of wisdom begins with a **turn**. One must be willing to change direction from the pursuit of foolishness and turn towards God and His wisdom. This response to wisdom's **rebuke** invites wisdom to **pour** itself out.

i. It seems that the description here is of the *spirit of wisdom*, not specifically the Holy Spirit. The two concepts do not contradict each other, but they are also not exactly the same.

d. **Because I have called and you refused**: This is the **rebuke** that wisdom offered. She promised that if she were rejected, she would **laugh at your calamity**. Rejected wisdom has nothing to offer the fool when **destruction comes like a whirlwind**.

i. "Wisdom does not laugh at disaster, but at the triumph of what is right over what is wrong *when your disaster happens*." (Waltke)

3. (28-33) The consequences of wisdom rejected.

"Then they will call on me, but I will not answer;
They will seek me diligently, but they will not find me.
Because they hated knowledge
And did not choose the fear of the LORD,
They would have none of my counsel
And despised my every rebuke.
Therefore they shall eat the fruit of their own way,
And be filled to the full with their own fancies.
For the turning away of the simple will slay them,
And the complacency of fools will destroy them;
But whoever listens to me will dwell safely,
And will be secure, without fear of evil."

a. **They will call on me, but I will not answer**: When wisdom is rejected, she has no alternative plan for the fool. In the time of crisis, the fool cannot expect to beg for and receive instant wisdom (**they will seek me diligently, but they will not find me**).

b. **And did not choose the fear of the LORD**: Since this **fear of the LORD** is the beginning of wisdom and knowledge (Proverbs 1:7, Job 28:28, Psalm 111:10, Proverbs 9:10, and Ecclesiastes 12:13), to reject this respect of God is to reject wisdom.

c. **Therefore they shall eat the fruit of their own way**: The consequences of rejecting wisdom cannot be avoided. The end result of this love of foolishness and scorn will be death (**will slay them**) and destruction (**will destroy them**).

i. "Eat as they baked, drink as they brewed. They that sow the wind of iniquity, shall reap the whirlwind of misery." (Trapp)

ii. **Turning away**: "The eleven other occurrences of *turning away* are all in Hosea or Jeremiah, always with reference to Israel's apostasy, faithlessness, and backsliding from God and from the Mosaic covenant." (Waltke)

iii. **Their own way**: "The reason for the sinner's ruin is placed again at his own door. He is wayward since he turns away from wisdom's beckoning voice. He despises the only cure." (Bridges)

iv. "If, elsewhere in the book, fool and scorner appear to be fixed types, it is their fault, not their fate: they are eating *of the fruit of their own way*." (Kidner)

d. **But whoever listens to me will dwell safely**: Those who do listen to wisdom's call will **be secure, without fear of evil**. Their fear of the LORD resulted in their having no **fear of evil**.

i. "And as a wicked man's mind is oft full of anxiety in the midst of all his outward prosperity and glory, so the mind of a good man is filled with peace and joy, even when his outward man is exposed to many troubles." (Poole)

ii. **Without fear of evil**: "*Death* shall lose its terrors, and become the Father's servant, ushering you into His presence. *Pain* and *suffering* shall but cast into relief the stars of Divine promise. *Poverty* will have no pangs, and no storms, no alarms." (Meyer)

Proverbs 2 – The Protective Power of Wisdom

Proverbs 2 is a unit to itself. "The 'alphabetic' poem is a single sentence consisting of 22 verses, matching the number of letters in the Hebrew alphabet, probably to suggest its completeness." (Bruce Waltke)

A. God's gift of wisdom.

1. (1-5) The search for wisdom.

> **My son, if you receive my words,**
> **And treasure my commands within you,**
> **So that you incline your ear to wisdom,**
> ***And* apply your heart to understanding;**
> **Yes, if you cry out for discernment,**
> ***And* lift up your voice for understanding,**
> **If you seek her as silver,**
> **And search for her as *for* hidden treasures;**
> **Then you will understand the fear of the Lord,**
> **And find the knowledge of God.**

a. **My son, if you receive my words**: In the first chapter of Proverbs Solomon began to speak to his son, instructing him in the ways of wisdom. Here he continues the teaching, appealing to his son to **receive my words** and to **treasure my commands**. Wisdom can never benefit us if it is not received and treasured.

i. "The search, strenuous as it must be, is not unguided. Its starting-point is revelation—specific (*words*) and practical (*commandments*); its method is not one of free speculation, but of treasuring and exploring received teachings so as to penetrate to their principles." (Kidner)

ii. "'Accept' [**receive**] is paralleled with 'store up' [**treasure**], a figure that implies that most teaching cannot be used immediately but that some time will pass before education's effects are felt." (Ross)

iii. **Treasure my commands within you**: "God's intention is that you and I make His wisdom our own. We are to learn it from the Bible. Nobody is to know it in our stead. Pastors are charged by God with helping us to grow, but we must make His Word *ours*, so as to keep it 'with' us." (Philipps)

iv. **Treasure my commands within you**: "He who has the rule of his *duty* only in his *Bible* and in his *head*, is not likely to be a steady, consistent character; his heart is not engaged, and his obedience, in any case, can be only *forced*, or done from a *sense of duty*: it is not the obedience of a *loving, dutiful child*, to an *affectionate father*. But he who has the word of God in his *heart*, works *from his heart*; his heart goes with him in all things, and he delights to do the will of his heavenly Father, because *his law is in his heart*." (Clarke)

b. **And apply your heart to understanding**: This implies *effort*. The **heart** must be *applied* to **understanding**. It won't happen by accident. This wisdom, **discernment**, and **understanding** must be sought out as if it were **silver** and **hidden treasures**.

i. In these few verses, Solomon described many ways that we must seek after wisdom.

- Receive.
- Treasure.
- Incline.
- Apply.
- Cry out, lift up the voice.
- Seek, search.

ii. The one who pursues wisdom in this way will not be disappointed. "But this search must be serious, strenuous. The way of wisdom is never revealed to triflers." (Morgan)

iii. "There must be willingness and desire to know (verses Proverbs 2:1-2). To this must be added diligence. The illuminative phrases are 'cry,' 'lift up thy voice,' 'seek,' 'search.' All indicate desire, expressing itself in devotion." (Morgan)

iv. **Apply your heart to understanding**: "Attention of body, intention of mind, and retention of memory, are indispensably desired of all wisdom's scholars; such as King Edward VI, who constantly stood up at the hearing of the word, took notes, which he afterwards diligently perused, and wrought the sermon upon his affections by meditation." (Trapp)

v. **Seek her as silver**: "Refers to silver as mined and smelted, not as a precious metal in its native state." (Waltke)

vi. **If you seek her as silver**: "With the same unwearied diligence, and earnest desire, and patient expectation under all delays, disappointments, and difficulties, which worldlings use in the purchase of riches, or in digging in mines of silver." (Poole)

vii. "How do men seek money? What will they not do to get rich? Reader, seek the salvation of thy soul as earnestly as the covetous man seeks wealth; and be ashamed of thyself, if thou be less in earnest after the *true riches* than he is after *perishing wealth*." (Clarke)

c. **Then you will understand the fear of the LORD**: Solomon established the principle that the **fear of the LORD** is the beginning of knowledge and wisdom (Proverbs 1:7). Here he teaches us that without the *effort* to seek out wisdom, we will lack in our **fear of the LORD** and **knowledge of God**.

i. **The knowledge of God**: "In short, 'knowledge of God' refers to personal intimacy with him through obedience to his word (cf. 1 Samuel 3:7)." (Waltke)

2. (6-9) The benefit of wisdom.

For the LORD gives wisdom;
From His mouth *come* knowledge and understanding;
He stores up sound wisdom for the upright;
***He is* a shield to those who walk uprightly;**
He guards the paths of justice,
And preserves the way of His saints.
Then you will understand righteousness and justice,
Equity *and* every good path.

a. **For the LORD gives wisdom**: This explains why the **fear of the LORD** is the foundation of wisdom, and an essential aspect of the pursuit of wisdom. True **wisdom** is found in Him, and He **gives** it.

b. **From His mouth come knowledge and understanding**: The most significant way God gives wisdom is from the words of **His mouth**. His word reveals **knowledge and understanding**. In His word **He stores up sound wisdom for the upright**.

c. **He is a shield to those who walk uprightly**: God not only gives wisdom in His word; He actively works to defend, guard and preserve those who walk in His ways.

d. **Then you will understand righteousness and justice**: The sense is that we *need* this defense from God to gain this proper **understanding**. There are so many wrong ideas about in the world that we will never hold on to what is wise and true without being defended against the false and foolish.

i. **Then you will understand righteousness and justice**: "He who is taught of God understands the whole law of *justice, mercy, righteousness, and truth*; God has written this on his heart. He who understands these things by *books* only is never likely to practise or profit by them." (Clarke)

ii. **Every good path**: "*Track* (*magal;* see Proverbs 2:15) refers to 'cart tracks,' 'wagon ruts.' While the earth is soft, wagon wheels press the trails that others are obliged to follow after it dries and hardens." (Waltke) We *will* make tracks, ruts, paths for our life – wisdom helps us to make good and useful "ruts" or habits.

B. The protective power of wisdom.

1. (10-11) The general statement.

When wisdom enters your heart,
And knowledge is pleasant to your soul,
Discretion will preserve you;
Understanding will keep you,

a. **When wisdom enters your heart**: Solomon mentioned the idea of *protection* relevant to wisdom (Proverbs 2:7-8). Now he explains that something happens when we gain wisdom; when we value God's **knowledge** (it is **pleasant to your soul**).

i. "Verses 10-11 assert that Wisdom gives both pleasure and surefootedness in life. The more wisdom one learns, the more one desires and enjoys it. The protection wisdom gives, moreover, is that it keeps its follower from making decisions that will later bring only regret." (Garrett)

ii. **Knowledge is pleasant to your soul**: "Spiritual joy mortifies sin. His mouth hankers not after homely provision that hath lately tasted of delicate sustenance. Pleasure there must be in the ways of God, because therein men let out their souls into God, that is the fountain of all good; hence they so infinitely distaste sin's tasteless fooleries." (Trapp)

b. **Discretion will preserve you**: We need God's protection to gain wisdom (Proverbs 2:7-8), but wisdom also protects us. **Understanding will keep you** from many foolish choices and harmful consequences in life.

2. (12-15) Wisdom rescues us from wicked men.

To deliver you from the way of evil,
From the man who speaks perverse things,
From those who leave the paths of uprightness
To walk in the ways of darkness;
Who rejoice in doing evil,
And delight in the perversity of the wicked;
Whose ways *are* crooked,
And *who are* devious in their paths;

a. **To deliver you from the way of evil**: Wisdom will keep us from going evil ways, and from associating with **the man who speaks perverse things**. Our fallen nature may be attracted to **perverse things**, but wisdom will guard us from that path, **from those who leave the paths of righteousness**.

i. "The promised protection is first defined as deliverance from apostate men who have opted for dark and crooked paths instead of the father's bright and straight ways." (Waltke)

b. **Who rejoice in doing evil, and delight in the perversity of the wicked**: Fallen nature is not only attracted to what is evil and perverse, it *rejoices* and *delights* in it. Shame is cast away and what is wrong and twisted is celebrated. This celebration of perversity is not unique to our time, but it certainly marks our present age.

i. **Delight in the perversity of the wicked**: "*They rejoice (yagilu)*, the outward parallel of their joy within, expresses exuberant, enthusiastic, spontaneous shouts of joy, like those heard in bawdy theaters and bloody stadiums." (Waltke)

c. **Whose ways are crooked, and who are devious in their paths**: Wisdom protects us from these evil men. If not protected by wisdom, their **crooked** ways will come to harm us, and we will suffer from their **devious** character.

3. (16-22) Wisdom rescues us from the immoral woman.

To deliver you from the immoral woman,
From the seductress *who* flatters with her words,
Who forsakes the companion of her youth,
And forgets the covenant of her God.
For her house leads down to death,
And her paths to the dead;
None who go to her return,
Nor do they regain the paths of life—
So you may walk in the way of goodness,
And keep *to* the paths of righteousness.
For the upright will dwell in the land,

And the blameless will remain in it;
But the wicked will be cut off from the earth,
And the unfaithful will be uprooted from it.

a. **To deliver you from the immoral woman**: Here Solomon especially spoke to his son (Proverbs 2:1), who could be easily deceived and trapped by **the immoral woman**. Wisdom could protect him from her.

i. The Bible's wisdom is much more sophisticated than much of popular thinking in today's world. Today there is the tendency to view things without nuance; for example, to think of all women as victims to men. This rejects the idea of **the immoral woman**, thinking that if there is a sexual liaison between a man and a woman, *he* must be the perpetrator and *she* must be the victim. The Bible recognizes that human beings and human relationships are far more complicated than that.

ii. **Immoral woman…seductress**: "Both these terms mean literally 'foreigner' or *stranger*, i.e., in such a context (cf. 16b), 'one who is outside the circle of [a man's] proper relations, that is, a harlot or an adulteress'." (Kidner)

b. **The seductress who flatters with her words**: Before Solomon described the **immoral woman** in any other way, he wrote of her as a **seductress** who uses **words** to seduce. The *Song of Solomon* shows us that King Solomon knew the power of the female form, but there is also great power in the flattering **words** of the **seductress**.

i. **Who flatters with her words**: "*Hechelikah*, she that *smooths* with her words. The original intimates the *glib, oily* speeches of a *prostitute*. The English *lick* is supposed to be derived from the original word." (Clarke)

ii. **Flatters**: "Comes from a root whose nominal derivative is used of David's five 'smooth' stones. The verb is used literally only of 'making smooth' metal (Isaiah 41:7). Once (Hosea 10:2) it is used metaphorically of a heart that is 'smooth' (i.e., deceitful)." (Waltke)

iii. "The subtlety of the appeal comes from flattering speech—the adulteress talks smoothly (see Proverbs 5:3). An example of such talk is found in Proverbs 7:14-20." (Ross)

c. **Who forsakes the companion of her youth**: The immoral woman Solomon had in mind had a past record of disloyalty and unfaithfulness. This was evident not only among men (**the companion of her youth**) but even more importantly in relation to God (**who forgets the covenant of her God**).

i. **Forgets the covenant of her God**: "Marriage is a mixed covenant, partly religious and partly civil: the parties tie themselves first to God, and then to one another. The bond is made to God, who also will be ready enough to take the forfeiture." (Trapp)

d. **For her house leads down to death**: *This* is an important part of wisdom's protection, to see where a path **leads**. Time with the flattering **seductress** seems wonderful, but wisdom helps us to understand where it **leads** – and that is **down to death**.

i. **Her house leads down to death**: "But how many, alas! by this means have lost their souls. Fleshly lusts, by a specialty, 'fight against the soul.' [1 Peter 2:12] And nothing hath so much enriched hell, saith one, as beautiful faces." (Trapp)

ii. Matthew Poole wrote of many ways that **her house leads down to death**: "By wasting a man's vital spirits, and shortening his life; by exposing him to many and dangerous diseases, which physicians have declared and proved to be the effects of inordinate lust; as also to the fury of jealous husbands or friends, and sometimes to the sword of civil justice, and undoubtedly, without repentance, to God's wrath and the second death."

iii. **Her house leads down to death**: "The woman who abandons herself to prostitution soon *contracts*, and generally *communicates*, that *disease*, which, above all others, signs the speediest and most effectual *passport* to the *invisible world*." (Clarke)

iv. **Her paths to the dead**: "Not only does she sink down to death, but her paths lead to the 'shades' (NIV, 'the spirits of the dead'). The 'shades' are the inhabitants of Sheol; the term describes the shadowy continuation of those who have lost their vitality and strength." (Ross)

v. **Her paths to the dead**: "Those who enter the house of the immoral woman, on the other hand, find only the ghosts of those who preceded them and discover too late that there is no exit." (Garrett)

e. **None who go to her return**: As with many statements in the Proverbs, this is not an absolute promise, but a true principle. Solomon had seen many go down the path of **death** with an immoral woman, never to **return** to the way of wisdom.

i. **Who go to her**: This phrasing is translated *go in to* [her] in Genesis 16:2 and *came in to* [them] in Genesis 6:4 as specifically referring to sexual intercourse.

ii. A life early given to promiscuity and sexual sin is much more difficult to reclaim. It is far better to never go down such paths. That is why Solomon warned, **none who go to her return**: "Adulterers and whoremongers are very rarely brought to repentance, but are generally hardened by the power and deceitfulness of that lust, and by God's just judgment, peculiarly inflicted upon such persons." (Poole)

f. **The unfaithful will be uprooted**: Solomon reminded his son of the consequences of the path of the seductress. It invites the discipline or the judgment of God, who according to His covenant with Israel promised that **the upright will dwell in the land**, but the **unfaithful will be uprooted from it**. These consequences give us a clear *choice* – one or the other.

i. "There's a price to pay if we would gain spiritual wisdom, but there's an even greater price to pay if we don't gain it. We must walk with God through the study of His Word." (Wiersbe)

ii. **For the upright will dwell in the land**: "Here the wise man speaks after the manner of Moses' law, under which he lived; [Deuteronomy 11:8]." (Trapp)

iii. "Here the wicked will be cut off because they defile the earth and threaten the relationship of the righteous with their God." (Waltke)

Proverbs 3 – Wisdom from Trusting God

A. My son, walk rightly with God.

1. (1-4) Walk rightly with God by valuing His word.

My son, do not forget my law,
But let your heart keep my commands;
For length of days and long life
And peace they will add to you.
Let not mercy and truth forsake you;
Bind them around your neck,
Write them on the tablet of your heart,
***And* so find favor and high esteem**
In the sight of God and man.

a. **Do not forget my law**: Solomon's advice as a father to his **son** in this section begins with a warning to never **forget** God's word (**my law**). Solomon didn't mean "**my law**" in the sense of his own personal decrees, but as God's word that he had internalized and made personal.

b. **Let your heart keep my commands**: Deciding to not **forget** God's word is more than a mental exercise of memory. It is also connected to a life of obedience, in which one does **keep** the **commands** of God. If one mentally remembers God's word yet fails to obey it, we could rightly say he or she has *forgotten* God's **commands**.

i. We note also that this obedience is one of the **heart**. Our goal in obedience is not mere outward conformity to God's will, but a **heart** that loves and obeys Him.

ii. "The heart is the first thing that wanders away from God, and it is also the first thing that returns to God." (Bridges)

c. **They will add to you**: There is a real benefit from this life and heart that obeys God. In principle, life and heart obedience bring **long life** and

peace. This is a blessed combination; **length of days** could be a curse and not a blessing without **peace**.

> i. We say *in principle* because this is largely how Proverbs was written and should be regarded. The principle of Proverbs 3:2 is not an absolute promise; there are some people who truly are given to obedience in both conduct and heart and die relatively young. Some godly persons have trouble living in **peace**. We regard these as true principles, not absolute promises.

d. **Let not mercy and truth forsake you**: Solomon wisely told his son to keep God's loyal love (**mercy**, the great Hebrew word *hesed*) and **truth** close. They should be so close that it would be as if they were a necklace on him at all times (**bind them around your neck**) and written **on the tablet of your heart**.

> i. Matthew Poole observed that **mercy and truth** could be understood both as God's mercy and truth to us and as the mercy and truth that is man's duty to show to others. Both are important and should never be forsaken.

> ii. "Mercy and truth are frequently joined together, as they are in God, as Psalms 25:10 57:3, etc., or in men, as 3:6 20:28 Hosea 4:1, and here." (Poole)

> iii. **Bind them...write them**: "Striking expressions for glorying in, meditating on and (7:3) acting by these principles." (Kidner) "By 'binding' and 'writing' the teacher is stressing that the teachings become a part of the disciple's nature." (Ross)

e. **So find favor**: The blessed, obedient life is magnetic. It enjoys the **favor** of the God it honors and attracts the **favor** of man.

> i. "*Favor* (*hen*, see 1:9), the common word for 'grace,' here denotes the positive disposition of heaven and earth toward the son because of his attractiveness. Like *hesed*, it cannot be compelled; it is extended voluntarily and unilaterally to preserve a valued relationship." (Waltke)

> ii. "This means that others will recognize the competence and intelligence of the wise individual." (Garrett)

> iii. Trapp on having **favor** before **man**: "As did Joseph, Moses, David. He was a man after God's own heart, and whatsoever he did pleased the people. It is God that gives credit; he fashioneth men's opinions, and inclineth their hearts, as Ezra oft acknowledges with much thankfulness. [Ezra 7:27-28]"

2. (5-6) Walk rightly with God by truly trusting Him.

Trust in the LORD with all your heart,
And lean not on your own understanding;
In all your ways acknowledge Him,
And He shall direct your paths.

a. **Trust in the LORD**: Solomon advised his son to live a life of **trust** in Yahweh. Solomon had found that God was *worthy* to be trusted. It is our nature to put our trust in something or someone, even if it is our self. Solomon told us to consciously put our **trust in the LORD**, the covenant God of Abraham, Isaac, and Jacob.

i. "The word translated 'trust' in verse 5 means 'to lie helpless, facedown.' It pictures a servant waiting for the master's command in readiness to obey, or a defeated soldier yielding himself to the conquering general." (Wiersbe)

ii. "To trust in God is to be unbottomed of thyself, and of every creature, and so to lean upon God, that if he fail thee thou sinkest." (Trapp)

b. **With all your heart**: If trust in God is to be true, it must be complete. To put half our trust in God and half our trust in self or something else is really failure to trust the LORD at all. We should endeavor to give God all our conscious trust.

i. "They trust not God at all that do it not alone. He that stands with one foot on a rock, and another foot upon a quicksand, will sink and perish as certainly as he that stands with both feet on a quicksand." (Trapp)

ii. This aspect troubles some because they fear there is some part of their **heart** that is not truly trusting God. We may sympathize with this concern, knowing that as imperfect people it is impossible for us to **trust in the LORD** perfectly. In principle, we gather that Proverbs 3:5-6 does not describe an objectively *perfect* trust in God, but a heart and life that does not consciously reject or defy God with unbelief.

iii. In fact, the following phrases will explain what Solomon intended with the phrase **with all your heart**.

iv. "This trust is not the mere cold assent of enlightened judgment. It is trust…with all your heart. It is a childlike, unwavering confidence in our Father's well-proved wisdom, faithfulness, and love." (Bridges)

c. **Lean not on your own understanding**: Trusting God with all our heart means to decide to put away our **own understanding** and instead to choose to trust God and His understanding, especially as declared in His word.

i. **Lean not**: "*Do not rely,* or lean as on a broken crutch, depicts what is meant by 'trust.'" (Waltke)

ii. "It is on GOD, not on *thyself,* that thou art commanded to *depend.* He who trusts in his own heart is a fool…. *Self-sufficiency* and *self-dependence* have been the ruin of mankind ever since the fall of Adam. The grand sin of the human race is their continual endeavour to *live independently of God.*" (Clarke)

d. **In all your ways acknowledge Him**: Trusting God with all our heart means to honor and **acknowledge** Him in all that we do. It is the choice to "invite" God into our everyday life and conduct. It is to practice the presence of God in the regular and sometimes mundane things that happen every day.

i. **In all your ways acknowledge**: "Ask counsel at his mouth, aim at his glory, be evermore in the sense of his presence, and light of his countenance." (Trapp)

e. **He shall direct your paths**: This is the great principle of God's response towards those who trust Him in the way described in the previous lines. When we **acknowledge Him** in our **ways**, He will **direct** our **paths** in the fulfillment of His will, into what is right before Him and pleasing to us.

i. More than a few are *afraid* to have God **direct** their **paths**. They would much rather direct themselves! This, fundamentally, is the heart that *does not* trust in the LORD with all the heart. The surrendered heart delights in God's direction and in God's paths.

ii. One of the most frequently asked questions among believers is, "How can I know the will of God?" In principle, Solomon gave a wonderful answer in Proverbs 3:5-6. When we:

- Decide to put our trust in the LORD.
- Decide to not trust in our own understanding, but give attention and priority to God's revealed word.
- Decide to acknowledge and honor God in all that we do.

When we do those things, we can trust that God will **direct** our **paths**. We can go forward in peace, believing that through His word, through the leading of the Holy Spirit, through the counsel of others, through godly common sense, and through life circumstances, God will **direct** our **paths**. We will walk along our way of life and come to see that we have been on the path God intended all along.

iii. G. Campbell Morgan gave his own testimony to the truth of Proverbs 3:5-6: "The measure in which I have trusted Jehovah and acknowledged Him, has been the measure of walking in the paths of real life."

3. (7-8) Walk rightly with God by a humble, reverent life.

Do not be wise in your own eyes;
Fear the LORD and depart from evil.
It will be health to your flesh,
And strength to your bones.

a. **Do not be wise in your own eyes**: We can regard this as an explanation of what it means to lean on one's own understanding (Proverbs 3:5). It is to regard *our* wisdom as better and greater than God's.

i. **Do not be wise in your own eyes**: "Be not puffed up with vain conceit of thine own wisdom, as if that were sufficient for the conduct of all thine affairs without direction or assistance from God, or without the advice of others." (Poole)

b. **Fear the LORD and depart from evil**: This is the natural result of trusting God. As we trust Him, we come to know Him better, leading to natural reverence and awe (to **fear the LORD**). As we trust Him, we are drawn more to God and further **from evil**.

c. **It will be health to your flesh**: A life of surrender and trust in God has real benefits to the **health** of the trusting one. It gives a greater sense of peace and **strength** that one would not have *apart* from a life of trust and surrender to God.

i. **Flesh** is literally *navel* and is usually taken as a center point referring to the entire body.

4. (9-10) Walk rightly with God in regard to your possessions.

Honor the LORD with your possessions,
And with the firstfruits of all your increase;
So your barns will be filled with plenty,
And your vats will overflow with new wine.

a. **Honor the LORD with your possessions**: This is another practical way to show that you do *trust in the LORD with all your heart* (Proverbs 3:5). When we truly trust Him, we can **honor** Him with generosity that realizes He is the great provider and God has inexhaustible resources.

i. Many commentators note that the word **honor** has a connection with sacrifice. "Commentaries note that this is the only place where Proverbs alludes to the ceremonial worship.... Proverbs is not so much concerning itself with ceremonial religion here as it is exhorting the reader to demonstrate gratitude toward and confidence in God (rather than in wealth)." (Garrett)

ii. "The third piece of advice is to give back to God some of one's wealth as a sacrifice in recognition that God gave it." (Ross)

b. **With the firstfruits of all your increase**: According to the principle of the sacrifice of the firstfruits, we should give to God the *first* and *best*. If we will truly **honor the Lord** with our giving, it won't be with the last and leftovers.

i. **Firstfruits**: "It takes on the technical sense of offering the best of material things." (Waltke)

ii. The principle of **firstfruits** also means that we give to God in active anticipation that He will provide more. We honor Him by thinking, "I can give You the first and the best because I know You can and will give much more."

iii. "The Old Testament Jews brought the Lord the firstlings of their flocks (Exodus 13:1-2) and the firstfruits of their fields (Leviticus 23:9-14), and in this way acknowledged His goodness and sovereignty." (Wiersbe)

c. **So your barns will be filled with plenty**: This is a wonderful principle. God is the master and distributor of unlimited resources. He knows how to prosper and take care of those who honor Him with the resources He has given to them.

i. **New wine**: "New wine, according to F. S. Fitzsimmonds, 'represents wine made from the first drippings of the juice before the winepress was trodden. As such it would be particularly potent.'" (Waltke)

B. My son, receive the hard lessons of wisdom.

1. (11-12) Receiving correction from God with the right heart.

My son, do not despise the chastening of the Lord,
Nor detest His correction;
For whom the Lord loves He corrects,
Just as a father the son *in whom* he delights.

a. **Do not despise the chastening of the Lord**: In giving advice to his son, Solomon taught him how to regard **correction** or discipline from God, the **chastening of the Lord**.

i. "The word *musar* [**chastening**] signifies *correction, discipline*, and *instruction. Teaching* is essentially necessary to show the man the *way* in which he is to go; *discipline* is necessary to render that *teaching* *effectual*; and, often, *correction* is requisite in order to bring the mind into *submission*, without which it cannot acquire *knowledge*." (Clarke)

ii. "When the father's admonitions are violated, the son can expect the Lord to back it up with a "spanking" to prevent the wrong from becoming habitual." (Waltke)

iii. We may **despise** God's chastening, "By accounting it an unnecessary, and useless, and troublesome thing." (Poole)

iv. The writer to the Hebrews quotes this passage in his encouragement that Christians should endure their own seasons of chastening and the discouragement that often comes with it. They could be encouraged in knowing that such suffering is a sign of sonship.

b. **Nor detest His correction**: This is when God either brings or allows some discomfort or affliction in the life of the believer for the good of:

- Exposing a sin or evil not previously seen.
- Showing the nature of the problem and need to address it.
- Discouraging the previous embrace of the sin or evil.
- Guiding to the rejection of sin or evil and embrace of God's best.

   i. The particular discomfort or affliction could come in many ways. God may do it through the inward conviction of the Holy Spirit. It may come through critics and adversaries. It may come through disappointing and sour circumstances. However it may come, it will not *feel* good, but before God could be allowed to *do* much good in the life of the believer.

   ii. "'Discipline' primarily involves teaching or training rather than punishment for wrongdoing. It is analogous to military training, in which, although the threat of punishment is present, even stern discipline is not necessarily retribution for offenses. Hardship and correction are involved, however, which are always hard to accept." (Garrett)

   iii. "The Lord's discipline is like that in a family, not in a school, let alone in a prison. The Lord corrects his children and does not treat them as criminals. 'I love the rod of my heavenly Father,' exclaimed the saintly Fletcher. 'How gentle are the stripes I feel. How heavy those I deserve.'" (Bridges)

c. **For whom the LORD loves He corrects**: Seen rightly, God's correction of His people is a wonderful sign of His *love*. In our instinctive desire for ease and comfort we often wish God would not correct us. Yet because He

loves and **delights** in us, according to His wisdom He will deal with our sins, weaknesses, and failings.

i. A father who truly loves his children will correct them appropriately. For a father to leave sins and failings uncorrected is not a sign of love; it is a sign of indifference and the selfish disregard that often accompanies indifference.

ii. "C. S. Lewis illustrates the truth by noting that an artist may not take much trouble over a picture drawn to amuse a child, but he takes endless effort over his great work of art that he loves." (Waltke)

iii. "Sometimes He chastens because we have rebelled and need to repent; other times He chastens to keep us from sinning and to prepare us for His special blessing. No matter how much the experience *hurts* us, it will never *harm* us, because God always chastens in love." (Wiersbe)

2. (13-18) The wonderful benefits of God's correction.

Happy *is* the man *who* finds wisdom,
And the man *who* gains understanding;
For her proceeds *are* better than the profits of silver,
And her gain than fine gold.
She *is* more precious than rubies,
And all the things you may desire cannot compare with her.
Length of days *is* in her right hand,
In her left hand riches and honor.
Her ways *are* ways of pleasantness,
And all her paths *are* peace.
She *is* a tree of life to those who take hold of her,
And happy *are all* who retain her.

a. **Happy is the man who finds wisdom**: Solomon longed for his son (and all who would read Proverbs) to seek after wisdom. In the fear of the Lord, **wisdom** and **understanding** (often the result of God's loving correction) would guide men and women into a truly **happy** life.

i. **Happy**: "'Blessed' describes heavenly bliss stemming from being right with God; it depicts the human condition of well being that comes with God's blessing or as a divine reward for righteousness." (Ross)

ii. **Happy**: "Is wisdom a sullen matron who entertains her followers only with sighs and tears? Does this mean that to gain the joys of the next life we must bid eternal farewell to the benefits of this life?... This is the world's creed, and it is a slander from the great liar." (Bridges)

b. **Her proceeds are better than the profits of silver**: Wisdom (especially that which comes from God's correction) is **better** than material gain. It imparts the kind of character and training that brings contentment and quality of life that money can't provide.

i. Solomon sought wisdom and God took care of the rest (1 Kings 3:9).

c. **All the things you may desire cannot compare with her**: This wisdom is greater than all kinds of riches – **silver**, **fine gold**, or **rubies**. To have the wisdom that comes from God's loving correction is to have something better than material wealth.

i. By inheritance from his father and through his own shrewd business dealings, Solomon was a fabulously wealthy man (2 Chronicles 9:22). In a way that few would ever know, Solomon knew that the blessings of relationship with God and godly character were greater than all that a man **may desire** of material things.

d. **Length of days is in her right hand**: In principle, wisdom brings many benefits. Wise people live longer, enjoy great prosperity (**riches**) and esteem (**honor**). They live lives marked by **pleasantness**, by **peace**, and by happiness (**happy are all who retain her**).

i. "Wisdom is here represented as a great and generous princess distributing gifts to her subjects." (Poole)

ii. **She is a tree of life**: "Alluding most manifestly to the tree so called which God in the beginning planted in the garden of Paradise, by eating the fruit of which all the wastes of nature might have been continually repaired, so as to prevent death for ever." (Clarke)

C. My son, value wise living before God and man.

1. (19-20) The wise Creator.

The LORD by wisdom founded the earth;
By understanding He established the heavens;
By His knowledge the depths were broken up,
And clouds drop down the dew.

a. **The LORD by wisdom founded the earth**: In His work of creation, God showed great **wisdom**. This is remarkably seen in both the large features and small details of creation. The universe around us has the marks of a brilliant Designer whose design shows His wisdom.

i. God's self-revelation through His creation is an important theme of Romans 1:18-20, which also describes the guilt of mankind in ignoring and rejecting God's self-revelation through what He created.

ii. "This section shows that the wisdom that directs life is the same wisdom that created the universe (see discussion on 8:20-31); to surrender to God's wisdom is to put oneself in harmony with creation, the world around one." (Ross)

b. **By understanding He established the heavens**: God's creative wisdom is seen in the smallest details of the single cell, but also in the expansive majesty of the **heavens**. In His great **understanding** God created a universe that some call "just right." According to physicists and scientists, we live in a *just right* universe.

i. **Established the heavens**: "Or *fitted* or *ordered* them; framed them in that exquisite order which now they have." (Poole)

ii. The universe has a just-right gravitational force. *If it were larger*, the stars would be too hot and would burn up too quickly and too unevenly to support life. *If it was smaller*, the stars would remain so cool, nuclear fusion would never ignite, and there would be no heat and light.

iii. The universe has a just-right speed of light. *If it were larger*, stars would send out too much light. *If it were smaller*, stars would not send out enough light.

iv. The universe has a just-right average distance between the stars. *If it were larger*, the heavy element density would be too thin for rocky planets to form, and there would only be gaseous planets. *If it were smaller*, planetary orbits would become destabilized because of the gravitational pull from other stars.

c. **By His knowledge the depths were broken up**: This is likely a reference to what happened at the flood described in Noah's day (Genesis 7:11). God knew that such a judgment was necessary, and He knew how to make it happen. The radical ecological changes suggested by the flood of Noah possibly set in motion our earth's modern hydrological system (**clouds drop down the dew**).

i. **Drop down the dew**: "The west wind after sunset brings enough moisture of the sea with it that during the night it falls in rich *dew* (*tal;* cf. Song of Solomon 5:2). In Canaan's almost rainless summer the land was dependent on this moisture for life, and so dew was more impressive to Orientals than to Westerners who, having a more abundant amount of rainfall, have less dependence on dew." (Waltke)

2. (21-22) Giving attention to God's wisdom.

My son, let them not depart from your eyes—
Keep sound wisdom and discretion;

So they will be life to your soul
And grace to your neck.

> a. **Let them not depart from your eyes**: Solomon told his **son** the importance of constant attention to God's **wisdom and discretion**. This requires not only a life-diligence, but also an appropriately surrendered heart that recognizes that God's **wisdom and discretion** are greater than my own.

> b. **They will be life to your soul**: Constant attention to God's **wisdom and discretion** brings real benefit to life.

3. (23-26) The safety of walking in God's wisdom.

Then you will walk safely in your way,
And your foot will not stumble.
When you lie down, you will not be afraid;
Yes, you will lie down and your sleep will be sweet.
Do not be afraid of sudden terror,
Nor of trouble from the wicked when it comes;
For the LORD will be your confidence,
And will keep your foot from being caught.

> a. **You will walk safely in your way**: In principle, God guides those who honor His wisdom into paths of safety. There is nothing safer than living in the wisdom and will of God.

> b. **The LORD will be your confidence**: The wise life can let go of fear (**you will not be afraid**) and in the release of anxiety know the blessing of **sleep**. Confident in God, we need not be afraid of **sudden terror** or **trouble from the wicked**.

> > i. **Your sleep will be sweet**: "Free from distracting cares and terrors, which ofttimes haunt sinners even in their sleep, because thy mind shall be composed and serene through the sense of God's favour and providence, and the conscience of thine own integrity." (Poole)

> > ii. "Wicked men's sleep is often troublesome, through the workings of their evil consciences; as our Richard III, after the murder of his own two innocent nephews, had fearful dreams." (Trapp)

> > iii. "When Peter was in prison, in chains, between two soldiers, on the eve of his expected execution, when there seemed but a step between him and death, he was able to lie down and not be afraid." (Bridges)

4. (27-30) Some lessons from God's wisdom.

Do not withhold good from those to whom it is due,
When it is in the power of your hand to do *so.*

Do not say to your neighbor,
"Go, and come back,
And tomorrow I will give *it*,"
When *you have* it with you.
Do not devise evil against your neighbor,
For he dwells by you for safety's sake.
Do not strive with a man without cause,
If he has done you no harm.

a. **Do not withhold good from those to whom it is due**: Here Solomon gave some practical examples of the lessons wisdom teaches. He began with the simple principle that we should do **good** when it **is in the power** of our hand to do so.

i. "Do not refuse a kindness when it is in thy power to perform it. If thou have the means *by thee*, and thy neighbour's necessities be pressing, do not put him off till the *morrow*. Death may take either him or thee before that time." (Clarke)

ii. **Those to whom it is due**: "May be laborers who have earned their pay, the poor who rightly plead for help, or suppliants at the city gates who call for justice." (Garrett)

iii. **To whom it is due**: "The Hebrew of 27a ('…from its owners') brings out the injustice, not merely inconsiderateness, of delay." (Kidner)

b. **Do not say to your neighbor**: The good we should do should be done *promptly*, while opportunity still exists. If we leave it to **tomorrow**, it may never happen – and will certainly not happen as soon as it could and should.

c. **Do not devise evil against your neighbor**: God's wisdom teaches us to treat others well. Since our own security and safety are connected to the good of our neighbor, then **for safety's sake** we should **not strive** with our neighbor when there is no cause (**if he has done you no harm**).

i. **Do not devise**: "*Do not plan* renders a verb meaning concretely 'to plow' and figuratively, always ethical, 'to prepare [i.e., plan]' good or evil deeds." (Waltke)

ii. "Do not be of a litigious, quarrelsome spirit. Be not under the influence of too nice a sense of honour. If thou must appeal to judicial authority to bring him that wrongs thee to reason, avoid all enmity, and do nothing in a spirit of revenge." (Clarke)

iii. "We must beware of becoming involved in quarrels (17:14; 18:6; 25:8-9) instead of pursuing peace (Romans 12:18). A spirit of strife is a great hindrance to holiness (Hebrews 12:14; Colossians 3:12-15) and is inconsistent for any of God's servants (2 Timothy 2:24). (Bridges)

5. (31-35) The benefit of a life that loves God's wisdom.

Do not envy the oppressor,
And choose none of his ways;
For the perverse *person is* an abomination to the LORD**,**
But His secret counsel *is* with the upright.
The curse of the LORD **is on the house of the wicked,**
But He blesses the home of the just.
Surely He scorns the scornful,
But gives grace to the humble.
The wise shall inherit glory,
But shame shall be the legacy of fools.

a. **Do not envy the oppressor**: Wisdom teaches us that though the way of the wicked may seem good and at times enviable, we should **choose none of his ways**. In honor to God, in love to others, and in wisdom of life we should never oppress others (as Jesus said in Matthew 10:25-28 and other passages).

b. **The perverse person is an abomination to the L**ORD: We should not envy or imitate the oppressor because God knows how and when to judge such wicked. God **blesses the home of the just**, but He also **scorns the scornful**. The temporary prosperity of the wicked should never make us envy or imitate them.

i. **The perverse person**: "The Lord abhors intrigue, but people who are candid and upright, who know the virtue of openness and simplicity, have his ear." (Waltke)

c. **He scorns the scornful, but gives grace to the humble**: This wonderful principle is repeated three times in the Bible (also in James 4:6 and 1 Peter 5:5). It shows how pride sets God in opposition to us, but humility invites the **grace** of God. We want to be **humble** and receive God's grace.

i. There is a sense in which Solomon spoke of *wisdom* and *humility* as being closely related. Those who are wise enough to see God as He really is and ourselves as we really are will have a natural and appropriate humility.

ii. James 4:6 and 1 Peter 5:5 quote the Septuagint translation of this verse, which – if anything – softened the force of the Hebrew phrasing here. "The verse uses a strong anthropomorphic idea: 'He mocks the proud mockers.' The LXX [Septuagint] has a softened interpretation: 'The Lord resists the proud'." (Ross)

d. **The wise shall inherit glory**: Whatever exaltation the wicked seem to have, it is only temporary. Their **legacy** shall be **shame**, but God has a destiny of **glory** for His wise, humble ones.

i. **Inherit glory**: "Not have it only, but inherit it…they shall have it as their proper, perfect, and perpetual right." (Trapp)

ii. "By contrast, fools *are those who acquire* or earn, not inherit, by their intractability, public *shame*." (Waltke)

Proverbs 4 – The Path of the Just and the Way of the Wicked

A. A father teaches his children.

1. (1-2) A plea to listen to a father's wisdom.

Hear, *my* children, the instruction of a father,
And give attention to know understanding;
For I give you good doctrine:
Do not forsake my law.

a. **Hear, my children**: Previously in Proverbs, Solomon spoke as a father to his son, perhaps with the principal heir in mind. Now the instruction is broadened to his **children** in general. This is the **instruction of a father** for the benefit of the **children**.

i. "So the home continues to be the prominent arena of learning as the parents in turn pass on the traditions (see Deuteronomy 6:6-9)." (Ross)

b. **Give attention to know understanding**: This appeal, and the appeal to **hear** in the first line, means there may be hesitancy or resistance on the part of the children that must be overcome by the appeal. Parents are often discouraged by a child's resistance to their wisdom and instruction, but it still must be spoken, and with heartfelt appeals.

c. **For I give you good doctrine**: The father had confidence in his instruction, no doubt because it was based on Scriptural wisdom. Confident that he spoke **good doctrine**, he could exhort them, "**do not forsake my law**."

2. (3-5) Guidance from previous generations: Get wisdom!

When I was my father's son,
Tender and the only one in the sight of my mother,
He also taught me, and said to me:

"Let your heart retain my words;
Keep my commands, and live.
Get wisdom! Get understanding!
Do not forget, nor turn away from the words of my mouth.

a. **When I was my father's son**: Solomon tenderly remembered the lessons *his* father **taught** him. This would be a special remembrance of any son with any father, but all the more so when we consider that Solomon's father was King David, the greatest of Israel's earthly kings.

i. "By recalling his own upbringing and citing his father, the teacher both identifies with the present struggles in his son's life and reinforces the paternal dignity of his words. These teachings have stood the test of time." (Garrett)

ii. **When I was my father's son**: Waltke explains that the sense here is of a *true son*, true in a spiritual and moral sense. Even as a rebellious child could be disowned in Israel (Deuteronomy 21:18-21 and 32:19-20), an obedient son was regarded as true in every sense.

iii. **The only one in the sight of my mother**: 1 Chronicles 3:5 indicates that Bathsheba had other sons through David, but Solomon was her special son, God's chose heir to the throne of Israel. "Though Abraham had other sons, only Isaac is called his *yahid* (Genesis 22:2, 12, 16) to emphasize the special status of Sarah's offspring." (Waltke)

iv. **He taught me**: "His [later] fall was therefore the more blameworthy, because he had been so piously educated." (Trapp)

v. "Those who receive from their parents direction in the fear of Jehovah, have that for which to be perpetually thankful. They can never escape its power. It may be that they will ultimately reject its appeal, but the fact that they have received it will create for them a way of escape from evil through all life's pilgrimage." (Morgan)

b. **Let your heart retain my words**: Before David spoke to Solomon, he cultivated a receptive **heart**. David didn't want his **words** to fall upon deaf ears or a hard **heart**, so he addressed this first.

i. Plainly said, if the king of Israel took the time to teach his children in this way, so does every father. "Parents, you must remember than an untaught child will be a living shame (Proverbs 29:15)." (Bridges)

c. **Keep my commands, and live**: One of the ways that David cultivated a receptive heart was to communicate the *importance* of his instruction. Because the teaching faithfully communicated God's truth, obedience to the **commands** of his father meant life or death for Solomon.

d. **Get wisdom**: Before David gave him the actual words of wisdom, he first encouraged the *pursuit* of wisdom in Solomon. We might say that this is even more important than any particular piece of wisdom, or it is one of the early lessons of wisdom. Value wisdom, pursue wisdom, sacrifice for wisdom, **get wisdom** and **understanding**.

i. **Get wisdom**: "A blunt way of saying: 'What it takes is not brains or opportunity, but decision. Do you want it? Come and get it.'" (Kidner)

ii. **Get wisdom**: Waltke explains that the verb **get** really has the sense *to buy* or *purchase*. "*Qana* means to acquire moveable goods through a financial transaction." The idea is that **wisdom** will cost something, but it is worth it.

iii. "'Get wisdom' suggests, 'buy wisdom,' because the Hebrew word carries the idea of a commercial transaction. There's a price to pay if you want to know God's truth and obey it." (Wiersbe)

e. **Do not forget, nor turn away from the words of my mouth**: Once wisdom is pursued and, in some sense, attained, it must be *kept*. It is possible to have wisdom for a time and then to **turn away** from it at a later time.

i. In this regard, we appreciate something of the irony and tragedy of Solomon's life. King David taught him well and Solomon received the lessons, valuing wisdom so much that he asked for it above all other things (1 Kings 3:7-12). Ironically and tragically, late in life, Solomon did **turn away** from the path of wisdom (1 Kings 11:1-13). Even the best lessons can, eventually, be rejected.

3. (6-9) The benefits of getting wisdom.

Do not forsake her, and she will preserve you;
Love her, and she will keep you.
Wisdom *is* the principal thing;
***Therefore* get wisdom.**
And in all your getting, get understanding.
Exalt her, and she will promote you;
She will bring you honor, when you embrace her.
She will place on your head an ornament of grace;
A crown of glory she will deliver to you."

a. **Do not forsake her, and she will preserve you**: Solomon continued in his remembrance of his father's teaching to him. King David taught Solomon that if he remained on the path of wisdom, and loved wisdom (**love her**), it would **preserve** him and keep him safe.

i. "The teacher uses feminine verbs to promise protection and safety. Here we find wisdom personified as a woman, at first reading like a bride that is to be loved and embraced (v. 8), but also having the qualities of an influential patron who can protect." (Ross)

b. **Wisdom is the principal thing**: King David communicated more than the *facts* of wisdom; he wanted Solomon to love and value and honor wisdom. Men and women often regard money or fame or romance as **the principal thing**; God's people should give a higher place to **wisdom**.

c. **Exalt her, and she will promote you**: The love and pursuit of wisdom is rewarded. She brings with her **honor** and **ornament**. Early in his life, Solomon was richly rewarded for his pursuit of wisdom (1 Kings 3:7-12).

i. **A crown of glory**: "A tiara, diadem, or crown, shall not be more honourable to the princely wearer, than sound wisdom-true religion-coupled with deep learning, shall be to the Christian and the scholar." (Clarke)

4. (10-13) Receive and take firm hold of wisdom's lessons.

Hear, my son, and receive my sayings,
And the years of your life will be many.
I have taught you in the way of wisdom;
I have led you in right paths.
When you walk, your steps will not be hindered,
And when you run, you will not stumble.
Take firm hold of instruction, do not let go;
Keep her, for she *is* your life.

a. **Hear, my son, and receive my sayings**: It seems that Solomon's remembrance of his father David's instruction ended at Proverbs 4:9. Now he once again speaks directly to his **son**, reminding him of the importance of the lessons learned.

i. **The years of your life will be many**: "Vice and intemperance impair the health and shorten the days of the wicked; while true religion, sobriety, and temperance, prolong them. The principal part of our diseases springs from 'indolence, intemperance, and disorderly passions.' Religion excites to *industry*, promotes *sober habits*, and destroys *evil passions*, and *harmonizes* the soul; and thus, by preventing many diseases, necessarily prolongs life." (Clarke)

b. **I have taught you in the way of wisdom**: We sense that Solomon received an appropriate satisfaction in fulfilling his duty to teach his son wisdom, even as his father taught him. This would guide his children well into the future (**when you run, you will not stumble**).

i. Parents often work hard to prepare their children to succeed in the world – to **run** well in the race of life. Without also working hard to impart God's wisdom to our children, we may set them to **run**, but also to **stumble** and to **be hindered**.

ii. "Living according to wisdom is like walking or running on a safe road, a course that will be free of obstacles, so that progress will be certain." (Ross)

iii. **I have led you in right paths**: "A track is not a road that has come into existence without people moving on it, but is that on which and in which people move. The son will be walking on an ancient and proved way." (Waltke)

c. **Keep her, for she is your life**: Again, Solomon emphasized the *value* we should have for wisdom. We should regard the love and pursuit of wisdom to be a **life** or death matter. We must **take firm hold** of wisdom because so much works to make us let go of her.

i. "The animated exhortation to **hold on to instruction** shows that it is a struggle to retain our principles. Feeble, indeed, is our hold when we are only interested in wisdom because it is a novelty." (Bridges)

B. Keeping the heart away from the path of the wicked.

1. (14-15) Avoid the path of the wicked

Do not enter the path of the wicked,
And do not walk in the way of evil.
Avoid it, do not travel on it;
Turn away from it and pass on.

a. **Do not enter the path of the wicked**: Solomon told his children to keep from *starting* on the **path of the wicked**. If a way is never entered, it never has to be remedied.

i. "The warning is to avoid evil ways and evil men by not even starting on the wicked path of life. Plaut rightly paraphrases: 'Don't take the first step, for you may not be master of your destiny thereafter.'" (Ross)

ii. "Never *associate* with those whose life is irregular and sinful; never *accompany* them in any of their acts of transgression." (Clarke)

b. **Do not walk in the way of evil**: If, through foolishness, the path of the wicked is entered, then one's steps should turn from it soon. With urgency, wisdom speaks and says **avoid it** and **turn away from it**. Every further step on the **way of evil** makes it more difficult to depart from that **path of the wicked**.

2. (16-19) Why the way of the wicked is to be avoided.

For they do not sleep unless they have done evil;
And their sleep is taken away unless they make *someone* fall.
For they eat the bread of wickedness,
And drink the wine of violence.
But the path of the just *is* like the shining sun,
That shines ever brighter unto the perfect day.
The way of the wicked *is* like darkness;
They do not know what makes them stumble.

a. **They do not sleep unless they have done evil**: Those on the path of wickedness are *committed* to their sin. They will sacrifice **sleep** and money and dignity and freedom to do their **evil**. They don't rest comfortably (**their sleep is taken away**) unless they draw others to their own path of wickedness. Sin becomes their food and drink (their **bread** and **wine**).

i. "By using hyperboles the teacher portrays the character of the wicked as those who are addicted to evil (Proverbs 4:16; cf. Psalm 36:4). They are so completely devoted to evil conduct that they cannot sleep until they find expression for it." (Ross)

ii. "The Bible does not hide the fact that one can become as zealous for evil as for good." (Kidner)

iii. "As empty stomachs can hardly sleep, so neither can graceless persons rest till gorged and glutted with the sweetmeats of sin, with the murdering morsels of mischief. The devil, their taskmaster, will not allow them time to sleep; which is very hard bondage." (Trapp)

b. **But the path of the just is like the shining sun**: The path of the wicked is dark and increasingly so. Yet the path of those who get wisdom – **the path of the just** – grows brighter. It **shines ever brighter unto the perfect day**.

i. "The path of the wicked is gloomy, dark, and dangerous; that of the righteous is open, luminous, and instructive. This verse contains a fine metaphor; it refers to the *sun* rising above the horizon, and the increasing twilight, till his beams shine full upon the earth." (Clarke)

ii. "*Nogah* refers to the light's bright gleam or radiance, as from the moon (Isaiah 4:5; 50:10) or stars (Joel 2:10; 4:15), and connotes that there are no clouds, not even a shadow, on this path." (Waltke)

iii. "This is not the feeble light of a candle, nor the momentary blaze of the meteor, but the grand illumination of heaven." (Bridges)

c. **The way of the wicked is like darkness**: Considering where each path leads should help a man or woman make the right choice. One of the tempter's chief strategies is to hide the consequences of our path, whether it is the **path of the just** or **the way of the wicked**.

3. (20-22) A plea to be heard.

My son, give attention to my words;
Incline your ear to my sayings.
Do not let them depart from your eyes;
Keep them in the midst of your heart;
For they *are* **life to those who find them,**
And health to all their flesh.

a. **My son, give attention to my words**: The lessons of wisdom can be given but never received. Solomon often exhorted his **son** to pay attention and to keep the lessons of wisdom before his **eyes**.

i. Proverbs 4:20-27 make mention of the body at least 11 times (eyes, feet, and heart are mentioned twice, and ear, flesh, mouth, lips, and eyelids once each). It is a section that speaks powerfully on how we can dedicate each part of our body to wisdom and God's honor. Later the Apostle Paul wrote of yielding the parts (members) of our body to God (Romans 6:12-13).

b. **Keep them in the midst of your heart**: Though it goes against our inherited sinful nature, we can and must cultivate a **heart** that loves wisdom and is focused upon her. If wisdom is regarded as only a system of rules and threats, then her purpose is never achieved. We should pray for and pursue wisdom **in the midst** of the **heart**.

i. "A neglected Bible is the melancholy proof of a heart that is alienated from God. For how can we have a spark of love for him if that Book that is full of his revealed glory is despised?" (Bridges)

c. **They are life to all who find them**: God's word – communicated through the **words** and **sayings** of this father to his children – brings **life** and **health**. The pursuit of wisdom is rewarded.

4. (23) Keep your heart.

Keep your heart with all diligence,
For out of it *spring* **the issues of life.**

a. **Keep your heart with all diligence**: Since wisdom belongs in the midst of the heart (Proverbs 4:21), it also is necessary to **keep** the **heart** in the sense of guarding it. In the sense Solomon meant here, the heart should be kept for *wisdom*, guarding it against the way of the wicked (Proverbs 4:19).

i. Especially from the perspective of the new covenant, which promises a new heart (Ezekiel 36:26), we can say that **keep your heart** implies a heart *worth* keeping – a new heart, one worth guarding.

ii. The heart is the reservoir, and change must begin there. If the reservoir is polluted, it does no good to fix the pipes and the valves.

iii. "The Bible warns us to avoid a double heart (Psalm 12:2), a hard heart (Proverbs 28:14), a proud heart (Proverbs 21:4), an unbelieving heart (Hebrews 3:12), a cold heart (Matthew 24:12), and an unclean heart (Psalm 51:10)." (Wiersbe)

b. **With all diligence**: This implies that it isn't easy to guard or **keep** one's heart. There will be many opportunities to give our heart to a person or a path that wisdom would warn against.

i. "As Satan keeps special watch here, so must we keep special watch as well. If the citadel is taken, the whole town must surrender. If the heart is captured, the whole man—affections, desires, motives, pursuits—will be handed over." (Bridges)

c. **For out of it spring the issues of life**: There is great reward to the one who guards their heart, keeping it for wisdom (as in Proverbs 4:21). They enjoy **life** flowing from their heart, like a pleasant and bountiful water spring. The unguarded heart sees a choking or restriction to the joy and pleasantness of life.

i. "The metaphor implies, according to Delitzsch, not only that life has its fountains in the heart, 'but also that the direction which it takes is determined by the heart.'" (Waltke)

ii. One of the great enticements to the way of the wicked (Proverbs 4:19) is that it is fun, pleasant, and will bring some sense of happiness. *This is a lie.* The same God who designed and created us is the God who guides us in and through His commands. Though it may not be immediately or instinctively apparent, *His commands are for our happiness and good.* Though guarding the heart with all diligence may mean saying a temporarily painful no to excitements and enticements on the way of the wicked, the overall result is happiness, joy, and pleasantness.

iii. "It is 'the wellspring of life' in that the capacity to live with joy and vigor ultimately comes from within and not from circumstances. The corrupt heart draws one down to the grave, but Wisdom protects the heart from that corruption." (Garrett)

iv. "If we pollute that wellspring, the infection will spread; before long, hidden appetites will become open sins and public shame." (Wiersbe)

5. (24-27) A plea to stay on the right path.

Put away from you a deceitful mouth,
And put perverse lips far from you.
Let your eyes look straight ahead,
And your eyelids look right before you.
Ponder the path of your feet,
And let all your ways be established.
Do not turn to the right or the left;
Remove your foot from evil.

a. **Put away from you a deceitful mouth**: To stay on the path of the just, one must give attention to what they *speak*. **Deceitful** and **perverse** words are used to cover deceitful and perverse actions and lead one further along the way of the wicked. If one could actually never speak in an impure or **perverse** way and determine to never do things that must be covered with **a deceitful mouth**, they would go a long way to avoiding the works of the wicked.

i. "Righteousness will control the tongue, avoiding twisted and crooked speech. This is the next logical step; for words flow out of the heart." (Ross)

ii. "Superficial habits of talk react on the mind; so that, e.g., cynical chatter, fashionable grumbles, flippancy, half-truths, barely meant in the first place, harden into well-established habits of thought." (Kidner)

b. **Let your eyes look straight ahead**: We often depart the path of the just out of distraction. The blinders used on horses do them much good and would do many of us good as well.

i. Jesus said that if we will be fit for His kingdom, we must keep our eyes forward, not distracted side to side or backwards (Luke 9:62).

c. **Ponder the path of your feet**: If one would consider the *destination* of their present path, it would lead to much more wise living. When we carefully **ponder** where we are headed, it helps to establish our wise direction and help us to not **turn to the right or the left**.

i. "The son must take care that every step conforms with that way; one false step could prove fatal. *Your foot (ragleka)* calls attention to every step taken in the road of life." (Waltke)

ii. "Of particular interest is Proverbs 4:27, the warning to swerve neither to the right nor to the left. Deuteronomy 5:32; 17:11; 28:14; and Joshua 23:6 are similar. The idea is that one should not be distracted from the way of wisdom." (Garrett)

Proverbs 5 – Warning Against Adultery

"This is a tremendous chapter, dealing with a delicate subject daringly, and, with great directness." (G. Campbell Morgan)

A. The warning against adultery.

1. (1-2) The call for attention.

My son, pay attention to my wisdom;
Lend your ear to my understanding,
That you may preserve discretion,
And your lips may keep knowledge.

> a. **My son, pay attention to my wisdom**: As previously, Solomon knew that his instruction would do most good when it was given **attention** and **ear**. Teachers must do what they can to gain, and hold, the attention of their learners.

> > i. In this chapter **wisdom** is "A man-to-man warning to avoid liaisons with loose women, a theme that is fairly common in the wisdom literature of the ancient Near East." (Ross)

> b. **That you may preserve discretion**: Solomon wanted his son to hold on to **discretion** and to **keep knowledge**. The idea is that the son started in these things, but must face the challenge of remaining in them throughout life.

> > i. If we ever gain **discretion**, it is difficult to **preserve**. This is especially true in regard to the sexual matters described in this chapter. "Many men's hearts are no better than stews and brothel houses, by reason of base and beastly thoughts and lusts that muster and swarm there, like the flies of Egypt." (Trapp)

2. (3) The allure of the immoral woman.

For the lips of an immoral woman drip honey,
And her mouth *is* smoother than oil;

a. **For the lips of an immoral woman drip honey**: This explains the reason why it was important for the son to hold on to discretion and knowledge – those things would be tested by the enticements of an **immoral woman**. **Honey** is sweet and **oil** is pleasant, and these represent the temptations of immorality.

b. **The lips of an immoral woman**: Solomon's phrasing is poetic and powerful. The figures of the **lips** and the **mouth** refer to the words an immoral woman may use in her enticements, and to her alluring kisses.

> i. The first steps towards immoral associations are almost always made by what is said or communicated. This speaks to the great need for men and women to guard their speech and communication with the opposite sex.

> ii. **Oil**: "The delightful oil symbolized gladness (Isaiah 61:3) and prosperity (Deuteronomy 33:24), and its absence indicated sorrow or humiliation (Joel 1:10)." (Waltke)

c. **Of an immoral woman**: Solomon here focused on the **immoral woman**, but it was not because he thought that men are always moral, or that it is mainly immoral women who seduce and corrupt moral men. Solomon – the author of the Song of Solomon – was far too wise and astute in the ways of romance and sexuality to believe that. Solomon focused on the **immoral woman** because he wrote this to his son (Proverbs 5:1) and sensed this was his greatest and closest moral danger.

> i. In other circumstances, he might have warned against *an immoral man*, and the principles of seduction he warned about can apply freely to women or men.

> ii. **Immoral woman**: "The 'adulteress' of v. 3 is literally the 'other woman,' that is, someone other than the man's wife." (Garrett)

d. **Honey…oil**: In Solomon's day some women had the ability to attract and allure men with the sweetness of **honey** and the pleasantness of **oil**. Operating outside the covenant of marriage, some of these women used that ability for their own advantage. They might gain something emotional, something material, something sensual, something romantic, or other potential gains. These women were a danger to be warned against.

> i. Our day is like Solomon's, or perhaps worse. Modern western culture is saturated with images of alluring women and their use of enticement to gain things that are sweet and pleasant to them.

3. (4-7) The danger of the immoral woman.

But in the end she is bitter as wormwood,
Sharp as a two-edged sword.
Her feet go down to death,
Her steps lay hold of hell.
Lest you ponder *her* path of life—
Her ways are unstable;
You do not know *them.*
Therefore hear me now, *my* children,
And do not depart from the words of my mouth.

a. **In the end she is bitter as wormwood**: Honey is sweet, but **wormwood** is **bitter**. The sweetness in the allure of the immoral woman becomes **bitter**, and her smooth, oil-like pleasantness becomes **sharp as a two-edged sword**.

> i. "It is a change from honey to wormwood, from the smoothness of oil to the sharpness of a sword, from the path of life to the highway of death." (Morgan)

> ii. "The image of the two-edged sword, literally a sword with more than one mouth, signifies that a liaison with this woman brings pain and destruction." (Ross)

b. **Her feet go down to death**: The path of the immoral woman leads to **death**. She promises to add life but ends up taking it away. The wise man will **ponder her path of life**.

c. **Her ways are unstable**: The decision to entice someone else into immorality is not a decision made by a stable person who desires the best for either self or the one enticed. Those led into immorality often feel they know the motives of their partner in sin, but Solomon rightly observed **you do not know them**.

- If the sexual immorality is desired out of a perceived impulse of love, maturity and stability would say, "If I really loved this person I would not act against their interest and my own. I will reject this immorality because I do in fact love them and will express my love only in ways that would honor God and His people."

- If the sexual immorality is desired out of desire for pleasure or adventure, maturity and stability would say, "My desire for pleasure and adventure must not reign supreme in my life. Whatever good I may think would come of this, it is not good and will not bring good."

d. **Hear me now, my children**: We sense the serious nature of Solomon's appeal. Perhaps he understood how adultery brought disaster to his father, King David (2 Solomon 11).

4. (8-14) The ruin adultery brings.

Remove your way far from her,
And do not go near the door of her house,
Lest you give your honor to others,
And your years to the cruel *one;*
Lest aliens be filled with your wealth,
And your labors *go* **to the house of a foreigner;**
And you mourn at last,
When your flesh and your body are consumed,
And say:
"How I have hated instruction,
And my heart despised correction!
I have not obeyed the voice of my teachers,
Nor inclined my ear to those who instructed me!
I was on the verge of total ruin,
In the midst of the assembly and congregation."

a. **Remove your way far from her**: Solomon didn't advise his son to stay in the immoral woman's presence and test his ability to resist her seductions. The best defense was distance; to not even **go near the door of her house**.

i. The Apostle Paul would write much later: *Flee also youthful lusts* (2 Timothy 2:22). The longer one stays in the presence of such enticement to evil, the worse the danger becomes.

ii. We must **remove** our **way far from her** not only in presence, but also in heart and mind. We must put away the pornography and enticements common to our day and work for a mind set on things above (Colossians 3:1-2, Philippians 4:8).

iii. "The New Testament echoes this practical, if seemingly unheroic, advice (2 Timothy 2:22; Matthew 5:28, 29), which could mean, in terms of detailed decision, e.g. 'change your job', 'change your newspaper', 'break with that set of friends.'" (Kidner)

iv. "Yea, the hypocrite, who outwardly abstains from gross sins, yet inwardly consenteth…in his heart and fancy, supposing himself with them, and desiring to do what they do. This is mental adultery, this is contemplative wickedness…. Surely as a man may die of an inward bleeding, so may he be damned for these inward boilings of lust and concupiscence, if not bewailed and mortified." (Trapp)

v. "He that would not be burnt must dread the fire; he that would not hear the bell, must not meddle with the rope." (Trapp)

b. **Lest you give your honor to others**: Solomon will describe many things that are lost through sexual immorality, and he began with **honor**. There is a valid sense of **honor** that the one who stays pure can have.

i. "People who commit sexual sins think their problems are solved ('She understands me so much better than my wife does!') and that life will get better and better. But disobedience to God's laws always brings sad consequences and sinners eventually pay dearly for their brief moments of pleasure." (Wiersbe)

c. **And your years to the cruel one**: Adultery and sexual immorality ruin lives. God's command that our sexual relationships remain only in the covenant of marriage was not given to take away from our life and enjoyment, but to add to it.

d. **Lest aliens be filled with your wealth**: In the modern world, many men know what it is like to lose their wealth because of adultery.

i. "The self-inflicted punishment of involving oneself with the unchaste wife is as bad as if the outsiders plundered the house (cf. Proverbs 1:10-14; Psalm 109:11b). Although sexual immorality today may not lead to slavery, it still leads to alimony, child support, broken homes, hurt, jealousy, lonely people, and venereal disease." (Waltke)

ii. "This sin is a purgatory to the purse, though a paradise to the desires." (Trapp)

iii. **And you mourn at last**: "The *mourning* here spoken of is of the most excessive kind: the word *naham* is often applied to the *growling of a lion*, and the *hoarse incessant murmuring* of the sea." (Clarke)

iv. **At last**: "The young man dreamed of pleasure, in wanton dalliance he hoped to find delight; but when the lamp or "At the last" began to shine, he saw rottenness in his bones, filthiness in his flesh, pains and griefs and sorrows, as the necessary consequence of sin." (Spurgeon)

e. **When your flesh and body are consumed**: Sexual immorality leads to disease and breakdown of health. Even the stress of living a double, deceptive life is enough to take away one's health.

i. "**Consumed** by those manifold diseases which filthy and inordinate lusts bring upon the body, of which physicians give a very large and sad catalogue, and the bodies of many adulterers give full proof." (Poole)

ii. "The point of these verses is clear: The price of infidelity may be high; for everything one works for—position, power, prosperity—

could be lost either through the avaricious demands of the woman or the outcry for restitution by the community." (Ross)

f. **How I have hated instruction!** One great price of sexual immorality is *regret*. When we see how empty the promises of sin are and how great the price for those sins is, deep sorrow and regret is a logical response. Many men and women, fallen into the snare of sexual immorality, have wondered: "How did I ever end up here? How could I be so foolish? How could I give up so much for what amounted to so little?"

i. Matthew Poole thought that these were not sincere words of repentance: "Which are not the words of a true penitent mourning for and turning from his sin, but only of a man who is grieved for the sad effects of his delightful lusts, and tormented with the horror of his own guilty conscience."

ii. John Trapp thought it *could* describe a true repentance: "Oh, what a wretch, what a beast, what a maddened devil was I, so woefully to waste the fat and marrow of my dear and precious time, the flower of mine age, the strength of my body, the vigour of my spirits, the whole of mine estate, in sinful pleasures and sensual delights! Lo, here is a kind of repentance which, though late, yet, if it were true, would be accepted,"

g. **In the midst of the assembly and congregation**: What the adulterer thought would remain secret was exposed. He entered his sin thinking, *no one will ever find out*. When it was exposed **in the midst of the assembly** his foolishness, betrayal, and lack of self-control were all public.

i. "I, who designed and expected to enjoy my lusts with secrecy and impunity, am now made a public example and shameful spectacle to all men, and that in the congregation of Israel, where I was taught better things, and where such actions are most infamous and hateful." (Poole)

ii. "No unclean person can have any assurance that his sin shall always be kept secret, no, not in this life. The Lord hath oft brought such - sometimes by terror of conscience, sometimes by frenzy - to that pass, that themselves have been the blazers and proclaimers of their own secret filthiness." (Trapp)

B. Find satisfaction in your own wife.

1. (15-19) God's provision in marriage.

Drink water from your own cistern,
And running water from your own well.
Should your fountains be dispersed abroad,

Streams of water in the streets?
Let them be only your own,
And not for strangers with you.
Let your fountain be blessed,
And rejoice with the wife of your youth.
As a loving deer and a graceful doe,
Let her breasts satisfy you at all times;
And always be enraptured with her love.

a. **Drink water from your own cistern**: Solomon reminded his son that God had provided his wife for his sexual needs. Instead of neglecting what God had given, he should renew his gratitude and focus upon what God has blessed.

i. "'Water' in v. 15, as in Song of Solomon 5:1, stands for quenching one's sexual thirst. Satisfying the sexual drive is likened to taking in solid food in Proverbs 30:20 and water and food in Proverbs 9:17." (Waltke)

ii. "Lust makes the heart hot and thirsty: God therefore sends men to this well, to this cistern." (Trapp)

iii. "Be satisfied with thy own wife; and let the wife see that she reverence her husband; and not tempt him by inattention or unkindness to seek elsewhere what he has a right to expect, but cannot find, at *home*." (Clarke)

b. **And running water from your own well**: God's provision for sexual need is found in the marital bed, which is pure before Him (Hebrews 13:4). It is like a pure, fresh spring (**running water**). Though some are dissatisfied with what God provides in marriage, that dissatisfaction is more a reflection on them than their spouse.

i. Ancient or modern, an over-sexualized culture promotes the idea that sexual satisfaction is mainly a physical sensation. While only a fool would deny the physical enjoyments of sex, a more mature mind sees that *intimacy* – the open, unhindered revelation, reception, and sharing of one's self with another – is also a great reward in a sexual relationship. When sex is reserved for the Biblical boundaries of marriage over the years and decades it says:

• I am here for you, and you are here for me.

• I am my beloved's and he is mine.

• I know you more than anyone else and yet I love you.

• You know me more than anyone else and yet you love me.

- Our children and home life are protected and safe.
- We are not slaves to our sexual desires; we live by principles greater than our sexual impulses.
- We will remain together and supportive of each other as we grow old.

ii. Individually, and especially collectively, these are benefits far greater than the experience of orgasm. This is sex with *meaning*, not only pleasure. The world, the flesh, and the devil do a masterful job in selling humanity the lie that sex focused only on pleasure is greater than what God promises in obedience to His plan: sex with *meaning*.

iii. "Strict fidelity is not an impoverishing isolationism: from such a marriage, blessing streams out in the persons and influences of a true family." (Kidner)

c. **Should your fountains be dispersed abroad**: Here the image changes, and the idea is that Solomon's son should regard his sexual activity to be like a supply of life-giving water that should be set in the right channel. It is for the satisfaction of his wife, and **not for strangers with you**.

i. Different interpreters take different approaches to this image of both the cistern and the fountains dispersed abroad. Some take it as a picture of fathering children outside of marriage or similar ideas. The best approach seems to be a contrast between *private* and *public*. God meant for sex to be enjoyed and celebrated in the privacy of marriage, not in the public or even commercial sphere.

ii. **Let them be only your own**: "The jussive *let them be* continues the admonition to find the sources of sexual pleasure from the privacy of marriage, not from springs with the common rabble. The privacy of conjugal love is underscored by *for yourself alone*." (Waltke)

iii. "What is at issue is private versus common property. The images of a cistern, well, or fountain are used of a wife (see Song of Songs 4:15) because she, like water, satisfies desires. Channels of water in the street would then mean sexual contact with a lewd woman." (Ross)

iv. "Solomon compares enjoying married love to drinking pure water from a fresh well, but committing sexual sin is like drinking polluted water from the gutter or sewer…. To commit sexual sin is to pour this beautiful river into the streets and the public squares. What waste!" (Wiersbe)

d. **Rejoice with the wife of your youth**: Solomon alluded to God's plan for marriage, even if he did not follow it himself (1 Kings 11:3). God's best for humanity is for a man to marry a wife in his **youth** and for him to **rejoice** with her for the rest of his days. Life circumstances mean there will be many different ways this is lived out, but when a man does marry a woman in his youth, God's best is for him to **rejoice** in her until death parts them.

> i. The exhortation to **rejoice with the wife of your youth** means there is an element of *choice* involved. There are times when a husband (or wife) needs to *choose* to **rejoice** in their spouse. Our affections are much more affected by where we choose to focus them than people realize.

> ii. We have no record that Solomon committed adultery, according to the technical definition of that sin. Solomon's 700 wives and 300 concubines (1 Kings 11:3) were all legal partners. Yet he obviously fell far short of God's plan for one man to be married to one woman and to find satisfaction in the wife of his youth. Solomon wrote about this ideal in the Song of Solomon, but never enjoyed it or did so only for a relatively brief time. Solomon's failure in this area shows that if a man is not satisfied with one woman – the wife of his youth – then he will not be satisfied with 1,000 women. If a man is not satisfied with the wife of his youth, the blame almost always is upon him and not upon the wife.

> iii. "Common sense would say that such brief liaisons with strangers give no time for intimacy—that requires a lifelong bonding with the wife of one's youth." (Ross)

> iv. "The adulterer watches the river turn into a sewer, but the faithful husband sees the water become wine!" (Wiersbe)

e. **Let her breasts satisfy you at all times**: Again, the point is made that God *has* provided a place for a man to satisfy his sexual needs – in the marriage, with the wife of his youth. It is easy to feel that real sexual satisfaction must be found *outside* the marriage, but this is an illusion and a deception.

> i. **Let her breasts satisfy you**: "The word *her breasts (daddeyha)* originated in infant's babble…it is associated with erotica in its only other uses (Ezekiel 23:3, 8, 21)." (Waltke)

> ii. "It is highly important to see sexual delight in marriage as God-given; and history confirms that when marriage is viewed chiefly as a business arrangement, not only is God's bounty misunderstood, but human passion seeks (cf. verse 20) other outlets." (Kidner)

iii. "God created sex not only for reproduction but also for enjoyment, and He didn't put the 'marriage wall' around sex to *rob* us of pleasure but to *increase* pleasure and *protect* it." (Wiersbe)

f. **And always be enraptured with her love**: The phrasing of this implies there is an element of choice involved. We usually think that being **enraptured with her love** is something that can happen to a person from the mystical force of love. Yet, we love what we choose to put our affections on and a husband can choose to be **enraptured** with love toward his wife, even if he fears love has diminished or died.

> i. **Enraptured**: "The husband should be 'captivated' by the love of his wife. The word *shagah* signifies a staggering gait and so here expresses the ecstatic joy of a 'captivated' lover. It may even suggest 'be intoxicated always with her love.'" (Ross)

> ii. The emphasis is on the *singular*, on one woman for one man. Though Solomon strayed far from this ideal (1 Kings 11:3), at least at one time in his life he recognized the value of it. "Sensual man can find a satisfaction from his wife that no other woman can give him. Marriage is here thought of as strongly monogamous." (Waltke)

> iii. "Ezekiel's wife was 'the delight of his eyes'; he took singular complacency in her company. This conjugal joy is the fruit of love, which therefore he commendeth to all married men, in the next words." (Trapp)

2. (20-23) The destiny of the man given to adultery.

For why should you, my son, be enraptured by an immoral woman,
And be embraced in the arms of a seductress?
For the ways of man *are* before the eyes of the LORD,
And He ponders all his paths.
His own iniquities entrap the wicked *man*,
And he is caught in the cords of his sin.
He shall die for lack of instruction,
And in the greatness of his folly he shall go astray.

a. **Why should you, my son, be enraptured by an immoral woman**: Solomon just described how God provided for a husband's sexual needs in marriage. That being the case, it makes no sense for a man to fall into the trap of the **immoral woman**. He should not fall into her trap or her embrace.

> i. "In view of the better way of conjugal bliss with the blessed wife, involvement with the unchaste wife is absurd." (Waltke)

b. **For the ways of man are before the eyes of the Lord**: This is an important reminder for any man dealing with the temptation of an immoral woman. It is human nature to think that such a sin may be excused if it is never made public. We often think sin can be excused if it is undiscovered, and many have been exceptionally tempted by what they think is a "risk free" opportunity. Solomon rightly reminds us that God sees all our ways, and before Him no sin is hidden. God **ponders all his paths**.

i. "Here, as everywhere, wisdom consists in recognizing that human life is ever under the observation...of Jehovah." (Morgan)

ii. **The ways of man**: "*Goings* (King James Version), or *paths* (Revised Standard, Revised Standard Version) (21b), are literally the (waggon-) tracks made by constant use; a better everyday term would be 'habits'." (Kidner)

c. **He is caught in the cords of his sin**: Sexual sin – especially the violation of the marriage covenant – is a sin that entraps and destroys. It brings death, not life (**he shall die**). It is God's care and compassion that gives us His **instruction** for our sexual conduct and expression.

i. **In the cords of his sin**: "Most people who follow unlawful pleasures, think *they can give them up whenever they please*; but sin *repeated* becomes *customary*; custom soon engenders *habit*; and habit in the end assumes the form of *necessity*; the man becomes *bound with his own cords*, and so is *led captive by the devil at his will*." (Clarke)

ii. "The lifelong occupation of the ungodly man is to twist ropes of sin. All his sins are as so much twine and cord out of which ropes may be made. His thoughts and his imaginations are so much raw material, and while he thinks of evil, while he contrives transgression, while he lusts after filthiness, while he follows after evil devices, while with head, and hand, and heart he pursues eagerly after mischief, he is still twisting evermore the cords of sin which are afterwards to bind him." (Spurgeon)

iii. "In other words, if the young man is not *captivated* by his wife but becomes *captivated* with a stranger in sinful acts, then his own iniquities will *captivate* him; and he will be led to ruin." (Ross)

iv. **Will die**: "Refers to eternal death in opposition to the eternal life of the righteous, not merely to either a premature death (see v. 11) or clinical death." (Waltke)

v. **In the greatness of his folly**: "Oh, what madmen are they that bereave themselves of a room in that city of pearl for a few dirty delights and carnal pleasures!" (Trapp)

Proverbs 6 – Wisdom to a Son on Debts and Work, Sin and Seduction

A. The foolishness of taking on other's debts.

1. (1-2) Taking debts of friends or strangers.

My son, if you become surety for your friend,
***If* you have shaken hands in pledge for a stranger,**
You are snared by the words of your mouth;
You are taken by the words of your mouth.

a. **If you become surety for your friend**: Solomon warned his **son** against guaranteeing the debts of others, whether they were a **friend** or a **stranger**. This was the promise to pay the debts of the friend or stranger if they failed to pay.

    i. This wasn't really like loaning someone money, nor exactly like cosigning a loan. In modern financial terms, it was more like guaranteeing someone's open line of credit. "The New Testament shows us Paul accepting Onesimus's past liabilities, but not his future ones (Philemon 18, 19)." (Kidner)

    ii. "If thou pledge thyself in behalf of another, thou takest the burden off him, and placest it on thine own shoulders; and when he knows he has got one to stand between him and the demands of law and justice, he will feel little responsibility; his spirit of exertion will become crippled." (Clarke)

    iii. "Even to the recipient, an unconditional pledge may be an unintended disservice by exposing him to temptation and to the subsequent grief of having brought a friend to ruin." (Kidner)

b. **You are snared by the words of your mouth**: To promise to pay the debts of another person is to put yourself in a trap. It is a promise made with **the words of your mouth** but will affect and afflict your wallet or purse.

> i. "Job 17:3 uses this circle of ideas to declare that Job is too bad a risk for anybody but God—and to plead that God will take him up (cf. Ps. 119:122). So a bridge is made in the Old Testament between the idea of material insolvency and spiritual." (Kidner)

> ii. "Our God, while he warns us against putting up security, has taken it on himself. May his name be praised for this! He has given us his Word, his bond, yes, his blood as security for sinners, which no power of hell can shake." (Bridges)

2. (3-5) What to do if you have taken the debt of another.

So do this, my son, and deliver yourself;
For you have come into the hand of your friend:
Go and humble yourself;
Plead with your friend.
Give no sleep to your eyes,
Nor slumber to your eyelids.
Deliver yourself like a gazelle from the hand *of the hunter,*
And like a bird from the hand of the fowler.

a. **Deliver yourself**: Solomon counseled his son that if he did make himself responsible for the debt of another person, he should do all he could to **deliver** himself. He should **humble** himself and **plead** to be released from his promise.

> i. **Humble yourself**: "Hebrew, *offer thyself to be trodden upon*, or *throw thyself down at his feet*. As thou hast made thyself his servant, bear the fruits of thine own folly, and humbly and earnestly implore his patience and clemency." (Poole)

b. **Deliver yourself like a gazelle from the hand of the hunter**: A **gazelle** would do anything to escape the **hunter**, and a **bird** would do anything to escape the **fowler**. Solomon tried to communicate the *urgency* his son should have in escaping responsibility for the debt of others.

> i. "Becoming surety is folly because the surety makes promises for the future that he cannot control (cf. Proverbs 27:1). Moreover, he has handed himself over to the debtor, who may unmercifully throw him into the hands of the creditor." (Waltke)

> ii. "Although we have no information on Israelite laws of surety, seizure of assets and home and even the selling of the debtor into slavery were common penalties for failure to make payment, and the cosigner could well have met the same fate." (Garrett)

B. The honor of hard work.

1. (6-8) The example of the ant.

Go to the ant, you sluggard!
Consider her ways and be wise,
Which, having no captain,
Overseer or ruler,
Provides her supplies in the summer,
***And* gathers her food in the harvest.**

a. **Go to the ant, you sluggard**: Solomon spoke wisdom to the **sluggard** – essentially, the lazy man or woman. That lazy person should learn from the **ant**, an insect proverbial for hard work.

i. The book of Proverbs speaks a lot about the value of hard work, and for good reason. The difference between success and failure, between potential disappointment or fulfillment is often hard work.

ii. "No insect is more *laborious*, not even the *bee* itself; and none is more *fondly attached* to or more *careful* of its young, than the ant." (Clarke)

iii. "Christ sends us to school to the birds of the air, and lilies of the field, to learn dependence upon divine providence, [Matthew 6:25-29] and to the stork, crane, and swallow, to be taught to take the seasons of grace, and not to let slip the opportunities that God putteth into our hands. [Jeremiah 8:7]." (Trapp)

b. **Having no captain, overseer or ruler**: The ant is **wise** and worthy of imitation because she works hard without having to be *told* to work hard. The ethic of diligence comes from within and does not have to be imposed by a **captain, overseer or ruler**.

i. "Aristotle also asserted that ants labor without rulers to direct them. Modern entomologists have discovered a perfect social organization among ants, but, as Plaut notes, this does 'not imply that there is a hierarchy of command.'" (Waltke)

c. **Provides her supplies in the summer**: The ant works hard when the work is to be done. In the **summer** and in the **harvest**, the work gets done. This means that the ant gives a good lesson in her **ways** and her wisdom.

i. "What a deal of grain gets she together in summer! What pains doth she take for it, labouring not by daylight only, but by moonshine also! What huge heaps hath she! What care to bring forth her store, and lay it drying on a sunshine day, lest with moisture it should putrefy." (Trapp)

2. (9-11) Warning the lazy man.

How long will you slumber, O sluggard?
When will you rise from your sleep?
A little sleep, a little slumber,
A little folding of the hands to sleep—
So shall your poverty come on you like a prowler,
And your need like an armed man.

a. **How long will you slumber, O sluggard?** Solomon asked the lazy man to give account for his ways. The thought is, "You want to sleep – **how long**? There is life to be lived and work to be done."

i. "The sluggard is the explicit audience, but the implicit audiences are the son and the gullible who are addressed in the book (see Proverbs 1:4-5). They are being warned against laziness through the sluggard's chastisement (see Proverbs 19:25)." (Waltke)

b. **When will you rise from your sleep?** Obviously, every person needs **sleep**. Solomon's advice is not that we should never sleep, but that we should not excessively sleep.

c. **A little sleep, a little slumber**: Solomon imagined the lazy man saying this. He claimed that he only needed a **little sleep**, but actually he needed to work more.

i. "Sleep is the defining characteristic of the sluggard (cf. Proverbs 20:13); for him the love of sleep is pure escapism—a refusal to face the world (Proverbs 26:14). In contrast to the sweet sleep of the laboring person (Proverbs 4:23; Eccl. 5:12), the sluggard's narcotic sleep ever craves still more sleep to escape the pain of living (Proverbs 19:15)." (Waltke)

d. **So shall your poverty come on you like a prowler**: The lazy man will find that **poverty** and **need** come upon him quickly. The sluggard loves to procrastinate and think things can always be done *later*. The hard worker can look forward to later; for the lazy man it will come **like a prowler**. When it comes, it will be **your poverty** – not one imposed by circumstances or misfortune, but through laziness.

i. **Poverty come on you**: "At least 14 proverbs relate idleness, either explicitly or implicitly, to poverty, the bitter end of the sluggard (cf. 20:13; 24:33-34). It is not riches the lazy person lacks; it is food, the necessity of life (cf. 19:15; 20:13; 23:21)." (Waltke)

ii. **Like an armed man**: "That is, with irresistible fury; and thou art not prepared to oppose it." (Clarke)

3. (12-15) The destiny of the wicked man.

A worthless person, a wicked man,
Walks with a perverse mouth;
He winks with his eyes,
He shuffles his feet,
He points with his fingers;
Perversity *is* in his heart,
He devises evil continually,
He sows discord.
Therefore his calamity shall come suddenly;
Suddenly he shall be broken without remedy.

a. **A worthless person, a wicked man**: Solomon moved from the idea of the lazy man (Proverbs 6:6-11) to the **worthless** and **wicked** man. These sinful characteristics are often related and combined.

b. **Walks with a perverse mouth**: One of the main features of the **worthless** and **wicked** person's manner of life (his walk) is the corruption of his speech. He has a **perverse mouth**, which mainly has the idea of crooked or corrupt, more than what we would think of as moral perversion. What he says isn't straight, honest, and right.

c. **Winks with his eyes**: With his **eyes**, his **feet**, and his **fingers**, the worthless and wicked man shows his crooked and dishonest character. **Evil** and **discord** come from his life.

d. **His calamity shall come suddenly**: Solomon did not directly attribute this **calamity** or breaking (**he shall be broken**) to the judgment of God, but it is implied. God knows how to set the cynical, crooked-speaking man or woman in their deserved place.

4. (16-19) Seven things the LORD hates.

These six *things* the LORD hates,
Yes, seven *are* an abomination to Him:
A proud look,
A lying tongue,
Hands that shed innocent blood,
A heart that devises wicked plans,
Feet that are swift in running to evil,
A false witness *who* speaks lies,
And one who sows discord among brethren.

a. **These six things...yes, seven**: Several times in the book of Proverbs, Solomon used this expression to give a list. Here the list is of things that **the LORD hates**, that are **an abomination to Him**.

i. "The 'six' and 'seven' of the opening statement have their explanation in the description. The six are first stated, and the seventh is that which results, namely, 'he that soweth discord among brethren.'" (Morgan)

ii. "The hissing sibilant sound resounds throughout the catalogue, especially in this verse: *ses* (six), *sane* ('hates'), *seba* ('seven'), and *napso* ('him')." (Waltke)

b. **Seven are an abomination to Him**: Solomon listed these seven sins.

- **A proud look**
- **A lying tongue**
- **Hands that shed innocent blood**
- **A heart that devises evil plans**
- **Feet that are swift in running to evil**
- **A false witness who speaks lies**
- **One who sows discord among brethren**

   i. Most of these sins are connected to something we do, in or through our body. The eyes have **a proud look**, the tongue lies, and so on. We are again reminded of what Paul wrote in Romans about presenting the parts of our body (our members) to God for the work of righteousness, not sin (Romans 6:13).

   ii. This collection of seven sins is also focused on how we treat others. We must honor God and worship Him in spirit and in truth, yet God is also concerned about how we treat others. Each of these are serious sins against others.

c. **One who sows discord among brethren**: This is presented as the result of the previous six or the ultimate among them. It is one of the highest among the things that God hates and regards as an abomination.

   i. "Seventh, the one *who unleashes conflicts* (see v. 14) again climactically brings the catalogue to its conclusion." (Waltke)

   ii. Adam Clarke describes this **one** as "he who troubles the peace of a family, of a village, of the state; all who, by lies and misrepresentations, strive to make men's minds evil-affected towards their brethren."

   iii. "None love a mischief-maker, and yet we are apt to think of the sin with something less than the Divine intolerance for it. We may take it as an unqualified certainty that no man in whose heart the fear of Jehovah prevails and rules, can ever sow discord among brethren." (Morgan)

iv. "A withering blast will fall on those who, mistaking prejudice for principle, cause divisions for their own selfish ends (Romans 16:17-18)." (Bridges)

C. The harm of the harlot.

1. (20-24) God's word can keep you from the evil woman's seduction.

My son, keep your father's command,
And do not forsake the law of your mother.
Bind them continually upon your heart;
Tie them around your neck.
When you roam, they will lead you;
When you sleep, they will keep you;
And *when* you awake, they will speak with you.
For the commandment *is* a lamp,
And the law a light;
Reproofs of instruction *are* the way of life,
To keep you from the evil woman,
From the flattering tongue of a seductress.

a. **Keep your father's command**: Solomon probably had in mind *both* the wisdom a father passed to his children and the word of God received and cherished by the parents. A wise child will keep God's word close, **upon your heart** and **around your neck**.

i. **Bind them**: "here it pictures him memorizing them in such a way that they are permanently impressed on his essential mental and spiritual being that prompts his every action." (Waltke)

ii. "Implicit in these verses is the basic understanding that a good home life—i.e., father and mother sharing the rearing of the children together—will go a long way to prevent the youth from falling into immorality." (Ross)

iii. "In chapters 5-7, each of the warnings against adultery is prefaced by an admonition to pay attention to the Word of God (Proverbs 5:1-2; 6:20-24; 7:1-5)." (Wiersbe)

b. **When you roam, they will lead you**: The word of God is living and active. When it is cherished and kept close, we benefit from its living power. It then will **lead** us, it will **keep** us, and it will **speak with** us. Anyone who wants God to **lead**, **keep**, or **speak** should begin with cherishing God's word.

i. Proverbs 6:22 presents God's word as a person who helps in many ways.

- A guide: **will lead you.**

- A guardian: **will keep you.**

- A companion: **will speak with you.**

ii. **Will speak with you**: "This Bible is a wonderful talking book; there is a great mass of blessed talk in this precious volume. It has told me a great many of my faults; it would tell you yours if you would let it. It has told me much to comfort me; and it has much to tell you if you will but incline your ear to it. It is a book that is wonderfully communicative; it knows all about you, all the ins and outs of where you are, and where you ought to be, it can tell you everything." (Spurgeon)

c. **The commandment is a lamp**: Solomon seems to quote Psalm 119:105 (*Your word is a lamp to my feet and a light to my path*). When given attention and properly valued, God's word brings light to us in our darkness.

d. **To keep you from the evil woman**: Here Solomon spoke to a specific place where wisdom from God's word can help. God's word and wisdom will never lead us to the **evil woman** or keep us with her. The light of God's word will wisely keep us from her and speak to us better things than her **flattering** words.

2. (25-29) The damage adultery does.

Do not lust after her beauty in your heart,
Nor let her allure you with her eyelids.
For by means of a harlot
A man is reduced **to a crust of bread;**
And an adulteress will prey upon his precious life.
Can a man take fire to his bosom,
And his clothes not be burned?
Can one walk on hot coals,
And his feet not be seared?
So *is* **he who goes in to his neighbor's wife;**
Whoever touches her shall not be innocent.

a. **Do not lust after her beauty in your heart**: Solomon granted that the immoral woman may have **beauty** to **lust** after. Wisdom and the word can help prevent one from being mastered by the desire of her beauty or her **allure**.

i. "It is a small praise to have a good face and a naughty nature - a beautiful countenance and a base life." (Trapp)

b. **Nor let her allure you**: In Solomon's day this **allure** normally took place in a personal encounter. In the modern world images constantly hope to **allure**. Wisdom and the word help us to see these alluring images for what they are: crooked lies that don't tell the truth about sex, relationships, or human nature.

> i. "The parallelism between 'do not covet her beauty' and 'and do not let her capture you with her eyes' suggests that coveting begins by allowing eye contact. Desiring comes into his heart through optical stimulation aroused by 'her beauty,' and more specifically by 'the pupils of her eyes,' followed by her sweet talk." (Waltke)

> ii. **With her eyelids**: "'Eyes' are singled out here because the painted eyes and the luring glances are symptoms of seduction (see 2 Kings 9:30)." (Ross)

c. **By means of a harlot a man is reduced to a crust of bread**: With her **beauty** and **allure**, the **harlot** promises to *add* something to the life of her customer. She promises excitement, pleasure, attention, or any number of other things. Yet she does not, and cannot, deliver on those promises; she takes away and does not give. The **adulteress will prey upon his precious life**.

> i. Several commentators favor translating Proverbs 6:26 with the thought of *comparing* the cost of a harlot and the cost of adultery. "The verse is best rendered, 'Although the price of a prostitute may be as much as a loaf of bread, / [another] man's wife hunts the precious life.'" (Garrett)

> ii. "This obviously is not meant to endorse going to a prostitute as opposed to having an affair with another man's wife but to show the complete folly of getting involved with another man's wife." (Garrett)

d. **Can a man take fire to his bosom, and his clothes not be burned?** Solomon's wisdom is brilliant in its clarity and simplicity. To take up with the harlot or adulteress is to play with **fire**, and to surely be **burned**. He warned, **whoever touches her shall not be innocent**.

> i. **He who goes in to his neighbor's wife**: "...that lieth with her, as the phrase signifies, Genesis 19:31; 29:21,23, etc. [**Whoever touches her**]...hath carnal knowledge of her, as this word is used, Genesis 20:6, 1 Corinthians 7:1." (Poole)

> ii. **Shall not be innocent**: "It is no good for such a man to later on complain about the strength of the temptation. Why did he not avoid it?" (Bridges)

3. (30-35) The disgrace adultery brings.

People do not despise a thief
If he steals to satisfy himself when he is starving.
Yet *when* he is found, he must restore sevenfold;
He may have to give up all the substance of his house.
Whoever commits adultery with a woman lacks understanding;
He *who* does so destroys his own soul.
Wounds and dishonor he will get,
And his reproach will not be wiped away.
For jealousy *is* a husband's fury;
Therefore he will not spare in the day of vengeance.
He will accept no recompense,
Nor will he be appeased though you give many gifts.

a. **People do not despise a thief**: Solomon considered how we may, in some way, excuse a **thief** who steals to survive. Yet even when that thief is caught, justice would require him to **restore** what he has stolen and more. The adulterer steals, but not out of necessity – and in such a way that true restitution is impossible.

i. **He must restore sevenfold**: "*i.e.,* Manifold, according as the law limiteth, though it be to the utmost of what the thief is worth. But what restitution can the adulterer make, should he make him amends with as much more? The thief steals out of want; the adulterer of wantonness." (Trapp)

ii. Though Solomon *contrasted* theft and adultery, there is an interesting link between them. Sexual immorality and adultery are like stealing. When we have sex with anyone other than our appointed partner in the covenant of marriage, we are stealing something from our spouse (present or future), from our illicit sexual partner, and from the present or future spouse of our illicit sexual partner. Paul confirmed this likeness in 1 Thessalonians 4:3-6, where he wrote that to commit sexual immorality is to *take advantage of* and to *defraud* our brother.

b. **He who does so destroys his own soul**: To commit adultery (and to commit sexual sin in general) is not only sin against God and others, but also against one's **own soul**, his own body (1 Corinthians 6:18-19). We usually think that the penalty for sexual immorality comes if the sin is exposed and known; wisdom and God's word tell us that it **destroys** whether it is exposed or not.

i. **Lacks understanding**: "King David was a brilliant strategist on the battlefield and a wise ruler on the throne, but he lost his common sense when he gazed at his neighbor's wife and lusted for her (2 Samuel 12)." (Wiersbe)

c. **Destroys his own soul**: Note that the blame is *upon the adulterer*. He may blame the temptress, his wife, his lusts, his desires, his circumstances, God, or the devil himself. Yet at the end of it all, he **destroys his own soul**.

> i. "The expression 'destroys himself' in v. 32 stresses that the guilty one destroys his own life." (Ross)

> ii. **Destroys his own soul**: "The vixen hunts for his life, but he is responsible for his self-destruction." (Waltke)

d. **His reproach will not be wiped away**: In *addition* to the ways that sexual immorality brings harm, it will also bring disgrace when it is discovered. The jealous husband will often **not spare in the day of vengeance** and will not be **appeased** in his anger.

> i. "**His reproach shall not be wiped away;** although it be forgiven by God, yet the reproach and scandal of it remains." (Poole)

> ii. **Accept no recompense**: "This is an injury that admits of *no compensation*. No *gifts* can satisfy a man for the injury his honour has sustained; and to take a *bribe* or a *ransom*, would be setting up *chastity* at a price." (Clarke)

> iii. "Though the court may sentence the adulterer to caning, shame, and loss of all his property, the cuckold will never be pacified and want nothing less than his death." (Waltke)

e. **Wounds and dishonor he will get**: Sexual immorality offers pleasure and excitement and often romance. It may or may not deliver those things, but even if it does, it will also bring **wounds and dishonor**. It brings **wounds** to one's body and soul, and **dishonor** in the family, congregation, and community.

> i. "He is wounded, but not like a soldier or Christian martyr. He is not full of honor but of **disgrace**. His name is full of **shame**." (Bridges)

> ii. "The picture of the adulterer as social outcast may seem greatly overdrawn. If so, the adjustment that must be made is to say that in any *healthy* society such an act is social suicide. Condonation, as distinct from forgiveness, only proves the adulterer to be part of a general decadence." (Kidner)

Proverbs 7 – The Story of Seduction

A. The importance of valuing wisdom.

1. (1-4) Keeping God's word and a father's wisdom close.

My son, keep my words,
And treasure my commands within you.
Keep my commands and live,
And my law as the apple of your eye.
Bind them on your fingers;
Write them on the tablet of your heart.
Say to wisdom, "You *are* my sister,"
And call understanding *your* nearest kin,

> a. **My son, keep my words**: As in the previous two sections warning against sexual immorality (Proverbs 5:1-4 and 6:20-24), Proverbs 7 begins with an emphasis on keeping and understanding God's word and a father's wisdom.

> b. **Keep my commands and live**: The implication is *not* that Bible reading provides a magical protection against sexual immorality. Yet if a person does **keep** God's written **commands**, they will not carry out this sin – and the keeping of the commands begins with knowing them, treasuring them, and meditating on them.

> > i. **As the apple of your eye**: "The familiar phrase 'apple of your eye' (v. 2) refers to the pupil of the eye which the ancients thought was a sphere like an apple. We protect our eyes because they're valuable to us, and so should we honor and protect God's Word by obeying it." (Wiersbe)

> c. **Write them on the tablet of your heart**: Solomon counseled his son to have a living, breathing *relationship* with the word of God. It should not

be only on his mind but also in his **heart**. He should love the word as his **sister** and **nearest kin**.

i. Morgan spoke of the power of truly regarding **wisdom** as a **sister** or **nearest kin**. "Thousands of men are kept from evil courses by the love and friendship of sisters, and women friends. Recognizing this, the father counsels his son to find strength against the seductions of evil, by cultivating that kind of defensive and defending familiarity with wisdom, which is typified by this love of a sister and of pure women."

2. (5) The benefit of keeping God's word and a father's wisdom close.

That they may keep you from the immoral woman,
From the seductress *who* flatters with her words.

a. **That they may keep you from the immoral woman**: The wisdom and power of God's word help to **keep** us from the immoral woman (or man). From God's word we learn the deception and strategy of sin and temptation. We learn the end result of sin and the wonderful benefits of obedience. God's word imparts the spiritual light and strength we need to obey God in this difficult area.

i. The task of keeping men and women from sexual immorality sometimes seems impossible. This is due to many factors, including:

- A secular, sexually saturated and permissive culture.
- The widespread availability of pornography.
- The disconnection of sex from pregnancy and reproduction.
- Laws making divorce easy and impossible to contest.
- Social media technology making anonymous meetings easier.
- Widespread prosperity that lessens the financial impact of family breakups.
- The large and growing gap between the time of puberty and the average time people get married.

ii. These factors are not all unique to the present day; Christianity was founded in a very sexually permissive culture. Yet they highlight the great need for Christian men and women to rely on the power and wisdom of God's word to remain pure. It also means that such purity, even in the sense of rededication to purity, is a great sacrifice and gift to the honor and glory of God.

b. **From the seductress who flatters with her words**: Immorality speaks and has **words** to draw us into sin. We need the corresponding and greater power of God's words to **keep** us from **the immoral woman** (or man).

B. A story of seduction.

1. (6-9) The young fool seeks the immoral woman.

For at the window of my house
I looked through my lattice,
And saw among the simple,
I perceived among the youths,
A young man devoid of understanding,
Passing along the street near her corner;
And he took the path to her house
In the twilight, in the evening,
In the black and dark night.

a. **At the window of my house**: As a skilled storyteller, Solomon explained how one day he **looked** out his window and saw a man **passing along the street**. The man was **simple**, **young**, and **devoid of understanding**.

b. **Simple**: As in Proverbs 1:4 and 1:22, this isn't stupidity, but inexperience and gullibility. The simple are uneducated in the ways of wisdom and need instruction. As Phillips commented on Proverbs 1:4, the simple man has his mind open, but in a gullible and dangerous way.

c. **Among the youths, a young man**: The idea is repeated twice for emphasis. This man does not have the experience of years to help guide him in the path of wisdom. He has all the passions, energy, and overconfidence of youth, and none of the wisdom the decades can bring.

i. Of course, it is not *only* the **young man** who faces the challenge of purity; men and women of every age have their own challenges to pure living. Yet these are often more severely felt in the life of the **young man**.

ii. Even when a **young man** has the desire for moral purity, there are many things that may make it difficult for a him to receive and live God's wisdom. These include:

- Youthful energy and sense of carelessness.
- The lack of life wisdom.
- The desire for, and gaining of, independence.
- Physical and sexual maturity that may run ahead of spiritual and moral maturity.
- Money and the freedom that it brings.
- Young women who may – knowingly or unknowingly – encourage moral impurity.

- The spirit of the age that both expects and promotes moral uncleanness for young men.
- The desire to be accepted by peers who face the same challenges.

iii. The world tells us, "Have your good time when you are young; get it all out of your system. When you are older you can settle down and be religious and proper." Yet God's wisdom can make (or *should* make) a huge difference in the life of a **young man**.

iv. God wants to spare the **young man** (and the older man) the bondage of sin. This reflects upon the power of *experience* to shape our *habits*. Surrender to any temptation; transfer it from the realm of mental contemplation to life experience, and that temptation instantly becomes *much more difficult to resist in the future*. Each successive experience of surrender to temptation builds a habit, reinforced not only spiritually, but also by brain chemistry. Such ingrained habits are more and more difficult to break the more they are experienced, and it is almost impossible to break such habits without *replacing* them with another habit.

d. **Devoid of understanding**: Because he is **simple** and **young**, his reservoir of wisdom and **understanding** is empty. He is the one who must, at all costs, *get wisdom* (Proverbs 4:5-7).

i. "Young, inexperienced, featherbrained, he is the very sort to need arming with borrowed wisdom." (Kidner)

ii. Psalm 119:9 gives remarkable wisdom to the young man: *How can a young man cleanse his way? By taking heed according to Your word.*

e. **He took the path to her house**: Lacking wisdom and experience, this man was an easy target for the immoral woman. Under cover of **the black and dark night**, he was foolish enough to pass **along** her **street**, then foolish enough to go **near her corner**. Soon he **took the path to her house**.

i. Given those conditions, it isn't difficult to finish the story. We know how it ends when someone positively pursues temptation in this manner. As part of the disciples' prayer, we are to pray *do not lead us into temptation* (Matthew 6:13). This one leads *himself* into temptation with sad and familiar results.

ii. **The black and dark night**: "Foolish men think to hide themselves from God, by hiding God from themselves." (Trapp)

2. (10-12) Meeting the immoral woman.

And there a woman met him,
With **the attire of a harlot, and a crafty heart.**

She *was* loud and rebellious,
Her feet would not stay at home.
At times *she was* outside, at times in the open square,
Lurking at every corner.

a. **There a woman met him**: Before he could actually reach her house, the immoral **woman met him**. She wasn't a prostitute, but she dressed like one (**the attire of a harlot**) and had the heart of one (**a crafty heart**). For her, sex was a transaction, not an experience of intimacy in marriage.

i. "Her bold attire matches her bold approach, for a harlot knows no shame (Proverbs 30:20). Her outward dress, which seems to promise her victim her body, conceals her secret intention to use him to gratify her own lusts." (Waltke)

ii. "Outwardly, she keeps nothing back; she is dressed, as we say, to kill; inwardly, she gives nothing away (10b, literally 'guarded of heart', meaning either hard, unyielding, or close, secretive)." (Kidner)

b. **She was loud and rebellious**: If the simple man cared to notice, this was not a woman of good and dignified character. Her heart or her body **would not stay at home** but looked for love and satisfaction **outside** the home.

i. **Rebellious**: "Indicates her rebellion against propriety for a life of profligacy. The original meaning of the verbal root can still be recognized in the imagery of the stubborn cow (Hosea 4:16); she chafes at restraint and revolts against the rules of proper society." (Waltke)

c. **Lurking at every corner**: Her availability and willingness for sex excited the young man. She wasn't hard to find or arrange a meeting with. His wisdom and ability to resist temptation would be tested by the presence of a willing and available woman.

i. "She is continually exposing herself, and showing by her gait and gestures *what* she is, and *what* she *wants*." (Clarke)

ii. When it comes to sexual purity, some people are outwardly pure because they have lacked, in their perception, low-risk opportunities. If a person quickly fails when they do encounter a willing and available partner for sexual immorality, it shows they were ready to fall and something was wrong even when they were, for a time outwardly pure.

3. (13-18) The seductive promises of the immoral woman.

So she caught him and kissed him;
With an impudent face she said to him:
"*I have* peace offerings with me;
Today I have paid my vows.

So I came out to meet you,
Diligently to seek your face,
And I have found you.
I have spread my bed with tapestry,
Colored coverings of Egyptian linen.
I have perfumed my bed
With myrrh, aloes, and cinnamon.
Come, let us take our fill of love until morning;
Let us delight ourselves with love.

a. **So she caught him and kissed him**: The idea is that she *trapped* him, and this is an accurate description of how many are ensnared in a sexually immoral relationship. They are pleased to be **caught**, and then soon feel trapped.

b. **With an impudent face she said to him**: The sexually immoral person shows a certain defiance and impudence. They insist on *their* way and *their* gratification. It was with this sense of arrogant defiance that she spoke the following words.

c. **I have peace offerings with me**: The sexually immoral woman Solomon described was not against religion, just against the moral code of the God of Abraham, Isaac, and Jacob. She favored a god who would receive her **peace offerings** while she lived as she pleased when it came to her sexual desires.

i. "She pretends religion to her filthy practices…. So did King Edward IV's holy whore, as he used to call her, that came to him out of a nunnery when he used to call for her." (Trapp)

ii. "She dared not play the harlot with man until she had played the hypocrite with God and stopped the mouth of her conscience with her fellowship offerings." (Gurnall, cited in Bridges)

iii. "Much light is cast on this place by the *fact* that the gods in many parts of the East are actually worshipped in *brothels*, and fragments of the *offerings* are divided among the wretches who fall into the snare of the prostitutes." (Clarke)

iv. The mention of **peace offerings** also suggested the food at her home would be good. "That she had plentiful and excellent provisions at her house for his entertainment. For the peace-offerings were to be of the best flesh, Leviticus 22:21, and a considerable part of these offerings fell to the offerers' share, wherewith they used to feast themselves and their friends." (Poole)

d. **I came out to meet you, diligently to seek your face**: By instinct or experience, the seductress knew the power of making this simple young man feel *desired*. She could catch him by displaying that she wanted him. For many people, that is all the seduction they need.

> i. "She appeals to the young man's male ego as she flatters him and makes him think he's very special to her. What she's offering to him she would never offer to anyone else!" (Wiersbe)

e. **I have spread my bed with tapestry**: She went on to allure him with the anticipation of the sensory experience, and that directly connected with her **bed**. She told the simple young man that he would experience wonderful touches, smells, and pleasures.

> i. "She designs to inflame his lust by the mention of the bed, and by its ornaments and perfumes." (Poole)

> ii. **Myrrh, aloes, and cinnamon**: "She now stimulates him with aphrodisiac smells; all three names for perfumes in this verse are also found in Song 4:14 as odiferous images of sexual love." (Waltke)

> iii. **With myrrh, aloes**: "This might have minded the young man that he was going to his grave; for the bodies of the dead were so perfumed. Such a meditation would have much rebated his edge, cooled his courage." (Trapp)

f. **Let us take our fill of love until morning**: Her invitations became more and more explicit, though still clouded in the misused word **love**. She offered him a kind of **love**, but certainly not the best or lasting love. It would be a **delight** and even last **until morning**, but bring pain, misery, and death in the end.

> i. Adam Clarke on verse 18: "The original itself is too gross to be literally translated; but quite in character as coming from the mouth of an abandoned woman."

4. (19-21) The successful seduction.

For my husband *is* not at home;
He has gone on a long journey;
He has taken a bag of money with him,
***And* will come home on the appointed day."**
With her enticing speech she caused him to yield,
With her flattering lips she seduced him.

a. **For my husband is not at home**: This makes clear what was hinted at before, that this was not a harlot but an adulterous woman. She betrayed her husband, her honor, her marriage vow, and her faithfulness to God.

i. She was careful to refer to her **husband** in ways that would not awaken the conscience of her target. She did not give her husband a name, and "she represents *my husband* by 'the man', not by 'my husband.'" (Waltke)

b. **He has gone on a long journey**: The final piece of her plan of seduction was to persuade the young, simple man that *this was safe and would have no consequence*. Many people are willing to commit sexual immorality when they feel there is little or no risk of being discovered, showing that their commitment to purity is rooted in external motivations, not internal motivations.

c. **With her enticing speech she caused him to yield**: At the end of it all, her seduction was successful. With her **enticing speech** and her **flattering lips** she convinced the simple young man to sin with her sexually. She used words and actions to successfully walk her victim through these steps of seduction:

- A well-chosen target (*simple…a young man devoid of understanding*, 7:7).
- Available to meet (*the path to her house…a woman met him*, 7:8, 7:10).
- Provocatively clothed (*with the attire of a harlot*, 7:10).
- Of bad character (*loud and rebellious*, 7:11).
- Looking to trap and seduce (*she caught him*, 7:13).
- Free with physical affection (*kissed him*, 7:13).
- Gave some recognition to religion (*peace offerings…paid my vows*, 7:14).
- Pursuit to make one feel desired (*I came out to meet you, diligently*, 7:15).
- Promise to please the senses (*I have spread my bed…I have perfumed my bed*, 7:16-17).
- Invitation to her bed (*I have spread my bed…I have perfumed my bed*, 7:16-17).
- Promises of love, delight, and sensual pleasure (*let us take our fill of love until morning; let us delight ourselves with love*, 7:18).
- Persuasion that the risk of discovery is very low (*my husband is not at home; he has gone on a long journey*, 7:19).

5. (22-23) The painful price of the immoral woman.

Immediately he went after her, as an ox goes to the slaughter,
Or as a fool to the correction of the stocks,
Till an arrow struck his liver.
As a bird hastens to the snare,
He did not know it *would cost* his life.

a. **Immediately he went after her**: The woman presented by Solomon in Proverbs 7 *would be* very difficult to resist. This is why we anticipated that **he went after her** as soon as he started on the path towards her house (Proverbs 7:8). Such strong temptation *can* be overcome by the power and presence of Jesus in the believer, but it is even better to keep one's self from the temptation itself.

b. **Immediately**: There was no delay. We sense he *begged* to be tempted this way, and so had no strength to stand against it.

i. "*Suddenly* (Proverbs 3:25; 6:15) fixes the moment of decision and implies that the gullible acted without reflection but allowed his glands to do his thinking for him." (Waltke)

c. **As an ox goes to the slaughter**: The promise of the sexually immoral woman and the anticipation of the simple young man was for sensual pleasure and delight. What was really waiting for him was **slaughter**; he was like an animal ripe for sacrifice or like **a fool** for **the correction of the stocks**.

i. "As the ox goes to the slaughter, unconscious of his fate, perhaps dreaming of rich pasture, or as a fool goes to the stock, careless and unfeeling, so does this poor deluded victim rush on with pitiable mirth or indifference." (Bridges)

ii. **Till an arrow struck his liver**: "The arrow piercing the liver may refer to the pangs of a guilty conscience that the guilty must reap along with spiritual and physical ruin." (Ross)

iii. **Like an ox...as a bird**: "Human beings are the only creatures in God's creation who can choose what kind of creatures they want to be. God wants us to be sheep (Psalm 23:1; John 10; 1 Peter 2:25), but there are other options, such as horses or mules (Psalm 32:9), or even hogs and dogs (2 Peter 2:22)." (Wiersbe)

d. **He did not know that it would cost his life**: The simple young man chose to only see and anticipate the sensual excitement and pleasure waiting for him with the sexually immoral woman. He did not reckon on the *cost* involved or supposed that the only cost came from being discovered.

i. "The temptress promises sexual love without erotic restraint, but she refuses to make the fundamental commitment of self to him that is required of true love. Her sort of eroticism leads to complications, even death, and so it must be rejected." (Waltke)

6. (24-27) Learning from the immoral woman.

Now therefore, listen to me, *my* children;
Pay attention to the words of my mouth:
Do not let your heart turn aside to her ways,
Do not stray into her paths;
For she has cast down many wounded,
And all who were slain by her were strong *men.*
Her house *is* the way to hell,
Descending to the chambers of death.

a. **Now therefore, listen to me**: The lesson had been presented, and needed a conclusion to reinforce the principle. The father once again asked for the **attention** of his children to this important matter.

b. **Do not let your heart turn aside to her ways**: Solomon understood that adultery and sexual immorality begin in the **heart**. They don't begin in the hormones or glands, and they don't begin in the heart in a romantic sense. In the sense that the **heart** describes our deepest loves and desires, a heart that does not properly love and desire God, but loves and desires pleasure more, will **turn aside** to sexual immorality.

c. **Do not stray into her paths**: If the **heart** is turned aside towards sexual immorality, the feet will find it easy to **stray** in that direction. It is far better for the line of godliness to be drawn at the heart; but if it is not, then it should be drawn at the path.

d. **For she has cast down many wounded**: Many, many people have had their reputations, their health, their money, and even their lives destroyed by sexual immorality. Many of these **were strong men** or women. God's word and a father's wisdom teach us to learn from their disaster and not repeat it for ourselves.

i. "The language of v. 26 is military in tone. The lady who was so desirable has slain whole armies." (Garrett)

ii. **Strong men**: "*Atsumim*, which we render *strong men*, may be translated *heroes*. Many of those who have distinguished themselves in the field and in the cabinet have been overcome and destroyed by their mistresses. History is full of such examples." (Clarke)

iii. "The valour of man hath oft been slaved by the wiles of a woman. Witness many of your greatest martialists, who conquered countries, and were vanquished of vices." (Trapp)

e. **Her house is the way to hell**: That wasn't how she saw it or described it (Proverbs 7:16-18), but it was true. Wisdom teaches us that things are not as they are often presented or perceived. Rare is the person who willingly, knowingly takes **the way to hell** and descends **to the chambers of death**. The power of temptation and the tempter lies in *concealing* this result, and wisdom sees what is concealed.

i. "Her bedroom is no ballroom, but a battlefield where corpses lie about and from where many are sent to the Netherworld." (Gemser, cited in Waltke)

ii. "In the hour of sin's glamor it is good for the soul to look through to the end which is in Sheol and the chambers of death. When the voice of the siren is heard, it is good to pause and listen to the moan of the breakers on the shore of darkness and death, for to that shore the way of impurity assuredly leads." (Morgan)

Proverbs 8 – In Praise of Wisdom

G. Campbell Morgan on Proverbs 8: "There is nothing greater or grander in all the Biblical literature, as setting forth the beauty and grace of that wisdom which has the fear of Jehovah as its chief part."

A. The call of wisdom.

1. (1-3) Wisdom cries out.

Does not wisdom cry out,
And understanding lift up her voice?
She takes her stand on the top of the high hill,
Beside the way, where the paths meet.
She cries out by the gates, at the entry of the city,
At the entrance of the doors:

a. **Does not wisdom cry out**: As before in the book of Proverbs, Solomon here wrote of wisdom as if she were a person – a noble, beautiful, helpful woman in contrast to the immoral woman described in Proverbs 7.

i. "The unchaste wife moves covertly at dusk and speaks falsely; Wisdom moves publicly and speaks direct and authoritative truth." (Waltke)

b. **She takes her stand on the top of the high hill**: Wisdom personified cries out as widely and broadly as possible. She speaks to those **beside the way** and **where the paths meet**. She makes her call in the most public of places, **by the gates, at the entry of the city**. *Wisdom is not hidden* – it cries out to all who will listen.

i. "A chapter which is to soar beyond time and space, opens at street-level, to make it clear, first, that the wisdom of God is as relevant to the shopping-centre (Proverbs 8:2-3) as to heaven itself (Proverbs 8:22)." (Kidner)

ii. "The important point is that wisdom is for ordinary people—she is not confined to the academic classroom or to sacred precincts of the temple. Nor is she high atop some mountain where only the hardiest and most determined will find her. To the contrary, she wants to attract all and be accessible to all." (Garrett)

iii. Adam Clarke saw something wonderful in wisdom's public proclamation, and something worthy to imitate. "There are, it is true, temples, synagogues, churches, chapels, etc.; but hundreds of thousands never frequent them, and therefore do not hear the voice of truth: *wisdom*, therefore, *must go to them*, if she wishes them to receive her instructions. Hence the zealous ministers of Christ go still to the *highways* and *hedges*, to the *mountains* and *plains*, to the *ships* and the *cottages*, to persuade sinners to turn from the error of their ways and accept that redemption which was procured by the sacrificial offering of Jesus Christ."

2. (4-11) The goodness wisdom promises.

"To you, O men, I call,
And my voice *is* to the sons of men.
O you simple ones, understand prudence,
And you fools, be of an understanding heart.
Listen, for I will speak of excellent things,
And from the opening of my lips *will come* right things;
For my mouth will speak truth;
Wickedness *is* an abomination to my lips.
All the words of my mouth *are* with righteousness;
Nothing crooked or perverse *is* in them.
They *are* all plain to him who understands,
And right to those who find knowledge.
Receive my instruction, and not silver,
And knowledge rather than choice gold;
For wisdom *is* better than rubies,
And all the things one may desire cannot be compared with her.

a. **To you, O men, I call**: Here Solomon spoke of wisdom personified. This is the message she presented to men and women, all who would listen to her.

i. "The loudness and the perseverance of the **voice** is that of an earnest friend who warns of danger. For would she have cried so loud or continued for so long if she had not loved your soul, if she had not known the wrath that was hanging over you, the hell that was before you?" (Bridges)

b. **You simple ones, understand prudence**: Wisdom doesn't give up on the **simple ones**. The simple man described in Proverbs 7 seems like a lost cause, but he doesn't have to be. *We can* learn the ways of wisdom and benefit from that learning.

c. **My mouth will speak truth**: When wisdom speaks, it is true. When people use lies they should not be trusted to communicate wisdom. Wisdom says of her words that there is **nothing crooked or perverse in them**. Because of this, the words can be understood; **they are all plain to him who understands**. There is clarity and a straightforward character to wisdom, one that contrasts with elaborate so-called hidden truths and mysteries.

   i. It could be said of the Scriptures in general, **they are all plain to him who understands**. Of course, there are deep and occasionally complicated passages, but the fundamental truths of the Bible are **plain** to those who trust God and honor His word. As the American author Mark Twain was reported to have said, *It's not the parts of the Bible I can't understand that bother me; it's the parts that I do understand.*

   ii. "It was a smart answer which M. Durant, a witty and learned minister of the Reformed Church of Paris, gave to a lady of suspected chastity, and now revolted: when she pretended the hardness of the Scripture, Why, said he, madam, what can be more plain than 'Thou shalt not commit adultery?' Had she not been failing in the practice of what she could not but know, she had found no cause to complain of the difficulty of that which she could not know." (Trapp)

d. **All the things one may desire cannot be compared with her**: Wisdom's value is above **silver**, **gold**, and **rubies**. Without wisdom, one may have the riches of this world and a miserable life. Early in his reign Solomon desired wisdom above all riches and was greatly blessed because of it (1 Kings 3:10-13).

B. Wisdom describes herself.

1. (12-21) What wisdom has and what wisdom gives.

"I, wisdom, dwell with prudence,
And find out knowledge *and* discretion.
The fear of the LORD is to hate evil;
Pride and arrogance and the evil way
And the perverse mouth I hate.
Counsel *is* mine, and sound wisdom;
I *am* understanding, I have strength.
By me kings reign,

And rulers decree justice.
By me princes rule, and nobles,
All the judges of the earth.
I love those who love me,
And those who seek me diligently will find me.
Riches and honor *are* with me,
Enduring riches and righteousness.
My fruit *is* better than gold, yes, than fine gold,
And my revenue than choice silver.
I traverse the way of righteousness,
In the midst of the paths of justice,
That I may cause those who love me to inherit wealth,
That I may fill their treasuries.

a. **I, wisdom, dwell with prudence**: Where **prudence** – self-control, good judgment – is found, there wisdom will be found. A life given to impulse and extremes will not gain, appreciate, or display wisdom.

i. **Prudence**: "Prudence is defined, *wisdom applied to practice*; so wherever true wisdom is, it will lead to action." (Clarke)

b. **The fear of the LORD is to hate evil**: Reverence for God (and the wisdom that comes from it) is not neutral towards evil. Like the God it respects, it hates evil, along with the **pride** and **arrogance** and **perverse mouth** that often express evil.

i. "God's people partake of the Divine nature, and so have God-like both sympathies and antipathies. They not only leave sin, but loathe it, and are at deadly feud with it." (Trapp)

c. **By me kings reign**: Many gain power, stay in power, and exercise power through gaining and using wisdom.

i. Adam Clarke had an interesting thought on the phrase **I have strength**. "Speaking still of wisdom, as communicating rays of its light to man, it enables him to bring every thing to his aid; to construct machines by which *one man* can do the work of *hundreds*. From it comes all *mathematical learning*, all *mechanical knowledge*; from it originally came the *inclined plane*, the *wedge*, the *screw*, the *pulley*, in all its *multiplications*; and the *lever*, in all its *combinations* and *varieties*, came from this wisdom. And as all these can produce prodigies of *power*, far surpassing all kinds of *animal energy*, and all the effects of the utmost efforts of muscular force."

d. **I love those who love me**: Those who **love** and pursue wisdom will find themselves rewarded. They will find wisdom (**those who seek me** diligently will find me) and the blessings wisdom brings (**riches and honor…righteousness**). It could even be said that wisdom seeks out her followers to bless them (**that I may cause those who love me to inherit wealth**).

    i. **Those who seek me diligently will find me**: "With sincere affection, and great diligence, and above all other persons or things in the world; which he mentions as the effect and evidence of their love; for otherwise all men pretend to love God." (Poole)

    ii. **Riches and honor are with me**: "Paradoxically when wealth is sought it corrupts, but when wisdom is sought, edifying wealth is given (cf. 1 Kings 3:4-15)." (Waltke)

2. (22-31) Wisdom's long history.

"**The LORD possessed me at the beginning of His way,**
Before His works of old.
I have been established from everlasting,
From the beginning, before there was ever an earth.
When *there were* **no depths I was brought forth,**
When *there were* **no fountains abounding with water.**
Before the mountains were settled,
Before the hills, I was brought forth;
While as yet He had not made the earth or the fields,
Or the primal dust of the world.
When He prepared the heavens, I *was* **there,**
When He drew a circle on the face of the deep,
When He established the clouds above,
When He strengthened the fountains of the deep,
When He assigned to the sea its limit,
So that the waters would not transgress His command,
When He marked out the foundations of the earth,
Then I was beside Him *as* **a master craftsman;**
And I was daily *His* **delight,**
Rejoicing always before Him,
Rejoicing in His inhabited world,
And my delight *was* **with the sons of men.**

    a. **The LORD possessed me at the beginning of His way**: God used wisdom and intelligence in the design of the universe. If we represent wisdom as a person, then it can be said that wisdom was with God in creation. In **the beginning, before there was ever an earth**, God used wisdom in making something out of nothing.

i. A phrase from Proverbs 8:22 (**The LORD possessed me at the beginning of His way**) became a key support for the teaching of an influential heretic in the early church. Arius of Alexandria spoke for and promoted the idea that Jesus Christ was *not* God (much in the way modern Jehovah's Witnesses believe). Arius used this verse from the Greek translation of the Hebrew Scriptures, which puts the phrase like this: *The Lord created me at the beginning of His way*. Arius argued that Jesus is the wisdom of God, and this verse spoke of His creation. If Jesus was created, then He had a beginning and was not eternal, and if not eternal, then not God.

ii. The errors of Arius were many. On this particular passage, he exaggerated the way that wisdom in Proverbs 8 *is* Jesus Christ. It is wonderfully true that Jesus is the wisdom of God, especially in His work on the cross (1 Corinthians 1:20-24), and that Jesus became for us wisdom from God (1 Corinthians 1:30), and in Jesus are hidden all the treasures of wisdom (Colossians 2:3). Yet it is a mistake to say that Proverbs 8 describes Jesus in a sort of direct correlation. Because Jesus *is* God, He has and expresses and demonstrates the wisdom of God; but the *woman* of Proverbs 8 does not directly describe Jesus.

iii. A second – and perhaps more fundamental error – of Arius on this passage was to translate the Hebrew word *qanah* as *created* or *birthed* instead of **possessed**. While there is *some* case to be made for the idea of *created* or *birthed*, on balance the best translation is **possessed**. We could say, "Proverbs 8 doesn't directly speak of Jesus in the sense Arius meant, and if even if it did, Proverbs 8:22 doesn't say that God the Father created or birthed the Son of God."

iv. "The verb *qanah* can mean either 'possess' or 'create.' The older versions chose 'possess'; otherwise it might sound as if God lacked wisdom and so created it before the world began. They wanted to avoid saying that wisdom was not eternal. Arius liked the idea of Christ as the meaning of wisdom and chose 'create' as the verb. Athanasius read 'constituted me as the head of creation.' The verb *qanah* occurs twelve times in Proverbs with the idea of acquire; but the Septuagint and Syriac have the idea of 'create.'" (Ross)

v. "The Arians (who denied the deity of Christ) appealed to Septuagint's 'created', to prove that Christ, the Wisdom of God, was not eternal. But our concern must be with the word's normal meaning, and with the general sense of the passage." (Kidner)

b. **Before the mountains were settled**: With poetic beauty, Solomon considered many different aspects of creation and how God used wisdom to design and arrange them all. Wisdom could say, **I was beside Him as a master craftsman**.

> i. The antiquity of wisdom has a real and practical application. If the whole created order is founded on God's wisdom, then to go against His wisdom is to go against all creation. "When we belong to Jesus Christ and walk in His wisdom, all of creation works for us; if we rebel against His wisdom and will, things start to work against us, as Jonah discovered when he tried to run away from the Lord." (Wiersbe)

> ii. **He assigned to the sea its limit**: "Wisdom has in mind that the Creator established unalterable laws or ordinances that set the boundaries for the earth that the hostile sea cannot transgress (see Job 38:8-11). The chaotic energy of the sea operates within strict limits." (Waltke)

> c. **Rejoicing in His inhabited world**: The created world is so marked by God's wise and good design and arrangement that wisdom rejoiced in it. Especially, wisdom was happy with God's creation of man (**my delight was with the sons of men**). We sometimes think that the creation of man was a *problem* with the design and creation of the world; in a sense, man was the *purpose* of creation.

C. Wisdom appeals for an audience.

1. (32-33) Asking for attention.

"Now therefore, listen to me, *my* children,
For blessed *are those who* keep my ways.
Hear instruction and be wise,
And do not disdain *it*.

> a. **Now therefore, listen to me, my children**: Having given her impressive résumé, now wisdom can make a reasoned appeal that we **listen** to her.

> b. **For blessed are those who keep my ways**: In sometimes subtle and sometimes obvious ways, the world, the flesh, and the devil want us to think that we will somehow lose by listening to wisdom and keeping her ways. The truth is that there is great *blessing* when we **keep** her **ways**.

> c. **Hear instruction and be wise**: Given that wisdom has proven herself to be good and reliable, and that she brings many blessings with her, we should give wisdom our attention and never **disdain it**.

2. (34-36) Wisdom's reward and the cost of folly.

Blessed is the man who listens to me,
Watching daily at my gates,
Waiting at the posts of my doors.

For whoever finds me finds life,
And obtains favor from the LORD;
But he who sins against me wrongs his own soul;
All those who hate me love death."

a. **Blessed is the man who listens to me**: This blessing comes to those who not only listen to wisdom but are willing to inconvenience themselves to seek her. They are willing to watch **daily at** her **gates** and wait **at the posts** of her **doors**. Their pursuit of wisdom is intentional, not accidental.

i. **Watching daily at my gates**: "Wisdom is represented as having a *school* for the instruction of men; and seems to point out some of the most *forward* of her *scholars* coming, through their intense desire to learn, even *before the gates were opened*, and waiting there for admission, that they might hear *every word* that was uttered, and not lose one accent of the heavenly teaching. *Blessed are such*." (Clarke)

b. **Whoever finds me finds life**: Wisdom here presents two incomparable gifts; **life** and **favor from the LORD**. To love true wisdom is to receive these; to reject wisdom is to wrong one's **own soul** and to **love death**.

i. **And obtains favor from the LORD**: "Which is better than life. God's favour is no empty favour; it is not like the winter's sun, that casts a goodly countenance when it shines, but gives little heat or comfort." (Trapp)

ii. **Love death**: "Not directly or intentionally, but by consequence, because they love those practices which they know will bring certain destruction upon them." (Poole)

Proverbs 9 – Wisdom's Feast and Folly's Funeral

A. The way of wisdom.

1. (1-6) Wisdom's generous invitation.

Wisdom has built her house,
She has hewn out her seven pillars;
She has slaughtered her meat,
She has mixed her wine,
She has also furnished her table.
She has sent out her maidens,
She cries out from the highest places of the city,
"Whoever *is* simple, let him turn in here!"
***As for* him who lacks understanding, she says to him,**
"Come, eat of my bread
And drink of the wine I have mixed.
Forsake foolishness and live,
And go in the way of understanding.

a. **Wisdom has built her house**: Proverbs 8 described wisdom as a woman with blessings and benefits for those who listened and obeyed. Now Solomon pictures wisdom as a woman of generous hospitality who invites all (**Whoever is simple, let him turn in here!**).

i. John Trapp wrote that **wisdom** here is literally in the plural. "Hebrew, Wisdoms, in the plural; and this, either *honoris causa,* for honour's sake, or else by an ellipsis, as if the whole of it were 'wisdom of wisdoms.'"

ii. **Built her house**: Adam Clarke described the general understanding of this figure from the early church fathers and medieval theologians: "The house built by wisdom is the holy *humanity of Jesus Christ*; the *seven pillars* are the *seven sacraments,* or the *seven gifts of the Holy Ghost,* or the *whole of the apostles, preachers, and ministers of the Church*; the *slain beasts* are the *sacrifice of Christ's body* upon the cross; and the *bread* and *mingled wine* are the *bread* and *wine* in the *sacrament of the Lord's Supper!*" Of this, Clarke wrote: "men have produced strange creatures of their own brain, by way of explanation."

b. **Hewn out her seven pillars**: The primary idea is that wisdom's **house** is large, well-appointed, and unshakable. Through the centuries, various commentators have not been able to resist seeing some symbolic meaning in **her seven pillars**.

> i. "i.e. many pillars; whereby is intimated both the beauty and the stability of the church. *Pillars*; prophets, and apostles, and ministers of holy things, which in Scripture are called pillars, as Galatians 2:9, and elsewhere." (Poole)

c. **Come, eat of my bread**: The customs and ethics of hospitality in the ancient near east made this invitation even more meaningful. Wisdom offers the **simple** and he **who lacks understanding** her provision, partnership, and protection.

> i. "So just as one would prepare a banquet and invite guests, wisdom prepares to press her appeal. All this imagery lets the simpleton know that what wisdom has to offer is marvelous." (Ross)

> ii. **Has slaughtered her meat**: "Slaughtering, like the difficult and responsible activity of building a house, was normally a man's job (cf. Genesis 18:7; Judges 6:19; 1 Samuel 25:11), but Wisdom is an extraordinary woman." (Waltke)

> iii. **Has mixed her wine**: "1. With spices, to make it strong and delightful, this mixed wine being mentioned as the best, Proverbs 23:29,30. Or, 2. With water, as they used to do in those hot countries, partly for refreshment, and partly for wholesomeness; whereby also may be intimated that wisdom teacheth us temperance in the use of our comforts. Hath also furnished her table with all necessaries, and now waits for the guests." (Poole)

> iv. "Among the ancient *Jews, Greeks*, and *Romans*, wine was rarely drank without being mingled with water; and among ancient writers we find several ordinances for this. Some direct *three parts* of water to *one of wine*; some *five* parts; and *Pliny* mentions some wines that required *twenty* waters: but the most common proportions appear to have been *three parts of water* to *two of wine*." (Clarke)

> v. **Sent out her maidens**: Several older commentators see here an allusion to those who would preach the gospel. "So ministers are called - in prosecution of the allegory, for it is fit that this great lady

should have suitable attendants - to teach them innocence, purity, and [diligence] as maidens, keeping the word in sincerity, and not adulterating and corrupting it." (Trapp)

d. **Eat of my bread and drink of the wine**: Several older commentators saw an allegorical reference to communion, the Lord's Table, in the mention of **bread** and **wine** in Proverbs 9:5. This is an example of taking the figures from Hebrew poetry and wisdom literature and over-allegorizing them.

i. "Lyrannus noteth on this chapter, that the Eucharist was anciently delivered in both kinds: but because of the danger of spilling the blood, the Church ordained that laymen should have the bread only. The Council of Constance comes in with a *non obstante* against Christ's institution, withholding the cup from the sacrament." (Trapp)

e. **Forsake foolishness and live**: Wisdom makes the invitation, but the **simple** must respond. They must be willing to **go in the way of understanding**.

i. "Just as food and drink give physical life, Solomon's teachings give spiritual life. This truth finds an even better realization in Jesus' invitation to the banquet in the kingdom of God (Luke 14:15-24). Wisdom has done her part; now the feckless and senseless must make a decision to feast and be healed." (Waltke)

ii. **Him who lacks understanding**: "Literally, *he that wanteth a heart*; who is without *courage*, is *feeble* and *fickle*, and *easily drawn* aside from the holy commandment." (Clarke)

2. (7-9) Those who reject and receive wisdom.

"He who corrects a scoffer gets shame for himself,
And he who rebukes a wicked *man only* harms himself.
Do not correct a scoffer, lest he hate you;
Rebuke a wise *man*, and he will love you.
Give *instruction* to a wise *man*, and he will be still wiser;
Teach a just *man*, and he will increase in learning.

a. **He who corrects a scoffer gets shame for himself**: Having given the generous invitation, wisdom explained the folly and fruitlessness of trying to impose wisdom on the unwilling. The **wicked man** and the **scoffer** won't receive wisdom and will often **hate** the one who tries to help.

i. **The scoffer**: "He is the person who will not live by wise and moral teachings and is not content to let others do so without his cynical mocking." (Ross)

ii. **Gets shame**: "*Shame* (King James Version, Revised Version): better, *abuse* (Revised Standard Version). The further one goes with folly or wisdom, the less or the more will one put up with the criticism which is wisdom's teaching-method." (Kidner)

iii. "Fools, scoffers, and the simple like to have their own way and be told they're doing fine, but wise men and women want the truth. Teach wise people and they'll accept the truth and become wiser; try to teach fools and they'll reject the truth and become even greater fools." (Wiersbe)

iv. Isaiah 28:10 is an example of the scorning and taunting of one who delivers the truth. "One observeth that that was a scoff put upon the prophet; and is as if they should say, Here is nothing but line upon line, precept upon precept. The very sound of the words in the original - *Zau le zau, kau lakau* - carries a taunt, as scornful people by the tone of their voice, and rhyming words, scorn at such as they despise." (Trapp)

v. **Do not correct a scoffer**: "Solomon gives us here the rule of Christian prudence…. Why should we correct and rebuke when more harm than good will be the result? Avoid irritations. Wait for the favorable opportunity." (Bridges)

b. **Give instruction to a wise man, and he will be still wiser**: In contrast, the **wise** and **just** man will benefit from wisdom's invitation. This is something of the sense of Jesus' words, *For whoever has, to him more will be given, and he will have abundance; but whoever does not have, even what he has will be taken away from him* (Matthew 13:12).

i. "Literally *give to the wise, and he will be wise*. Whatever you give to such, they reap profit from it. They are like the bee, they extract honey from every flower." (Clarke)

ii. "David loved Nathan the better while he lived for dealing so plainly with him, and named him a commissioner for the declaring of his successor. [1 Kings 1:32-35]" (Trapp)

3. (10-12) The beginning and benefits of wisdom.

"The fear of the LORD is the beginning of wisdom,
And the knowledge of the Holy One *is* understanding.
For by me your days will be multiplied,
And years of life will be added to you.
If you are wise, you are wise for yourself,
And *if* you scoff, you will bear *it* alone."

a. **The fear of the LORD is the beginning of wisdom**: The statement of Proverbs 1:7 is repeated again, here towards the end of this section of the book of Proverbs. Though Proverbs is a book that focuses on practical life, it is founded on this important principle: wisdom begins with a right relationship with God.

   i. **Knowledge of the Holy One**: "Holy is here in the plural number, importing the Trinity of Persons, as likewise Joshua 24:19." (Trapp) "The plural can express excellence or comprehensiveness, like the plural word for Deity: Elohim." (Kidner)

   ii. **The Holy One**: "This title for the Lord underscores his 'otherness,' the sphere of his sacredness, separated from the mundane, the common, and the profane." (Waltke)

b. **The fear of the LORD**: This is a real **fear**, but in the sense of awe and reverence. It honors God as He really is – holy, just, and creator of all. It is not a cowering or servile fear, but it is a kind of fear nonetheless.

c. **The beginning of wisdom**: Wisdom has a starting place, and it is in the recognition and honor of God. This means those who do not recognize or honor God fall short of true wisdom in some way or another.

   i. "We are ever beginning; every morning we start afresh; every task we take up is a new start; every venture in joy or in effort, must have its commencement. Then let every beginning be in the fear of Jehovah. That is Wisdom, and it leads in the way of Wisdom." (Morgan)

   ii. "There is an old saying which runs, 'Well begun is half done.' This is true indeed when the beginning is inspired and conditioned by the fear of Jehovah." (Morgan)

d. **By me your days will be multiplied**: Wisdom brings her benefits to those who receive her. Finding wisdom's start through the fear of the LORD will always be rewarded.

e. **If you are wise, you are wise for yourself**: Solomon explained how wisdom and folly directly affect the individual. Sometimes we seek wisdom more for others than ourselves; Solomon reminded us that wisdom is **for yourself**; the scoffer will not gain from the wisdom of others. When he is foolish he will **bear it alone**.

   i. Perhaps there is something like this also implied: "Don't seek wisdom to please others. That isn't a right or sufficient motivation. You are the one who will most benefit from the wisdom you seek after, so let the motivation come from you and not from another."

ii. "This is perhaps the strongest expression of individualism in the Bible. Such statements (cf. Ezekiel 18; Galatians 6:4-5) are not meant to deny that people benefit or suffer from each other's characters (cf. Proverbs 10:1), but to emphasize that the ultimate gainer or loser is the man himself." (Kidner)

B. The way of folly.

1. (13-15) The seat of the foolish woman.

A foolish woman is clamorous;
***She is* simple, and knows nothing.**
For she sits at the door of her house,
On a seat *by* the highest places of the city,
To call to those who pass by,
Who go straight on their way:

a. **A foolish woman is clamorous**: Using symbolic figures, Solomon now presented the foolish way that rejects wisdom. Wisdom is like a gracious woman offering generous hospitality (Proverbs 9:1-12). Folly is like a **clamorous**, unpleasant woman – one who is **simple, and knows nothing** – looking for friends.

i. **Clamorous**: "Speaks loudly, that she may be heard; and vehemently, that persons might be moved by her persuasions." (Poole)

b. **She sits at the door of her house**: Foolishness can be found in the home, but also in **the highest places of the city**. Wisdom works hard to make a wonderful meal and offer impressive hospitality; folly **sits at the door** and makes her **call to those who pass by** in either place.

i. **On a seat**: "Probably chairs were so rare that only the highest nobleman owned one. In Elizabethan times chairs were a luxury. Common people sat on stools and benches, the gentry used cushions on the floor, and even the grandest ballroom rarely held more than one chair. Only the nobleman himself sat on it. When a teacher was raised to the position of professor, he was presented with an actual chair as a symbol of his elevated status in the world of learning. So also in Proverbs the chair or throne symbolizes a seat of honor (cf. 16:12; 20:8, 28; 25:5; 29:14)." (Waltke)

ii. **Who go straight on their way**: "Who were going innocently and directly about their business without any unchaste design; for others needed none of those invitations or offers, but went to her of their own accord. And besides, such lewd persons take a greater pleasure in corrupting the innocent." (Poole)

2. (16-18) The call of the foolish woman.

"Whoever *is* simple, let him turn in here";
And *as for* him who lacks understanding, she says to him,
"Stolen water is sweet,
And bread *eaten* in secret is pleasant."
But he does not know that the dead *are* there,
***That* her guests *are* in the depths of hell.**

a. **Whoever is simple, let him turn in here**: Folly imitates the call wisdom makes to the simple (Proverbs 9:4). She works to keep those she already has, the **simple** and **him who lacks understanding**. Folly has her own training program to bring her victims further along their path.

i. "Wisdom says, 'Let the simple turn in to me.' No, says Folly, 'Let the simple turn in to me.' If he turn in to *Wisdom*, his folly shall be taken away and he shall become wise; if he turn in to *Folly*, his darkness will be thickened, and his folly will remain." (Clarke)

b. **Stolen water is sweet**: This is the message of folly, explaining how *good* it is to be *bad*. Things gained through transgression are more **sweet** and **pleasant** than what may be rightfully obtained.

i. "If Proverbs 9:10 is the motto of the wise, here is that of the sophisticated." (Kidner)

ii. "Forbidden pleasures are most pleasing to sensualists, who count no mirth but madness; no pleasure, unless they may have the devil to their playfellow." (Trapp)

iii. "When Augustine describes how he stole fruit from the pear tree, he says that he did not do it because he was hungry, as he threw away most of the fruit, but for the mere pleasure of sin as sin. He did it to break God's law." (Bridges)

iv. **Stolen water is sweet**: "I suppose this to be a proverbial mode of expression, importing that *illicit pleasures are sweeter than those which are legal*. The meaning is easy to be discerned; and the conduct of multitudes shows that they are ruled by this adage. On it are built all the *adulterous intercourses* in the land." (Clarke)

v. **Water...bread**: "A contrast is intended between the rich fare offered by Wisdom and the ordinary food tendered by the foolish woman." (Waltke)

c. **But he does not know that the dead are there**: There is *some* truth in the idea that transgression can make something feel better. There is some genuine allure in the excitement, independence, camaraderie, and pleasure in breaking God's command and wisdom's counsel. Sin has its pleasures for a season (Hebrews 11:25). Yet folly's path has an end: **the dead are there…her guests are in the depths of hell**. Accepting folly's invitation is to accept ultimate death and permanent misery for a few hours or days of what is **sweet** and **pleasant**. What they eat on earth will be digested in hell.

i. "Folly allures her victim with the half-truth that sin gives pleasure (cf. Hebrews 11:25), but, like Satan (cf. Genesis 3:4), she denies the connection between sin and death." (Waltke)

ii. "She calls to the same simple ones and invites them to her house. But if they accept her invitation, they'll be attending a funeral and not a feast—and it will be their own funeral!" (Wiersbe)

iii. "In every city, on every street, by every door of opportunity, these two voices of wisdom and folly are appealing to men. To obey the call of wisdom is to live. To yield to the clamor of folly is to die. How shall we discern between the voices? By making the fear of Jehovah the central inspiration of life. By yielding the being at its deepest to Him for correction and guidance." (Morgan)

Proverbs 10 – Contrasting Lives, Contrasting Destinies

Proverbs 10:1

The proverbs of Solomon:
A wise son makes a glad father,
But a foolish son *is* the grief of his mother.

a. **The proverbs of Solomon**: Proverbs 10 begins a new section of the book. In some sense, the first nine chapters have been an introduction. It can be said that the collection of Solomon's proverbs begins here as a series of two-phrase, single verse, wisdom sayings. This arrangement continues through Proverbs 22:16. From the start of Proverbs 10:1 through at least Proverbs 22:16, this commentary will treat each proverb individually.

i. We sense *some* kind of arrangement in these proverbs; they may be sometimes grouped in sets of two, three, or four proverbs linked by a theme. For example, Proverbs 10:4 and 10:5 may have been arranged next to each other because both deal with the theme of hard work.

ii. Yet understanding the manner and nature of the arrangement is difficult if not impossible, and different commentators often see different arrangements. In this look at Proverbs, any such connections between individual proverbs are left to the reader to make, and each verse will be treated as its own proverb.

iii. "No exposition is possible save to take each proverb and consider it in its separate value. In the majority of instances this is unnecessary, because they are self-evident expositions of one abiding truth." (Morgan)

b. **A wise son**: Solomon himself was the ultimate **wise son**, receiving and valuing wisdom above all other things (1 Kings 3). When King David saw this heart in his son, it no doubt made him **a glad father**.

c. **A foolish son**: Many of the proverbs work on the principle of contrast. This proverb contrasts the **foolish son** with the **wise son**. Ironically, we could say that Solomon ultimately turned out to be **a foolish son** (1 Kings 11), though it was long after the death of **his mother**.

d. **Is the grief of his mother**: Our wisdom or folly affects more than ourselves. Wisdom benefits more than the individual, and folly grieves more than the individual.

> i. **The grief of his mother**: "The occasion of her great sorrow, which is decently ascribed to the mothers rather than to the fathers, because their passions are most vehement, and make deepest impression in them." (Poole)

Proverbs 10:2

Treasures of wickedness profit nothing,
But righteousness delivers from death.

a. **Treasures of wickedness profit nothing**: We are reminded of the parable Jesus told of the rich fool (Luke 12:16-21). That rich fool gathered great wealth but was not *rich toward God* (Luke 16:21).

b. **Righteousness delivers from death**: Being right with God brings a benefit that money can't buy.

Proverbs 10:3

The Lord will not allow the righteous soul to famish,
But He casts away the desire of the wicked.

a. **Will not allow the righteous soul to famish**: This is one of the blessings that money can't buy that we might think of from the previous verse. Significantly, the principle is directed to the **soul**. The **soul** can flourish even when the body is afflicted.

b. **He casts away the desire of the wicked**: Ultimately, to be **wicked** and in opposition to God is to have desire frustrated. To be righteous and to inherit eternal life is to have desire fulfilled.

Proverbs 10:4

He who has a slack hand becomes poor,
But the hand of the diligent makes rich.

a. **A slack hand**: This describes the lazy man or woman, who does not put forth their hand energetically to do their work. We should do all that we can heartily, as unto the Lord (Colossians 3:23).

b. **The hand of the diligent makes rich**: Hard work is normally rewarded, and prosperity often comes to those who work for it.

i. "Industry was the law of paradise (Genesis 2:15), and although it now bears the stamp of the Fall (Genesis 3:19), it is still a blessing and under God's providence brings **wealth**." (Bridges)

Proverbs 10:5

He who gathers in summer *is* a wise son;
He who sleeps in harvest *is* a son who causes shame.

a. **He who gathers in summer**: The ant was previously presented as an example of hard work in the summer (Proverbs 6:6-8). The idea here is of a **wise son** who shows his wisdom by working hard.

i. **Gathers in summer**: "A well chosen season is the greatest advantage of any action, which, as it is seldom found in haste, so it is too often lost in delay. The men of Issachar were in great account with David, because 'they had understanding of the times, to know what Israel ought to do,' and when to do it; [1 Chronicles 12:32]." (Trapp)

ii. "Joseph seized his opportunity to prepare and preserve his life for an otherwise barren future (Genesis 41:46-57; cf. John 9:4)." (Waltke)

b. **He who sleeps in harvest**: To sleep when there is work to be done is laziness and folly, and **causes shame** to self and to others.

i. "All the work of the field should be done in the *season suitable to it*. If *summer* and *harvest* be neglected, in vain does a man expect the fruits of *autumn*." (Clarke)

ii. "It is as much the will of God that the young should gather knowledge as that the farmer should gather his harvest." (Bridges)

Proverbs 10:6

Blessings *are* on the head of the righteous,
But violence covers the mouth of the wicked.

a. **Blessings are on the head of the righteous**: This was especially true in the context of the old or Mosaic covenant, where God promised to bless obedience and curse disobedience (Deuteronomy 27-28).

b. **Violence covers the mouth of the wicked**: Instead of blessing, **violence** will come to **the wicked**.

i. "But it is simpler to take it as the man's evil, written, as we say, all over his face." (Kidner)

Proverbs 10:7

The memory of the righteous *is* blessed,
But the name of the wicked will rot.

a. **The memory of the righteous is blessed**: The heroes of faith in Hebrews 11 are good examples of righteous men and women whose memory is **blessed**.

b. **The name of the wicked will rot**: If the wicked are remembered at all, it will be as a stinking, rotten thing. Our present path in a **righteous** direction or in a **wicked** direction will end either in blessedness or rottenness, each answering to the path. Every man and woman can choose if they will be remembered to praise or remembered to shame.

i. "The very name of the wicked is as offensive as putrid carrion." (Clarke)

Proverbs 10:8

The wise in heart will receive commands,
But a prating fool will fall.

a. **The wise in heart will receive commands**: Wisdom gives the humility to be instructed and to **receive commands** from God and those in rightful authority.

i. **Will receive commands**: "*i.e.,* Submit to God's holy word without replies and cavils. This is check to the brave gallants of our age, which exercise their ripe heads and fresh wits in wrestling with the truth of God, and take it for a glory to give it a foil." (Trapp)

b. **A prating fool will fall**: Here, the **fool** is the opposite of the **wise in heart**. In their disobedience they **will fall**.

i. **A prating fool**: "In the Hebrew he is called a fool of lips, either because he discovers the folly of his heart by his lips, and thereby exposeth himself to the mischief here following; or because he is without heart, as is said of Ephraim, Hosea 7:11, or his heart is little worth, as is said here, Proverbs 10:20; or because he speaks rashly, without any consideration." (Poole)

Proverbs 10:9

He who walks with integrity walks securely,
But he who perverts his ways will become known.

a. **He who walks with integrity walks securely**: The man or woman who lives with nothing to hide, with no double life, can walk with **integrity**. There is no anxiety from the fear of having sin and compromise discovered.

i. There is a story – sometimes attributed to the British author Conan Doyle – about a man who sent a letter to others with only these words: *All is discovered; flee at once.* He said a businessman who received the letter fled at once and was never seen again. **He who walks with integrity** lives free from the fear of such discovery.

b. **He who perverts his ways will become known**: The man or woman who walks a crooked life will have it revealed. Jesus said, *there is nothing covered that will not be revealed, and hidden that will not be known* (Matthew 10:26).

Proverbs 10:10

He who winks with the eye causes trouble,
But a prating fool will fall.

a. **He who winks with the eye causes trouble**: The idea of **winks** here is of one who does not take wickedness and folly seriously.

i. **Winks with the eye**: "That secretly and cunningly designs mischiefs against others, as this phrase is used, Psalms 35:19 Proverbs 6:13." (Poole)

b. **The prating fool will fall**: The **fool** will continue along their path until they **fall**.

Proverbs 10:11

The mouth of the righteous *is* a well of life,
But violence covers the mouth of the wicked.

a. **The mouth of the righteous is a well of life**: A **righteous** man speaks life-giving words, most often to others and sometimes to himself.

i. "The dependence of life on water is experienced existentially all over the earth, especially in the ancient Near East, where it is in short supply. Flowing well water is particularly precious (cf. Jeremiah 2:13), and people gather around it. The open, benevolent speech of the righteous is just as necessary for a community, offering everyone abundant life—temporal, intellectual, moral, and spiritual." (Waltke)

b. **Violence covers the mouth of the wicked**: The **wicked** man or woman brings harm and hurt with their words. They take away life.

Proverbs 10:12

Hatred stirs up strife,
But love covers all sins.

a. **Hatred stirs up strife**: The constant stirring up of **strife** and controversy is evidence of **hatred**.

i. **Stirs up strife**: "Upon every slight occasion, by filling men with suspicions and surmises, whereby they imagine faults where there are none, and aggravate every small offence." (Poole)

b. **Love covers all sins**: Peter quoted this in 1 Peter 4:8. We could say this is true in two senses, in that love covers the sins of others, and that love covers the sins of the one who loves. **Hatred** brings trouble, but **love** brings healing.

> i. There certainly is a place for the confrontation and exposure of sin. "This stress on reconciliation is balanced by other passages warning us against hushing up our own sins (Proverbs 28:13) or shirking the giving of a rebuke (e.g. Proverbs 27:5, 6)." (Kidner)

> ii. "In this collection 'conceal' is not used in the bad sense of maliciously hiding something (unlike Proverbs 10:6, 11) but in a good sense of forgiving or not finding fault (Proverbs 11:13; 12:16, 23; 17:9; 28:13; note especially Proverbs 10:12)." (Garrett)

> iii. **Covers all sins**: "On the contrary, love conciliates; removes aggravations; puts the best construction on every thing; and pours *water*, not *oil*, upon the *flame*." (Clarke)

> iv. "**Love covers**, overlooks, speedily forgives, and forgets. Full of candor and inventiveness, it puts the best construction on doubtful matters and does not expose the faults of a brother. Oh, let us put on the Lord Jesus in his spirit of forbearing, sacrificial love, and let us forgive as we have been forgiven by Christ." (Bridges)

Proverbs 10:13

Wisdom is found on the lips of him who has understanding,
But a rod *is* for the back of him who is devoid of understanding.

a. **Wisdom is found**: When a person has wisdom, it will be found on their **lips**. The words they speak reveal the wisdom they possess, as Jesus said: *Out of the abundance of the heart the mouth speaks* (Matthew 12:34).

b. **A rod is for the back**: The ones who lack wisdom must be corrected by pain, represented by **a rod** used to strike those who misbehave.

> i. "*A rod* (*sebet*) denotes a part of a tree from which a staff or weapon could be made." (Waltke)

> ii. "He that *can learn*, and *will not learn*, should be *made to learn*. The rod is a most powerful instrument of knowledge. Judiciously applied, there is a lesson of profound wisdom in every *twig*." (Clarke)

Proverbs 10:14

Wise *people* store up knowledge,
But the mouth of the foolish *is* near destruction.

a. **Wise people store up knowledge**: Wisdom takes knowledge and makes it accessible for the future. This can be done in many ways – memorization, note taking, and the use of modern digital technology.

b. **The mouth of the foolish is near destruction**: The foolish man is a contrast to the wise man, and his rejection of **knowledge** puts him **near destruction**.

Proverbs 10:15

The rich man's wealth *is* his strong city;
The destruction of the poor *is* their poverty.

a. **The rich man's wealth is his strong city**: This principle observes that wealth gives a measure of protection and provision in this world to the **rich** man.

> i. "Half of the ten occurrences of *wealth* (*hon*; see Proverbs 3:9) in Solomon's proverb instruct the youth to prize it (Proverbs 12:27; 13:7; 19:14; 29:3; cf. 19:4), and the other half not to trust it." (Waltke)

b. **The destruction of the poor**: In this world, poverty puts the poor man at a great disadvantage, sometimes leading to their **destruction**.

> i. "This is a plain recognition of the power of wealth, and the paralysis of poverty. It is a wholesome corrective to much nonsense talked today about the blessings of poverty. Wealth may become a curse, but poverty is inherently a destruction." (Morgan)

> ii. "You may be called to forgo wealth; you must certainly rate it below honesty. But don't affect to despise it; don't embrace poverty out of laziness or romanticism." (Kidner)

Proverbs 10:16

The labor of the righteous *leads* to life,
The wages of the wicked to sin.

a. **The labor of the righteous leads to life**: For the **righteous** man or woman, **labor** is life-giving and **leads to life**. They understand that our calling to co-labor with God (1 Corinthians 3:9) is a life-giving gift.

b. **The wages of the wicked to sin**: Wickedness has a "reward," and it is **sin** and the judgment due to it (Romans 6:23 – *the wages of sin is death*).

Proverbs 10:17

He who keeps instruction *is in* the way of life,
But he who refuses correction goes astray.

a. **He who keeps instruction**: Wisdom and **instruction** must not only be gained but also *kept*. That keeping will bring one **in the way of life**.

b. **He who refuses correction**: To **refuse correction** is the opposite of keeping instruction. It is to reject instruction and will lead to going **astray**.

Proverbs 10:18

Whoever hides hatred *has* lying lips,
And whoever spreads slander *is* a fool.

a. **Whoever hides hatred**: It's common for those who are motivated by **hatred** to hide their motivation and therefore lie. In our modern day, very few people will ever admit to the sin of hatred.

i. **Whoever hides hatred**: "This is a common case. How many, when full of resentment, and deadly hatred, meditating revenge and cruelty, and sometimes even murder, have pretended that they *thought nothing of the injury they had sustained*; had *passed by the insult*, etc.! Thus *lying lips* covered the malevolence of a wicked heart." (Clarke)

b. **Whoever spreads slander is a fool**: This explains one way that someone filled with **hatred** lies. They do it by spreading slander: false and unsupported accusations against others. That person is a **fool** because God knows all and will judge righteously.

Proverbs 10:19

In the multitude of words sin is not lacking,
But he who restrains his lips *is* wise.

a. **In the multitude of words sin is not lacking**: For many people, the more they talk the more they will **sin**. There is much more potential sin in talking than in listening.

b. **He who restrains his lips is wise**: Many of us could bless others, and keep ourselves from sin, simply by speaking less and restraining our **lips**.

Proverbs 10:20

The tongue of the righteous *is* choice silver;
The heart of the wicked *is worth* little.

a. **The tongue of the righteous is choice silver**: The words that the **righteous** one speaks are full of goodness and benefit, like **choice silver**. For many people, the greatest riches they treasure in their hearts are the kind and encouraging things others have said to them.

b. **The heart of the wicked is worth little**: There are great hearts and small hearts, and a **wicked** heart is certainly small. Thankfully, God still loves the **heart of the wicked** and wants to transform that heart into something greater.

Proverbs 10:21

The lips of the righteous feed many,
But fools die for lack of wisdom.

a. **The lips of the righteous feed many**: Solomon likely meant this in a symbolic sense, the idea being that they are "fed" by the good and beneficial words spoken by the **righteous** man or woman.

b. **Fools die for lack of wisdom**: The fool's rejection of **wisdom** will not go unpunished, and ultimately leads to death.

Proverbs 10:22

The blessing of the LORD makes *one* rich,
And He adds no sorrow with it.

a. **The blessing of the LORD makes one rich**: There are many who have been blessed with riches and are wise enough to receive those riches as God's blessing. They understand that *every good gift and every perfect gift is from above and comes down from the Father of lights* (James 1:17).

i. Bridges compared this principle with that of Proverbs 10:4: "The one notes the primary source of wealth; the other points to the instrumental source of wealth. Neither can be effective without the other. The sluggard looks for prosperity without diligence; the atheist looks for prosperity only from being **diligent**."

b. **He adds no sorrow with it**: This is a greater blessing upon a smaller blessing. To receive riches from God is to be blessed; to have riches without the **sorrow** that often come with them is an even greater blessing. There are many rich people who are miserable and have great **sorrow** along with their riches.

i. **Adds no sorrow with it**: "Those three vultures shall be driven away that constantly feed on the wealthy worldling's heart - care in getting, fear in keeping, grief in losing the things of this life. God giveth to his, wealth without woe, store without sore, gold without guilt." (Trapp)

ii. "Lot's covetous choice was fraught with bitterness (Genesis 13:10-11; 14:12; 19:15; 2 Peter 2:8). Ahab wore a crown but lay on his sickbed discontent (1 Kings 21:4). The rich man's rejection of Christ was the source of present and everlasting sorrow (Luke 18:23-25)." (Bridges)

Proverbs 10:23

To do evil *is* like sport to a fool,
But a man of understanding has wisdom.

a. **To do evil is like sport**: The **fool** regards **evil** as entertainment, as **sport**. Not only is it meant for enjoyment, but there is also a competitive aspect to evil among fools, with each trying to outdo the other.

i. "Evil conduct to the fool is 'like sport' (*kishoq*; New International Version, 'pleasure'), literally, like a laugh; like child's play, it is so easy." (Ross)

b. **A man of understanding has wisdom**: The man or woman of **wisdom** sees evil for what it is and avoids it.

i. "A man of understanding finds sport in wisdom. That is, he gets out of wisdom the same satisfaction that a fool gets out of wickedness." (Morgan)

ii. "As strong people delight in performing feats of strength and musicians find joy in their virtuosity, the competent person finds delight in constructive work." (Waltke)

Proverbs 10:24

The fear of the wicked will come upon him,
And the desire of the righteous will be granted.

a. **The fear of the wicked will come upon him**: The **wicked** man or woman knows that all is not right and that their day of accountability will come. They therefore live in **fear** and these fears will one day **come upon** them.

b. **The desire of the righteous will be granted**: The **righteous** man or woman also has a sense of what is to come, but it is rightly filled with optimism and hope. Their godly **desire** will be granted (Psalm 37:4).

Proverbs 10:25

When the whirlwind passes by, the wicked *is* no *more*,
But the righteous *has* an everlasting foundation.

a. **When the whirlwind passes by, the wicked is no more**: As with the previous proverb, this phrase emphasizes the unstable and dangerous place the **wicked** stand in. Trouble (**the whirlwind**) comes to all people, but the wicked have no foundation to stand on when it comes.

i. "As tornadoes that sweep every thing away before them; so shall the wrath of God sweep away the wicked; it shall leave him neither branch nor root." (Clarke)

b. **The righteous has an everlasting foundation**: Like the illustration used of the wise man who built upon the rock (Matthew 7:24-27), the

righteous man has a firm, **everlasting foundation** and can withstand the **whirlwind**.

Proverbs 10:26

As vinegar to the teeth and smoke to the eyes,
So *is* the lazy *man* to those who send him.

a. **As vinegar to the teeth and smoke to the eyes**: The idea is of constant and extreme irritation, and of disappointed expectation.

i. "The drinker expected sweet wine but instead received sour vinegar. *As smoke to the eyes* infers the same points of comparison. A person preparing food expected a constructive fire to prepare the meal but received smoke and tears instead." (Waltke)

b. **So is the lazy man to those who send him**: The one who sends a **lazy** man to do the work will be irritated by their laziness and lack of concern for hard work. The sense is that the **lazy man** irritates his managers more than himself.

i. "This little proverb portrays the aggravation in sending a lazy servant on a mission—it could be a confusing, unpleasant ordeal." (Ross)

ii. "The sluggard can disappoint and provoke his earthly master. So we must ensure that we are not sluggards to our heavenly Master.... The slothful minister is accountable to the one who sends him. When he hears the Master's call to go into his vineyard, he disobeys at his peril (Matthew 20:7; 25:30)." (Bridges)

Proverbs 10:27

The fear of the Lord prolongs days,
But the years of the wicked will be shortened.

a. **The fear of the Lord prolongs days**: The one who fears and honors God will enjoy the blessing of a longer life. Sinful habits, guilt, and ungodly anxiety all take years from one's life.

b. **The years of the wicked will be shortened**: This is one of the many prices that the **wicked** man or woman must pay.

Proverbs 10:28

The hope of the righteous *will be* gladness,
But the expectation of the wicked will perish.

a. **The hope of the righteous will be gladness**: God has a glorious future **hope** for His **righteous**. They have **gladness** in their destiny, if not now then in eternity.

b. **The expectation of the wicked will perish**: The **wicked** man or woman faces a future where all desires and expectations for good will be disappointed.

> i. **The expectation of the wicked**: "A wicked man is always imposing on himself by the *hope of God's mercy* and *final happiness*; and he continues *hoping*, till he dies without receiving that *mercy* which alone would entitle him to that *glory*." (Clarke)

> ii. "As Esau came from hunting, with his head full of hopes, but went away with his heart full of blanks, and his face full of blushing." (Trapp)

Proverbs 10:29

The way of the LORD is strength for the upright,
But destruction *will come* to the workers of iniquity.

a. **The way of the LORD is strength**: God's path is blessed and good for those who are set upon it. When we are weak, we can ask God for His strength (Isaiah 40:31) as we walk on **the way of the LORD**.

b. **Destruction will come**: Those who work **iniquity** will find they have built *nothing*. Only **destruction** will come from all their effort.

Proverbs 10:30

The righteous will never be removed,
But the wicked will not inhabit the earth.

a. **The righteous will never be removed**: God's **righteous** men and women have a wonderful future to look forward to, secure and immoveable.

b. **The wicked will not inhabit the earth**: Jesus promised that the meek would inherit the earth (Matthew 5:5), but certainly not the **wicked**.

Proverbs 10:31

The mouth of the righteous brings forth wisdom,
But the perverse tongue will be cut out.

a. **The mouth of the righteous brings forth wisdom**: God's **righteous** men and women are known for the **wisdom** they speak. A person's heart is often revealed by their words.

b. **The perverse tongue will be cut out**: Those who speak in a crooked or twisted way can only expect to be left without a word. They misused their ability to speak; God will make sure they are no longer able to use it.

> i. "This probably alludes to the punishment of *cutting out the tongue for blasphemy, treasonable speeches, profane swearing*, or such like.... Were the tongue of every *shrew* or *scold* to be extracted, we should soon have much less *noise* in the world." (Clarke)

Proverbs 10:32

The lips of the righteous know what is acceptable,
But the mouth of the wicked *what is* perverse.

a. **The lips of the righteous know what is acceptable**: God's **righteous** men and women have a sense of discernment in what they say.

b. **The mouth of the wicked what is perverse**: As righteous men and women are skilled in saying what is acceptable, so the wicked have a talent to speak what is crooked or **perverse**.

i. "The wicked man knows as well what is *perverse*, and that he speaketh forth. As the love of God is not in his heart, so the law of kindness is not on his lips." (Clarke)

Proverbs 11 – Blessings to the Righteous and Upright

Proverbs 11:1

Dishonest scales are an abomination to the LORD,
But a just weight is His delight.

a. **Dishonest scales are an abomination**: The term **abomination** was reserved for terrible, horrific things. This shows just how deeply God cares about simple honesty and fairness. He regards **dishonest scales** as an **abomination**.

b. **A just weight is His delight**: To the degree that God condemns the **dishonest** who defraud, to the same degree He has **delight** in just and fair business practices.

i. The Law of Moses clearly commanded God's people to have honest scales (Leviticus 19:35-36 and Deuteronomy 25:13-16).

Proverbs 11:2

When pride comes, then comes shame;
But with the humble *is* wisdom.

a. **When pride comes, then comes shame**: The proud man or woman fears **shame**. Ironically, they cultivate **shame** and disgrace for themselves. One significant reason for this is that God resists the proud (James 4:6 and 1 Peter 5:5).

b. **With the humble is wisdom**: There is great **wisdom** in humility because it recognizes the truth about God and the truth about self, especially in relation to others. This humility is an important foundation for true **wisdom**.

i. **The humble**: "*Lowly* (King James Version, Revised Version) is a rare word, found only here and (as a verb) in Micah 6:8 ('walk humbly with thy God'), where it suggests the biddable spirit that is the opposite of the insubordination just considered." (Kidner)

ii. "The humble man looks for nothing but justice; has the meanest opinion of himself; expects nothing in the way of commendation or praise; and can never be disappointed but in receiving praise, which he neither expects nor desires." (Clarke)

Proverbs 11:3

The integrity of the upright will guide them,
But the perversity of the unfaithful will destroy them.

a. **The integrity of the upright will guide them**: The man or woman who lives with **integrity** – a trustworthy life lived without shame or secrets – is recognized as **upright** and will have their **integrity** to **guide them**.

b. **The perversity of the unfaithful will destroy them**: The false and crooked ways of the **unfaithful** will bring those who practice them to destruction.

Proverbs 11:4

Riches do not profit in the day of wrath,
But righteousness delivers from death.

a. **Riches do not profit in the day of wrath**: The book of Proverbs recognizes the benefit of riches, but also their limitations. Earthly wealth is useless **in the day of wrath**.

i. John Trapp used a historical example to illustrate the truth that **riches do not profit in the day of wrath**: "Wherefore should I die, being so rich? Said that wretched Cardinal Henry Beaufort, Bishop of Winchester, in Henry VI's time. Fie, quoth he, will not death be hired? Will money do nothing? His riches could not reprieve him."

b. **But righteousness delivers from death**: We can, and should, use our present earthly wealth to store up treasure in heaven (Luke 12:33-34), which *will* bring **profit in the day of wrath**.

Proverbs 11:5

The righteousness of the blameless will direct his way aright,
But the wicked will fall by his own wickedness.

a. **The righteousness of the blameless will direct his way aright**: The **blameless** man or woman finds some rest in the confidence that God's guiding eye is upon the righteous.

b. **The wicked will fall by his own wickedness**: The **wicked** man or woman has no such confidence. God does not need to specially intervene in the **fall** of the wicked; he or she can **fall by his own wickedness**.

Proverbs 11:6

The righteousness of the upright will deliver them,
But the unfaithful will be caught by *their* lust.

a. **The righteousness of the upright will deliver them**: The **upright** will have their reward; their **righteousness** will be blessed, and they will be delivered.

b. **The unfaithful will be caught by their lust**: As the **upright** are delivered, the **unfaithful** will be **caught** – and by their own **lust**, receiving the penalty of their own **unfaithful** desires.

Proverbs 11:7

When a wicked man dies, *his* expectation will perish,
And the hope of the unjust perishes.

a. **His expectation will perish**: The **wicked** man or woman often expects blessing and goodness, but that **expectation** will **perish** when they die and face the judgment to come on all men and women (Hebrews 9:27).

b. **The hope of the unjust perishes**: The hopes of the wicked end up only being wishes, and wishes that are bitterly disappointed.

i. "That is to say, the expectation or hope of the wicked lies wholly on this side of the grave, and perishes at death." (Morgan)

ii. "*Hope* was not made for the *wicked*; and yet they are the very persons that most abound in it! They hope to be saved, and get at last to the kingdom of God; though they have their face towards perdition, and refuse to turn. But their hope goes no farther than the *grave*." (Clarke)

Proverbs 11:8

The righteous is delivered from trouble,
And it comes to the wicked instead.

a. **The righteous is delivered from trouble**: God promises deliverance to His **righteous** ones. Whatever trouble they experience in this life is only temporary, and they will see His deliverance in this life and especially in the life to come.

b. **It comes to the wicked instead**: For the righteous, this life is the worst **trouble** they will ever experience. For the wicked, their greatest **trouble** is yet to come.

i. "The Israelites were delivered out of the trouble of the Red Sea, but the Egyptians were drowned by it (Exodus 14:21-28). Mordecai was rescued from the gallows, on which Haman was then hanged (Esther 5:14; 7:10). Peter was snatched from death, while his persecutors and jailers were condemned." (Bridges)

Proverbs 11:9

The hypocrite with *his* mouth destroys his neighbor,
But through knowledge the righteous will be delivered.

a. **With his mouth destroys his neighbor**: One of the identifying marks of the **hypocrite** is that they destroy people with their words. Sincere love looks to build others up, not to destroy them.

i. "Haman, under the pretense of loyalty, sought to destroy a whole nation (Esther 3:8-13). Ziba, under the same false cover, wanted to destroy his neighbor (2 Samuel 16:1-4; compare 19:26-27)." (Bridges)

b. **Through knowledge the righteous will be delivered**: God's deliverance comes to the **righteous** through their **knowledge**, both in the sense of wisdom and in the sense of personal relationship with God.

Proverbs 11:10

When it goes well with the righteous, the city rejoices;
And when the wicked perish, *there is* jubilation.

a. **When it goes well with the righteous, the city rejoices**: God gives favor among men with His **righteous** ones (Proverbs 3:4), and the community **rejoices** when they are blessed.

i. "When such men are encouraged and advanced into places of power and trust, the city rejoiceth; the citizens or subjects of that government rejoice, because they confidently expect justice and tranquility, and many other benefits, by their administration of public affairs." (Poole)

ii. "However drab the world makes out virtue to be, it appreciates the boon of it in public life." (Kidner, cited in Ross)

b. **When the wicked perish, there is jubilation**: As much as the community rejoices over the blessing of the righteous, they also celebrate the calamity and end of the **wicked**. **Wicked** men and women are not missed when they pass.

i. "Rome rejoiced at the death of Nero, and the public rejoiced in the French Revolution at the death of Robespierre." (Waltke)

Proverbs 11:11

By the blessing of the upright the city is exalted,
But it is overthrown by the mouth of the wicked.

a. **The city is exalted**: When good comes to the **upright**, it is good for the entire community. Their **blessing** and prosperity extend beyond themselves.

b. **It is overthrown by the mouth of the wicked**: The words of **the wicked** can even destroy a city, leading to its overthrow.

i. This **mouth of the wicked** can overthrow a city either spiritually or politically. It can be done through the promotion of spiritual or social deception. "Whether he be a seedsman of sedition or a seducer of the people, a Sheba or a Shebna, a carnal gospeller or a godless politician, whose drift is to formalise and enervate the power of truth, till at length they leave us a heartless and sapless religion." (Trapp)

Proverbs 11:12

He who is devoid of wisdom despises his neighbor,
But a man of understanding holds his peace.

a. **He who is devoid of wisdom despises his neighbor**: The way of **wisdom** is also the way of love and respect. When one **despises his neighbor**, it isn't evidence of superior **wisdom** and discernment, but a failure of true wisdom.

b. **A man of understanding holds his peace**: Men and women of wisdom (**understanding**) recognize there is a time and place to hold back one's outrage. They know when love and respect should compel them to hold **their peace**.

Proverbs 11:13

A talebearer reveals secrets,
But he who is of a faithful spirit conceals a matter.

a. **A talebearer reveals secrets**: The unfaithful gossip, the uncontrolled talker (**a talebearer**) loves the power and intrigue of revealing **secrets**. For them, such **secrets** are a form of power that they use for their own advancement.

i. **A talebearer**: "Or, *he that goeth about* (from one place or person to another, as the manner of such is) *telling tales*, making it his business to scatter reports, revealeth secrets." (Poole)

ii. "It is not safe to be close to this cruel man who trifles with the happiness of his fellow creatures. For as readily as he betrays a confidence about a neighbor to us, so he will betray a confidence about us to someone else." (Bridges)

b. **He who is of a faithful spirit conceals a matter**: The man or woman of wisdom – those **of a faithful spirit** – knows there is an appropriate time to conceal **a matter**. There are times when love and wisdom guide to privacy.

Proverbs 11:14

Where *there is* no counsel, the people fall;
But in the multitude of counselors *there is* safety.

a. **Where there is no counsel, the people fall**: People need leadership and guidance. God has given systems and structures of authority, and those in leadership need to be able to give wise **counsel**.

b. **In the multitude of counselors there is safety**: There is great value and **safety** in receiving opinions and input from **the multitude of counselors**. No man or woman has all gifts and wisdom, and a **multitude of counselors** may work well to bring greater wisdom and **safety** in decisions.

i. "One special thing the primitive Christians prayed for the emperor was, that God would send him *Senatum fidelem,* a faithful council." (Trapp)

Proverbs 11:15

He who is surety for a stranger will suffer,
But one who hates being surety is secure.

a. **He who is surety for a stranger will suffer**: To promise to pay the debts of a **stranger** is to invite trouble. It is never a surprise when one suffers because of such a foolish promise.

b. **One who hates being a surety is secure**: There is security in being responsible only for one's own debts, for the things that they have control over.

Proverbs 11:16

A gracious woman retains honor,
But ruthless *men* retain riches.

a. **A gracious woman retains honor**: A mark of a truly **gracious woman** is that she carries with herself a sense of **honor** and dignity.

i. **A gracious woman**: "Hebrew, a *woman of grace and favour,* i.e. one who by her meekness, and modesty, and prudence, and other virtues, renders herself acceptable and amiable to God and to men." (Poole)

b. **Ruthless men retain riches**: Character and **honor** are important to the **gracious woman**, but all the **ruthless** care about is **riches**. Wealth is their god.

> i. Some believe that **ruthless men** does *not* have a negative sense in this proverb, and that it simply speaks of the reward that comes to the strong. "The method of this proverb is of comparison rather than of contrast, the idea being that a 'gracious woman' will defend honor with the same strength and persistency as 'violent men,' or 'strong men,' as the Authorized Version had it, will retain riches. The word 'violent' here suggests evil rather than good." (Morgan)

Proverbs 11:17

The merciful man does good for his own soul,
But *he who is* cruel troubles his own flesh.

a. **The merciful man does good for his own soul**: The one who shows mercy to others will be shown mercy (2 Samuel 22:26), and this is good for the **soul**.

> i. **The merciful man**: "The kindness spoken of is *hesed*, steadfast love, like God's." (Kidner)

b. **He who is cruel troubles his own flesh**: The one who is unmerciful and **cruel** to others will find that it **troubles** himself. The measure men use for others will also be measured to them (Matthew 7:2).

> i. "The word 'trouble' may recall Joshua 7:25-26—Achan troubled Israel." (Ross)

Proverbs 11:18

The wicked *man* does deceptive work,
But he who sows righteousness *will have* a sure reward.

a. **The wicked man does deceptive work**: When someone works with deception and dishonesty, it is evidence of wickedness. The wise and honest person knows that work must be done in a way marked by honesty and integrity.

b. **He who sows righteousness will have a sure reward**: Those who do their work in **righteousness** – marked by honesty and integrity – will see the **sure reward** of their work. Their righteous work is like good seed that has been sown.

Proverbs 11:19

As righteousness *leads* to life,
So he who pursues evil *pursues it* to his own death.

a. **As righteousness leads to life**: For Solomon, this was a self-evident fact. Using the same logic, he could have written, "As the sun rises in the east." The path of **righteousness** is a path **to life**.

b. **He who pursues evil pursues it to his own death**: The way of **evil** is also a path, and it leads to **death**. Many people sacrifice a lot in their pursuit of the evil way, but their only reward is the destination of **death**.

i. **Pursues evil**: "That follows it hotfoot - as Asael followed Abner; that is, wholly carried after it, and thinks to have a great catch of it, that works 'all uncleanness with greediness.' [Ephesians 4:19]." (Trapp)

Proverbs 11:20

Those who are of a perverse heart *are* an abomination to the LORD,
But *the* blameless in their ways *are* His delight.

a. **Those who are of a perverse heart are an abomination to the LORD**: There is a sense in which we are the *victims* of sin, but another and perhaps greater sense in which we are the willing participants and perpetrators of sin. God is right to regard the **perverse heart** of man as an **abomination** before Him.

b. **The blameless in their ways are His delight**: Men and women can **delight** God. Especially from a new covenant perspective, we see that **the blameless in their ways** are those who have been forgiven and declared righteous because of the person and work of Jesus Christ. These are those who **are His delight**, God delights in them as He delights in His own Son.

i. We can say that this proverb hints at the transformation the new covenant promised. "The proverb calls for a transformation of human affections to correspond with God's affections. One must be sincere in his heart and constant in his way. No in-between ground is granted." (Waltke)

Proverbs 11:21

Though they join **forces, the wicked will not go unpunished;**
But the posterity of the righteous will be delivered.

a. **Though they join forces, the wicked will not go unpunished**: Individually, man is not strong enough to resist God; *collectively* man is also not strong enough to resist God. God judged mankind when they joined forces to resist God in the days of the Tower of Babel (Genesis 11:1-9).

b. **But the posterity of the righteous will be delivered**: God's blessing will be upon His **righteous** ones, and upon their descendants (their **posterity**).

Proverbs 11:22

As **a ring of gold in a swine's snout,**
So is **a lovely woman who lacks discretion.**

a. **As a ring of gold in a swine's snout**: Solomon used a humorous and absurd word picture. No one would think of putting a **ring of gold in a swine's snout**; the ornament doesn't match the thing adorned.

b. **So is a lovely woman who lacks discretion**: It doesn't fit to put a golden ring in a pig's snout; even so it doesn't fit to have a **lovely woman** who does not have the wisdom or self-control that mark **discretion**. The power and influence of that woman's beauty aren't enough to make up for her folly.

i. **Lacks discretion**: "The word is literally 'taste'; this can mean physical taste (Exodus 16:31), intellectual discretion (1 Samuel 25:33—Abigail had it), or ethical judgment (Psalm 119:66). Here the description is probably of a woman with no moral sensibility, no propriety— unchaste." (Ross)

ii. "Note that the woman has actually *abandoned discretion; an immoral way of life is implied.*" (Garrett)

iii. "It implies that she has turned herself into a boorish animal in her dress, speech, and behavior. In fact, she is worse than a pig. The sow by nature is boorish, but this woman 'turns aside' from her dignity. The misplaced ornaments, instead of enhancing her beauty, make her look foolishly wasteful, grotesque, and repulsive. Instead of gaining honor by her natural gift, she wins ridicule (11:16). The proverb instructs youth to give priority to inner grace, not outward beauty." (Waltke)

iv. "If the thought of the contrast be carried out a little, it will be recognized that the swine will speedily destroy the luster of the gold, and so a woman lacking discretion will surely destroy her own beauty." (Morgan)

Proverbs 11:23

The desire of the righteous *is* only good,
But **the expectation of the wicked *is* wrath.**

a. **The desire of the righteous is only good**: The good character of a **righteous** man or woman is reflected in their desires. They **desire** that which is good.

b. **The expectation of the wicked is wrath**: The **good** desires of the righteous will be fulfilled, and that which is due to the **wicked** will come to them.

Proverbs 11:24

There is *one* who scatters, yet increases more;
And there is *one* who withholds more than is right,
But it *leads* to poverty.

a. **There is one who scatters, yet increases more**: This refers to the generous man or woman who **scatters**, yet not in the sense of wasteful distribution. This is Biblical generosity, which is like the scattering of seed (2 Corinthians 9:8-13) that will later bring a great harvest (**increases more**). We never lose when we give generously unto God and His work.

b. **There is one who withholds more than is right**: To be stingy and to hold on to **more than is right** is to lead **to poverty**. When we are selfish and ungenerous with what God has given us, we should expect that God would grant less to us – leading eventually **to poverty**.

Proverbs 11:25

The generous soul will be made rich,
And he who waters will also be watered himself.

a. **The generous soul will be made rich**: God has promised to bless the **generous soul** and will do so with riches in this world, the next, or both.

i. **The generous soul**: "Hebrew, *the soul of blessing*; that man who is a blessing to others, who blesseth them, i.e. doeth good to them, as blessing is oft used for a gift, as Genesis 33:11 1 Samuel 25:27 2 Corinthians 9:5." (Poole)

ii. **Rich** is literally *fat*, and so translated in the King James Version (*The liberal soul will be made fat*). "Especially in countries where people have little to eat, the metaphor 'to be fattened' connotes wealth, abundance, full satisfaction, and health (cf. Deuteronomy 31:20)." (Waltke)

b. **He who waters will also be watered himself**: When we give, God knows how to give unto us. We can't water others without being **watered** ourselves. We are never the loser for our God-guided generosity. Jesus told us that *it is more blessed to give than to receive* (Acts 20:35).

i. "If I want to get water I must give water. Though that seems a strange way of self-serving I pray you try it." (Spurgeon)

ii. "The minister is refreshed by his own message of salvation to his people. The Sunday school teacher learns many valuable lessons in the work of instruction. Every spiritual gift, every active grace, is increased by exercise, while its efficiency withers by neglect." (Bridges)

Proverbs 11:26

The people will curse him who withholds grain,
But blessing *will be* on the head of him who sells *it*.

a. **The people will curse him who withholds grain**: This has in mind the *seller* of grain who refuses to sell hoping to manipulate the market and gain a much higher price later. Such a selfish man or woman will not only be opposed by God but also cursed by **the people**. God is a remarkably generous God; selfishness comes from the fallen nature of man.

i. "The grain trader had larger stores at his disposal, which he presumably could hold back in times of shortage to raise the price." (Waltke)

ii. This verse doesn't establish a regulated price for grain, yet it protects the buyer by warning the seller of the eventual consequences of their action. **People will curse him**.

iii. Charles Spurgeon thought this spoke to how we should regard financial markets and transactions: "Laws which interfere between buyer and seller, master and workman, by any form of law, are blunders and nuisances. Parliaments and princes have hung on to the antiquated absurdity of regulating prices, but the Holy Ghost does nothing of the kind. All the attempts of men to control the price of bread and wheat is sheer folly, as the history of France may well prove. The market goes best when it is left alone, and so in our text, there is no law enacted and no penalty threatened, except that which the nature of things makes inevitable. God knows political economy, whether men do or not, and leaving the coarse machinery of police regulations, he puts the offender under a form of self- acting legislature which is far more efficient."

b. **Blessing will be on the head of him who sells it**: The one who does good by providing **grain** and goods for sale will be blessed by the community. This proverb doesn't refer to someone who *gives away* grain but simply to someone who **sells it**, making it available at a fair and good price.

i. The principle is spiritual as well as practical. When we distribute instead of hoarding, **blessing** will come. Spurgeon applied this to the "distribution" of the gospel in the 19th century missionary movement and the blessing that came to churches because of it. "Mark this, from the day when Fuller, Carey, Sutcliffe, and others, met together to send out missionaries to India the sun began to dawn of a gracious revival which is not over yet, for bad as the state of the Churches now is, yet it is marvellously an improvement upon anything before the age of missions.... I believe that the neglect of sending the word to the heathen brought a blight and a curse upon the Churches, which is now happily removed."

Proverbs 11:27

He who earnestly seeks good finds favor,
But trouble will come to him who seeks *evil*.

a. **He who earnestly seeks good finds favor**: God honors the one who **earnestly seeks good**, and that one may be blessed with **favor** with God and among men. This is especially true when the **good** sought is God Himself (Deuteronomy 4:29, Matthew 7:7).

b. **Trouble will come to him who seeks evil**: Seeking **good** brings favor, but seeking **evil** brings **trouble**. The **trouble** is often simply *finding* the **evil** that one seeks.

i. **Him who seeks evil**: "The ceaseless energy of Satan's servants in seeking **evil** puts to shame our indifference!" (Bridges)

Proverbs 11:28

He who trusts in his riches will fall,
But the righteous will flourish like foliage.

a. **He who trusts in his riches will fall**: Proverbs teaches us the value of money and wealth but also teaches us to never trust in **riches**. To put trust in riches is to invite our own **fall**.

i. "Riches were never true to any that trusted to them." (Trapp)

b. **The righteous will flourish like foliage**: The **righteous** man or woman does not trust in riches, but in God. This leads to a truly flourishing life.

Proverbs 11:29

He who troubles his own house will inherit the wind,
And the fool *will be* servant to the wise of heart.

a. **He who troubles his own house will inherit the wind**: To bring trouble to one's own family is to prepare a future full of storm and difficulty. To **inherit the wind** is to have a future of storm and trouble.

i. "Achan, after whom the Valley of Achor was named (Joshua 7:26), provides a classic example of the proverb. Nabal, by selfishly hoarding his food and water for his own men, hung disaster over his household, but Abigail, by her wisdom, saved it (1 Samuel 25:17, 33)." (Waltke)

b. **The fool will be servant to the wise of heart**: Because God's blessing is on the **wise** God will lift up **the wise of heart**. The foolish man or woman should expect to end up working for the wise man or woman.

Proverbs 11:30

The fruit of the righteous *is a* tree of life,
And he who wins souls *is* wise.

a. **The fruit of the righteous is a tree of life**: A **righteous** life bears fruit, and it gives **life** to others. The New Testament will later speak of the fruit of the Spirit in the life of God's people (Galatians 5:22-23, Ephesians 5:9). This is **fruit** like a **tree of life** to others. It brings shade and sustenance to others.

> i. "The fruit of the righteous – that is to say his life – is not a thing fastened upon him, but it grows out of him…. Look to it more and more that your religion is real, true, natural, vital – not artificial, constrained, superficial, a thing of times, days, places, a fungus produced by excitement, a fermentation generated by meetings and stirred by oratory. We all need a religion which can live either in a wilderness, or in a crowd; a religion which will show itself in every walk of life, and in every company." (Spurgeon)

b. **He who wins souls is wise**: One of the greatest exercises of wisdom is to win souls to God and His kingdom. It takes wisdom to love, give, and winsomely answer those who have yet to come into God's kingdom.

- We use the word *win* in romance; to win souls, you must love them.
- We use the word *win* in war; to win souls is a battle.
- We use the word *win* in sports; to win souls is a competition.

> i. "God himself wins not souls without wisdom, for the eternal plan of salvation was dictated by an infallible judgment, and in every line of it infinite skill is apparent…. There is as much wisdom to be seen in the new creation as in the old. In a sinner saved, there is as much of God to be beheld as in a universe rising out of nothing." (Spurgeon)

> ii. **He who wins souls**: "Hebrew, *that catcheth souls*, as a fowler doth birds; that maketh it his design and business, and useth all his skill and diligence, to gain souls to God, and to pluck them out of the snare of the devil." (Poole)

> iii. "The phrase 'to win souls (i.e. people)' can, however, also mean 'to take lives', when the context demands it (as in 1 Kings 19:4)…. But the Old Testament knows the metaphor of capturing people with ideas or influences…and the promise, 'thou shalt catch men', was doubly apt if it was meant to awaken echoes of this proverb." (Kidner)

> iv. "It is implied in our text that there are souls which need winning. Ah me, all souls of men are lost by nature." (Spurgeon)

v. "'He that winneth souls is wise.' I do not ask you how he did it. He sang the gospel, and you did not like it, but if he won souls he was wise. Soul-winners have all their own ways, and if they do but win souls they are wise. I will tell you what is not wise, and will not be thought so at the last, namely to go about the churches doing nothing yourself and railing at all the Lord's useful servants." (Spurgeon)

Proverbs 11:31

If the righteous will be recompensed on the earth,
How much more the ungodly and the sinner.

a. **If the righteous will be recompensed on the earth**: We see that many times God's **righteous** men and women see at least something of the reward of their righteousness while they are still **on the earth**. A **righteous** life is a blessed life.

b. **How much more the ungodly and the sinner**: The **righteous** will receive their reward, and often on this earth. It is sobering to consider **how much more** is this true of **the ungodly and the sinner**.

Proverbs 12 – Words, Deeds, and Destiny

Proverbs 12:1

Whoever loves instruction loves knowledge,
But he who hates correction *is* stupid.

a. **Whoever loves instruction**: Wisdom tells us to keep learning and to **love instruction** and **knowledge**. A humble willingness to be taught (**instruction**) shows a true love of **knowledge**.

i. "If we find that we are upset when our faults are pointed out to us, that shows we lack not only grace but understanding. We are behaving as if we were stupid.... Oh, for a teachable spirit to sit at the feet of our divine Master and learn from him." (Bridges)

b. **He who hates correction is stupid**: The proud man or woman who is unwilling to receive **correction** reveals his or her own rejection of knowledge.

i. **Hates correction**: "That sapless fellow Nabal would hear nothing; there was no talking to him, no dealing with him; but as [the] horse and mule that have no understanding. [Psalms 32:9]." (Trapp)

ii. **Is stupid**: "Discovereth himself to be a most foolish and stupid creature, because he is an enemy to himself and to his own happiness." (Poole)

Proverbs 12:2

A good *man* obtains favor from the LORD,
But a man of wicked intentions He will condemn.

a. **A good man obtains favor from the LORD**: Obedience to God leads to deeper relationship with Him (1 John 1:6-7). This principle was especially true under the old covenant, with its promises of blessings for obedience and curses for disobedience (Deuteronomy 27-28).

i. John Trapp on verse 2, regarding Martin Luther: "And on a time praying for the recovery of a godly useful man, among other passages, he let fall this transcendent rapture of a daring faith, *Fiat mea voluntas*, 'Let my will be done'; and then falls off sweetly, *Mea voluntas, Domine, quia tua;* 'My will, Lord, because thy will!'"

b. **A man of wicked intentions He will condemn**: God sees the heart and sees **wicked intentions** before they result in action, and even if they never result in action.

Proverbs 12:3

A man is not established by wickedness,
But the root of the righteous cannot be moved.

a. **A man is not established by wickedness**: Many men seek to advance and establish themselves through treating others badly. Lying, cheating, and deception are common when someone seeks to advance or establish himself. This is never God's way and can never enjoy His blessing.

i. "Evil is always variable: it has no *fixed principle*, except the *root* that is in the human heart; and even that is ever assuming *new forms*. Nothing is *permanent* but *goodness*; and that is *unchangeable*, because it comes from GOD." (Clarke)

b. **The root of the righteous cannot be moved**: God establishes His **righteous** ones in a firm, permanent way. Their **root** goes down deep and holds strong.

i. **Cannot be moved**: This idea is repeated many times in the Scriptures. "'God is my rock, I shall not be greatly moved.' [Psalms 62:2] Nay, 'I shall not be moved at all.' [Proverbs 12:3] 'The gates of hell cannot do it.' [Matthew 16:18] 'None can pluck them out of God's hands,' [John 10:28] for he 'hath laid help upon one that is mighty.' [Psalms 89:19]" (Trapp)

Proverbs 12:4

An excellent wife *is* the crown of her husband,
But she who causes shame *is* like rottenness in his bones.

a. **An excellent wife is the crown of her husband**: A man may achieve success in many areas of life, but unless there is happiness in the home, all other achievements are empty. To have **an excellent wife** and all the home happiness that she brings is a true **crown** of success.

i. "The modern sense of *virtuous* (King James Version, Revised Version) [**excellent**] does no justice to the Hebrew term's root idea of strength and worth…. The modern phrase, 'she has a lot in her', expresses something of the meaning." (Kidner)

b. **She who causes shame is like rottenness**: A wife that brings **shame** to the husband and the family seems to take away life and happiness instead of bringing it.

i. "The ignoble wife invisibly saps his strength and vitality and deconstructs him from within." (Waltke)

ii. "A 'crown' is a symbol of honor and renown; but the negative side, using the figure of 'decay in his bones,' is that the disgrace will eat away her husband's strength and destroy his happiness." (Ross)

Proverbs 12:5

The thoughts of the righteous *are* right,
***But* the counsels of the wicked *are* deceitful.**

a. **The thoughts of the righteous are right**: The **righteous** man or woman is not only right in their actions, but even in their **thoughts**. They know something of what it means to be transformed by the renewing of the mind (Romans 12:1-2).

b. **The counsels of the wicked are deceitful**: As for the **wicked**, it is more than their actions that are **deceitful**; their **counsels** (thinking, thoughts) are also full of deception and error.

i. **The counsels of the wicked**: "Not their rash thoughts only, but also their deliberate ones are how to circumvent others, or to cloak their own wickedness." (Trapp)

Proverbs 12:6

The words of the wicked *are*, "Lie in wait for blood,"
But the mouth of the upright will deliver them.

a. **Lie in wait for blood**: The **wicked** plot violence and are ready to ambush others for their own unrighteous gain.

i. "The vivid picture of 'lying in wait for blood' conveys that the wicked make a trap by their false accusations." (Ross)

b. **The mouth of the upright**: The **upright** man or woman will find their rescue in the good and wise words that they speak.

Proverbs 12:7

The wicked are overthrown and *are* no more,
But the house of the righteous will stand.

a. **The wicked are overthrown**: Having no root in righteousness, the **wicked** cannot and will not stand. They will one day be **overthrown** and simply perish.

b. **The house of the righteous will stand**: God will preserve His own **righteous** men and women. They and their **house** will endure that which would overthrow the house of the wicked.

Proverbs 12:8

A man will be commended according to his wisdom,
But he who is of a perverse heart will be despised.

a. **Will be commended according to his wisdom**: Wise men and women will be recognized and honored for their **wisdom**. The more **wisdom**, the greater the commendation. This is often true in this world, but always true in the world to come.

b. **Will be despised**: The one with a crooked or twisted heart will not receive praise, but instead will be **despised**. This present age often shows this to be true, and the coming age will certainly show it so.

Proverbs 12:9

Better *is the one* who is slighted but has a servant,
Than he who honors himself but lacks bread.

a. **Better is the one who is slighted but has a servant**: To receive an insult or be **slighted** is never pleasant, but wisdom sees that if one has enough in this world to have **a servant**, they shouldn't be so proud as to despair over an insult.

i. **Has a servant**: "Hath but one servant. Or rather, *is servant to himself*, hath none to wait upon him or work for him but himself, that getteth bread by his own labours." (Poole)

b. **Than he who honors himself but lacks bread**: The proud man who promotes his own honor can't eat his self-exaltation. Honoring self isn't the way to either prosperity or happiness.

i. "Nothing is so despicable as to be proud when there is nothing to be proud about." (Bridges)

ii. Kidner suggested an alternative translation: "But the Revised Standard Version, following the Septuagint, [and the] Syriac, reads the same Hebrew consonants to mean: *Better is a man of humble standing who works for himself than one who plays the great man but lacks bread.* This is stronger, and gives more content to the word 'better'."

Proverbs 12:10

A righteous *man* regards the life of his animal,
But the tender mercies of the wicked *are* cruel.

a. **A righteous man regards the life of his animal**: God cares for the animals (Matthew 10:29, Psalm 104:27). The **righteous** or godly man will also show care and compassion to **his animal**. There is a true sense in which the animal is **his**, and God gives him authority over the animal; but he is to exercise that authority with care and compassion.

i. "Verse 10 teaches that a good man cares for those who provide for him, even if they are only animals. The wicked only exploit." (Garrett)

ii. "I once in my travels met with the *Hebrew* of this clause on the *sign board* of a public inn: *yodea tsaddik nephesh behemto.* 'A righteous man considereth the life of his beast;' which, being very appropriate, reminded me that I should feed my horse." (Clarke)

b. **The tender mercies of the wicked are cruel**: Even the supposed **mercies** of the wicked have their own cruel self-interest in mind. The **righteous man** is kind even to his animals; the **wicked** man can be cruel even in his kindness.

i. "The wicked, influenced by Satan, can show no other disposition than what is in their master. If they *appear* at any time *merciful*, it is a *cloak* which they use to cover purposes of cruelty." (Clarke)

Proverbs 12:11

He who tills his land will be satisfied with bread,
But he who follows frivolity *is* devoid of understanding.

a. **He who tills his land**: The one who does the hard work of farming will be **satisfied with bread**. Under God's blessing, they will enjoy the result of their labor.

b. **He who follows frivolity**: The one who lives for the vain and superficial things of life lacks something worse than bread; he is **devoid of understanding**.

i. "The proud person is Satan's throne, and the idle man his pillow. He sits in the former and sleeps quietly on the latter." (Swinnock, cited in Bridges)

Proverbs 12:12

The wicked covet the catch of evil *men,*
But the root of the righteous yields *fruit.*

a. **The wicked covet the catch of evil men**: It is in the nature of the **wicked** to **covet** what others have, even if it is the **catch of evil men**. In this they sin in the covetousness and the longing for what has been gained by **evil men**.

b. **The root of the righteous yields fruit**: God's **righteous** men and women don't need to covet the catch of evil men, because they are like fruit-bearing trees. Fruit comes from their very **root**, from who they are.

Proverbs 12:13

The wicked is ensnared by the transgression of *his* lips,
But the righteous will come through trouble.

a. **The wicked is ensnared**: What a wicked man says (**the transgression of his lips**) will eventually get him into trouble. It will become a snare he is trapped in.

i. "A man who deals in *lies* and *false oaths* will sooner or later be found out to his own ruin. There is another proverb as true as this: *A liar had need of a good memory*; for as the *truth* is not in *him*, he *says* and *unsays*, and often *contradicts himself*." (Clarke)

b. **The righteous will come through trouble**: The **righteous** man or woman will certainly experience **trouble** but will **come through** it. As Jesus said, *in the world you will have tribulation, but be of good cheer; I have overcome the world* (John 16:33).

Proverbs 12:14

A man will be satisfied with good by the fruit of *his* mouth,
And the recompense of a man's hands will be rendered to him.

a. **A man will be satisfied with good**: A righteous man finds blessing comes to his life by what he says (**the fruit of his mouth**). His good, kind, and encouraging words will bring life to himself and others.

b. **The recompense of a man's hands will be rendered to him**: A man will receive what he has worked for, whether it be for good or evil. God's judgments are true and fitting.

Proverbs 12:15

The way of a fool *is* right in his own eyes,
But he who heeds counsel *is* wise.

a. **The way of a fool is right in his own eyes**: The **fool** almost always thinks they are on the right path. It is difficult for them to think carefully and accurately about the path of their life.

b. **He who heeds counsel is wise**: The **wise** man or woman understands the value of **counsel** and does not look only to what **is right in his own eyes**. The **wise** person understands that it is helpful to get another set of "**eyes**" on one's **way**.

Proverbs 12:16

A fool's wrath is known at once,
But a prudent *man* covers shame.

a. **A fool's wrath is known at once**: The fool does not have the self-control to wait and let the immediate anger pass before making a response. The fool does most things out of impulse without thought.

b. **A prudent man covers shame**: The wise and **prudent** man knows that there are many times when the right thing to do is to *cover* shame. They thoughtfully respond to situations instead of making an immediate, impulsive response.

i. "It is not so much that the wise man represses anger or feelings but that he is more shrewd in dealing with it." (Ross)

Proverbs 12:17

He *who* speaks truth declares righteousness,
But a false witness, deceit.

a. **He who speaks truth declares righteousness**: The words of the wise are filled with **truth** and therefore reflect God's **righteousness**.

b. **But a false witness, deceit**: The **false witness** doesn't speak the **truth**, and promotes **deceit** instead of **righteousness**.

Proverbs 12:18

There is one who speaks like the piercings of a sword,
But the tongue of the wise *promotes* health.

a. **There is one who speaks like the piercings of a sword**: Some people have the terrible ability to speak in a manner that stabs and slices others. Their words are like the slashing and **piercings of a sword**, bringing hurt instead of healing.

i. "How keenly have the servants of God suffered from this sword! Many will speak daggers without compunction who would be afraid to use them." (Bridges)

b. **The tongue of the wise promotes health**: **Wise** men and women are able to bring **health** and healing by the words they speak.

Proverbs 12:19

The truthful lip shall be established forever,
But a lying tongue *is* but for a moment.

a. **The truthful lip shall be established forever**: God looks after those who love the truth and speak the truth. Under His blessing, they will be **established forever**.

b. **The lying tongue is but for a moment**: It often seems that the **lying tongue** wins the day and is stronger than the **truthful lip**. The judgments of the God of truth will show how temporary the success of the **lying tongue** is.

i. **But for a moment**: "The lying tongue may continue to utter its falsehood for long years by the calendars of men, but when you place those years by the side of the ages of God, they are as a moment, as the winking of the eye, as nothing." (Morgan)

ii. "*Truth* stands for ever; because its *foundation* is indestructible: but *falsehood* may soon be detected; and, though it gain credit for a while, it had that credit because it was supposed to be *truth*." (Clarke)

iii. "It is truth which abides. A lie must perish. In a world still largely mastered by lies, it is difficult at times to believe this. Yet to review the history of the race is to have evidence of it. Lies are always perishing." (Morgan)

Proverbs 12:20

Deceit is in the heart of those who devise evil,
But counselors of peace have joy.

a. **Deceit is in the heart**: Those who **devise evil** and practice it have **deceit** in their heart before it is ever evident in their actions. There is something corrupt in their core that finds expression outwardly.

b. **Counselors of peace have joy**: There is a happiness and contentment (**joy**) that comes to those who speak words of peace. This *shalom* is within the **counselors of peace**, and so they are able to give it to others.

i. "Significantly, Proverbs always represents counselors as in a group (Proverbs 11:14; 15:22; 24:6)." (Waltke)

Proverbs 12:21

No grave trouble will overtake the righteous,
But the wicked shall be filled with evil.

a. **No grave trouble will overtake the righteous**: God's **righteous** men and women will certainly experience trouble. Yet God promised to manage the degree of trouble, the duration of trouble, and the depth of the trouble. Especially seen in the light of eternity, **no grave trouble will overtake the righteous**.

b. **The wicked shall be filled with evil**: In contrast, the **wicked** will receive the result of their wickedness. They will not be rescued from their trouble; because they pursued **evil**, they will be **filled with evil**.

Proverbs 12:22

Lying lips *are* an abomination to the LORD,
But those who deal truthfully *are* His delight.

a. **Lying lips are an abomination**: The God of truth loves the truth and regards the **lips** that spread lies as offensive, an **abomination**.

b. **Those who deal truthfully are His delight**: The same God who regards lies as an **abomination** takes **delight** in those who value and tell the truth. Wisdom's lesson is plain: *stop lying and start telling the truth.*

Proverbs 12:23

A prudent man conceals knowledge,
But the heart of fools proclaims foolishness.

a. **A prudent man conceals knowledge**: It is a mark of wisdom and prudence to not reveal all that we know, especially if it may harm or disgrace others.

i. "Someone who is careful in what he says will be equally careful about whom he confides in." (Garrett)

b. **The heart of fools proclaims foolishness**: The wise man or woman knows restraint, but the fool does not. It is in the nature of fools to proclaim their foolishness. What is in the heart will eventually be revealed.

i. "Fools, however, proclaim their folly everywhere. They are dogmatic in arguments when wiser men are cautious. They teach when they should be learning." (Bridges)

Proverbs 12:24

The hand of the diligent will rule,
But the lazy *man* will be put to forced labor.

a. **The hand of the diligent will rule**: This is both according to the blessing of God (who rewards the **diligent**) and the nature of the world and society. Hard working people achieve and come to places of leadership.

i. "So, Christian, be diligent. Spend and be spent in Christ's service. Your privileges will be enlarged. Your God will be honored. Your crown will be secure." (Bridges)

b. **The lazy man will be put to forced labor**: Because he is unfit to rule over others or even himself, **the lazy man** will be ruled over by others.

i. "Diligence at work determines success and advancement. To put it bluntly, the diligent rise to the top and the lazy sink to the bottom." (Ross)

ii. **The lazy man**: "Hebrew, *the deceitful*. So he calls the slothful, because deceit and idleness are commonly companions, and such men seek to gain by fraud what they either cannot or will not get by honest labour." (Poole)

Proverbs 12:25

Anxiety in the heart of man causes depression,
But a good word makes it glad.

a. **Anxiety in the heart of man causes depression**: Solomon considered an inward cause of **depression**. It may come from fear and **anxiety** within a man's or woman's **heart**. This is why God so often tells us to *be anxious for nothing* (Philippians 4:6) and pray about everything.

b. **But a good word makes it glad**: An anxious heart can be helped by a simple **good word**. Encouragement costs little from the one who gives it, but can do enormous good for the one who receives it.

i. "The 'kind word' probably includes encouragement, kindness, and insight—saying that which the person needs to gain the proper perspective and renew hope and confidence." (Ross)

ii. Think of the many times Jesus spoke a simple **good word** and made others **glad**:

- *Son, be of good cheer; your sins are forgiven you* (Matthew 9:2).
- *Your sins are forgiven* (Luke 7:48).
- *Daughter, be of good cheer; your faith has made you well* (Luke 8:48).
- *Neither do I condemn you; go and sin no more* (John 8:11).

iii. Our simple words of encouragement can encourage and guide beyond all our imagining. "A single good or favourable word will remove despondency." (Clarke)

Proverbs 12:26

The righteous should choose his friends carefully,
For the way of the wicked leads them astray.

a. **The righteous should choose his friends carefully**: This is good advice for both **the righteous** and those who have the wisdom to seek after righteousness. It has been rightly said, *show me your friends and I will show you your future.*

b. **For the way of the wicked leads them astray**: Bad friends can have a significant impact for evil and many people have been led **astray** towards **the way of the wicked** because of unwise and undiscerning friendships. The power of friendship can also work for good, and good friends can help one on *the way of wisdom.*

Proverbs 12:27

The lazy *man* does not roast what he took in hunting,
But diligence *is* man's precious possession.

a. **The lazy man does not roast what he took in hunting**: Using a somewhat humorous illustration, Solomon showed that the **lazy man** does not finish the job. He went to all the trouble of hunting and capturing the prey, but will never enjoy the fruit of his work because he is too **lazy** to do it.

i. "Just as one who might hunt but never cook what he finds, so the lazy person never completes a project." (Ross)

b. **Diligence is man's precious possession**: There are many **precious** things a man or woman can have, but **diligence** is near the top of the list. Many great things are accomplished with little talent but great **diligence**.

Proverbs 12:28

In the way of righteousness *is* life,
And in *its* pathway *there is* no death.

a. **In the way of righteousness is life**: It is a common belief that the **way of righteousness** is boring or unpleasant. This is a deception of the world, the flesh, and the devil. The truth is that **in the way of righteousness is life**.

b. **In its pathway there is no death**: The **life** righteousness brings is not only for the present but also for eternity. Those who walk **in the way of righteousness** will receive and know eternal life, beginning now into eternity.

i. "The practice of justice and godliness, though it expose a man to some dangers and inconveniences in the world, yet it will certainly lead him to life and happiness, whereas the end of all wicked courses is death and destruction." (Poole)

Proverbs 13 – The Value of Correction

Proverbs 13:1

A wise son *heeds* his father's instruction,
But a scoffer does not listen to rebuke.

a. **A wise son heeds his father's instruction**: The fact that Solomon delivered this proverb to his own son does not make it any less true. Children are **wise** to listen to instruction from their parents.

b. **A scoffer does not listen to rebuke**: The **scoffer** is fool enough to reject all guidance and therefore never learns.

i. **Does not listen**: "Or, Heareth and jeereth; – as Lot's sons-in-law, as Eli's sons, and afterwards Samuel's." (Trapp)

ii. **Instruction...rebuke**: "The change to a stronger word in the second line—('rebuke')—shows that he does not respond to any level of discipline." (Ross)

Proverbs 13:2

A man shall eat well by the fruit of *his* mouth,
But the soul of the unfaithful feeds on violence.

a. **A man shall eat well by the fruit of his mouth**: Wise and good speech brings blessings of many different kinds, including the blessing of prosperity.

b. **The soul of the unfaithful feeds on violence**: Those who are **unfaithful** to God and His wisdom may find themselves supported by or through **violence**.

i. **Feeds on violence**: "Shall have that violence and injury returned upon themselves, which they have offered to others in word or deed." (Poole)

Proverbs 13:3

He who guards his mouth preserves his life,
***But* he who opens wide his lips shall have destruction.**

a. **He who guards his mouth preserves his life**: Wise and good words can preserve life. This is true both in a moment of crisis and over a lifetime.

 i. **Guards his mouth**: "As the guard keepeth the gates in a siege. God hath set a double guard of lips and teeth before this gate, and yet, unless he himself set the watch, and keep the door, all will be lost." (Trapp)

 ii. "The old Arab proverb is appropriate: 'Take heed that your tongue does not cut your throat'." (Ross)

b. **He who opens wide his lips shall have destruction**: To speak too much is usually to find trouble, leading to **destruction**. Wisdom will guard the mouth and the words it speaks.

 i. "How often have the foolish, headstrong, and wicked, forfeited their lives by the *treasonable* or *blasphemous* words they have spoken! The *government of the tongue* is a *rare* but useful talent." (Clarke)

 ii. "It has often been remarked that God has, given us *two* EYES, that we may SEE *much; two* EARS, that we may HEAR *much*; but has given us but ONE *tongue*, and that fenced in with teeth, to indicate that though we *hear* and *see much*, we should *speak* but *little*." (Clarke)

Proverbs 13:4

The soul of a lazy *man* desires, and *has* nothing;
But the soul of the diligent shall be made rich.

a. **The soul of a lazy man desires**: It isn't that the **lazy man** or woman lacks desire; they *wish* for many things. Yet they have **nothing** because they cannot or will not apply themselves to the work required to take desires to reality.

 i. "The sluggard craves the fruit of diligence without the diligence that gains it." (Bridges)

 ii. "Affection without endeavour is like Rachel - beautiful, but barren." (Trapp)

b. **The soul of the diligent shall be made rich**: As in most places in Proverbs, **soul** here is used in the sense of "life," without so much reference to the non-material aspect of one's being. Yet, it is true that diligence in spiritual things leads to spiritual riches and blessing.

i. "We often hear many religious people expressing a *desire to have more of the Divine life*, and yet never get *forward* in it. How is this? The reason is, they *desire*, but do not *stir themselves up* to lay hold upon the Lord." (Clarke)

Proverbs 13:5

A righteous *man* hates lying,
But a wicked *man* is loathsome and comes to shame.

a. **A righteous man hates lying**: The **righteous man** or woman doesn't just love truth and avoid the lie; they actually hate **lying**. Being godly, they have some of the love of the truth and hatred of the lie that God Himself has.

b. **A wicked man is loathsome**: The implication is that **wicked** men and women love the lie, and this makes them **loathsome** and repulsive. This will surely bring them **to shame**.

i. **Comes to shame**: "Makes himself contemptible and hateful to all that know him; there being scarce any reproach which men more impatiently endure, and severely revenge, than that of being called or accounted a liar." (Poole)

Proverbs 13:6

Righteousness guards *him whose* way is blameless,
But wickedness overthrows the sinner.

a. **Righteousness guards him whose way is blameless**: A **blameless** life – certainly not *free* of sin, but a life of general righteousness and integrity – is honored and blessed by God. It is both the **righteousness** of God Himself and the **righteousness** of the **blameless** that **guards** them.

b. **Wickedness overthrows the sinner**: Even as the blameless man or woman's own **righteousness guards** them, so the sin of the sinner **overthrows** them. Deeds can reflect destiny.

i. **The sinner**: "Hebrew, *the man of sin*, who giveth up himself to wicked courses." (Poole)

Proverbs 13:7

There is one who makes himself rich, yet *has* nothing;
***And* one who makes himself poor, yet *has* great riches.**

a. **There is one who makes himself rich, yet has nothing**: Material riches and wealth may be of little account for happiness in this world and especially in the world to come. One may work hard to make **himself rich** yet find at the end of it all that he has **nothing**. Solomon wrote about these principles in Ecclesiastes.

i. "Our own age abounds with men who have made themselves rich, and yet have nothing. They have amassed great wealth, and yet it has no purchasing power in the true things of life. It cannot insure health, it brings no happiness, it often destroys peace." (Morgan)

b. **And one who makes himself poor, yet has great riches**: There are those who willingly make themselves **poor** on a material level, and do so out of generosity to others or out of fixed spiritual priorities. Such ones have **great riches** in this life and in the life to come.

i. Morgan saw the key to this proverb in its use of *self* in both the first and second lines. "To make *self* rich, is *to* destroy the capacity for life. To make *self* poor, by enriching others, is to live."

ii. The greatest occasion of anyone making **himself poor**, yet gaining **great riches** through it was that of Jesus Christ. *For you know the grace of our Lord Jesus Christ, that though He was rich, yet for your sakes He became poor, that you through His poverty might become rich* (2 Corinthians 8:9).

Proverbs 13:8

The ransom of a man's life *is* his riches,
But the poor does not hear rebuke.

a. **The ransom of a man's life is his riches**: A **man's life** can be measured in many ways. One of those measurements – though by no means the best measurement – is **his riches**. In a time of crisis, a man's **riches** may well **ransom** his life.

i. **His riches**: "They may help a man out at a dead lift, and get him a release out of captivity, or a lease of his life. 'Slay us not,' say they, [Jeremiah 41:8] 'for we have treasures in the field. So he forebore, and slew them not among their brethren.'" (Trapp)

ii. **The ransom of a man's life**: "But what can a person give in exchange for his soul (Matthew 16:26)? It is too precious to be redeemed with corruptible silver and gold (1 Peter 1:18). When all the treasures of earth were insufficient for this ransom, the riches of heaven were poured out (1 Peter 1:19; Hebrews 10:5-8)." (Bridges)

b. **The poor does not hear rebuke**: Most commentators take this in a *positive* sense, with the idea that the **poor** will never find himself in the same trouble as the rich man who must **ransom** his life with **his riches**.

i. Morgan explains the thought in the positive sense: "That is to say that if wealth has its advantages, so also has poverty. The rich man by his wealth may be able to conserve his life, but the poor man escapes the very dangers into which the rich are brought."

ii. "Those who have riches have often much trouble with them; as they had much trouble to *get* them, so they have much trouble to *keep* them. In despotic countries, a rich man is often accused of some capital crime, and to save his life, though he may be quite innocent, is obliged to give up his riches; but the *poor*, in such countries, are put to no trouble." (Clarke)

iii. If taken in a negative sense, then here Solomon considered those whose poverty comes from their moral failings. Certainly, not everyone who is **poor** is in that condition because of their unwillingness to **hear rebuke**, but some are. Their foolish rejection of wisdom leads them to poverty.

Proverbs 13:9

The light of the righteous rejoices,
But the lamp of the wicked will be put out.

a. **The light of the righteous rejoices**: Righteousness – godliness as expressed in real life – is associated with **light** and with rejoicing. There is something wrong with the person who claims to be **righteous** yet rarely has evidence of **light** and rejoicing.

b. **The lamp of the wicked will be put out**: The **righteous** are associated with **light**, but the **wicked** with darkness. The darkness conceived of here is one that is *imposed* by the judgment of a righteous God (**will be put out**).

i. "The proverb contrasts the enduring wealth of the righteous with the extinction of the wicked and implicitly their wealth." (Waltke)

Proverbs 13:10

By pride comes nothing but strife,
But with the well-advised *is* wisdom.

a. **By pride comes nothing but strife**: **Pride** – excessive self-focus and self-regard – constantly generates **strife**. When people are focused on their own exaltation they will always attempt to advance themselves at the expense of others.

i. **Nothing but strife**: "Pride is a dividing distemper; gouty swollen legs keep at a distance; bladders blown up with wind spurt one from another, and will not close; but prick them, and you may pack a thousand of them in a little room." (Trapp)

ii. "Perhaps there is not a *quarrel* among *individuals* in private life, nor a *war* among nations, that does not proceed from *pride* and *ambition....* It was to destroy this *spirit of pride*, that Jesus was manifested in the *extreme of humility* and *humiliation* among men. The salvation of Christ is a *deliverance* from *pride*, and a being clothed with *humility*. As far as we are *humble*, so far we are *saved*." (Clarke)

b. **With the well-advised is wisdom**: Those who listen to and receive the counsel of others walk in **wisdom**.

Proverbs 13:11

Wealth *gained by* dishonesty will be diminished,
But he who gathers by labor will increase.

a. **Wealth gained by dishonesty will be diminished**: This may be because God's blessing is not upon **wealth gained by dishonesty**, or because such wealth was not **gained** by the habits of life that earn and retain wealth.

i. "The metaphor of getting money from a vapor suggests what English speakers call 'easy money,' including tyranny, injustice, extortion, lies, and windfalls, at the expense of others." (Waltke)

ii. "Wealth that is not the result of *honest industry* and *hard labour* is seldom permanent. All fortunes acquired by speculation, lucky hits, and ministering to the pride or luxury of others, etc., soon become dissipated. They are not gotten in the way of Providence, and have not God's blessing, and therefore are not permanent." (Clarke)

b. **He who gathers by labor will increase**: This happens with God's blessing on honest **labor** and in the practice of habits that normally earn, retain, and **increase** wealth.

Proverbs 13:12

Hope deferred makes the heart sick,
But *when* the desire comes, *it is* a tree of life.

a. **Hope deferred makes the heart sick**: The strength of **hope** sustains the heart; when hope's fulfillment is long delayed (**deferred**), it can make **the heart sick**.

i. "How many see we lie languishing at hope's hospital, as he at the pool of Bethesda!" (Trapp)

ii. "Plaut elaborates that people can bear frustration only so long; they must have encouragement to continue (p. 153). Perhaps believers should make it part of their task to help others realize their hopes whenever possible." (Ross)

b. **When the desire comes, it is a tree of life**: When hope's **desire** finally is fulfilled it brings long-sustained **life**. This principle reminds us that though hope's delayed fulfillment may even make **the heart sick**, it is worth it to endure the sense of sickness for the goodness of the fulfillment when it comes.

Proverbs 13:13

He who despises the word will be destroyed,
But he who fears the commandment will be rewarded.

a. **He who despises the word will be destroyed**: This principle may be fulfilled through the direct judgment of God upon those who commit the terrible sin of despising His **word**, or by the natural consequences of such folly.

b. **He who fears the commandment will be rewarded**: The one who not only understands and obeys but also properly respects and reverences God's word (**fears the commandment**) will **be rewarded** both in this life and the life to come.

i. **Word** and **commandment**: "The use of these two terms has religious significance: they most often refer to Scripture. Kidner says that their use is a 'reminder that revealed religion is presupposed in Proverbs.'" (Ross)

ii. **Fears the commandment**: "As Queen Elizabeth…who, when the Bible was presented to her as she rode triumphantly through London after her coronation, received the same with both her hands, and kissing it, laid it to her breast, saying that it had ever been her delight, and should be her rule of government." (Trapp)

Proverbs 13:14

The law of the wise *is* a fountain of life,
To turn *one* away from the snares of death.

a. **The law of the wise is a fountain of life**: God's word (**the law of the wise**) is a continual source of **life** for all who will receive it.

b. **To turn one away from the snares of death**: This is one way that God's word brings life. Understanding and obeying God's word will keep **one away** from many things that trap and destroy, both spiritual and material.

i. **Snares of death**: "Suggests that death is like a hunter." (Ross)

ii. **The snares of death**: "There is only one fountain of life, but there are many snares of death (cf. 2 Tim. 2:24-26)." (Waltke)

Proverbs 13:15

Good understanding gains favor,
But the way of the unfaithful *is* hard.

a. **Good understanding gains favor**: This happens both from the blessing of God and simply from the way people relate and socialize with each other. Men and women of **good understanding** are more welcome among others because of the way they deal with people.

b. **The way of the unfaithful is hard**: Those who reject wisdom, and live lives **unfaithful** to God and man, will find life **hard**. They find many more obstacles and difficulties in their path and receive less help from others along the way.

i. This recalls a contemporary proverb, supposedly attributed to the actor John Wayne: *Life is hard; it's harder when you're stupid.*

ii. **The way of the unfaithful is hard**: "They dream of a flowery path, but they make for themselves a hard way…'I was held before conversion,' said Augustine, 'not with an iron chain, but with the obstinacy of my own will.'" (Bridges)

iii. "Never was a truer saying; most sinners have *more pain* and *difficulty* to get their souls damned, than the righteous have, with all their cross-bearings, to get to the kingdom of heaven." (Clarke)

Proverbs 13:16

Every prudent *man* acts with knowledge,
But a fool lays open *his* folly.

a. **Every prudent man acts with knowledge**: The wise and **prudent** man or woman not only has knowledge, but they act with it. Wisdom is more than in their mind, it is in their life.

b. **A fool lays open his folly**: The **folly** of the **fool** is plain for the world to see. It is **open** before God and man.

i. "Lacking this prudence, a fool exposes his folly. He pours out his wrath, vaunts his vanity, exposes his thoughtlessness, and exercises no judgment." (Bridges)

Proverbs 13:17

A wicked messenger falls into trouble,
But a faithful ambassador *brings* health.

a. **A wicked messenger falls into trouble**: It could be often said that the **wicked** person **falls into trouble**, but this is even more so of the **messenger**, who has the responsibility to relay the message. This is a warning to those who are, or wish to be, messengers of God's truth.

i. "The messenger is an example of a person charged with a serious responsibility. Those who are reliable are appropriately rewarded, but those who are not soon find themselves in serious trouble." (Garrett)

ii. "'The professional courier had to be courageous and bold and his training must have included the study of military strategy and tactics.' They also enjoyed an extraordinary status that entitled them to privileged treatment: 'Their names are amongst those of the very few names of officials which have come down to us in the literature.' They were authorized to speak in the 'I' style of the client." (Waltke)

b. **A faithful ambassador brings health**: An **ambassador** is a special kind of messenger, and those who are **faithful** in that duty bring goodness to others and to themselves. This is a blessing for those who are, or wish to be, ambassadors of God.

Proverbs 13:18

Poverty and shame *will come* to him who disdains correction,
But he who regards a rebuke will be honored.

a. **Poverty and shame will come to him who disdains correction**: We all make mistakes, but the man or woman who cannot be corrected will remain in their mistakes and never learn from them. This often leads to **poverty and shame**.

i. Waltke observed that Proverbs shows us that "There are many causes of poverty: laziness (Proverbs 10:4-5; 12:24; 13:4; 15:19; 19:15; 20:4, 13; 21:25), love of pleasure and luxury (Proverbs 21:17; 28:19), a propensity to talk instead of getting down to work (Proverbs 14:23), wickedness in general (Proverbs 13:25), and meanness (Proverbs 11:24). This proverb points to a more fundamental problem, namely, the refusal, like that of the horse and mule (Psalm 32:9), to listen to the instructions that correct these flaws."

ii. "Poverty due to moral failure brings disgrace, but poverty with virtue (Proverbs 17:1; 19:1), such as from injustice (Proverbs 13:23), is not disgraceful." (Waltke)

iii. "Proverbs takes a balanced position; it neither dehumanizes the poor on the grounds that they are to blame for all their troubles nor absolves the individual of personal responsibility." (Garrett)

b. **He who regards a rebuke will be honored**: A **rebuke** never feels good, but when we properly regard it and learn from it, we will not repeat the same mistakes over and over. This leads to honor in this life and the life to come.

> i. **Regards a rebuke**: "That considers it seriously, receiveth it kindly, and reformeth himself by it, shall be honoured, and enriched…Or if he do not always gain riches, he shall certainly have honour both from God and men." (Poole)

Proverbs 13:19

A desire accomplished is sweet to the soul,
But *it is* an abomination to fools to depart from evil.

a. **A desire accomplished is sweet to the soul**: When our desires are fulfilled – especially when they are **accomplished** through hard work, discipline, and sacrifice – this **is sweet to the soul** and brings great life satisfaction.

b. **It is an abomination to fools to depart from evil**: The fool is so in love with his or her **evil** that they regard it as a terrible thing (**an abomination**) to **depart** from that evil. This shows that **evil** and folly are not surface problems; they are bound up deep within a person's being.

> i. "Men will not pay the price of departing from evil, and so fail of the sweetness of fulfilled desire." (Morgan)

> ii. "A person's life depends on finding his drives and appetites satisfied. The frustrated fool goes from failure to failure, but the gratified righteous go from strength to strength." (Waltke)

> iii. "Holiness makes heaven; sin makes hell. So which place are the ungodly suited for? Hating holiness means that you are fit for hell." (Bridges)

Proverbs 13:20

He who walks with wise *men* will be wise,
But the companion of fools will be destroyed.

a. **He who walks with wise men will be wise**: Good companions bring much good and wisdom to life. When we choose to associate ourselves with **wise men** and women, we will grow in wisdom.

b. **The companion of fools will be destroyed**: It is taken for granted that the **companion of fools** is a fool and will remain rooted in their folly. Their choice of companions proves their folly and shows their destiny: destruction.

i. Kidner quoted John Knox's translation of the Latin Vulgate: *Fool he ends that fool befriends.*

Proverbs 13:21

Evil pursues sinners,
But to the righteous, good shall be repaid.

a. **Evil pursues sinners**: By their very nature, **sinners** will pursue evil. Yet it is also true that **evil pursues sinners**. The power of evil and the evil one desire to keep **sinners** in their grasp.

b. **To the righteous, good shall be repaid**: The "reward" of **sinners** is for evil to chase after them. God's **righteous** men and women have a much better destiny. **Good** shall be granted to them as they reap what they have sowed (Galatians 6:7).

i. We remember the promise Jesus made: *So Jesus answered and said, "Assuredly, I say to you, there is no one who has left house or brothers or sisters or father or mother or wife or children or lands, for My sake and the gospel's, who shall not receive a hundredfold now in this time— houses and brothers and sisters and mothers and children and lands, with persecutions—and in the age to come, eternal life."* (Mark 10:29-30)

ii. "God shall repay good. Now he is a liberal paymaster, and all his retributions are more than bountiful. Never did any yet do or suffer aught for God, that complained of a hard bargain. God will recompense your losses." (Trapp)

iii. We also remember another of Jesus' promises: *Whoever gives one of these little ones only a cup of cold water in the name of a disciple, assuredly, I say to you, he shall by no means lose his reward.* (Matthew 10:42)

Proverbs 13:22

A good *man* leaves an inheritance to his children's children,
But the wealth of the sinner is stored up for the righteous.

a. **A good man leaves an inheritance to his children's children**: The blessing on the life of a **good man** is great enough that, upon his death, he has enough to give **an inheritance** not only to his children but to his grandchildren. This also shows the *generosity* of the **good man.**

i. More importantly, the good man passes an inheritance to his children and grandchildren greater than material wealth. He gives something money can't buy: the gift of a good parent and grandparent, and the example of goodness and all that goodness entails.

ii. "He files many a *prayer* in heaven in their behalf, and his good *example* and *advices* are remembered and quoted from generation to generation." (Clarke)

b. **The wealth of the sinner is stored up for the righteous**: The **sinner** may have wealth, and this may be a discouragement to **the righteous**. Yet confident in the judgments of God, the **righteous** know that all things are theirs and God can, if He wishes, transfer the **wealth of the sinner** to **the righteous**.

Proverbs 13:23

Much food *is in* the fallow *ground* of the poor,
And for lack of justice there is waste.

a. **Much food is in the fallow ground of the poor**: Most commentators understand this as a proverb in sympathy with the poor in both its first and second lines. In this thinking, the **fallow ground of the poor** exists *because of* the **lack of justice** mentioned in the second line.

i. "This is the declaration of an abiding truth that there is sustenance in the land, but men are excluded from it by injustice." (Morgan) "According to this proverb, the lack of food for the hard-working poor is due to tyranny, not the environment." (Waltke)

ii. Yet it is possible that the first line of this proverb rebukes those who are poor because of their lack of work or initiative. A wise man or woman might look at a piece of **fallow ground** and see **much food** that can be gained with hard work. Others may only see the hard work and disruption to a lazy life.

iii. Adam Clarke understood this as a rebuke of the lazy poor: "O, how much of the *poverty* of the *poor* arises from their own want of management! They have little or no economy, and no foresight. When they get any thing, they speedily spend it; and a *feast* and a *famine* make the chief *varieties* of their life."

b. **For lack of justice there is waste**: The second line of this proverb speaks clearly of things that are wasted because **justice** does not prevail. When hard work is justly rewarded, and laziness is allowed its natural penalty there will be much less **waste**.

Proverbs 13:24

He who spares his rod hates his son,
But he who loves him disciplines him promptly.

a. **He who spares his rod hates his son**: The **rod** is a figure of correction (as previously in Proverbs 10:13), here including but not limited to the appropriate physical discipline of children. The one who refuses to discipline his child may *feel* they avoid it out of compassion for the child, but they are mistaken. The harm is potentially so great that it could be said that he **hates his son**.

> i. **Hates his son**: "His fond affection is as pernicious to him as his or another man's hatred could be." (Poole)

> ii. "It is as if one should be so tender over a child as not to suffer the wind to blow upon it, and therefore hold the hand before the mouth of it, but so hard as he strangles the child." (Trapp)

b. **He who loves him disciplines him promptly**: Proper discipline for a child comes from both wisdom and love. Such correction will be done **promptly**, reinforcing the connection between the correction and error of the child.

> i. "Ephesians 6:4 warns against undue severity; but the obligation remains. Proverbs itself exalts the place of tenderness, constructiveness and example, in this relationship: see, e.g., 4:3, 4, 11." (Kidner)

> ii. "The proverb is based on several assumptions. First, that the home is the basic social unit for transmitting values (cf. Exodus 20:12). Second, that parents have absolute values, not merely valuations. Third, that folly is bound up in the heart of the child (Proverbs 22:15; cf. Genesis 8:21). Fourth, 'that it will take more than just words to dislodge it.' (Waltke)

Proverbs 13:25

The righteous eats to the satisfying of his soul,
But the stomach of the wicked shall be in want.

a. **The righteous eats to the satisfying of his soul**: This principle was even more treasured in ancient times when only the relatively wealthy were able to eat as much as they pleased at a meal. God's blessing on **the righteous** man or woman is often so great that they have material abundance that does them good.

> i. It also speaks to having a **soul** that *can* be satisfied. "His desires are all moderate; he is contented with his circumstances, and is pleased with the lot which God is pleased to send." (Clarke)

> ii. "Although the word is used literally, in this gnomic proverb it can also be used metaphorically for the satisfying of the spiritual appetite." (Waltke)

b. **The stomach of the wicked shall be in want**: This may be because of the judgment of God upon **the wicked**, but it is also true that the **wicked** and foolish life creates its own scarcity.

i. "Elijah was fed, first by ravens, afterwards by a widow, while the wicked country of Israel went hungry." (Bridges)

ii. "The wicked, though he use all *shifts* and *expedients* to acquire earthly good, not sticking even at *rapine* and *wrong*, is frequently in real want, and always dissatisfied with his portion. A *contented mind is a continual feast*. At such feasts he eats not." (Clarke)

iii. This principle was especially true according to the terms of the old covenant. "Abundance of food indicates a right relationship to the Lord and the community, but a lack of it signifies a failed relationship (cf. Proverbs 10:3; Deuteronomy 28:48, 57; Jeremiah 44:18; Ezekiel 4:17)." (Waltke)

Proverbs 14 – The Contrast Between Wisdom and Folly

Proverbs 14:1

The wise woman builds her house,
But the foolish pulls it down with her hands.

a. **The wise woman builds her house**: Wisdom **builds**. It looks at what is and wisely considers how to make it better. Many homes have been made by a godly, **wise woman** who looks after the home and **builds** it.

i. "By her prudent and industrious management she *increases property* in the family, *furniture* in the *house*, and *food* and *raiment* for her household. This is the true *building of a house*. The *thriftless* wife acts differently, and the opposite is the result." (Clarke)

b. **The foolish pulls it down**: Folly tears **down**. Instead of supporting and building what is, folly shows its destructive nature. The **woman** of a home has tremendous power to make it a better or worse place.

i. **With her hands**: "As the husband is as the head from whom all the sinews do flow, so she is as the hands into which they flow, and enable them to do their office." (Trapp)

ii. "Note the foolish woman—her idleness, waste, love of pleasure, lack of all forethought and care.... We see her house torn down in confusion. It would have been a sad result if this had been done by an enemy. But it is the doing, or rather undoing, of her own hands." (Bridges)

Proverbs 14:2

He who walks in his uprightness fears the LORD,
But *he who is* perverse in his ways despises Him.

a. **He who walks in his uprightness fears the LORD**: One who is *upright* through their heritage, past habits, and general course of life still has the decision to *walk* in their uprightness. Doing this demonstrates that they do fear **the LORD**.

> i. The first line of this proverb communicates the New Testament attitude towards Christian obedience. Our call is to *be* what we *are*. Jesus has made us new creatures in Christ; He has made us upright. Our duty is to walk in that **uprightness**.

b. **He who is perverse in his ways despises Him**: The disobedient man shows that he really **despises** God and His authority. They say, *we will not have this Man to reign over us* (Luke 19:14). This displays the sinfulness of sin; it is often not only weakness, it is deep-seated rebellion against God.

Proverbs 14:3

In the mouth of a fool *is* a rod of pride,
But the lips of the wise will preserve them.

a. **In the mouth of a fool is a rod of pride**: The **fool** deserves the rod of correction (Proverbs 10:13). In the word picture used here, the **rod** of correction is made of the fool's **pride**, and it comes from his own **mouth**.

> i. "The fool's pride finds a rod in his mouth that lashes himself—he is his own worst enemy—and others." (Waltke)

> ii. "Here it is a rod of pride. Sometimes it strikes against God and sometimes against men…. Were this iron rod to rule the earth, who could tolerate it?" (Bridges)

b. **The lips of the wise will preserve them**: The **mouth of a fool** brings punishment to the fool, but the **wise** man or woman is rescued (**preserved**) by their own wise words.

Proverbs 14:4

Where no oxen *are*, the trough *is* clean;
But much increase *comes* by the strength of an ox.

a. **Where no oxen are, the trough is clean**: Where there is no work being accomplished, there is no mess or disorder to deal with. If you have **oxen**, they will bring a good measure of mess and work with them.

b. **But much increase comes by the strength of an ox**: Yet, *the mess an ox brings is worth it*. There is much good (**increase**) that comes from the impressive **strength of an ox**. Those who insist that there *never* be mess or disorder will miss the **increase** that comes from good things that can be a bit messy.

i. This is an important principle when it comes to church life and Christian community. There are some who, out of good intentions, are obsessed with making sure there is *never* any kind of "mess" to address among believers. Each and every expression of spiritual life must be hyper-regulated and suspiciously watched with the expectation of grave error. Not only is this an offense against Christian liberty, but it also creates an environment where, spiritually speaking, there is little **increase** – because no one will tolerate any mess in the trough.

ii. "Orderliness can reach the point of sterility. This proverb is not a plea for slovenliness, physical or moral, but for the readiness to accept upheaval, and a mess to clear up, as the price of growth. It has many applications to personal, institutional and spiritual life, and could well be inscribed in the minute-books of religious bodies, to foster a farmer's outlook, rather than a curator's." (Kidner)

iii. Adam Clarke used this proverb to describe seven reasons why oxen were superior to horses as farm animals, concluding: "In all large farms *oxen* are greatly to be preferred to *horses*. Have but patience with this most patient animal, and you will soon find that *there is much increase by the strength* and labour *of the ox.*"

Proverbs 14:5

A faithful witness does not lie,
But a false witness will utter lies.

a. **A faithful witness does not lie**: This simple and straightforward statement has much spiritual instruction in it. Jesus called His followers to be His witnesses (Acts 1:8). One of the primary responsibilities of a witness is to simply *tell the truth* and to **not lie**. When we have a genuine faith and experience in the person and work of Jesus Christ, we can give simple, true witness to Him.

b. **A false witness will utter lies**: Again, this simple statement points to a great spiritual truth. We should *never* be a **false witness** for Jesus Christ and utter **lies** about who He is and what He has done in our life.

i. **Will utter lies**: "Is or will be a false witness, when occasion requires it. Having debauched his conscience by daily lying, he is thereby prepared and disposed to false witness-bearing." (Poole)

Proverbs 14:6

A scoffer seeks wisdom and does not *find it*,
But knowledge *is* easy to him who understands.

a. **A scoffer seeks wisdom and does not find it**: When someone **seeks wisdom and does not find it**, it is evidence that they are likely a **scoffer** – someone whose pursuit of **wisdom** and the truth is cynical and superficial.

> i. "Such may *seek wisdom*; but he never can find it, because he does not seek it *where* it is to be found; neither in the *teaching of God's Spirit*, nor in the *revelation* of his will." (Clarke)

b. **Knowledge is easy to him who understands**: Jesus promised, *Ask, and it will be given to you; seek, and you will find; knock, and it will be opened to you* (Matthew 7:7). This is a promise to the sincere seeker, the one **who understands**.

Proverbs 14:7

Go from the presence of a foolish man,
When you do not perceive *in him* the lips of knowledge.

a. **Go from the presence of a foolish man**: Earlier Proverbs (such as Proverbs 13:20) spoke of the danger of foolish friends. Here the encouragement is to avoid **the presence of a foolish man** altogether.

> i. "One cannot increase in knowledge by associating with a fool— nothing comes from nothing, as many can affirm." (Ross)

b. **When you do not perceive in him the lips of knowledge**: The fool and the wise man can almost always be known by their words. This is a wonderful and often neglected way to discern if someone is wise or a fool.

Proverbs 14:8

The wisdom of the prudent *is* to understand his way,
But the folly of fools *is* deceit.

a. **The wisdom of the prudent is to understand his way**: The **prudent** man or woman carefully considers and understands **his way**. They know the path they are on, their point upon the path, and their progress along the way.

> i. **The wisdom of the prudent**: "It consists not in vain speculations, nor in a curious prying into other men's matters, nor in cunning arts of deceiving others; but in a diligent study of his own duty, and of the way to true and eternal happiness." (Poole)

b. **The folly of fools is deceit**: This explains one reason why **folly** and **fools** can be popular. Their attraction is based on **deceit**, in the same way that the bait deceives the fish into ignoring the hook.

Proverbs 14:9

Fools mock at sin,
But among the upright *there is* **favor.**

a. **Fools mock at sin**: This is in the nature of **fools** and their folly. They think sin is a light thing, worthy to be mocked. Their mockery of sin is connected with their lack of the fear of the LORD (Proverbs 1:29 and 8:13).

i. "But he that makes a *sport* of *sinning*, will find it *no sport* to suffer the vengeance of an eternal fire." (Clarke)

b. **But among the upright there is favor**: Those who are **upright** before God and man find **favor** among God and men.

i. "Fools do wrong and scoff at making reparations, but they find no divine or mutual favor and acceptance." (Waltke)

Proverbs 14:10

The heart knows its own bitterness,
And a stranger does not share its joy.

a. **The heart knows its own bitterness**: There is pain and **bitterness** enough for every **heart**. The sense is that though one's **heart knows its own bitterness**, it is difficult for anyone else to know the pain and bitterness of another's **heart**.

i. "We may not judge our brethren as though we understood them, and were competent to give a verdict upon them. Do not sit down, like Job's friends, and condemn the innocent." (Spurgeon)

b. **A stranger does not share its joy**: What was true regarding the **bitterness** of life in the first line of this proverb is also often true regarding the **joy** of life. It can be difficult for someone else to truly **share** the **joy** of another's heart.

i. "No less personal is the heart's joy. It lies deep within. Michal could understand David's bravery, but not his joy. She knew him as a man of war, not as a man of God." (Bridges)

ii. Spurgeon listed and described many joys that are personal in nature, and therefore often **a stranger does not share** them.

- The **joy** of sin forgiven.
- The **joy** of sin conquered.
- The **joy** of restored relationship with God.
- The **joy** of accepted service.
- The **joy** of answered prayer.

- The **joy** of usefulness for God.
- The **joy** of peace in time of trouble.
- Highest of all: the **joy** of communion with God.

Proverbs 14:11

The house of the wicked will be overthrown,
But the tent of the upright will flourish.

a. **The house of the wicked will be overthrown**: Whatever is built on a poor foundation cannot stand, especially against the storm of God's coming judgment.

b. **The tent of the upright will flourish**: The **wicked man** boasts of his great **house** and looks down upon his **upright** neighbor who lives in only a **tent**. Yet the **tent of the upright** is more secure than the **house of the wicked**.

i. "The tent is by no means used for any kind of dwelling but refers to a nomadic tent. It is a bell tent, supported in the middle by a wooden pole and composed of several dark, goatskin curtains. It was fastened down to pegs with cords." (Waltke)

Proverbs 14:12

There is a way *that seems* right to a man,
But its end *is* the way of death.

a. **There is a way that seems right to a man**: Proverbs often speaks of the **way**, the path of life a man or woman walks upon. Solomon observed that this **way** often **seems right to a man**. His path of life seems fine to him, and he wonders why God or anyone else would have a different opinion.

i. "The issue then is how deceptive evil is. It might promise and deliver happiness, power, and the good life, but it cannot sustain what it gives." (Ross)

b. **But its end is the way of death**: Though it **seems right**, *it isn't right* – it leads to **death**. Wisdom understands that what may **seem right to a man** isn't necessarily right; it can in fact be the **way of death**.

i. This proverb reminds us that **the way of death** is rarely clearly marked. "The safety and destiny of a road are not always as they appear (Matt. 7:13, 14). The deceptive road leads as certainly to death as the plainly marked one." (Waltke)

ii. This makes plain our need for a revelation from God. We can't entirely trust our own examination and judgment. To really know we are on the way of life (instead of the **way of death**), we need to fear the LORD and receive His wisdom, especially as revealed in His word.

iii. The principle of this proverb is so important that God repeated it again at Proverbs 16:25.

Proverbs 14:13

Even in laughter the heart may sorrow,
And the end of mirth *may be* grief.

a. **Even in laughter the heart may sorrow**: The person who often laughs is not always happy. The outward expression of **laughter** may be used to mask great **sorrow** in the heart.

i. "The design of the proverb is to declare the vanity of all worldly joys and comforts, and to teach men moderation in them, and to persuade us to seek for more solid and durable joys." (Poole)

b. **The end of mirth may be grief**: Laughter and **mirth** may do more than mask **sorrow**; they may very well end in **grief**. We are grateful for laughter and godly **mirth**, but not if they keep us from the fear of the LORD and the wisdom associated with it.

Proverbs 14:14

The backslider in heart will be filled with his own ways,
But a good man *will be satisfied* from above.

a. **The backslider in heart will be filled with his own ways**: Those who decline in their relationship and obedience to God will suffer from it, even if their decline is only **in heart**. Their own backsliding **ways** will come upon them.

i. **The backslider**: "The first part of his name is 'backslider.' He is not a back runner, nor a back leaper, but a backslider, that is to say he slides back with an easy, effortless motion, softly, quietly, perhaps unsuspected by himself or anybody else." (Spurgeon)

ii. "Every spot does not mean that you have leprosy. Every sin does not indicate that you are a backslider." (Bridges)

iii. "What is implied in being *filled with his own ways*? Having his soul *saturated* with folly, sin, and disappointment." (Clarke)

iv. "The story of Judas has been written over and over again in the lives of other traitors. We have heard of Judas as a deacon, and as an elder; we have heard Judas preach, we have read the works of Judas the bishop, and seen Judas the missionary. Judas sometimes continues in his profession for many years, but, sooner or later, the true character of the man is discovered." (Spurgeon)

b. **A good man will be satisfied from above**: The wise ones who do **good** enjoy God's blessing and the satisfaction that comes from Him.

i. "Which simply means that whatever may be within a man, in the deepest region of his personality, will sooner or later be wrought out into actual experience and visibility." (Morgan)

Proverbs 14:15

The simple believes every word,
But the prudent considers well his steps.

a. **The simple believes every word**: The man or woman who lacks wisdom (**the simple**) has little ability to discern truth from falsehood. They believe everyone, especially if they seem sincere.

i. "To believe every word of God is faith. To believe every word of man is credulity.… An indiscriminate faith is, therefore, fraught with mischief. The world was ruined by this weakness (Genesis 3:1-6)." (Bridges)

b. **The prudent considers well his steps**: The wise man or woman doesn't believe everything is as it first appears. While they do think carefully about others, they give even more consideration to their own **steps**.

Proverbs 14:16

A wise *man* fears and departs from evil,
But a fool rages and is self-confident.

a. **A wise man fears and departs from evil**: The **wise man** appreciates **evil** for what it is and keeps himself far from it. He does not overestimate or test his own strength in resisting **evil**; he **departs** from it.

b. **A fool rages and is self-confident**: Instead of godly fear, the **fool rages** with uncontrolled temper and outbursts. Despite his bad temper, he is **self-confident**. The self-confidence of fools is a mystery and a marvel.

Proverbs 14:17

A quick-tempered *man* acts foolishly,
And a man of wicked intentions is hated.

a. **A quick-tempered man acts foolishly**: In the previous proverb the fool raged; here his quick temper leads him to act out his foolishness. The wise man has the self-control to not react immediately and out of bad temper.

i. **Quick tempered-man**: "*Ketsar appayim*, 'short of nostrils:' because, when a man is angry, his *nose is contracted*, and drawn up towards his eyes." (Clarke)

b. **A man of wicked intentions is hated**: The love that fools and wicked men have for each other is limited. The **man of wicked intentions** is understood to be untrustworthy and therefore **hated**.

Proverbs 14:18

The simple inherit folly,
But the prudent are crowned with knowledge.

a. **The simple inherit folly**: As someone gains an inheritance as that which is due to them, so **the simple inherit folly**. For those who willfully reject wisdom, **folly** is due.

b. **The prudent are crowned with knowledge**: A wise (**prudent**) man or woman enjoys the benefits of their wisdom. **Knowledge** sits upon them as a graceful and noble crown.

Proverbs 14:19

The evil will bow before the good,
And the wicked at the gates of the righteous.

a. **The evil will bow before the good**: In this present age, it often feels that the **evil** win and sometimes triumph over the good. With true wisdom, Solomon reminds us that ultimately **evil will bow** in submission **before the good**.

i. "Ultimately the wicked will acknowledge and serve the righteous. The figure used here is of a conquered people kneeling before their victors awaiting their commands." (Ross)

ii. "The Egyptians and Joseph's brothers bowed before Joseph. The proud Pharaoh and his people bowed before Moses. The saints will judge the world (1 Corinthians 6:2)." (Bridges)

b. **The wicked at the gates of the righteous**: As if they came in humble surrender to the leaders of the city, the **wicked** will **bow** at the **gates of the righteous**.

Proverbs 14:20

The poor *man* is hated even by his own neighbor,
But the rich *has* many friends.

a. **The poor man is hated even by his own neighbor**: This is another of the proverbs that honestly describes the benefits of wealth. When a person is **poor**, they don't have as many friends and maybe their **own neighbor** may hate them.

    i. "This is a humbling but common illustration of natural selfishness.... But Jesus was deliberately the poor man's friend. How endearing is Jesus' love!" (Bridges)

b. **The rich has many friends**: This is a simple fact of life. The **friends** of the **rich** might be insincere friends, but there are more of them.

Proverbs 14:21

He who despises his neighbor sins;
But he who has mercy on the poor, happy *is* he.

a. **He who despises his neighbor sins**: Men and women are made in the image of God, and therefore we are commanded to love our neighbor (Leviticus 19:18, Matthew 22:39). To despise is to hate, so to despise your neighbor is to sin.

b. **He who has mercy on the poor, happy is he**: The generous heart is the happy heart. The link between the first and second lines of this proverb shows that whoever **has mercy on the poor** should never do it in a superior manner that would show they despise the **poor** they say they help.

Proverbs 14:22

Do they not go astray who devise evil?
But mercy and truth *belong* to those who devise good.

a. **Do they not go astray who devise evil?** Doing **evil** is an obvious sin, but even the plotting and devising of **evil** leads us astray. God cares about our heart and mind as well as our outward actions (Matthew 5:21-32).

    i. **Devise evil**: "Hebrew, That plough it and plot it, that dig it and delve it, that whet their wits and beat their brains about it - do not these err?" (Trapp)

b. **But mercy and truth belong to those who devise good**: The wicked will plot their evil, but wisdom leads us to **devise good** for others and ourselves. This will bring the blessings of **mercy and truth** into our lives.

    i. "Wicked as it is to do evil, it is far more wicked to plot evil. Children of God, do you show the same diligence and determination in planning to do good?" (Bridges)

Proverbs 14:23

In all labor there is profit,
But idle chatter *leads* only to poverty.

a. **In all labor there is profit**: As a principle, hard work is always rewarded. Even if there is not an immediate **profit** from the work, there is reward from God and in the building and demonstration of character.

b. **But idle chatter leads only to poverty**: If **labor** leads to **profit**, then anything that distracts from labor – such as **idle chatter** – will keep profits away, and lead to **poverty**. We can imagine a group of employees gathered together with **idle chatter** and entertaining conversation leading to no **profit** for their employer.

i. "People should be more afraid of idle talk than of hard work. Or, to put it another way, do not just talk about it—Do it!" (Ross)

ii. "Great talkers are do-littles, for the most part…. And 'why stand you looking upon one another? Get you down to Egypt,' said Jacob to his sons. [Genesis 42:1-2]" (Trapp)

Proverbs 14:24

The crown of the wise is their riches,
***But* the foolishness of fools *is* folly.**

a. **The crown of the wise is their riches**: Solomon was smart enough to know that riches can come in several ways. He knew that one of the ways **riches** came was through wisdom and hard work. When this is the case, those **riches** are like a **crown of the wise**, both evidence and reward of their wisdom.

b. **The foolishness of fools is folly**: For those who reject wisdom, the only crown they get is more **folly**. Their **foolishness** is multiplied.

Proverbs 14:25

A true witness delivers souls,
But a deceitful *witness* speaks lies.

a. **A true witness delivers souls**: This is true on an everyday life level, where truth brings light, blessing, and freedom. Where lies and false reports dominate, **souls** will be in darkness and bondage. This is also true on a spiritual or ministry level, where God will use the **true witness** of the preacher to rescue **souls**.

i. "A man who will trim the facts for you will trim them as easily against you; and a career or a life may hang on a word." (Kidner)

b. **A deceitful witness speaks lies**: Those who spread such **lies** and false reports fail to do the good of a **true witness** and they practice the evil of their **lies**.

i. "This proverb appears to have legal proceedings in view. Honesty in court is not a mere fine point of law; people's lives depend upon it." (Garrett)

Proverbs 14:26

In the fear of the Lord there is strong confidence,
And His children will have a place of refuge.

a. **In the fear of the Lord there is strong confidence**: One might think that **fear** always leads to a loss of **confidence**. But that isn't how it works with **the fear of the Lord**. Our honor, reverence, and sense of awe towards Him moves us from self-confidence and towards **strong confidence** in God's love and greatness.

b. **His children will have a place of refuge**: God always provides Himself as a refuge for **His children** (*God is our refuge and strength, a very present help in trouble*, Psalm 46:1).

Proverbs 14:27

The fear of the Lord is a fountain of life,
To turn *one* away from the snares of death.

a. **The fear of the Lord is a fountain of life**: One might think that **fear** always leads to less life, not more. But that isn't how it works with **the fear of the Lord**. Proper **fear of the Lord** is rooted in understanding who God is and who we are in relation to Him. That itself is like a **fountain of life**.

b. **To turn one away from the snares of death**: There are many additional benefits that come from a proper **fear of the Lord**, and one of those is to have a greater measure of God's watchful care and protection.

Proverbs 14:28

In a multitude of people *is* a king's honor,
But in the lack of people *is* the downfall of a prince.

a. **In a multitude of people is a king's honor**: Kings focus on the glory and strength useful and apparent in this world. With that focus, the more people the better. The greater the **multitude of people**, the greater is the **king's honor**.

i. "A prince's power varies with the size of his empire. This statement is generally true of empires; from a human viewpoint political power is based on the number of people in the party." (Ross)

ii. Related to spiritual things and Christian ministry, the principle of this proverb shows the weakness of a worldly, humanistic view of ministry. It is of the carnal, worldly wisdom of kings to understand large crowds as the only *real* measure of success. We imagine that the Apostle Paul might rephrase this line: *In a multitude of people is a king's honor, but in love, faithfulness, and sacrificial service is an apostle's honor.* A **multitude of people** in ministry is never to be despised, but we should have a *greater* measure of success than that.

b. **In the lack of people is the downfall of a prince**: If there are no people to govern, there won't be much governing. In the ancient world, rulers thought much about increasing the populations in their governed realm.

i. "The proverb, however, must be held in tension with the biblical teaching that large numbers are of little value with the Lord's presence (e.g., Psalm 33:16-17)." (Waltke)

Proverbs 14:29

He who is **slow to wrath has great understanding,**
But *he who is* **impulsive exalts folly.**

a. **He who is slow to wrath has great understanding**: There is great wisdom in the ability to control one's response to provoking situations. Being *quick* **to wrath** brings many regrets.

b. **He who is impulsive exalts folly**: The **impulsive**, uncontrolled person who quickly reacts without thinking lives in a way that **exalts** foolishness.

Proverbs 14:30

A sound heart *is* **life to the body,**
But envy *is* **rottenness to the bones.**

a. **A sound heart is life to the body**: If **heart** here meant the physical organ that beats in the chest, any medical doctor would agree. Yet Solomon had in mind **heart** as a metaphor for our innermost being. When we are **sound** on the inside, it brings health and **life** to the whole **body**.

b. **Envy is rottenness to the bones**: The presence of **envy** is presented as a contrast to **a sound heart**. **Envy** corrupts us from within and can poison many otherwise good things.

i. "The proverb teaches that to nurse a resentment is bad for body as well as soul: it is no sacrifice when we renounce it." (Kidner)

Proverbs 14:31

He who oppresses the poor reproaches his Maker,
But he who honors Him has mercy on the needy.

a. **He who oppresses the poor reproaches his Maker**: To oppress the **poor** is to sin against them, but it is also to sin against and to insult God

Himself. To oppress and despise the poor is to despise **his Maker**, the one in whose image all humanity was made.

b. **He who honors Him has mercy on the needy**: The one who **honors** and loves God will reflect God's own **mercy on the needy**. A cold, mean heart towards the poor shows a lack of honor towards God.

i. "Verse 31 stands in the ancient Near Eastern tradition of warning rulers not to trample upon the rights of the poor; the king who ignores this advice will soon find himself without a nation." (Garrett)

Proverbs 14:32

The wicked is banished in his wickedness,
But the righteous has a refuge in his death.

a. **The wicked is banished in his wickedness**: Godliness and wisdom are useful for many things, and one of their great benefits is the way that they make for good *community*. Yet the **wicked** will be **banished**, being of no benefit and of definite danger to the community.

b. **The righteous has a refuge in his death**: The **righteous** man or woman enjoys refuge in the community, but also even unto **his death**. God will demonstrate His care for **the righteous**.

i. The Old Testament in general and the Book of Proverbs in particular don't have much specific information or confidence in the life to come. There are rare flashes of this confidence, and **a refuge in his death** is one of those. "Job and the Psalms show occasional glimpses, such as this, of what lies normally beyond their view." (Kidner)

Proverbs 14:33

Wisdom rests in the heart of him who has understanding,
But *what is* in the heart of fools is made known.

a. **Wisdom rests in the heart of him who has understanding**: The idea is that **wisdom** finds a suitable home **in the heart** of those who have wisdom (**understanding**). It isn't like a temporary visitor; it comes and **rests in the heart**.

i. "True wisdom sets its throne in the heart." (Bridges)

b. **What is in the heart of fools is made known**: The wisdom of a wise man's heart will be revealed; so will the folly of the fool's **heart**. What we *are* is eventually evident in what we *do*.

Proverbs 14:34

Righteousness exalts a nation,
But sin *is* a reproach to *any* people.

a. **Righteousness exalts a nation**: Because **righteousness** is to follow God's will and God's way, it will always exalt a person, a family, a neighborhood, a city, a state, or even **a nation**. This is both because of the natural consequences of **righteousness** and because of God's active response of blessing.

i. Many things may, in human perspective, exalt a nation. Military might, economic prosperity, status among nations, cultural influence, and athletic victory may each make a nation seem exalted. Yet ultimately, none of those things match **righteousness** as a way a nation is *truly* exalted. One might say that the most patriotic thing a citizen might do is repent of their **sin** and then receive and pursue God's **righteousness** in their life.

b. **But sin is a reproach to any people**: When a **people** reject **righteousness** and choose **sin**, it will bring **reproach** and insult upon them. We never gain through our rejection of God and our embrace of **sin**.

i. "No nation is so low as not to sink even lower under sin. The strongest nations are given an indelible blot if they are overcome by sin. What an enemy an ungodly man is to his country. He may talk eloquently about his patriotism, but even if God should elevate him in his work, he will only bring disgrace on his people." (Bridges)

Proverbs 14:35

The king's favor *is* toward a wise servant,
But his wrath *is against* him who causes shame.

a. **The king's favor is toward a wise servant**: On a human level, there is nothing greater than the **favor** of those in places of power and prestige such as kings. Having that **favor** is one of the rewards of wisdom.

i. "What will the solemn day of reckoning bring to me? May I, may we all be found to be wise servants to the best of Kings." (Bridges)

b. **His wrath is against him who causes shame**: Kings are allergic to **shame**. Their power and presence rests upon the image of success and majesty. Therefore, to cause **shame** is to gain the **wrath** of the kings of this world.

i. **Causes shame**: "Both to himself, by his foolish management of the king's affairs committed to him; and to the king, who made so foolish a choice of a servant." (Poole)

ii. "The saying is a bracing reminder not to blame luck or favouritism but one's own shortcomings, for any lack of recognition. Moffatt gives the sense well: 'The king favours an able minister; his anger is for the incompetent.'" (Kidner)

iii. We are forever grateful that the *King of Kings* (1 Timothy 6:15 and Revelation 19:16) did not despise the shame of our sin, but bore it in Himself on the cross.

Proverbs 15 – The Words of the Wise

Proverbs 15:1

A soft answer turns away wrath,
But a harsh word stirs up anger.

a. **A soft answer turns away wrath**: When people come to us in **wrath**, we are often tempted to be harsh in response. Wisdom shows us the value of a **soft answer**, one without sharp edges or points. That kind of answer can actually turn **away wrath**.

i. "Soft speech is like oil on bruised skin to soften and heal it (cf. Judges 8:1-3); painful speech has the effect of oil poured on fire (cf. 1 Kings 12:1-16)." (Waltke)

ii. "Pride and passion on both sides strike together like two flints. We indulge in sarcasm as if we would rather lose a friend than miss scoring a point in the argument. All this the world excuses. But the Gospel sets before us our Savior's example and imbues us with his spirit; so we should be careful not to provoke a chafed or wounded spirit." (Bridges)

b. **A harsh word stirs up anger**: A **harsh** response to **wrath** often only **stirs up** more **anger**. It may feel good at the moment but ends up making the situation worse, not better.

i. "Many conflicts arise not because the issues separating the parties are so great but because of the temperaments people bring to a confrontation." (Garrett)

ii. "How was Saul enkindled by Doeg, and David by Nabal's currishness! Rehoboam, with one churlish breath, lost ten tribes." (Trapp)

iii. "Gideon in Judges 8:1-3 is a classic example of the soft answer that brings peace, whereas Jephthah illustrates the harsh answer that leads to war (Judges 12:1-6)." (Ross)

Proverbs 15:2

The tongue of the wise uses knowledge rightly,
But the mouth of fools pours forth foolishness.

a. **The tongue of the wise uses knowledge rightly**: The **wise** man or woman will show their right use of **knowledge** by the words they say. The words of their **tongue** demonstrate their wisdom.

i. **Uses knowledge rightly**: "Expressing what he knows prudently and gracefully; taking due care both what, and when, and to whom, and in what manner he speaks." (Poole)

ii. "This is very difficult to know: - *when* to *speak,* and *when* to be *silent; what* to *speak,* and *what* to leave *unspoken*; the *manner* that is best and most suitable to the *occasion,* the *subject,* the *circumstances,* and the *persons….* Even *wise counsel* may be *foolishly* given." (Clarke)

b. **The mouth of fools pours forth foolishness**: A fool will be revealed by their words. It isn't enough for a man or woman to claim they have wisdom in their heart or mind; what they say proves either their wisdom or folly.

i. **Pours forth**: "Hebrew, Bubbleth it out; blurteth it out, as a fountain casteth out its waters, with a great force and swiftness." (Trapp)

Proverbs 15:3

The eyes of the LORD are in every place,
Keeping watch on the evil and the good.

a. **The eyes of the LORD are in every place**: Wisdom understands that we are always under the eye of God. He sees us **in every place**, even when we are hidden to human eyes.

i. **The eyes of the LORD**: "The eyes of Christ are 'as a flaming fire.' [Revelation 1:14] And the school of nature teacheth that the fiery eye needs no outward light, that sees *extra mittendo,* by sending out a ray." (Trapp)

ii. "So how will I meet these eyes? Will I meet them as a rebel or as a child?" (Bridges)

b. **Keeping watch on the evil and the good**: God takes note of *both* **the evil and the good**. He will deal with the **evil** according to His righteous judgment, and He will bless and reward **the good**. Among men, **evil** is often unpunished and **good** is often unrewarded – but God sees and notes all.

i. We might say that God has night vision and sees all that happens under the cover of darkness.

ii. **Keeping watch**: "The word employed describes a very active and purposeful seeing. The statement is far more than that God sees; it is that He is investigating, observing…. He is keeping watch upon the evil. It is never out of His sight. It loves the darkness rather than the light, but He sees as well in the darkness as in the light." (Morgan)

iii. **And the good**: "The Lord's eyes also see the good. He sees them in outward destitution, in secret retirement, in deep affliction. He pierces the prison walls. He is with them in the furnace and in the storm." (Bridges)

Proverbs 15:4

A wholesome tongue *is* a tree of life,
But perverseness in it breaks the spirit.

a. **A wholesome tongue is a tree of life**: Good words are like a **tree** that continually brings **life** from its shade and fruit. Our words have the power to do far more good than we often think.

b. **Perverseness in it breaks the spirit**: If someone's tongue is perverse (twisted, crooked, corrupt) instead of **wholesome**, their words will break **the spirit** of others. Our words have the power to do far more harm than we often think.

Proverbs 15:5

A fool despises his father's instruction,
But he who receives correction is prudent.

a. **A fool despises his father's instruction**: Proverbs is written as advice from a father to his children. **A fool** would despise the wisdom that comes from a godly parent and God's word.

i. "One's attitude toward parental teaching will determine one's lifelong attitude toward authority and instruction." (Garrett)

b. **He who receives correction is prudent**: Learning wisdom is more than learning facts; it is to receive **correction**. If what we learn *only* confirms what we already know, it probably isn't wisdom we are learning.

Proverbs 15:6

***In* the house of the righteous *there is* much treasure,**
But in the revenue of the wicked is trouble.

a. **In the house of the righteous there is much treasure**: Because wisdom and godliness tend to bring prosperity, this is generally true of material **treasure**. Thankfully, the **treasure** in **the house of the righteous** isn't only material; the greater **treasure** is spiritual.

i. "Every righteous man is a rich man, whether he hath more or less of the things of this life." (Trapp)

b. **In the revenue of the wicked is trouble**: Even what the **wicked** man or woman earns (**the revenue**) can be a problem. Instead of **treasure**, they have **trouble**.

i. **Revenue of the wicked**: "Though he may obtain great revenues, yet they are attended with much trouble and vexation; either because they are strangely blasted and taken from them, or because they are imbittered to them by their own insatiable desires, or tormenting cares and fears, or the horrors of their guilty consciences, or by divers other ways." (Poole)

Proverbs 15:7

The lips of the wise disperse knowledge,
But the heart of the fool *does* not *do* so.

a. **The lips of the wise disperse knowledge**: The **wise** man or woman will spread (**disperse**) knowledge and wisdom. It is within them and will be given to others by the words they say.

b. **The heart of the fool does not do so**: Since wisdom isn't in the **heart of the fool**, it won't be on their **lips** either. They are unable to spread the blessing of wisdom to others through their words.

Proverbs 15:8

The sacrifice of the wicked *is* an abomination to the LORD,
But the prayer of the upright *is* His delight.

a. **The sacrifice of the wicked is an abomination to the LORD**: Without godliness, religious ritual, such as **sacrifice,** can be **an abomination** to God. As Samuel said to Saul, *Behold, to obey is better than sacrifice* (1 Samuel 15:22).

b. **The prayer of the upright is His delight**: The godly man or woman delights God with their **prayer**. The **wicked** one goes to the trouble and expense of offering a **sacrifice**, but it does not **delight** God in the way the **prayer of the upright** does.

Proverbs 15:9

The way of the wicked *is* an abomination to the LORD,
But He loves him who follows righteousness.

a. **The way of the wicked is an abomination to the LORD**: God rejects the religious ceremonies of **the wicked** (Proverbs 15:8); therefore, much more does God consider the sinful life of **the wicked** as **an abomination**.

b. **He loves him who follows righteousness**: The one who lives and **follows righteousness** does so in surrender and love to God, and they do what Jude advised; they keep themselves in the love of God (Jude 21).

Proverbs 15:10

Harsh discipline *is* for him who forsakes the way,
***And* he who hates correction will die.**

a. **Harsh discipline is for him who forsakes the way**: When a man or woman departs from God's path (**the way**), in mercy God will send them **harsh discipline**. This **discipline** is a warning and opportunity to change one's ways.

b. **He who hates correction will die**: The one who rejects God's loving and merciful **correction** seals his own fate and sets his own course. They are on the way of death and will remain there.

i. "He that is embittered by rebukes, and not bettered by chastisements, shall die…they that will not obey that sweet command, 'Come unto me all ye that labour and are heavy laden,' shall one day have no other voice to obey but that terrible [word], 'Go ye cursed into everlasting flames.'" (Trapp)

ii. "*The one who hates correction will die* (see Proverbs 5:23; 10:21) an eternal death without God, the tragic and inevitable end of apostates who have become hardened against truth." (Waltke)

Proverbs 15:11

Hell and Destruction *are* before the LORD;
So how much more the hearts of the sons of men.

a. **Hell and Destruction are before the LORD**: These two destinies are symbolically pictured as persons who are **before the LORD** to serve His purpose. The sobering truth is that God has a plan and a purpose for both **Hell and Destruction**.

i. "Sheol and Abaddon represent the remote underworld and all the mighty powers that reside there (see Proverbs 27:20; Job 26:6; Psalm 139:8; Amos 9:2; Revelation 9:11)." (Ross)

ii. God can see what we cannot. **Hell and Destruction** are presently invisible to us, but they **are before the LORD**. If we *could* see **Hell and Destruction**, we would think and live much differently. "We, silly fishes, see one another jerked out of the pond of life by the hand of death; but we see not the frying pan and the fire that they are cast into, that 'die in their sins,' and refuse to be reformed." (Trapp)

iii. "God's surveillance extends to the realm of the dead in the depths of the earth, as remote from heaven as possible, and he will be met in every corner of this pitch-black place shrouded in mystery and secrecy and of no apparent value to humanity or God." (Waltke)

b. **How much more the hearts of the sons of men**: If God has a plan and a purpose for those two destinies, it is **much more** true that He has a plan and purpose for humanity (**the sons of men**).

i. "This is a simple method of drawing attention to God's perfect knowledge of all the deepest and hidden things. If that which is most full of mystery to us is perfectly known to Him, how well He must know our hearts." (Morgan)

ii. "And not only so, but we have known cases in which the thoughts of men have been revealed from the pulpit. I have sometimes seen persons nudge with their elbow, because they have got a smart hit, and I have heard them say, when they went out, 'That is just what I said to you when I went in at the door.' 'Ah!' says the other, 'I was thinking of the very thing he said, and he told me of it.' Now, if God thus proves his own Omniscience by helping his poor, ignorant servant, to state the very thing, thought and done, when he did not know it, then it must remain decisively proved that God does know everything that is secret, because we see he tells it to men, and enables them to tell it to others." (Spurgeon)

Proverbs 15:12

A scoffer does not love one who corrects him,
Nor will he go to the wise.

a. **A scoffer does not love one who corrects him**: Because the fool and the **scoffer** hate correction, they will hate (**not love**) the one who brings it.

i. **Does not love one who corrects him**: "As Ahab did Micaiah; Herodias, John Baptist; the Pharisees, our Saviour." (Trapp)

b. **Nor will he go to the wise**: In rejecting correction, the **scoffer** rejects wisdom and will remain trapped in his folly.

Proverbs 15:13

A merry heart makes a cheerful countenance,
But by sorrow of the heart the spirit is broken.

a. **A merry heart makes a cheerful countenance**: If someone has happiness and joy, it should be seen on their face. They should have a **cheerful countenance**.

i. "This cheerfulness, however, is very different from the noisy mirth of the ungodly. The word *cheerful* was often used by the old writers. It was Foxe's favorite description of the holy joy of the martyrs." (Bridges)

b. **By sorrow of heart the spirit is broken**: Those who have deep **sorrow of heart** will display their **broken** spirit. We can observe both the happy and the sad with understanding and sympathy for both the **merry heart** and those with **sorrow of heart**.

i. "The words used here stress the pain and the depression with a note of despair." (Ross)

Proverbs 15:14

The heart of him who has understanding seeks knowledge,
But the mouth of fools feeds on foolishness.

a. **The heart of him who has understanding seeks knowledge**: The scoffer avoids wisdom's correction (Proverbs 15:12), but the one with **understanding** and wisdom in his or her heart will seek after more wisdom.

i. **Seeks knowledge**: "As a hungry man seeks meat, or a covetous man gold, the more he hath, the more he desires." (Trapp)

b. **The mouth of fools feeds on foolishness**: In this sense, the normal course of humanity is that the wise become wiser and that **fools** feed on more **foolishness**.

i. "Let fools feed on foolishness, as swine do on swill, as flies do on blotches, as carrion kites do on stinking carcasses." (Trapp)

Proverbs 15:15

All the days of the afflicted *are* evil,
But he who is of a merry heart *has* a continual feast.

a. **All the days of the afflicted are evil**: To live in **days** of affliction is to know the trouble and **evil** of life and this fallen world.

b. **He who is of a merry heart has a continual feast**: When a **merry heart** instead of an **afflicted** heart marks our attitude towards life, there is a sense of continual bounty and enjoyment.

i. **A continual feast**: "Hath constant satisfaction and delight in all conditions, yea, even in affliction." (Poole)

ii. "It is a full feast, a lasting feast; not for a day, as that of Nabal, not for seven days, as that of Samson, no, nor of hundred and eighty days, as that of Ahasuerus, but a durable continual feast, without intermission of solace, or interruption of society." (Trapp)

Proverbs 15:16

Better *is* a little with the fear of the LORD,
Than great treasure with trouble.

a. **Better is a little with the fear of the LORD**: Especially in our materialistic and consumer age, we constantly want *more,* and we fear living with **little**. Yet life is better with **little** if lived with reverence and honor to God (**the fear of the LORD**).

i. "If saints be sad, it is because they are too busy here below, and, Martha-like, troubled about many things, with neglect of that one thing necessary." (Trapp)

b. **Than great treasure with trouble**: To have **great treasure** and great **trouble** is not a good life. Because **the fear of the LORD** spares us from much **trouble**, it is better to have that than **great treasure**.

i. "Riches, though well got, are but as manna, those that gathered less had no want, and those that gathered more, it was but a trouble and annoyance to them." (Trapp)

Proverbs 15:17

Better *is* a dinner of herbs where love is,
Than a fatted calf with hatred.

a. **Better is a dinner of herbs where love is**: The presence of **love** makes up for a lot. We can live on a humble diet but can never flourish without **love**.

i. "Riches and poverty are more in the heart than in the hand. He is wealthy who is contented. He is poor who wants more." (Bishop Hall, cited in Bridges)

b. **Than a fatted calf with hatred**: One may enjoy the extravagant abundance of a **fatted calf**, but **hatred** will spoil it all. Nothing really makes up for a lack of **love**.

i. "*A fattened ox* (see Proverbs 7:22; 14:4) represents the king of domesticated animals at its very best and functions as a synecdoche for the finest foods (cf. Luke 15:23)." (Waltke)

Proverbs 15:18

A wrathful man stirs up strife,
But *he who is* slow to anger allays contention.

a. **A wrathful man stirs up strife**: When **strife** is stirred up, it doesn't happen by accident. Usually, the cause is a **wrathful man** or woman who **stirs up strife**.

b. **He who is slow to anger allays contention**: The wise man or woman is **slow to anger**, and they have a way of bringing peace and smoothing over **contention** instead of stirring up **strife**.

Proverbs 15:19

The way of the lazy *man is* like a hedge of thorns,
But the way of the upright *is* a highway.

a. **The way of the lazy man is like a hedge of thorns**: Those who are **lazy** may not see it in themselves. Often, they may more easily see the *result* of their laziness, which is a life filled with constant trouble and irritations **(like a hedge of thorns)**.

i. "Because he is *slothful*, he imagines *ten thousand* difficulties in the way which cannot be surmounted; but they are all the creatures of his own *imagination*, and that imagination is formed by his *sloth*." (Clarke)

ii. Many times, Proverbs reminds us of what serious sin laziness is.

- Laziness is *theft* – you live off the work of others.
- Laziness is *selfishness* – you live for yourself and comfort.
- Laziness is *neglect of duty* – you don't do what you should.

iii. In his sermon titled *The Hedge of Thorns and the Plain Way*, Charles Spurgeon used Proverbs 15:19 in a spiritual sense, speaking to those who are *spiritually* lazy: "The spiritual sluggard does not believe after that practical fashion. He says, 'It is true;' but he acts as if it were false. He is too much a sluggard to become an infidel; he is too lethargic to argue against the truth which condemns him; he nods assent, it is the nod of sleep." Spurgeon went on to describe the life of the spiritually lazy man:

- His spiritual life is lived as if he were asleep.
- He once gave an effort to forsake sin but did not follow through.
- His spiritual life is a hard way, full of thorns.
- Spiritual things seem long and dreary.
- The Christian life is full of thorny perplexities, problems, and misery.
- He may find that his way to heaven is blocked.

b. **The way of the upright is a highway**: The wise man or woman – **upright** and hardworking before the LORD – does not know the same constant troubles and irritations of life that the **lazy man** must endure. Life for the **upright** is much smoother and more efficient in its progress.

i. "Unthinking persons suppose that the sluggard lives a happy life, and travels an easy road. It is not so.... Labour of a holy sort has ten thousand times more joy in it than purposeless leisure." (Spurgeon)

Proverbs 15:20

A wise son makes a father glad,
But a foolish man despises his mother.

a. **A wise son makes a father glad**: A **father** is made glad by a **wise son**, both for the blessing of knowing there is good for the son, and because it vindicates the father's trust in God and training of the son in wisdom.

b. **A foolish man despises his mother**: The **foolish man** or woman brings disgrace to his parents, and their rejection of the parents' wisdom shows they despise their **mother** and father.

i. "Tragically the person who needs their instruction, out of his exaggerated opinion of his self-importance, feels that he is better than his godly parents and so is intractable and incorrigible." (Waltke)

Proverbs 15:21

Folly *is* joy *to him who is* destitute of discernment,
But a man of understanding walks uprightly.

a. **Folly is joy to him who is destitute of discernment**: For the fool, his foolishness (**folly**) is something to take pleasure in. He only hates his **folly** when they have to pay the bitter consequences of it. Otherwise, it **is joy to him**.

b. **A man of understanding walks uprightly**: With wisdom, our life is ordered and upright. The wise man or woman finds **joy** in what is good and upright.

i. "His sincerity supplies him with serenity; the joy of the Lord, as an oil of gladness, makes him lithe and nimble in ways of holiness." (Trapp)

Proverbs 15:22

Without counsel, plans go awry,
But in the multitude of counselors they are established.

a. **Without counsel, plans go awry**: The difference between success and failure can often be found in those who plan with or **without counsel**. Wisdom understands that other people also have wisdom.

i. "Our wisdom lies in self-distrust, or at least allowing for the possibility that we may often be wrong! So it is most expedient, especially in important matters, to seek experienced counsel." (Bridges)

b. **In the multitude of counselors they are established**: Normally there is more insight from many people than from one. Getting many eyes to see and many minds to think about **plans** can often see those plans **established** and successful.

Proverbs 15:23

A man has joy by the answer of his mouth,
And a word *spoken* in due season, how good *it is!*

a. **A man has joy by the answer of his mouth**: Right and wise words have the potential and power to bring great **joy** to one's self and to others.

b. **A word spoken in due season, how good it is**: The value in a **good** word is often not only found in its *content* but also in its *timing*. The right word at the right time (**in due season**) is a powerful force for good.

i. "This proverb sets forth the satisfaction of being able to say the right thing at the right moment." (Morgan)

Proverbs 15:24

The way of life *winds* upward for the wise,
That he may turn away from hell below.

a. **The way of life winds upward for the wise**: One of the great benefits of a life of wisdom is that, generally, life gets better as the years go on. The progress of their life **winds upward** and not down; they move from glory to glory (2 Corinthians 3:18).

b. **That he may turn away from hell below**: The progress of a wise life isn't just in what it heads toward (**upward**), but also in what it moves away from. Heaven becomes closer and **hell** becomes further distant behind.

i. **Upward...below**: "A recognition of the two forces of which man is ever conscious the upward pull and the downward pull with a declaration that wisdom consists in answering the upward." (Morgan)

ii. **From hell below**: "Or, *from the lowermost hell*; not *from the grave*, as this word is elsewhere used, for no wisdom can prevent that; but from hell properly so called, as this word is elsewhere used, as hath been formerly observed." (Poole)

Proverbs 15:25

The LORD will destroy the house of the proud,
But He will establish the boundary of the widow.

a. **The LORD will destroy the house of the proud**: Those who choose pride set themselves against God (James 4:6 and 1 Peter 5:5), and God will set Himself against them. They and their **house** will be targets of God's destruction.

b. **He will establish the boundary of the widow**: The **widow** is the picture and representative of a humble, needy person who looks to and depends on God. She represents the opposite of **the proud**, and God takes special care of those who humbly depend on Him.

> i. "When they were too weak to have a voice, God spoke for the poor and needy through Moses (cf. Deuteronomy 19:14; 27:17), the prophets (Hosea 5:10), and the sages (Job 24:2; Proverbs 15:25; 22:28)." (Waltke)

> ii. "The story of Naboth (1 Kings 21) illuminates the saying; but it is relevant to all kinds of exploitation." (Kidner)

Proverbs 15:26

The thoughts of the wicked *are* an abomination to the LORD,
But *the words* of the pure *are* pleasant.

a. **The thoughts of the wicked are an abomination to the LORD**: Wickedness doesn't begin with actions; it begins in the heart and **thoughts**. There is certainly a sense in which our actions are more important than our thoughts, but our actions *begin* in our thoughts, so what we think is also important to God.

> i. "How little most people think they are responsible for their thoughts. They live as if they were on their own and so can indulge themselves without any restraints." (Bridges)

> ii. "*Thoughts*…in the first line, mean 'plans', and the contrasted language of the second line emphasizes the fact that such plans are hateful to God even before they issue in words or deeds." (Kidner)

b. **The words of the pure are pleasant**: Solomon knew that a person's thoughts would be ultimately revealed by their **words**. God hears the **words of the pure** and is pleased, contrasting with the **thoughts of the wicked**.

Proverbs 15:27

He who is greedy for gain troubles his own house,
But he who hates bribes will live.

a. **He who is greedy for gain troubles his own house**: Many of those who are **greedy for gain** justify it with the excuse that they do it for their family. This is not wise, because being **greedy for gain** will ultimately bring trouble to one's **house**.

i. "The 'greedy man' is the one who wants a big cut, who is in a hurry to get rich, and who is not particular how it happens." (Ross)

ii. "The Papists propose rewards to such as shall relinquish the Protestant religion and turn to them…. Thus they tempted Luther, but he would not be hired to go to hell; and thus they tempted that noble Marquis of Vicum, nephew to Pope Paul V, who left all for Christ and fled to Geneva, but he cried out, Let their money perish with them that prefer all the world's wealth before one day's communion with Jesus Christ and his despised people." (Trapp)

b. **He who hates bribes will live**: The one who **hates bribes** is set as a contrast to the one who is **greedy for gain**. The **greedy** man or woman will do anything for more money and loves **bribes** if they can bring more money. God's blessing is on men and women of integrity who hate **bribes** and other dishonest ways of doing business.

Proverbs 15:28

The heart of the righteous studies how to answer,
But the mouth of the wicked pours forth evil.

a. **The heart of the righteous studies how to answer**: The idea behind the phrase "**how to answer**" is simply what one says in response. God's **righteous** ones – men and women of wisdom – think beforehand what they should and will say. Their words are not based only on impulse and reaction.

b. **The mouth of the wicked pours forth evil**: There is little self-control when it comes to the **mouth of the wicked**. **Evil** words and ideas simply pour out of their **mouth**, with no wise thought beforehand.

i. "The advice is to say less but better things." (Ross)

Proverbs 15:29

The LORD is far from the wicked,
But He hears the prayer of the righteous.

a. **The LORD is far from the wicked**: Men and women who are **wicked** do their best to separate themselves from God, and in this sense, God is **far from** them. There is another sense, especially in light of the work of Jesus, in which God draws near to **the wicked** to offer redemption and wisdom (Romans 5:8).

i. "But this farness or nearness respects not God's essence, which is every where, but his gracious and helpful presence." (Poole)

ii. "Proverbs does not envision the wicked as repenting; if they did, they would be righteous." (Waltke)

b. **He hears the prayer of the righteous**: God draws near to those who draw near to Him (James 4:8). The **prayer of the righteous** man or woman is effective before God (James 5:16).

Proverbs 15:30

The light of the eyes rejoices the heart,
***And* a good report makes the bones healthy.**

a. **The light of the eyes rejoices the heart**: The **eyes** are something like a lamp to the whole body (Matthew 6:22-23). When the **eyes** are full of **light** it brings happiness and contentment to the **heart** and the whole body.

i. "*The light of the eyes* may perhaps refer to the radiant face of a friend (cf. Proverbs 16:15); if so, the two lines of the proverb will be speaking of the heartwarming effect that persons and facts, respectively, can bring." (Kidner)

b. **A good report makes the bones healthy**: Good news cheers the spirit and brings health to the body. The ultimate fulfillment of this is the gospel – the good news, the **good report** of what God did in Jesus Christ to demonstrate His love for us and to rescue us (1 Corinthians 15:1-8).

Proverbs 15:31

The ear that hears the rebukes of life
Will abide among the wise.

a. **The ear that hears the rebukes of life**: Not every **ear** will listen to correction, but there is a blessing to those that do. Also, **life** has its own **rebukes** for those who have the **ear** to hear. In general, life rewards wisdom and **rebukes** folly.

i. **Hears the rebukes of life**: "That receives it gratefully and obeys it. 'Advice is for them that will take it,' so says one of our own old proverbs; and the meaning here is nearly the same." (Clarke)

ii. "The way we receive a rebuke tests our character. It reveals if we possess the graces of humility, sincerity, and self-knowledge." (Bridges)

b. **Will abide among the wise**: One of the more important aspects of wisdom is the simple ability to hear and learn. If we can't learn, we can never **abide among the wise**.

Proverbs 15:32

He who disdains instruction despises his own soul,
But he who heeds rebuke gets understanding.

a. **He who disdains instruction despises his own soul**: To refuse wisdom and the **instruction** that comes from wisdom is to hate one's **own soul**. Those who reject wisdom hurt many people, but most of all themselves.

b. **He who heeds rebuke gets understanding**. To hear and heed **rebuke** is to get and grow in wisdom (**understanding**). Receiving **rebuke** is rarely pleasant, but it is worth it for the wisdom it brings.

i. **Heeds rebuke**: "Correction is infinitely preferable to the poison of sweet flattery." (Bridges)

ii. **Gets understanding**: "Hebrew, *possesseth an heart*, which the Hebrews make the seat of wisdom." (Poole)

Proverbs 15:33

The fear of the Lord is the instruction of wisdom,
And before honor *is* humility.

a. **The fear of the Lord is the instruction of wisdom**: A common and foundational theme in Proverbs is repeated here. **Wisdom** begins in the **fear of the Lord**, and true wisdom flows from it.

b. **And before honor is humility**: An essential aspect of **the fear of the Lord** is **humility**. To properly fear God is to see and recognize Him as He really is. When we see and recognize who we really are, **humility** comes.

i. **Before honor is humility**: "Luther observed that ever, for most part, before God set him upon any special service for the good of the church, he had some sore fit of sickness. Surely, as the lower the ebb, the higher the tide; so the lower any descend in humiliation, the higher they shall ascend in exaltation; the lower this foundation of humility is laid, the higher shall the roof of honour be overlaid." (Trapp)

ii. "*Humility*; whereby men submit to God, and yield to men, which gains them love and respect; whereas pride procures them hatred and contempt from God and men." (Poole)

iii. "Paradoxically, the one who grants himself no glory before the glorious God in the end is crowned with the glory and wealth that give him social esteem." (Waltke)

Proverbs 16 – Of Righteousness and Kings

Proverbs 16:1

The preparations of the heart *belong* **to man,**
But the answer of the tongue *is* **from the LORD.**

 a. **The preparations of the heart belong to man**: God plans and prepares, and because man is made in the image of God (Genesis 1:27), it is in the nature of man to make **preparations of the heart**.

 b. **But the answer of the tongue is from the LORD**: When wisdom is given voice (**the answer of the tongue**), it is **from the LORD** – beyond the **preparations** of man's heart.

  i. "A somewhat obscure proverb which recognizes that man has to exercise his own reason in making his plans, but that he is dependent on the Lord for the answer of the tongue." (Morgan)

Proverbs 16:2

All the ways of a man *are* **pure in his own eyes,**
But the LORD weighs the spirits.

 a. **All the ways of a man are pure in his own eyes**: By instinct, men and women justify themselves and see their own **ways** as **pure**. Some of the most criminal and violent people have thought themselves **pure** in their **own eyes**.

  i. "They who are best acquainted with mankind will tell you that self-righteousness is not the peculiar sin of the virtuous, but that most remarkably, it flourishes best where there appears to be the least soil for it." (Spurgeon)

 b. **But the LORD weighs the spirits**: Despite the constant self-justification of men and women, God fairly and accurately **weighs the spirits** of all. God knows and God measures.

i. "The conclusion of the matter is that we deceive ourselves so easily and therefore cannot fully evaluate ourselves. God, by his Spirit and through his Word, provides the penetrating evaluation." (Ross)

Proverbs 16:3

Commit your works to the LORD,
And your thoughts will be established.

a. **Commit your works to the LORD**: Every man and woman should **commit** their **works to the LORD**. They should depend on God in their works and they should do those works as unto the LORD (Colossians 3:23).

i. **Commit your works**: "Hebrew, *Roll*, etc., as a man rolls a burden to another, which is too heavy for himself, imploring his help. Refer all thy actions and concerns to God, and to his glory." (Poole)

ii. "The admonition *commit to* (*golel,* literally 'roll to/upon' cf. Genesis 29:3, 8, 10; Psalm 22:8 37:5) connotes a sense of finality; roll it unto the Lord and leave it there." (Waltke)

iii. "Our activities and *plans* (**thoughts**) will be no less our own for being his: only less burdensome (*commit* is literally 'roll', as in Psalm 37:5), and better made." (Kidner)

b. **Your thoughts will be established**: Usually, we think of committing our **thoughts** or plans to the Lord, *then* committing our works to Him. Here Solomon reversed that order, and told us to first commit our works, then trust that our **thoughts** and plans **will be established**.

Proverbs 16:4

The LORD has made all for Himself,
Yes, even the wicked for the day of doom.

a. **The LORD has made all for Himself**: God, as creator of all things, has the right to claim **all** things **for Himself**.

b. **Yes, even the wicked for the day of doom**: God's plan and providence includes the destiny of the **wicked**. He has appointed them for **the day of doom**.

i. "The general meaning is that there are ultimately no loose ends in God's world: everything will be put to some use and matched with its proper fate. It does not mean that God is the author of evil." (Kidner)

ii. "He does not *make* the *wicked* or *ungodly man*; but when *man has made himself such*, even *then* God bears with him. But if he repent not, when the measure of his iniquity is filled up, he shall fall under the wrath of God his Maker." (Clarke)

iii. John Trapp was among those who believed that this proverb did *not* teach the predestination of the damned: "For God may, to show his sovereignty, annihilate his creature; but to appoint a reasonable creature to an estate of endless pain, without respect of his desert, cannot agree to the unspotted justice of God."

Proverbs 16:5

Everyone proud in heart *is* an abomination to the LORD;
***Though they join* forces, none will go unpunished.**

a. **Everyone proud in heart is an abomination to the LORD**: God resists the **proud** (James 4:6 and 1 Peter 5:5) and regards them as an **abomination**. The proud man or woman imitates Satan in his proud rebellion against God (Isaiah 14:12-15).

b. **Though they join forces, none will go unpunished**: One proud man or woman cannot succeed against God, but neither can many proud men or women. Even if they **join forces** against God as they did at Babel (Genesis 11:1-9), they will not **go unpunished**, even as at Babel.

Proverbs 16:6

In mercy and truth
Atonement is provided for iniquity;
And by the fear of the LORD one departs from evil.

a. **In mercy and truth atonement is provided**: God in His **mercy and truth** has provided **atonement** for **iniquity**. God's **mercy** prompted the great sacrifice of Jesus Messiah on the cross, and His **truth** made it necessary to make atonement in a way that honored the righteousness of God.

i. "This may be misunderstood, as if a man, by *showing mercy* and *acting according to truth*, could atone for his own iniquity. The Hebrew text is not ambiguous: *bechesed veemeth yechapper avon*; 'By mercy and truth he shall atone for iniquity.' *He* – God, *by* his *mercy*, in sending his son Jesus into the world, – 'shall make an atonement for iniquity' according to his *truth* – the word which he declared by his holy prophets since the world began." (Clarke)

ii. To paraphrase a thought from Bridges: *Mercy engages; truth fulfills. The ransom is provided by mercy and accepted by truth. Both sat together in the eternal council. In Jesus, both entered into the world together.*

iii. Some commentators believe that this refers to *man's* **mercy and truth** but are careful to point out that it does not teach the idea of self-atonement or self-salvation. "The second line indicates that the mercy (*hesed*) *and truth* (better, *loyalty and faithfulness*, Revised Standard

Version) are man's here, not God's…. This is not a denial of grace, but a characteristic demand for 'fruits that befit repentance'." (Kidner)

b. **By the fear of the LORD one departs from evil**: The great principle of **the fear of the LORD** is not only the beginning of wisdom (Proverbs 1:7, 9:10), it is also the foundation of a God-honoring life. To live in the **fear of the LORD** is to depart **from evil**.

Proverbs 16:7

When a man's ways please the LORD,
He makes even his enemies to be at peace with him.

a. **When a man's ways please the LORD**: It is possible for a man or woman to live a life that pleases God. This isn't the idea that we can be perfectly pleasing to God before our salvation is completed in resurrection and glorification. Instead, the idea is that in general, a man or woman can honor and **please the LORD** with their life.

b. **He makes even his enemies to be at peace with him**: One of God's blessings on the man or woman who pleases Him is to give them **peace** with others, even extending to their **enemies**.

i. "God is the guardian…of all that fear and love him; and it is truly astonishing to see how wondrously God works in their behalf, raising them up friends, and turning their enemies into friends." (Clarke)

ii. "A lifestyle pleasing to God disarms social hostility." (Ross)

Proverbs 16:8

Better *is* a little with righteousness,
Than vast revenues without justice.

a. **Better is a little with righteousness**: Sometimes those who are righteous in this world have **little** of the material comforts of this world.

b. **Than vast revenues without justice**: Someone who has great wealth (**vast revenues**) but little **righteousness** is worse off than the righteous man or woman who has **little** materially in this world. **Vast revenues without justice** can never give a peaceful conscience, freedom from guilt and sin, the love and joy of God, and a hundred other things the righteous enjoy.

i. It isn't that the only two options in life are to have either **little with righteousness** or **vast revenues without justice**. It's that when those two options are compared, the first is clearly better.

ii. "Was not the widow of Zarephath richer with her scanty fare than Jezebel in her royal attire?… If godliness is great riches in this life, what will it be in eternity?" (Bridges)

Proverbs 16:9

A man's heart plans his way,
But the LORD directs his steps.

a. **A man's heart plans his way**: This is not a bad thing. We, as the God in whose image we are made, think about and plan our **way**. Many people would do well to more carefully plan their **way**.

b. **But the LORD directs his steps**: We plan as we can and should, but we should never think that our ability to plan makes us lord over our lives. It is the LORD who **directs** our **steps**. Every plan we make should be held in humility before God and in surrender to His ultimate will.

i. "A man may plan his road to the last detail, but he cannot implement his planning, unless it coincides with Yahweh's plan for him." (Waltke)

ii. "A man can and does devise his own way under the direction of his heart. If desire be evil, the way devised is evil. If desire be good, the way devised is good. But that is not all the truth about life. This is also true: 'Jehovah directeth his steps'…. That is to say that no man can step outside the government of God, no man can devise a way that enables him to escape from God." (Morgan)

iii. This is true with both good and bad **plans**. "The point is the contrast between what we actually plan and what actually happens— God determines that. As Paul later said, God is able to do abundantly more than we ask or think (Ephesians 3:20)." (Ross)

iv. "As rational agents we think, consult, act freely. We are dependent agents, and the Lord exercises his own power in permitting, overruling, or furthering our actions. Thus man proposes, and God disposes." (Bridges)

Proverbs 16:10

Divination *is* on the lips of the king;
His mouth must not transgress in judgment.

a. **Divination is on the lips of the king**: The word **divination** is used here not in the sense of seeking occult or demonic guidance. It is used simply in the sense of wise guidance, the wisdom that should be **on the lips of the king**.

i. "Hebrew, *divination*, which is sometimes taken in a good sense for prudence, as it is Isaiah 3:2. A great sagacity and piercing judgment to discern dubious and difficult cases." (Poole)

ii. **Divination**: "The word *qesem* is used throughout the Bible in the negative sense of 'divination'; here it seems merely to mean his words from an oracular sentence, as if he speaks for God (see Numbers 22:7; 23:23; and, for a popular opinion of such, 2 Samuel 14:20)." (Ross)

b. **His mouth must not transgress in judgment**: The same **lips** that must speak wisdom and discernment should not also be used to go beyond God's wisely appointed boundaries of **judgment**.

    i. "The Old Testament lends no support to the idea that the king can do no wrong; rather, he is a man under authority: Deuteronomy 17:18-20." (Kidner)

Proverbs 16:11

Honest weights and scales *are* the LORD's;
All the weights in the bag *are* His work.

a. **Honest weights and scales are the LORD's**: Fair business and measures are so pleasing to God that it can be said that **honest** measures belong to Him. All of *God's* measurements and assessments are fair and true. The proper measure does not come from the king, nor does it belong to the king. The right measure comes from God and belongs to Him.

    i. "*Balance* [**weights**] refers to a stationary balance with beams and bolts, *and scale* (see Proverbs 11:1) possibly refers to the hand-held balance." (Waltke)

b. **All the weights in the bag are His work**: This assumes that the **weights in the bag** are those mentioned in the previous line – **honest weights and scales**. Fair and honest business is God's business, **His work**.

    i. "Verse 11 does not mention the king and is theologically important in that, using the concrete image of scales and measures, it teaches that the principle of justice is derived from God. Equity is not a human invention, and thus kings do not have the authority to suspend or violate the laws of fairness." (Garrett)

Proverbs 16:12

***It is* an abomination for kings to commit wickedness,**
For a throne is established by righteousness.

a. **It is an abomination for kings to commit wickedness**: Solomon admitted that it was *possible* for **kings to commit wickedness**. Some think that because someone is a king or leader all they do is justified. Sadly, Solomon became a king who committed **wickedness** (1 Kings 11:1-10).

b. **A throne is established by righteousness**: The righteous life of a king invites God's blessing upon his life and reign. Because of this great potential and influence, it is an even greater sin for **kings to commit wickedness**.

i. "If this proverb had been written later, after the monarchy had disintegrated, there would have been a greater variance between the ideal and the real. But coming from the golden age of Solomon, the ideal was still credible." (Ross)

Proverbs 16:13

Righteous lips *are* the delight of kings,
And they love him who speaks *what is* right.

a. **Righteous lips are the delight of kings**: In their positions of authority, it is important for **kings** to hear from those who speak honestly and wisely. Therefore, they find **delight** in **righteous lips**.

i. It is always important for **kings** and leaders to hear the truth from others and not mere flattery. "Most princes are held by their parasites, who soothe them up in their sins, and smooth them up with fair words, which soak into them as oil doth into earthen vessels." (Trapp)

b. **They love him who speaks what is right**: Even when a man speaks what may be difficult for the king to hear, the one who **speaks what is right** will gain the **love** and respect of those who are in authority.

Proverbs 16:14

As messengers of death *is* the king's wrath,
But a wise man will appease it.

a. **As messengers of death is the king's wrath**: When a king or man of authority is angry, his reaction can bring **death** or a death-like fear to others. This is true of earthly kings; it is much truer of the King of Kings. To be the target of His wrath is to receive **messengers of death**.

i. "Solomon's kingdom is said to be established only after he rid his realm of the wrongdoers (1 Kings 2:22-46)." (Waltke)

ii. "Queen Elizabeth was so reserved, that all about her stood in a reverent awe of her very presence and aspect, but much more of her least frown or check; wherewith some of them, who thought they might best presume of her favour, have been so suddenly daunted and planet stricken that they could not lay down the grief thereof but in their grave." (Trapp)

b. **But a wise man will appease it**: Wisdom can help us have the right reaction even in the difficult moments when a king or person of authority is angry and shows their **wrath**. The **wise man** or woman will especially know how to **appease** the wrath of the King of Kings – not by their own works and merits, but by receiving what God has provided in the person and work of Jesus Messiah.

Proverbs 16:15

In the light of the king's face *is* life,
And his favor *is* like a cloud of the latter rain.

a. **In the light of the king's face is life**: The approval and favor of an earthly king could mean success or failure for anyone in his kingdom. To have his shining countenance give approval (**the light of the king's face**) meant you were safe in the king's favor and had **life**.

i. "The saying describes the benefits of having a king who is pleased with his subjects. The king's brightened face signifies his delight and thus means life for those around him (as opposed to his wrath)." (Ross)

b. **His favor is like a cloud of the latter rain**: The welcome and approval of a king is like life-giving rain, especially the **latter rain** which ensured a good harvest. This proverb is especially true regarding the King of Kings. The favor of His countenance is a blessing to receive (Numbers 6:25) and it gives **light** and **life**.

i. "As acceptable as those clouds which bring the latter rain, whereby the fruits are filled and ripened a little before the harvest; of which see Deuteronomy 11:14, Job 29:23, James 5:7." (Poole)

ii. "The early rains prepare the ground for plowing and sowing and the latter rains provide the last bit of moisture on which the cereal harvest depends." (Waltke)

Proverbs 16:16

How much better to get wisdom than gold!
And to get understanding is to be chosen rather than silver.

a. **How much better to get wisdom than gold**: The riches of this world have their uses, but it is better to have **wisdom than gold**. Wisdom is much more helpful and useful in this life, and it is far more profitable for the life to come.

i. "Who believes this, though spoken by the wisest of men, under Divine inspiration?" (Clarke)

b. **To get understanding is to be chosen rather than silver**: One should make the main pursuit of one's life to gain **wisdom** and **understanding** in the fear of the Lord. This has value far more than **gold** or **silver**, but it also often leads to material prosperity as it did for Solomon (1 Kings 3:5-15).

i. "Wisdom and wealth are not incompatible; but this comparison is between wealth without wisdom and wisdom without wealth." (Ross)

Proverbs 16:17

The highway of the upright *is* to depart from evil;
He who keeps his way preserves his soul.

a. **The highway of the upright is to depart from evil**: The **upright** man or woman knows that the path of their life – their **highway** – should move away from evil, not towards it or with it.

b. **He who keeps his way preserves his soul**: The one who walks well upon the right way will find his life preserved. He will stay away from the **evil** way that may cost him his life, his **soul**.

Proverbs 16:18

Pride *goes* before destruction,
And a haughty spirit before a fall.

a. **Pride goes before destruction**: God is opposed to the proud (James 4:6 and 1 Peter 5:5) and the proud man or woman is an abomination to God (Proverbs 16:5). With God so set against the proud, no wonder that **pride goes before destruction**.

i. "The special evil of pride is that it opposes the first principle of wisdom (the fear of the Lord) and the two great commandments." (Kidner)

ii. "A bulging wall is near a downfall. Swelling is a dangerous symptom in the body; so is pride in the soul." (Trapp)

iii. "So far as any man is proud, he is kin to the devil, and a stranger to God and to himself." (Baxter, cited in Bridges)

b. **And a haughty spirit before a fall**: One of the many ways that **pride** is evident is in a **haughty spirit** – an attitude that communicates superiority over other people. Those who think themselves higher than others are ready to **fall** under the fair judgment of God.

i. "The proverb gives the strong impression of saying the same thing twice…. In this way its truth is underscored and clarified; the proud are defined more precisely as the haughty in spirit." (Waltke)

Proverbs 16:19

Better *to be* of a humble spirit with the lowly,
Than to divide the spoil with the proud.

a. **Better to be of a humble spirit with the lowly**: Because pride is an abomination to God (Proverbs 16:5) and leads to destruction (Proverbs 16:18), it isn't so bad to live among the **lowly** and to have a **humble spirit**.

b. **Than to divide the spoil with the proud**: A **humble** life among the **lowly** is **better** than having reward (**spoil**) among **the proud**. This is because **proud** people are not pleasant company, and because it is never good to join those whom God is set against.

i. "A humble man is worth his weight in gold; he hath far more comfort in his losses than proud giants have in their rapines and robberies." (Trapp)

Proverbs 16:20

He who heeds the word wisely will find good,
And whoever trusts in the LORD, happy *is* he.

a. **He who heeds the word wisely will find good**: Obedience to God – to heed His **word** and to do it **wisely** – will always bring **good**. This thought also suggests that there are *unwise* or *foolish* ways to heed the word, perhaps as the religious leaders in Jesus' day could *strain out a gnat and swallow a camel* (Matthew 23:24).

b. **Whoever trusts in the LORD, happy is he**: The **good** that the obedient **will find** also comes because they have a true and confident trust in God. They can happily and calmly rest in the good God who loves and cares for them.

i. "I have read a story of an old Doctor of the Church, who, going out one morning, met a beggar, and said to him, 'I wish you a good day.' 'Sir,' said he, 'I never had an ill day in any life.' 'But,' said the Doctor, 'your clothes are torn to rags, and your wallet seems to be exceedingly empty.' Said he, 'My clothes are as good as God wills them to be, and my wallet is as full as the Lord has been pleased to make it, and what pleases him pleases me.' 'But,' said the Doctor, 'suppose God should cast you into hell?' 'Indeed, sir,' said he, 'but that would never be; but if it were, I would be contented, for I have two long and strong arms – faith and love – and I would throw these about the neck of my Savior, and I would never let him go, so that if I went there, he would be with me, and it would be a heaven to me.' Oh, those two strong arms of faith and love! if you can but hang about the Savior's neck, indeed, you may fear no ill weather." (Spurgeon)

Proverbs 16:21

The wise in heart will be called prudent,
And sweetness of the lips increases learning.

a. **The wise in heart will be called prudent**: Those who are **wise in heart** will demonstrate it in their life. Others will see it and call them **prudent** or wise. This is another reminder that true wisdom is demonstrated in life; it isn't only having good or true thoughts in one's mind.

b. **The sweetness of the lips increases learning**: The phrase **sweetness of the lips** doesn't have to do with good tasting food or pleasant kisses. Like many proverbs, it refers to wise and well-spoken words, perhaps with a touch of eloquence. Such speaking **increases learning**, both in the speaker and those who hear him or her.

i. **The sweetness of the lips**: "Eloquence added to wisdom; the faculty of expressing a man's mind fitly, and freely, and acceptably." (Poole)

ii. "Wise teachers choose their words carefully and in so doing enhance the learning experience for their students. The wisdom of the true sage not only benefits the disciples morally but is a joy to receive as well." (Garrett)

Proverbs 16:22

Understanding *is* a wellspring of life to him who has it.
But the correction of fools *is* folly.

a. **Understanding is a wellspring of life to him who has it**: Wisdom (**understanding**) brings life to the wise man or woman. It is like a continually flowing **wellspring of life**.

b. **The correction of fools is folly**: Wisdom brings life, but it is usually foolish to try to correct a fool. As soon as a fool decides to receive **correction**, they have started not being a fool and leaving their **folly**.

Proverbs 16:23

The heart of the wise teaches his mouth,
And adds learning to his lips.

a. **The heart of the wise teaches his mouth**: Our wisdom is shown by what we speak, and by the control we have over the words that come from our mouths. Godliness and wisdom are evident when they teach the **mouth** what to say and not say.

b. **And adds learning to his lips**: Wisdom is shown by a heart and mind that are continually **learning**. When **learning** is added to the **lips** (the words one says), then a person truly has wisdom and is growing in it.

Proverbs 16:24

Pleasant words *are like* a honeycomb,
Sweetness to the soul and health to the bones.

a. **Pleasant words are like a honeycomb**: There is wonderful power in our **words** to bring blessing and pleasantness to others. In ancient Biblical culture, nothing was as sweet as honey from the **honeycomb**, and **pleasant words** can be just as sweet and wonderful.

> i. **Like a honeycomb**: "One might recall, in line with the use of this imagery, how Jonathan's eyes brightened when he ate the honeycomb (1 Samuel 14:27); such is the uplifting effect of pleasant words." (Ross)

b. **Sweetness to the soul and health to the bones**: Encouraging and **pleasant words** bring enjoyment to the whole person (**the soul**) and **health** to the body (**the bones**).

Proverbs 16:25

There is a way *that seems* right to a man,
But its end *is* the way of death.

a. **There is a way that seems right to a man**: Some people walk a path of life that they know is wrong, and many proverbs speak to that person. Others walk a path of life that **seems right** to them, and they are mistaken. It isn't enough to feel good about our path or to follow our heart on life's way. God's revelation and word are always truer and safer than what **seems right to a man**.

b. **But its end is the way of death**: Taking the wrong **way** – even if it **seems right to a man** – isn't an innocent mistake. This is because the wrong path ends in **death**. The **end** of the wrong path isn't temporary trouble or inconvenience; **its end is the way of death**.

> i. The repetition of this proverb (also at Proverbs 14:12) emphasizes its greatness and importance. "And think not this a vain repetition; but know that it is thus redoubled, that it may be the better remarked and remembered. Nothing is more ordinary or more dangerous than self-delusion…. To warn us therefore of this greatest wickedness, it is that this sentence is reiterated." (Trapp)

Proverbs 16:26

The person who labors, labors for himself,
For his *hungry* mouth drives him *on*.

a. **The person who labors, labors for himself**: The Bible recognizes the principle of personal property (Exodus 20:15) and that the reward of work properly belongs to the worker (**labors for himself**). This argues against schemes of forced communal living, either on a small or national scale. It also argues against excessive taxation, because it does not say *the person who labors, labors for his government*.

b. **For his hungry mouth drives him on**: When people are rewarded with the benefit of their own work, they know that their work can fill their

hungry mouths. When it isn't necessary to work in order to fill a **hungry mouth**, much less work will be done.

i. "That is to say that hunger will make a man work when nothing else will. This is in harmony with the apostolic principle, 'If a man will not work, neither let him eat.'" (Morgan)

ii. "*A worker's appetite works for him; his mouth urges him on...*this is welcome realism (cf. 2 Thessalonians 3:10-12), though it is not the last word on incentives: cf. Ephesians 4:28; 6:7." (Kidner)

iii. "Though work is tiring and frustrating in this fallen world, nevertheless the drive to gratify his appetites prods the diligent person to productive efforts.... God and the wise do not frustrate these primal, productive drives and appetites by denying them gratification (Proverbs 10:3) or by gratifying them apart from work (cf. Proverbs 3:27; 10:3a; 1 Thessalonians 4:11; 2 Thessalonians 3:10)." (Waltke)

Proverbs 16:27

An ungodly man digs up evil,
And *it is* on his lips like a burning fire.

a. **An ungodly man digs up evil**: The sense is that for the **ungodly man**, the evil he casually finds isn't enough to satisfy his desire. He **digs up evil**, finding the effort to pursue evil.

i. **Digs up evil**: "A wicked man labours as much to bring about an evil purpose, as the *quarryman* does to dig up stones." (Clarke)

ii. John Trapp relates how the enemies of both Augustine and Beza dug up their old sins and tried to discredit them on account of those sins.

b. **It is on his lips like a burning fire**: When an **ungodly man digs up evil**, he can't keep it to himself. He has to spread it to others, so he casts it from **his lips** as if it were **a burning fire**.

i. "What he finds he spreads; his speech is like scorching fire—the simile speaks of the devastating effect of his words." (Ross)

Proverbs 16:28

A perverse man sows strife,
And a whisperer separates the best of friends.

a. **A perverse man sows strife**: Twisted, **perverse** people love to sow **strife** the way a farmer sows seeds. When there is much strife, there is some **perverse** person sowing the strife.

i. **Sows**: "It is, appropriately, the word used of the release of flaming foxes in the Philistines' corn, Judges 15:5." (Kidner)

b. **A whisperer separates the best of friends**: This is one way that the **perverse man sows strife** – by whispering gossipy words. The strife they sow is so powerful that it can separate **the best of friends**. Often, such people show they are **perverse** because they count it a victory and an accomplishment to sow such strife and to separate even **the best of friends**.

  i. **Whisperer**: "…denotes a malicious gossip who misrepresents a situation and by his calumny aims to besmirch and to defame others behind their backs. In 17:9 the talebearer also implicitly repeats a matter without confronting the wrong doer directly." (Waltke)

Proverbs 16:29

A violent man entices his neighbor,
And leads him in a way *that is* not good.

  a. **A violent man entices his neighbor**: The **violent man** may do this by encouraging partnership in his violent works, or by inviting a violent response from **his neighbor**.

  b. **Leads him in a way that is not good**: Violence often leads to **a way that is not good**. Sometimes the threat or presence of strength is necessary to prevent violence, but often violence leads to **a way that is not good**.

Proverbs 16:30

He winks his eye to devise perverse things;
He purses his lips *and* brings about evil.

  a. **He winks his eye to devise perverse things**: This is likely connected to the previous verse. The *violent man* of Proverbs 16:29 may entice his neighbor as he **winks his eye**, treating it as a light and clever thing to **devise perverse things**.

  i. "The winking eye and pursed lips of v. 30 may be taken either as signals among conspirators or as a general statement of shiftiness in the facial mannerisms of scheming people." (Garrett)

  ii. **To devise perverse things**: "Wicked men are great students; they beat their brains and close their eyes that they may revolve and excogitate mischief with more freedom of mind. They search the devil's skull for new devices, and are very inventive to invent that which may do harm." (Trapp)

  b. **He purses his lips and brings about evil**: With expressions of contempt, the violent man **brings about evil**. He does not seriously consider the bad effects of his actions.

  i. **Winks his eye…purses his lips**: "Often people who are planning wicked things betray themselves with malicious expressions. Two expressions are depicted here: winking the eye and pursing the lips. Facial expressions often reveal whether someone is plotting something evil." (Ross)

Proverbs 16:31

The silver-haired head *is* a crown of glory,
***If* it is found in the way of righteousness.**

a. **The silver-haired head is a crown of glory**: The cultural setting of its time, there was nothing unusual about this statement. Ancient cultures were sensible enough to honor and value the wisdom and experience of old age. They saw the white hair of the elderly as a **crown of glory**.

i. **Silver-haired head**: "It is often considered a blessing (Genesis 15:15; 25:8), but not always (Hosea 7:9), and is treated with respect (Leviticus 19:32)." (Waltke)

b. **If it is found in the way of righteousness**: This is a helpful and necessary follow-up statement to the first line of this proverb. It isn't age itself that brings **a crown of glory** to a person, but age **in the way of righteousness**. The sad truth is that age itself does not make all people better and certainly not godlier.

i. "There is something commendable about old age that can remember a long walk with God through life and can anticipate unbroken fellowship with him in glory." (Ross)

Proverbs 16:32

He who is **slow to anger *is* better than the mighty,**
And he who rules his spirit than he who takes a city.

a. **He who is slow to anger is better than the mighty**: There is someone **better** than the **mighty** man who can defeat many others on the field of combat. It is the man (or woman) who has control over his own anger, who can (when it is wise and necessary) be **slow to anger**.

i. "There have been many kings who had conquered nations, and yet were slaves to their own passions. Alexander, who conquered the world, was a slave to *intemperate anger*, and in a fit of it slew *Clytus*, the best and most intimate of all his friends, and one whom he loved beyond all others." (Clarke)

ii. "A great conflict and a glorious victory are set out here. The heart is the field of battle. All its evil and powerful passions are deadly foes. They must be met and triumphed over in God's strength." (Bridges)

b. **And he who rules his spirit than he who takes a city**: Under God's wisdom and strength, to rule one's own **spirit** is a greater accomplishment than to conquer a city. Some who can conquer cities should first be concerned with conquering self.

i. Matthew Poole thought of three reasons why **he who rules his spirit** was better than **he who takes a city**.

- He conquers though he fights a stronger enemy.
- He conquers by his own hands, and not through other people.
- He conquers without the injury and ruin of others.

ii. "How much better Valentinian the emperor, who said, upon his deathbed, that among all his victories one only comforted him; and being asked what that was, he answered, I have overcome my worst enemy, mine own naughty heart." (Trapp)

iii. "This is a proverb that is constantly quoted, and very little believed. If men only recognized that there is more valor and heroism in self-control than in doughty deeds which others acclaim in song and story, how different our world would be." (Morgan)

Proverbs 16:33

The lot is cast into the lap,
But its every decision *is* from the LORD.

a. **The lot is cast into the lap**: This was something similar to the rolling of dice. To cast the lot was to use some tool of chance to make a choice. The **lot** was used to divide the land of Israel among the tribes (Numbers 26:55, Joshua 14:2) and to arrange the workers for the temple (1 Chronicles 24:5). The disciples used lots to fill the vacancy left by Judas (Acts 1:26).

b. **Its every decision is from the LORD**: The idea is *not* that every single event in life is a message from God, *nor* is it that we should use games of chance to determine God's will. To **cast** the **lot** was a way to commit the decision to God, and when we commit our decisions to Him, God guides us (Proverbs 3:5-6).

i. "The Old Testament use of the word *lot* shows that this proverb (and Proverbs 18:18) is not about God's control of all random occurrences, but about his settling of matters properly referred to him." (Kidner)

ii. Waltke connected Proverbs 16:33 back to 16:32: "Ultimately, the Lord, not the disciple's self-possession alone, rules his destiny, as illustrated by 'the lot.'"

Proverbs 17 – Wisdom, Justice, and Family

Proverbs 17:1

Better *is* a dry morsel with quietness,
Than a house full of feasting *with* strife.

a. **Better is a dry morsel with quietness**: There is nothing appealing about a **dry morsel**. Yet the blessing of **quietness** and peace is so great, that it can make **a dry morsel** seem better than the alternative presented.

> i. "Peace and contentment, and especially *domestic peace*, are beyond all other blessings." (Clarke)

> ii. "Ponder every thought that may disturb contentment. If you have fewer comforts than you used to have, or fewer comforts than other people have, or fewer comforts than you desire, do you not still have more than you deserve?" (Bridges)

b. **Than a house full of feasting with strife**: A home **full of feasting** would be wonderful; but *not* with constant **strife**. Peace and **quietness** in the home are so valuable that they make up for many other comforts denied.

> i. "Its precise antithetic parallels contrasts a dinner party consisting of a dry bite of bread that had not been dipped into a dish of savory sauce of oil, vinegar or the like (cf. Proverbs 19:24), but nevertheless enjoyed in security, with an unlimited royal banquets but plagued with strife." (Waltke)

> ii. "Abundance often brings a deterioration of moral and ethical standards as well as an increase in envy and strife." (Ross)

Proverbs 17:2

A wise servant will rule over a son who causes shame,
And will share an inheritance among the brothers.

a. **A wise servant will rule over a son who causes shame**: It is natural that **a son** should rule; the trust one has in family is often greater than the trust one has servants. Yet, should a son cause **shame**, God knows how to replace that son with a **wise servant**. The **son** has his natural place, but God does not see that natural place as giving absolute right to lead and may give leadership to a **wise servant** instead.

b. **And will share an inheritance among the brothers**: Should the son prove to cause shame and if it is in God's will, God is able to even lift up a **wise servant** to a place of leadership and **inheritance among the brothers.**

i. "Contrary to judicial law and custom, one's virtue, not the privilege of birth, ultimately counts for more in social and economic standing." (Waltke)

Proverbs 17:3

The refining pot *is* for silver and the furnace for gold,
But the LORD tests the hearts.

a. **The refining pot is for silver and the furnace for gold**: There are appropriate places where things are tested and purified. **Silver** and **gold** each have their place of **refining** and purification.

b. **The LORD tests the hearts**: The most appropriate place for the human heart to be tested and purified is with **the LORD** Himself. His word and His truth give a wise, loving standard that will both examine and refine the inner man or woman.

i. "Two important thoughts are suggested by this proverb. First, that the heart will yield to no force other than that of God. Dross in metal may be discovered and expurged by fire, but evil in the heart can be discovered and dealt with only by God. Second, Jehovah does try the heart." (Morgan)

ii. "He therefore tries us, that he may make us know what is in us, what dross, what pure metal; and that all may see that we are such as, for a need, can 'glorify him in the very fires,' [Isaiah 24:15]." (Trapp)

Proverbs 17:4

An evildoer gives heed to false lips;
A liar listens eagerly to a spiteful tongue.

a. **An evildoer gives heed to false lips**: When it comes to lies spoken by **false lips**, evil people not only spread them, they also receive them. They seem to love to embrace a lie.

i. "It is an ill sign of a vicious nature to be apt to believe scandalous reports of godly men. If men loved not lies, they would not listen to them." (Trapp)

ii. "An evil heart is disposed and ever ready to receive evil; and liars delight in lies." (Clarke)

iii. "Evil words die without a welcome; and the welcome gives us away." (Kidner)

b. **A liar listens eagerly to a spiteful tongue**: Those who lie love to listen to lies as well as speak them. It should concern us if we love to hear lies and gossip about others.

i. "This proverb contains a comparison between an evil-doer and an evil-speaker, and showeth their agreement in the same sinful practice of being greedy to hear false and wicked speeches." (Poole)

ii. "Both the liar and his willing audience have no taste for truth." (Waltke)

iii. "Taking gossip seriously is itself a form of malice practiced by those who have no respect for the truth." (Garrett)

Proverbs 17:5

He who mocks the poor reproaches his Maker;
He who is glad at calamity will not go unpunished.

a. **He who mocks the poor reproaches his Maker**: Some people find it easy to mock **the poor**. They love to think of themselves as better than those who have less than they do. Such people should understand that when they mock the poor, they despise (reproach) the One who made both the poor and themselves. The fact that both **the poor** and the well-off have the same **Maker** should give the richer person greater sympathy and greater sense.

i. "The first part of this proverb does not teach, as is so often stated, that poverty is from God. Rather, it recognizes the inherent rights of every man in God, notwithstanding his poverty." (Morgan)

b. **He who is glad at calamity will not go unpunished**: To be **glad** at anyone's **calamity** shows an unloving, unsympathetic heart. Anyone who despises their fellow man this way should expect God to answer and defend the weaker one.

i. "He who is pleased to hear of the misfortune of another will, in the course of God's just government, have his own multiplied." (Clarke)

ii. John Trapp relates in his commentary how cruelly some take joy in the persecution, suffering, and death of innocent people – and how certainly judgment will come upon such.

Proverbs 17:6

Children's children *are* the crown of old men,
And the glory of children *is* their father.

a. **Children's children are the crown of old men**: Grandchildren are like a **crown** of glory for a grandparent. They can give an almost indescribable sense of pleasure and satisfaction.

i. "The proverb pictures them gathered around the aged parent like a crowning diadem." (Waltke)

b. **The glory of children is their father**: This is true both as a fact and as an aspiration. It is natural for **children** to **glory** in their **father**, and fathers should live and parent in such a way that would cause their children to **glory** in them.

i. "Behind this apparently innocuous proverb is a profound assertion of the psychological interdependence of the generations. Elders derive a sense of pride from their descendants, and children get their self-worth from parents. On the other hand, one generation can cause shame and a sense of worthlessness in another." (Garrett)

ii. "These fine family fruits need cultivating and protecting. A neglected crop, riddled with mutual antipathy, is seen in Isaiah 3:5; Micah 7:6; 2 Timothy 3:2-4." (Kidner)

Proverbs 17:7

Excellent speech is not becoming to a fool,
Much less lying lips to a prince.

a. **Excellent speech is not becoming to a fool**: It isn't that **excellent speech** is not desired from the **fool**, but that it is such an unexpected surprise. Since people usually express their wisdom or folly by what they *say*, it seems strange and almost inappropriate if a **fool** should say something wise and eloquent.

i. "God likes not fair words from a foul mouth. Christ silenced the devil when he confessed him to be the Son of the most high God." (Trapp)

b. **Much less lying lips to a prince**: Any leader (**a prince**) should be so known for truthfulness that it is regarded as a strange surprise that they would lie. This is a lofty and rarely reached standard among leaders, especially political leaders.

i. "A dishonest leader is worse than an arrogant fool. A comparison shows which of two things is worse." (Ross)

Proverbs 17:8

A present *is* a precious stone in the eyes of its possessor;
Wherever he turns, he prospers.

a. **A present is a precious stone in the eyes of its possessor**: It is human nature to regard **a present** as something **precious**. In this context the **present** may be a *bribe*, because the same Hebrew word is used. This proverb may simply state the fact that a bribe usually works.

i. "The proverb is expressing this reality from the viewpoint of the one giving the bribe—it works." (Ross)

b. **Wherever he turns, he prospers**: The gain one receives from a gift (or bribe) so delights them that it accomplishes the purpose of the gift.

i. "In the latter clause there is an evident allusion to *cut stones*. Whithersoever you *turn them*, they *reflect the light*, are *brilliant* and *beautiful*." (Clarke)

Proverbs 17:9

He who covers a transgression seeks love,
But he who repeats a matter separates friends.

a. **He who covers a transgression seeks love**: There is a time and a place for the exposure of sin (Ephesians 5:11), but often the sins of others should be tactfully and lovingly covered. The exposure of all belongs to God, not man (Luke 12:3).

b. **He who repeats a matter separates friends**: To uncover someone's sin by repeated it to others will ruin relationships and divide friendships.

i. **Repeats** "…may indicate either tale-telling or…harping on a matter." (Kidner)

Proverbs 17:10

Rebuke is more effective for a wise *man*
Than a hundred blows on a fool.

a. **Rebuke is more effective for a wise man**: Because a **wise man** or woman will respond to **rebuke** and learn from it, it can be truly **effective** for him or her.

b. **Than a hundred blows on a fool**: Correction may be administered deeply and repeatedly to the **fool**, yet they will not receive it. The problem is not in the correction itself (though the fool will likely blame it); the problem is in the **fool**.

i. "The finer the disposition, the less is needed to correct it." (Morgan)

Proverbs 17:11

An evil *man* seeks only rebellion;
Therefore a cruel messenger will be sent against him.

a. **An evil man seeks only rebellion**: The instinctive response of **rebellion** belongs to the **evil**, not to the wise. Those who seek **only rebellion** can offer nothing wise and good to replace that which they rebel against.

b. **A cruel messenger will be sent against him**: Repeated **rebellion** invites **cruel** retaliation. The **evil man** should not be surprised when it comes.

i. "This expression could refer to a pitiless messenger that the king would send; but it also could refer to storms, pestilence, or any misfortune that was God's messenger of retribution." (Ross)

Proverbs 17:12

Let a man meet a bear robbed of her cubs,
Rather than a fool in his folly.

a. **Let a man meet a bear robbed of her cubs**: A mother **bear** is notoriously angry and dangerous when she is **robbed of her cubs**. No sensible person would want to **meet** a mother bear under such conditions.

b. **Rather than a fool in his folly**: A foolish man in the midst of his foolish actions can be more dangerous than a mother bear who lost **her cubs**. The wise man or woman will stay away from such **a fool in his folly**.

i. "The human, who is supposed to be intelligent and rational, in such folly becomes more dangerous than the beast that in this case acts with good reason." (Ross)

Proverbs 17:13

Whoever rewards evil for good,
Evil will not depart from his house.

a. **Whoever rewards evil for good**: It is plainly wrong to give **evil** to those who deserve **good**. It discourages those who do **good** and encourages those who do not. It upsets God's moral order to have good punished.

i. "To render good for evil is divine, good for good is human, evil for evil is brutish, evil for good is devilish." (Trapp)

b. **Evil will not depart from his house**: God sees when His moral order is offended and will answer it. The one who gives **evil** to the **good** can expect their own home to be troubled by **evil**.

i. "As many persons are guilty of the sin of *ingratitude*, and of paying *kindness* with *unkindness*, and *good* with *evil*, it is no wonder we find so much *wretchedness* among men; for God's word cannot fail; evil shall not depart from the houses and families of such persons." (Clarke)

ii. "This proverb was very near the bone: both parents of Solomon had so repaid the devoted Uriah, and had duly received the sentence of line 2: see 2 Samuel 12:10ff." (Kidner)

Proverbs 17:14

The beginning of strife *is like* releasing water;
Therefore stop contention before a quarrel starts.

a. **The beginning of strife is like releasing water**: The nature of liquid **water** makes it difficult to restrain. Once it is released it will go in unexpected and uncontrolled ways. This is like **the beginning of strife**. Once an argument or battle has begun, it is difficult to control its course, and like uncontrolled water, it can cause great damage.

i. "The verse likens the beginning of a bitter conflict involving the pent up arrogance and anger of a fool to a person who digs a hole in a dam or opens a sluice. The seepage starts from a small aperture, but under built up pressure it quickly bursts open and the small leak turns into a raging, uncontrolled cataclysm that gets out of hand and does irreparable damage." (Waltke)

ii. "Opening such a sluice lets loose more than one can predict, control or retrieve." (Kidner)

b. **Therefore stop contention before a quarrel starts**: Because **strife** and **contention** are difficult to control and cause great damage, wisdom sees that it is much better to **stop contention before** it ever starts.

i. "Do therefore here as the Dutchmen do by their banks; they keep them with little cost and trouble, because they look narrowly to them, and make them up in time. If there be but the least breach, they stop it presently, otherwise the sea would soon flood them." (Trapp)

Proverbs 17:15

He who justifies the wicked, and he who condemns the just,
Both of them alike *are* an abomination to the LORD.

a. **He who justifies the wicked, and he who condemns the just**: This is the same kind of upset of God's moral order as mentioned previously in Proverbs 17:13. Justice requires the opposite outcome – that the **wicked** are condemned and that the **just** are justified.

b. **Both of them alike are an abomination to the LORD**: God sees the violation of justice on both sides. God never thinks that *all* should be equally condemned or justified; but that the appropriate answer be given to both the **wicked** and the **just**.

i. "A self-evident statement, and yet one that needs to be made, for in every age there have been those who fall into both forms of wrong." (Morgan)

ii. "The proverb corrects the popular misconception that it is better to set free ten guilty persons than to condemn one innocent person. Both *are an abomination to the Lord*." (Waltke)

Proverbs 17:16

Why *is there* in the hand of a fool the purchase price of wisdom,
Since *he has* no heart *for it*?

a. **Why is there in the hand of a fool the purchase price of wisdom**: Wisdom has a **price**, and Solomon imagined a **fool** who was ready to pay that price. We might say that the **price of wisdom** begins with the fear of the Lord. The **price of wisdom** also involves humility and willingness to receive correction.

i. "The fool has no interest in obtaining wisdom in the way that it must be obtained." (Ross)

b. **Since he has no heart for it**: It would be strange to find the **price of wisdom** in the **hand of a fool**, because then that person would no longer be a **fool**. The nature of the **fool** requires that they have **no heart** to pay the **price of wisdom**.

Proverbs 17:17

A friend loves at all times,
And a brother is born for adversity.

a. **A friend loves at all times**: A true **friend** will not only love when it is easy, but **at all times**. What used to be called *fair-weather friends* – those who are friends only when the weather is pleasant and fair – are not true friends at all.

i. "Ahithophel has deserted David, and Judas has sold his Lord. The greatest of kings who have been fawned upon by their courtiers while in power, have been treated as if they were but dogs in the time of their extremity." (Spurgeon)

ii. "That eminent servant of God, Jonathan Edwards, when he was at his last, said, 'Where is Jesus of Nazareth, my old and faithful friend? I know he will be with me now that I need his help,' and so he was, for that faithful servant died triumphant." (Spurgeon)

b. **A brother is born for adversity**: A true **brother** (here used in a sense beyond the literal blood relation) will show himself in a time of **adversity**.

 i. Morgan on the principle of this proverb: "Let it be applied. Then two startling questions will arise. First, a question as to whether I am really a friend to anyone; and second, a question as to how many real friends I have."

 ii. Charles Bridges had an even better application: "We must look to our Lord for the best example in this matter. We see the Son of God taking on our nature so that he might be our friend and brother (Hebrews 2:14). The mystery of this friendship is beyond our imagination."

 iii. "The ancient Jews applied this proverb to Christ, adducing it as a testimony that the divine Messiah would by his incarnation become the Brother of man." (Bridges)

Proverbs 17:18

**A man devoid of understanding shakes hands in a pledge,
And becomes surety for his friend.**

a. **A man devoid of understanding shakes hands in a pledge**: Wisdom guards us against foolish partnerships.

b. **And becomes surety for his friend**: It is responsibility enough to honor our own debts. Wisdom warns us against taking responsibility for the debts of others.

Proverbs 17:19

**He who loves transgression loves strife,
And he who exalts his gate seeks destruction.**

a. **He who loves transgression loves strife**: There are those who love both **transgression** and **strife**. They love it when God's laws are sinfully transgressed and when there is conflict.

b. **He who exalts his gate seeks destruction**: Those who exalt the leadership of those who love **transgression** and **strife** are promoting **destruction**. Such people should never sit in the **gate** of respect, leadership, and authority.

 i. "The man who builds a high gate exalts himself above his neighbor and assumes a lifestyle beyond his rank." (Bridges)

 ii. "Possibly *gate* is here taken for the *mouth*; and the *exalting of the gate* may mean proud boasting and arrogant speaking, such as has a tendency to kindle and maintain strife. And this interpretation seems to agree better with the scope of the context." (Clarke)

Proverbs 17:20

He who has a deceitful heart finds no good,
And he who has a perverse tongue falls into evil.

a. **He who has a deceitful heart finds no good**: The one filled with deceit will only find corruption and deceit in others.

b. **He who has a perverse tongue falls into evil**: Wicked and foolish words not only display the evil of someone's heart, they also lead them **into** greater **evil**.

Proverbs 17:21

He who begets a scoffer *does so* to his sorrow,
And the father of a fool has no joy.

a. **He who begets a scoffer does so to his sorrow**: To be the parent of a foolish **scoffer** (one who foolishly doubts and rejects the truth) is to have **sorrow**. Parents should do all they can to *not* raise scoffers, beginning with believing and living out the truth themselves.

b. **The father of a fool has no joy**: There is no pleasure in seeing that your child is a **fool**. There is both the pain of the consequences of the child's folly and the regret of wondering if one parented effectively.

i. "No more than William the Conqueror had in his ungracious children, or Henry II, who, finding that his sons had conspired against him with the king of France, fell into a grievous passion, cursing both his sons, and the day wherein himself was born; and in that distemperature departed the world, which himself had so oft distempered." (Trapp)

Proverbs 17:22

A merry heart does good, *like* medicine,
But a broken spirit dries the bones.

a. **A merry heart does good, like medicine**: It has been said – no doubt based on this proverb – that laughter is the best **medicine**. Truly, a cheerful and **merry heart** is good for more than the personality; it is good for the body.

b. **A broken spirit dries the bones**: Those who are defeated and **broken** in spirit will see the effect in their health and experience of life. It will feel to them that their life has withered and dried up. This was the feeling David described in Psalm 32:1-4.

i. "'Bones' figuratively represents the body (encased in the bony frame): fat bones means a healthy body (Proverbs 3:8; 15:30; 16:24), but dry bones signify unhealthiness and lifelessness (cf. Ezekiel 37:1-14)." (Ross)

ii. "A broken spirit in an evangelical sense is God's precious gift. It is stamped with his special honor. But here a crushed spirit describes a brooding spirit of despondency that always looks on the dark side of things. If this is linked to religion, it flows from a narrow and perverted view and a spurious humility centered on the self. It has the effect of drying up the bones." (Bridges)

Proverbs 17:23

A wicked *man* accepts a bribe behind the back
To pervert the ways of justice.

a. **A wicked man accepts a bribe behind the back**: It is wrong to receive a **bribe**, an illegal and unjust payment to get around normal laws and procedures and to buy favor from officials. This shows a fundamental corruption and lack of integrity.

i. "The corrupt official defies God who has placed him over the community to protect the poor. He shows he is conscious of his guilt by accepting the sly bribe, which is concealed from public scrutiny and opprobrium, but it is not concealed from God." (Waltke)

b. **To pervert the ways of justice**: When favor and a desired outcome depends on bribe money and not fairness and righteousness, justice is perverted. Then, no one can or should have confidence in the system of laws and **ways of justice**.

Proverbs 17:24

Wisdom *is* in the sight of him who has understanding,
But the eyes of a fool *are* on the ends of the earth.

a. **Wisdom is in the sight of him who has understanding**: The sense seems to be that the wise see things in the light of their wisdom. Their wisdom makes everything else clearer and able to be understood.

b. **The eyes of a fool are on the ends of the earth**: The fool doesn't see things with the eyes of wisdom. They have their **eyes** everywhere (**the ends of the earth**) *except* where they should be.

i. "Wisdom is within the *sight* and *reach* at every man: but he whose *desires* are scattered abroad, who is always aiming at impossible things, or is of an unsteady disposition, is not likely to find it." (Clarke)

ii. "The contrast here is between 'before the face of him' and 'the ends of the earth.' While it is a sure sign of weakness to see only the things that are near, it is a yet surer sign of folly to be forever looking at far-off things, to the neglect of those close at hand." (Morgan)

iii. "As a student who is hearing nothing of what his teacher says might let his eyes rove to every corner of the classroom, so the fool who is inattentive to the instruction of Wisdom is said to have his eyes on the ends of the earth." (McKane, cited in Ross)

iv. "His eyes are on the ends of the earth, rolling and wandering from one object to another. His thoughts are scattered. He has no definite objective, no certain way of life. Talent, cultivation of mind, and improvement of opportunity are all frittered away. He cares about those things that are furthest from him and with which he has the least concern." (Bridges)

v. "This diversion is a great friend to the enemy. Our enemy's great object is to turn the mind away from what is immediate to what is indefinite, from what is plain and important to what is unsearchable, from what is personal to what is irrelevant. Many trifles take the place of the one thing that is needful." (Bridges)

Proverbs 17:25

A foolish son *is* a grief to his father,
And bitterness to her who bore him.

a. **A foolish son is a grief to his father**: The thought in this proverb is similar to that in Proverbs 17:21. Parents may find great **grief** in the **foolish** character of their children.

b. **And bitterness to her who bore him**: Because of the maternal instinct and bond, there is a special pain and **bitterness** that belongs to the mother of a **foolish son** or daughter.

Proverbs 17:26

Also, to punish the righteous *is* not good,
***Nor* to strike princes for *their* uprightness.**

a. **To punish the righteous is not good**: God's moral order insists that the **righteous** be rewarded and the wicked be punished. To upset this or reverse it **is not good**.

b. **Nor to strike princes for their uprightness**: If a leader is upright, he should never be punished – especially by striking. **Uprightness** should be rewarded and honored, not punished.

Proverbs 17:27

He who has knowledge spares his words,
***And* a man of understanding is of a calm spirit.**

a. **He who has knowledge spares his words**: Both wisdom and folly are often revealed by one's words. Yet, in the case of wisdom, it may be revealed by the **knowledge** of when to keep quiet. We should never think that the wise man or woman reveals their wisdom by talking a lot.

b. **A man of understanding is of a calm spirit**: The peace and contentment that properly come to the wise is described here as a **calm spirit**. To be constantly agitated and upset is a mark of folly, not wisdom.

Proverbs 17:28

Even a fool is counted wise when he holds his peace;
***When* he shuts his lips, *he is considered* perceptive.**

a. **Even a fool is counted wise when he holds his peace**: This continues the idea from the previous proverb. There is a wonderful way that **even a fool** can be considered **wise** – to not speak.

i. **Is counted wise**: "The dry advice of 28 is not purely ironical: the fool who takes it is no longer a complete fool." (Kidner)

b. **When he shuts his lips, he is considered perceptive**: If the fool cared about being **considered perceptive**, this gives an easy way for it to happen.

i. One is reminded of Abraham Lincoln's witty saying: "It is better to keep your mouth shut and let them think you a fool than to open your mouth and remove all doubt."

Proverbs 18 – Wisdom in Getting Along with Others

Proverbs 18:1

A man who isolates himself seeks his own desire;
He rages against all wise judgment.

a. **A man who isolates himself seeks his own desire**: To cut one's self off from family, friends, and community is often to express a selfish **desire**. It shows an unwillingness to make the small (and sometimes large) sacrifices to get along with others.

i. "The Mishnah uses this passage to teach the necessity of not separating from the community, because people have responsibilities as social beings (*Aboth* 2:4)." (Ross)

b. **He rages against all wise judgment**: God designed us after His own triune nature; He designed us to live in community. The instinct many have for isolation must not be over-indulged; it is **against all wise judgment**.

i. "The protest of this proverb is against the self-satisfaction which makes a man separate himself from the thoughts and opinions of others. Such a one finally 'rages against,' or 'quarrels with all sound wisdom.'" (Morgan)

Proverbs 18:2

A fool has no delight in understanding,
But in expressing his own heart.

a. **A fool has no delight in understanding**: The wise man or woman has great satisfaction in knowledge, **understanding**, and wisdom. This is not so with the **fool**; they find **no delight** in wisdom.

i. "He is wilful, and so stands as a stake in the midst of a stream; lets all pass by him, but he stands where he was. It is easier to deal with twenty men's reasons, than with one man's will." (Trapp)

b. **But in expressing his own heart**: What *does* **delight** the **fool** is **expressing his own heart**. If he asks questions it is to show how clever he is rather than to learn. He is focused on self instead of God, and his folly flows from this wrong priority and wrong place to find **delight**.

i. "It is a fact that most vain and foolish people are never satisfied in company, but in showing their own *nonsense* and *emptiness*." (Clarke)

ii. **Expressing his own heart**: "The verb occurs in *Hithpael* elsewhere only in connection with the drunken Noah indecently uncovering himself (Genesis 9:21; cf.)." (Waltke)

Proverbs 18:3

When the wicked comes, contempt comes also;
And with dishonor *comes* reproach.

a. **When the wicked comes, contempt comes also**: The **wicked** *brings* **contempt** with them; the proud, superior attitude that thinks itself better than others and looks at those thought to be lesser with scorn. Yet it can also be said that **contempt** *follows* the **wicked** because God will scorn those who scorn others.

b. **With dishonor comes reproach**: The **wicked** bring insults (**reproach**) upon those they consider dishonorable.

Proverbs 18:4

The words of a man's mouth *are* deep waters;
The wellspring of wisdom *is* a flowing brook.

a. **The words of a man's mouth are deep waters**: The idea isn't that everyone's speech is deep and meaningful. Instead, the idea is that we reveal the depths of our heart by **the words** of our **mouth**.

i. "That is, the wise sayings of a wise man are like *deep waters*; howsoever much you pump or draw off, you do not appear to lessen them." (Clarke)

b. **The wellspring of wisdom is a flowing brook**: When the **wellspring** of a man's being is rooted in **wisdom**, it will then flow out from their **words**.

i. **Deep waters...flowing brook**: "Fitly are the words of the wise resembled to waters, saith one, inasmuch as they both wash the minds of the hearers, that the foulness of sin remain not therein, and water them in such sort that they faint not, nor wither by a drought and burning desire of heavenly doctrine." (Trapp)

Proverbs 18:5

It is not good to show partiality to the wicked,
Or to overthrow the righteous in judgment.

a. **It is not good to show partiality to the wicked**: This is obvious to the person with a moral compass. Yet there are many reasons why someone might be tempted **to show partiality to the wicked**. They may do it out of misplaced compassion, out of a desire to please others, because of some kind of bribe, or many other reasons.

i. "We must not, in judicial cases, pay any attention to a man's *riches, influence, friends, offices*, etc., but judge the case according to its own merits. But when the *wicked* rich man opposes and oppresses the poor *righteous*, then all those things should be utterly forgotten." (Clarke)

b. **Or to overthrow the righteous in judgment**: When one shows **partiality to the wicked**, they will **overthrow the righteous in judgment** whether they intend to or not. Each aspect of injustice is sin.

i. "For justice to happen, the *cause* must be heard, not the *person*. Let the person be punished for his wickedness, not the wickedness be covered for the person's sake. When one is partial to the wicked, the rights of God are despised, and the claims of his justice are thrown away." (Bridges)

Proverbs 18:6

A fool's lips enter into contention,
And his mouth calls for blows.

a. **A fool's lips enter into contention**: It is in the nature of the fool to argue. Their words often bring them **into contention**.

b. **His mouth calls for blows**: The contentious words of the fool invite punishment, and sometimes this punishment will be physical correction, the **blows** of the rod of correction.

Proverbs 18:7

A fool's mouth *is* his destruction,
And his lips *are* the snare of his soul.

a. **A fool's mouth is his destruction**: The words of the fool show his folly, but they also work towards **his destruction**. Many a fool has been ruined because of his foolish words.

b. **His lips are the snare of his soul**: As in most places in Proverbs, **snare** here speaks of the life of being of the fool. It includes the inner spiritual self but is not restricted to it. The fool's life is trapped – caught in a **snare** – by his foolish words.

i. "It is most remarkable that the apostle Paul, when analyzing man's depravity, focuses on the little member and all that is linked to it—the throat, the tongue, the lips, and the mouth (Romans 3:13-14)." (Bridges)

Proverbs 18:8

The words of a talebearer *are* like tasty trifles,
And they go down into the inmost body.

a. **The words of a talebearer are like tasty trifles**: The gossip and evil reports brought by the **talebearer** are almost impossible to resist. Those who should know better find it difficult to tell the **talebearer** to stop talking. The importance of this proverb is expressed in its repetition, being repeated in Proverbs 26:22.

i. Yet the *damage* the **talebearer** brings is great. "He that takes away a man's good name kills him alive, and ruins him and his posterity; being herein worse than Cain, for he, in killing his brother, made him live for ever, and eternalised his name." (Trapp)

ii. "Unlike the fool's insolent speech that hurts himself in hurting others, gossip destroys the relationship of others, even the closest friends." (Waltke)

iii. "The words of a gossip [**talebearer**] in an unguarded moment may inflict irreparable injury. This evil may be welcomed in certain circles that thrive on scandal. But that does not alter the real character of a gossip, who is detested by both God and man." (Bridges)

b. **They go down into the inmost body**: When we receive the **words of a talebearer**, they normally have an effect on us. The words **go down into** us and often change the way we think and feel about people, even if what the **talebearer** says isn't true or isn't confirmed. God gave a strong word regarding the confirmation of testimony (Deuteronomy 19:15, 2 Corinthians 13:1, 1 Timothy 5:19).

i. Once we start eating these **tasty trifles**, it is hard to stop. "When such tasty bits are taken into the innermost being, they stimulate the desire for more." (Ross)

ii. Instead of eating the **tasty trifles** of the **talebearer**, "Jeremiah sets a better model: he ate God's word and delighted in it (Jeremiah 15:16; cf. Colossians 3:12-20)." (Waltke)

Proverbs 18:9

He who is slothful in his work
Is a brother to him who is a great destroyer.

a. **He who is slothful in his work**: There are times of entertainment or leisure where perhaps laziness can be excused. There is never an excuse to be lazy or **slothful** in **work**. As previously noted at Proverbs 15:19:

- Laziness is *theft* – you live off the work of others.

- Laziness is *selfishness* – you live for yourself and comfort.

- Laziness is *neglect of duty* – you don't do what you should.

b. **Is a brother to him who is a great destroyer**: We often think of laziness as a fairly innocent sin, but it is not. The lazy man is a close associate (**brother**) to the one who brings great destruction.

i. "It means that in life there can be no neutrality. Every man lives in the midst of a conflict between good and evil. He must and does take part therein. If he is not helping Jehovah against the mighty, he is helping the mighty against Jehovah" (Morgan). Morgan also noted this principle in other Biblical passages.

- "It was in the mind of Deborah when she cursed Meroz for not coming to the help of Jehovah against the mighty."

- "It found explicit statement when our Lord said: 'He that gathereth not with me scattereth'"

- "James recognized it when he wrote: 'To him that knoweth to do good and doeth it not, to him it is sin.'"

ii. "This proverb applies this principle to work. Constructive work is the law of human life and progress. There· is an active principle of destruction operating in the history of man; and· he who is a slacker at his work, who does not put into it all his strength, is a brother to the man who in wickedness sets himself to the activity of destruction. No living being can be merely a spectator. Each works or wastes. Not to work well, is to aid the process of waste." (Morgan)

iii. If a person is given management over a large estate and ruins it through vandalism and outright destruction, it is easy to see them as a **great destroyer**. Yet if the same person allows it to fall into disrepair and uselessness through neglect and laziness, they also are a **great destroyer** – they just did it another way. *Laziness destroys.*

Proverbs 18:10

The name of the LORD is a strong tower;
The righteous run to it and are safe.

a. **The name of the LORD is a strong tower**: God provides a wonderful and strong defense. This is rooted not in a magical saying of His name as if it were a charm or a spell, but in **the name of the LORD** as a declaration of His character, His person. In all that He is and all that He stands for, Yahweh (**the LORD**) is **a strong tower**.

i. "This is the only place in Proverbs where 'the name of the LORD' is found; it signifies the attributes of God, here the power to protect (cf. Exodus 34:5-7)." (Ross)

ii. Because the name of Yahweh represents His character in all its aspects, the believer can think about the aspects of God's character and find a strong, safe refuge in them. It can be as simple as this:

• LORD, You are a God of love – so I find refuge in Your love.

• LORD, You are a God of mercy – so I find refuge in Your mercy.

• LORD, You are a God of strength – so I find refuge in Your strength.

• LORD, You are a God of righteousness – so I find refuge in Your righteousness.

iii. "Numberless are those castles in the air to which men hasten in the hour of peril: ceremonies lift their towers into the clouds; professions pile their walls high as mountains, and works of the flesh paint their delusions till they seem substantial bulwarks; but all, all shall melt like snow, and vanish like a mist." (Spurgeon)

iv. **A strong tower**: "Within these walls, which of us needs to worry that the sharpest arrow can harm us? We realize our security from external trouble as we exercise our faith. We are safe from God's avenging justice, from the curse of the law, from sin, from condemnation, from the second death." (Bridges)

b. **The righteous run to it and are safe**: God invites all to find refuge in His name; *whoever calls upon the name of the Lord shall be saved* (Joel 2:32, Acts 2:21, and Romans 10:13). Those who humbly **run** to God and find refuge with Him are His **righteous** ones, so it is **the righteous** who **run to it**.

i. "All creatures run to their refuges when hunted…. Run therefore to God, by praying and not fainting. [Luke 18:1] This is the best policy for security." (Trapp)

ii. **Run to it**: "This running appears to me to imply, that they have nothing to carry. A man who has a load, the heavier the load may be, the more will he be impeded in his flight. But the righteous run, like racers in the games, who have thrown off everything, their sins they leave to mercy, and their righteousness to the moles and bats." (Spurgeon)

Proverbs 18:11

The rich man's wealth *is* his strong city,
And like a high wall in his own esteem.

a. **The rich man's wealth is his strong city**: In contrast to the righteous who find their strong tower in God and His character, the **rich man** (here used in the sense of the man who trusts in his riches, who is *only* rich and nothing else) finds refuge in his **wealth**.

i. Such a man who trusts in his own riches has *no* refuge when they fail. "A wicked man beaten out of earthly comforts is as a naked man in a storm, and an unarmed man in the field, or a ship tossed in the sea without an anchor, which presently dasheth upon rocks, or falleth upon quicksands." (Trapp)

b. **Like a high wall in his own esteem**: The rich man sees his **wealth** as safe and sure as a **high wall** around a **strong city**. Yet this is only in **his own esteem**; both the LORD and the wise know that **wealth** is not a truly **strong city** and not a **high wall**.

i. "Wealth does afford a measure of protection, but the danger of wealth is precisely that it gives its possessor the illusion of greater security than it can provide." (Garrett)

Proverbs 18:12

Before destruction the heart of a man is haughty,
And before honor *is* humility.

a. **Before destruction the heart of man is haughty**: Since pride leads the way to destruction (Proverbs 16:18), we should expect that the **haughty** heart is ready to receive its just **destruction**.

i. "There is no wisdom in a self-exaltation. Other vices have some excuse, for men seem to gain by them; avarice, pleasure, lust, have some plea; but the man who is proud sells his soul cheaply. He opens wide the flood-gates of his heart, to let men see how deep is the flood within his soul; then suddenly it floweth out, and all is gone – and all is nothing, for one puff of empty wind, one word of sweet applause – the soul is gone, and not a drop is left." (Spurgeon)

b. **And before honor is humility**: Wise people know that **humility** leads the way to **honor**. If you want **destruction**, be **haughty**; if you want **honor**, show **humility**.

i. "It is not humility to underrate yourself. Humility is to think of yourself, if you can, as God thinks of you." (Spurgeon)

ii. "Very likely the most humble man in the world won't bend to anybody. John Knox was a truly humble man, yet if you had seen him march before Queen Mary with the Bible in his hand, to reprove her, you would have rashly said, 'What a proud man!' (Spurgeon)

iii. "The humility and exaltation of Jesus provides the classic example of this truth (see Isaiah 52:13-53:12; Philippians 2:1-10)." (Ross)

Proverbs 18:13

He who answers a matter before he hears *it*,
It *is* folly and shame to him.

a. **He who answers a matter before he hears it**: It is common to give a quick, impulsive answer to questions and problems. We respond without thinking, or without hearing the full story, sometimes more interested in what we hope to say than what the **matter** before us really is.

i. This is "a special snare of the self-important." (Kidner)

b. **It is folly and shame to him**: To whatever extent we do this, it is foolish and shameful. It is **folly** because a wrong or misguided answer is likely; it is **shame** because we do not represent ourselves well in doing so.

i. "There are many also that *give judgment* before they hear the whole of the cause, and express an *opinion* before they hear the state of the case. How absurd, stupid, and foolish!" (Clarke)

Proverbs 18:14

The spirit of a man will sustain him in sickness,
But who can bear a broken spirit?

a. **The spirit of a man will sustain him in sickness**: Many who have labored long under **sickness** have felt themselves sustained – sometimes miraculously so – by the strength of their **spirit**.

i. "Christian principle strengthens natural strength. Outward troubles are bearable, yes, more than bearable, if there is peace within." (Bridges)

b. **Who can bear a broken spirit?** When the **spirit** is **broken**, instead of giving life it proves to be something few people can **bear**.

i. "In physical sickness one can fall back on the will to live; but in depression the will to live may be gone, and there is no reserve for physical strength. The figure of a 'crushed' spirit suggests a broken will, loss of vitality, despair, and emotional pain. Few things in the human experience are as difficult to cope with as this." (Ross)

ii. "There are some who have been greatly wounded, no doubt, through sickness. A wounded spirit may be the result of diseases which seriously shake the nervous system. Let us be very tender with brethren and sisters who got into that condition. I have heard some say, rather unkindly, 'Sister So-and-so is so nervous, we can hardly speak in her presence.' Yes, but talking like that will not help her; there are many persons who have had this trying kind of nervousness greatly aggravated by the unkindness or thoughtlessness of friends. It is a real disease, it is not imaginary. Imagination, no doubt, contributes to it, and increases it; but, still, there is a reality about it. There are some forms of physical disorder in which a person lying in bed feels great pain through another person simply walking across the room. 'Oh!' you say, 'that is more imagination 'Well, you may think so, if you like; but if you are ever in that painful condition, – as I have been many a time, – I will warrant that you will not talk in that fashion again." (Spurgeon)

Proverbs 18:15

The heart of the prudent acquires knowledge,
And the ear of the wise seeks knowledge.

a. **The heart of the prudent acquires knowledge**: The wise desire more wisdom and knows how to get it. They show their **prudence** (wisdom) by seeking and getting more **knowledge**.

b. **The ear of the wise seeks knowledge**: Wise men and women seek after wisdom with all their being – their **heart** and their **ear** are given over to the pursuit of more wisdom.

i. "By paralleling 'heart' and 'ears,' the verse stresses the full acquisition of knowledge: the ear of the wise listens to instruction, and the heart of the wise discerns what is heard to acquire knowledge." (Ross)

Proverbs 18:16

A man's gift makes room for him,
And brings him before great men.

a. **A man's gift makes room for him**: A previous proverb (Proverbs 17:8) spoke of a *present* in the sense of a bribe, but a different word is used here. This proverb is a simple recognition of fact: generosity and politeness open many doors.

i. "*Matan* ('gift') is more general than 'bribe' (*soh ad* as in Proverbs 17:8, 23).… Here the proverb simply says that a gift can expedite matters but says nothing about bribing judges." (Ross)

ii. "This Jacob [Genesis 43:11] knew well, and therefore bade his sons take a present for the governor of the land, though it were but of every good thing a little. So Saul, [1 Samuel 9:7] when to go to the man of God to inquire about the asses." (Trapp)

iii. "It can also be an innocent courtesy or eirenicon [gift to reconcile], like the present (*minhah*) sent to the captain in 1 Samuel 17:18, or to Esau or Joseph (Genesis 32:20; 43:11)." (Kidner)

b. **And brings him before great men**: It is true that a **gift** can be effective in gaining an audience of even **great men**. We are grateful that no gift is required to come **before** the greatest Man, the Man Christ Jesus who offers His work as mediator without cost (1 Timothy 2:5, Romans 5:1-2).

i. "Blessed be God! We do not lack any gifts to bring before him. Our welcome is free. The door of access is forever open. Our treasure of grace in his unchanging favor is unfathomable." (Bridges)

Proverbs 18:17

The first *one* to plead his cause *seems* right,
Until his neighbor comes and examines him.

a. **The first one to plead his cause seems right**: This is a strong and familiar principle. When we hear the first side of a dispute or a debate, we often think **the first one to plead his cause seems right**, and we are quick to take their side against the other.

b. **Until his neighbor comes and examines him**: The judgment is very different when the other side is heard from **his neighbor**. The second voice may confront **the first one to plead his cause** and give both sides of the story.

i. "Any man may, in the first instance, make out a fair tale, because he has the choice of circumstances and arguments. But when the neighbour cometh and searcheth him, he examines all, dissects all, swears and cross-questions every witness, and brings out truth and fact." (Clarke)

ii. "Thus the proverb teaches the equality of disputants and instructs the disciple not only to hear both sides of an argument but to demand direct cross-examination before rendering a decision (cf. Deuteronomy 19:16-18)." (Waltke)

iii. With this principle in mind, it is important that we argue for and defend Biblical truth in a way that can stand before the examination of others. Giving arguments that sound convincing but can be easily exposed or answered by an adversary do no good in defending and advancing God's kingdom.

Proverbs 18:18

Casting lots causes contentions to cease,
And keeps the mighty apart.

a. **Casting lots causes contentions to cease**: When there is an argument or dispute, appealing to an outside authority to solve the matter can make **contentions to cease**. In this case, the outside authority is the **casting** of **lots**, but the principle can be applied to other agreed-upon authorities.

i. "Verse 18 speaks of a practice that was widely practiced and highly regarded in ancient Israel, the casting of lots to settle disputed matters. The intent is to give the controversy over to God." (Garrett)

ii. "Today God's word and spiritual leaders figure prominently in divine arbitration (1 Corinthians 6:1-8)." (Ross)

b. **And keeps the mighty apart**: When an outside authority settles the contention, it can keep **mighty** warriors from fighting and killing each other.

Proverbs 18:19

A brother offended *is harder to win* than a strong city,
And contentions *are* like the bars of a castle.

a. **A brother offended is harder to win than a strong city**: There is a price to pay in offending **a brother**. To **win** him back to friendship and cooperation is difficult, more than we often think. Therefore, we avoid offending our **brother**, doing so only if necessary and doing all we can to be blameless so that whatever offense is taken is because of him and not us.

i. "If we take the words according to the *common version*, we see them express what, alas! we know to be too generally true: that when brothers fall out, it is with extreme difficulty that they can be reconciled. And fraternal enmities are generally strong and inveterate." (Clarke)

ii. "It is as if the closer the relationship, the wider the breach. The thread, once snapped, is not easily joined." (Bridges)

b. **Contentions are like the bars of a castle**: The conflict and **contentions** that come from a **brother offended** can be as difficult to break as **the bars of a castle**. They also may imprison those caught in the **contentions**.

i. "The proverb so understood is a forceful warning of the strength of the invisible walls of estrangement, so easy to erect, so hard to demolish." (Kidner)

ii. "Chrysostom gives this rule: 'Have but one enemy, the devil. With him never be reconciled; with your brother never fall out.'" (Bridges)

Proverbs 18:20

A man's stomach shall be satisfied from the fruit of his mouth;
From the produce of his lips he shall be filled.

a. **A man's stomach shall be satisfied from the fruit of his mouth**: For some, it is possible for them to make their living by what they say. They satisfy their **stomach** and perhaps that of their family **from the fruit of** the **mouth**.

b. **From the produce of his lips he shall be filled**: What he says shall fill his stomach and fulfill his financial obligations.

i. At the same time, this proverb "forces the thought that whatever a person dishes out, whether beneficial or harmful, he himself will feed on it to full measure through what his audience in return dishes out to him." (Waltke)

Proverbs 18:21

Death and life *are* in the power of the tongue,
And those who love it will eat its fruit.

a. **Death and life are in the power of the tongue**: The previous proverb said how what a man speaks could provide for his stomach. Here the idea is extended to remind us that **the tongue** not only has the power of provision but also of **death and life**.

i. "The Midrash mentions this point, showing one way it can cause death: 'The evil tongue slays three, the slanderer, the slandered, and the listener' (*Midrash Tehillim* 52:2)." (Ross)

ii. "Solomon doth vary his words: he speaketh sometimes of the 'mouth,' sometimes of the 'lips,' sometimes of the 'tongue,' as Proverbs 18:21, to show that all the instruments or means of speech shall have, as it were, their proper and just reward." (Trapp)

b. **Those who love it will eat its fruit**: Those who are wise enough to **love** and appreciate the power of what a man says will be blessed and will **eat** the pleasant **fruit** of wise and effective speech.

Proverbs 18:22

He who **finds a wife finds a good** *thing,*
And obtains favor from the L<small>ORD</small>.

a. **He who finds a wife finds a good thing**: God brought together the first husband and wife in Genesis 2:21-25. In this God gave marriage between a man and woman as a gift to humanity, both as a whole and a blessing on an individual level.

i. Some commentators believe that this proverb *implies* **finds a** *good* **wife** (such as John Trapp and Allen Ross); others insist it does not (such as Matthew Poole and Adam Clarke).

ii. "Although it does not say it, the verse clearly means a 'good' wife." (Ross)

iii. "For a wife, though she be not the best of her kind, is to be esteemed a blessing, being useful both for society of life, Genesis 2:18, and for the mitigation of a man's cares and troubles, and for the prevention of sins." (Poole)

iv. "*Marriage*, with all its troubles and embarrassments, is a blessing from God; and there are *few cases* where a *wife of any sort* is not better than none…. As to *good wives* and *bad wives*, they are relatively so, in general; and most of them that have been *bad* afterwards, have been *good* at first; and we well know the best things may deteriorate, and the world generally allows that where there are matrimonial contentions, there are *faults on both sides*." (Clarke)

b. **And obtains favor from the** L<small>ORD</small>: In Genesis 2:18 God said that it was not good for man to be alone. His gift of Eve to Adam was a demonstration of God's **favor**, and He still gives that gift of **favor**. In the modern western world, the cultural incentives for marriage seem to become weaker year by year, but God's declaration of **good** and the giving of His **favor** doesn't depend on cultural incentives.

i. "As with the first man, the Creator gives each fractured male with whom he is pleased one wife to complete the abundant life he intended." (Waltke)

ii. "The wording, especially in the Hebrew, strikingly resembles that of Proverbs 8:35, and so suggests that after wisdom itself, the best of God's blessings is a good wife." (Kidner)

Proverbs 18:23

The poor *man* uses entreaties,
But the rich answers roughly.

a. **The poor man uses entreaties**: It is sadly true that often, when a person is **poor** in money or influence, all they can do is beg for favor and justice.

i. "Speaks supplications; comes in a submissive manner; uses a low language, as a broken man. How much more should we do so to God…creeping into his presence with utmost humility and reverence." (Trapp)

b. **The rich answers roughly**: The **rich** man or **woman** can speak boldly – even *rudely* – because they have resources of money and influence. Solomon here described the world as it is, not as it should be. We sense in this proverb a quiet plea to make a better world than what is described in the proverb.

i. **Answers roughly**: "Speaketh proudly and scornfully, either to the poor, or to others that converse with him, being puffed up with a conceit of his riches, and of his self-sufficiency." (Poole)

ii. "The well-bred man of the world, who is all courtesy and refinement in his own circle, is often insufferably rude to those who are under him." (Bridges)

iii. "Was Jesus not as considerate to blind Bartimaeus as to the nobleman of Capernaum? All classes of people alike shared in his tenderest sympathy." (Bridges)

Proverbs 18:24

A man *who has* friends must himself be friendly,
But there is a friend *who* sticks closer than a brother.

a. **A man who has friends must himself be friendly**: This is a basic but often ignored principle. If you want **friends**, you should **be friendly** to others.

b. **There is a friend who sticks closer than a brother**: Even when a man **has friends**, there is something that will disappoint in human friendship. The flesh and blood friends of this world are important and a blessing, but we need the **friend who sticks closer than a brother** – Jesus Christ Himself, who called us no longer servants but friends (John 15:14-15).

i. "The bond of real friendship is often closer than the natural tie. The friendship between David and Jonathan is such an example." (Bridges)

ii. The transition between the plural (**friends**) and the singular (**a friend**) is significant. "It is better to have one good, faithful friend than numerous unreliable ones." (Ross)

iii. We apply this to Jesus our Friend as a spiritual principle; it is likely that Solomon did not have the Messiah in mind. "In many cases the genuine friend has shown more attachment, and rendered greater benefits, than the natural brother. Some apply this to *God*; others to *Christ*; but the text has no such meaning." (Clarke)

iv. "The friend whose loyalty transcends the solidarity of blood is realized in Jesus Christ (cf. John 15:12-15; Hebrews 2:11, 14-18)." (Waltke)

v. "Now I have a question to ask: that question I ask of every man and every woman in this place, and of every child too – Is Jesus Christ your friend? Have you a friend at court – at heaven's court? Is the Judge of quick and dead your friend? Can you say that you love him, and has he ever revealed himself in the way of love to you? Dear hearer, do not answer that question for thy neighbor; answer it for thyself. Peer or peasant, rich or poor, learned or illiterate, this question is for each of you, therefore, ask it. Is Christ my friend?" (Spurgeon)

Proverbs 19 – Fools and Family Life

Proverbs 19:1

Better *is* the poor who walks in his integrity
Than *one who is* perverse in his lips, and is a fool.

a. **Better is the poor who walks in his integrity**: Previous proverbs have been critical of **the poor**, but here Solomon recognized that not all poverty is caused by moral failure or weakness. There are definitely **poor** people who walk in their **integrity**.

i. "Often men put under their feet those whom God carries in his heart. Man honors the perverse for their riches and despises the poor because of their poverty." (Bridges)

b. **Than one who is perverse in his lips, and is a fool**: The Book of Proverbs is honest about the disadvantages of poverty. Yet it also recognizes that being **poor** is in no way the *worst* thing a person can be. It is far worse to be a **fool** who speaks twisted, **perverse** things.

i. "Once again a proverb correlates poverty with piety and wealth with impiety. The poor may be miserable for the moment, but the unethical rich are miserable for eternity. Thus the proverb teaches the pilgrim to walk by faith, not by sight." (Waltke)

Proverbs 19:2

Also it is not good *for* a soul *to be* without knowledge,
And he sins who hastens with *his* feet.

a. **It is not good for a soul to be without knowledge**: When a person (**a soul**) has no wisdom (is **without knowledge**), it is never **good**. It may be common, but it is not **good**.

b. **And he who sins hastens with his feet**: Solomon listed a second thing that was not **good** – the one who rushes toward sin (**hastens with his feet**). On this side of eternity, we will also struggle with sin, but we don't have to run towards it. We should be those who battle against sin, not run towards it.

Proverbs 19:3

The foolishness of a man twists his way,
And his heart frets against the Lord.

a. **The foolishness of a man twists his way**: it is true that a fool is foolish because they are twisted, crooked. Yet it also true that the foolish man finds his way more and more twisted. **Foolishness** leads to more twistedness.

b. **His heart frets against the Lord**: God intended us to be at peace with Him, but because of rebellion (both inherited and chosen), we are in many ways **against the Lord**. The foolish man or woman has no peace in God; their **heart frets against the Lord**. They are angry and perhaps bitter against God for their twisted way.

i. "Fools will try to blame God when they ruin their lives…The fool is not willing to accept failure as his own. Of course, to blame God is also folly." (Ross)

ii. "Such is the pride and blasphemy of a proud spirit. The criminal blames the judge for his righteous sentence." (Bridges)

Proverbs 19:4

Wealth makes many friends,
But the poor is separated from his friend.

a. **Wealth makes many friends**: When a person is wealthy, it draws **many** people to them in friendship. Yet these friendships may not be sincere or meaningful.

i. "Although a crowd, each one forms the friendship out of what he can gain, not for what he can give. The proverb anticipates the Lord's teaching to use of money to win friends and an eternal reward in the kingdom of God (Luke 18:1-9)." (Waltke)

b. **The poor is separated from his friend**: The wealthy man has advantages and draws **many friends**, but the **poor** man does not have these advantages. Their would-be friends find it easy to separate from them.

Proverbs 19:5

A false witness will not go unpunished,
And *he who* speaks lies will not escape.

a. **A false witness will not go unpunished**: The first idea in this proverb is probably that of the law court, and in the court, it is essential that the **false witness** be punished. Justice depends upon it. This principle extends beyond the court of law into our daily life. God loves the truth and wants us to speak the truth.

b. **He who speaks lies will not escape**: Among men, sometimes the **false witness** and liars escape the discovery and penalty of their sin. With God, **he who speaks lies will not escape**. Jesus said our every word would be held to account (Matthew 12:36).

> i. "This is a statement made in faith, for perjurers may escape human justice. Even the stern law of Deuteronomy 19:18-21 availed nothing for Naboth—or for Jesus." (Kidner)

Proverbs 19:6

Many entreat the favor of the nobility,
And every man *is* a friend to one who gives gifts.

a. **Many entreat the favor of the nobility**: When someone is of high status and importance (**of the nobility**), many people want their **favor**. There are advantages in having the **favor** of influential people.

b. **Every man is a friend to the one who gives gifts**: Many people who offer friendship do so out of selfish motives. They want the benefit of the **favor of the nobility** and the **gifts** that others may offer.

Proverbs 19:7

All the brothers of the poor hate him;
How much more do his friends go far from him!
He may pursue *them with* words, *yet* they abandon *him.*

a. **All the brothers of the poor hate him**: To be poor is often to be rejected by men, even by **brothers** and **friends**. What a contrast to Jesus, who Himself became poor (2 Corinthians 8:9) to draw near to us in our poverty and need.

b. **He may pursue them with words, yet they abandon him**: By nature, people run from the poor person, even when he tries to persuade and **pursue them with words**. In contrast, God pursues the poor and needy.

Proverbs 19:8

He who gets wisdom loves his own soul;
He who keeps understanding will find good.

a. **He who gets wisdom loves his own soul**: The possession and pursuit of **wisdom** is so good and helpful to us that we can and should get wisdom simply out of self-interest. In so doing we love our **own soul**, our own life.

> i. **Loves his own soul**: "Or *loveth himself,* because he procures great good to his soul, or to himself, as it follows; as sinners, on the contrary,

are said to *hate their souls*, Proverbs 29:24, because they bring mischief upon them." (Poole)

b. **He who keeps understanding will find good**: Wisdom isn't just something to *get*; it is also something to *keep*. We **find good** when we *keep* **understanding**.

Proverbs 19:9

A false witness will not go unpunished,
And *he who* speaks lies shall perish.

a. **A false witness will not go unpunished**: The words and sense of this proverb were previously presented in Proverbs 19:5. The repetition reminds us that this is an *important* principle. In the law court and in daily life, God wants us to be people of the truth and so He promised that **a false witness will not go unpunished**.

b. **He who speaks lies shall perish**: This speaks to the certainty of God's justice towards those who lie. Revelation 21:8 warns that *liars* are among those who will have *their part in the lake which burns with fire and brimstone, which is the second death*.

Proverbs 19:10

Luxury is not fitting for a fool,
Much less for a servant to rule over princes.

a. **Luxury is not fitting for a fool**: The sense is that there are some wisdom-rejecting fools who enjoy **luxury**, but it doesn't seem right. It isn't **fitting** for a **fool** to live in luxury.

b. **Much less for a servant to rule over princes**: Solomon spoke according to the wisdom of the natural man, which places great trust in nobility and family lineage. This is one of the proverbs that the gospel and the new covenant turn on its head, where those who would be great should be as servants and not as **princes** (Matthew 20:26 and 23:11).

i. "The slave, who is incompetent both by disposition and training, will be drunk from the feeling of power and his rulership will develop into unbearable despotism. The consequences for the community are only incompetence, mismanagement, abuse of power, corruption, injustice; in brief, social chaos (cf. Ecclesiastes 10:5-7)." (Waltke)

ii. "The slave has the same rational power as his sovereign. But lesser habits of mind make him unfit to rule. There are, however, exceptions to this, as in the case of Joseph." (Bridges)

Proverbs 19:11

The discretion of a man makes him slow to anger,
And his glory *is* to overlook a transgression.

a. **The discretion of a man makes him slow to anger**: It isn't necessarily weakness or lack of courage that makes a man **slow to anger**. It may be wisdom, here described as **discretion**.

b. **His glory is to overlook a transgression**: A wise man or woman knows that they have been forgiven much, and this shapes how they deal with others. They don't act as if they must hold everyone accountable for every **transgression** but know when to **overlook a transgression**.

i. "The virtue which is indicated here is more than a forgiving temper; it includes also the ability to shrug off insults and the absence of a brooding hypersensitivity." (McKane, cited in Ross)

ii. "The manlier any man is, the milder and readier to pass by an offence. This shows that he hath much of God in him (if he do it from a right principle), who bears with our evil manners, and forgives our trespasses, beseeching us to be reconciled." (Trapp)

Proverbs 19:12

The king's wrath *is* like the roaring of a lion,
But his favor *is* like dew on the grass.

a. **The king's wrath is like the roaring of a lion**: The roar of a **lion** is terrifying in itself, even without the understanding that destruction will swiftly follow. The same is true for the **wrath** of a king or any other influential person. It is much *truer* regarding the wrath of God or the wrath of the Lion of the Tribe of Judah (Revelation 5:5).

i. "Hebrew, Of a young lion, which, being in his prime, roars more terribly; sets up his roar with such a force that he amazeth the other creatures whom he hunteth, so that, though far swifter of foot than the lion, they have no power to fly from him." (Trapp)

ii. "There is nothing more dreadful than the roaring of this tyrant of the forest. At the sound of it all other animals tremble, flee away, and hide themselves. The *king* who is above law, and rules without law, and whose will is his own law, is like the *lion*." (Clarke)

b. **His favor is like the dew on the grass**: This means the king's **favor** is refreshing and life-giving; it also means that it is fleeting, as **the dew on the grass**. The favor of God is certainly refreshing and life-giving, but it is *not* fleeting, as if God were an impossible-to-please tyrant.

i. "Dew, which in the climatic conditions of Palestine was essential to the survival of vegetation in the hot, dry summer, is a gift from God." (Waltke)

ii. "This proverb would advise the king's subjects to use tact and the king to cultivate kindness." (Ross)

Proverbs 19:13

A foolish son *is* the ruin of his father,
And the contentions of a wife *are* a continual dripping.

a. **A foolish son is the ruin of his father**: It is grieving to any parent to have a **foolish son** or daughter. This may run from grief to **ruin** as the grief destroys the father's health and life, or as the father ruins himself to rescue the **foolish son**.

b. **The contentions of a wife are a continual dripping**: This proverb of sympathy for a man's problems as a **father** now looks at a man's potential problem as a husband. A wife who often contends (fights, argues) with her husband is like a **continual dripping** in at least three ways.

• It is an always-present annoyance and trouble.

• It wastes and destroys, eroding good and valuable things.

• It points to some underlying, more basic problem.

i. "The man who has got such a wife is like a tenant who has got a *cottage* with a *bad roof*, through every part of which the rain either *drops* or *pours*. He can neither *sit, stand, work*, nor *sleep*, without being exposed to these *droppings*. God help the man who is in such a case, with *house* or *wife*!" (Clarke)

ii. "Like as a man that hath met with hard usage abroad thinks to mend himself at home, but is no sooner sat down there but the rain, dropping through the roof upon his head, drives him out of doors again. Such is the case of him that hath a contentious wife - a far greater cross than that of ungracious children, which yet are the father's calamities and heart breaks." (Trapp)

iii. "Delitzsch passes on an Arab proverb told him…'Three things make a house intolerable: *tak* (the leaking through of rain), *nak* (a wife's nagging) and *bak* (bugs).'" (Kidner)

Proverbs 19:14

Houses and riches *are* an inheritance from fathers,
But a prudent wife *is* from the LORD.

a. **Houses and riches are an inheritance from fathers**: There are good things a man may receive as an **inheritance**, including material things such as **houses and riches**. A man is blessed to have such things.

b. **A prudent wife is from the** LORD: A gift beyond the **inheritance** one may receive from **fathers** is this gift from God – a **prudent wife**. A wife of wisdom, self-control, and appropriate living is a greater gift than **houses and riches**. A wife who is *not* **prudent** may waste whatever wealth a man has. Every man with a **prudent**, wise wife should give thanks to the LORD.

i. **From the** LORD: "Nature makes a woman, election a wife; but to be prudent, wise, and virtuous is of the Lord. A good wife was one of the first real and royal gifts bestowed on Adam." (Trapp)

ii. "Thus the proverb instructs the disciple to look to God (Proverbs 15:8, 29; 16:3; cf. Genesis 24:14) and find his favor through wisdom to obtain from him a competent wife (Proverbs 8:35; 18:22).... As a result, when a man has a competent wife, he praises God, not himself." (Waltke)

iii. "The verse does not answer questions about unhappy marriages or bad wives; rather, it simply affirms that when a marriage turns out well, one should credit God." (Ross)

Proverbs 19:15

Laziness casts *one* into a deep sleep,
And an idle person will suffer hunger.

a. **Laziness casts one into a deep sleep**: There are many problems with **laziness**, and one of them is that it leads to more **laziness**, sending the lazy man into a **deep sleep**. There is no work to be done from a **deep sleep**.

i. "Laziness plunges him into a state of being so deep in sleep that he is totally unconscious of his situation. Unaware of his tragic situation and unable to arouse himself, the sluggard neglects his source of income and so hungers. His fate is similar to that of drunkards and the gluttons (Proverbs 23:21)." (Waltke)

b. **An idle person will suffer hunger**: There is a great price to be paid from **laziness**, one of those prices is the **hunger** one suffers as one's needs are *not* met through hard work. The lazy man or woman puts themselves in a trap of **sleep** and **hunger**.

Proverbs 19:16

He who keeps the commandment keeps his soul,
***But* he who is careless of his ways will die.**

a. **He who keeps the commandment keeps his soul**: Obedience to the word and **commandment** of God is of real, practical benefit. Obedience guards and **keeps** the life, the **soul** of the wise man or woman who lives according to God's word.

b. **He who is careless of his ways will die**: To abandon wisdom and live **careless** in our **ways** is to invite death. God gave His **commandment** to give us life and to keep us from death.

Proverbs 19:17

He who has pity on the poor lends to the LORD,
And He will pay back what he has given.

a. **He who has pity on the poor lends to the LORD**: When we give to the **poor** (expressing our love and **pity** towards them), we aren't wasting our money. It is like lending money **to the LORD** Himself.

i. "Their just and gracious Creator takes it upon himself to assume their indebtedness and so he will repay the lender in full." (Waltke)

b. **He will pay back what he has given**: God will never be in debt to any man. He will never be in a position where He owes anything as a matter of debt. Therefore, to lend **to the LORD** is to ensure blessing in return. God will certainly **pay back what** we give in compassion to the poor. God promises that we will never be the loser for generous and compassionate giving.

i. "God will never be in your debt. He is exact and punctilious in His repayment. No man ever dared to do His bidding in respect to any case of need, and found himself the poorer…. Was not Ruth's love to Naomi well compensated?" (Meyer)

ii. "O what a word is this! God makes himself debtor for every thing that is given to the *poor*! Who would not *advance much* upon such *credit*? *God will pay it again*. And in no case has he ever forfeited his word." (Clarke)

iii. "This promise of reward does not necessarily signify that he will get his money back; the rewards in Proverbs involve life and prosperity in general." (Ross)

Proverbs 19:18

Chasten your son while there is hope,
And do not set your heart on his destruction.

a. **Chasten your son while there is hope**: There is not an endless window of opportunity to **chasten** and wisely discipline our children. Age and circumstances limit the opportunity for effective training, so it must be done **while there is hope**. There may come the time when you wish you had done much more to **chasten your son** or daughter.

i. "It is far better that the child should cry under healthy correction than that parents should later cry under the bitter fruit to themselves and their children of neglected discipline." (Bridges)

b. **Do not set your heart on his destruction**: To fail to **chasten your son** in the opportune season is to actually work for **his destruction**. Many parents bring much **destruction** to their children through *neglect*, not outright abuse.

i. "Psychologically healthy parents do not consciously desire to kill their children. But if they do not employ the God-given means of verbal reproof to prevent acts of folly and corporal punishment to prevent their repetition, they are in fact unwittingly party to the worst punishment, his death." (Waltke)

Proverbs 19:19

A man of great wrath will suffer punishment;
For if you rescue *him*, you will have to do it again.

a. **A man of great wrath will suffer punishment**: Out of control anger brings many problems and costs. Among the fruit of the spirit is *self-control* (Galatians 5:23), and wisdom does not lead a person to be of **great wrath**.

i. "He punishes himself. Wounded pride and resentment leave the wretched criminal brooding in his room. He suffers an intolerable burden of self-inflicted punishment." (Bridges)

b. **For if you rescue him, you will have to do it again**: The person who can't control their anger will run into trouble **again** and again. To **rescue** them once isn't enough, because the problem is more *in them* than in the circumstances that they blame for their anger. It is better for them to face the consequences of their action and hope they learn something from it.

i. "An ungovernable temper will repeatedly land its owner in fresh trouble." (Kidner)

Proverbs 19:20

Listen to counsel and receive instruction,
That you may be wise in your latter days.

a. **Listen to counsel and receive instruction**: One of the first marks of wisdom is the readiness to receive more wisdom. A teachable person, one who will **listen to counsel and receive instruction**, has already made much progress on the path of wisdom.

b. **That you may be wise in your latter days**: The bad effects of the foolish rejection of wisdom may not be seen for many years. Yet in the **latter days** of a man or woman's life, it will be clear whether or not they learned wisdom's lessons and if they did **listen to counsel**. If you want to be **wise** later in life, *start now*.

Proverbs 19:21

There are many plans in a man's heart,
Nevertheless the LORD's counsel—that will stand.

a. **There are many plans in a man's heart**: It is in the nature of men (and women) to plan and prepare for the future. Some of the plans may be wise and some may be foolish, but **there are many plans in a man's heart**.

b. **Nevertheless, the LORD's counsel – that will stand**: Man makes his plans, *and he should*. Yet every plan should be made with an appreciation of God's overall wisdom, work, and will.

i. James would later explain this principle this way: *Come now, you who say, "Today or tomorrow we will go to such and such a city, spend a year there, buy and sell, and make a profit"; whereas you do not know what will happen tomorrow. For what is your life? It is even a vapor that appears for a little time and then vanishes away. Instead you ought to say, "If the Lord wills, we shall live and do this or that."* (James 4:13-15)

ii. "This is a perfectly self evident assertion, but, as such, important as to warrant a pause in reading it. The one thing in the heart that may be depended upon is the counsel or guidance of Jehovah." (Morgan)

Proverbs 19:22

What is desired in a man is kindness,
And a poor man is better than a liar.

a. **What is desired in a man is kindness**: It is not that **kindness** is the highest or only virtue for the people of God. Yet, in many ways, it is the one most **desired** by others, especially in a modern world.

b. **A poor man is better than a liar**: This proverb shows that **kindness**, though valuable, is not the only virtue. To be a man or woman of *truth* – to not be a **liar** – is also of great value. This proverb reminds us that though we should pursue and value **kindness**, we should not treat it as the only valued virtue among God's people.

Proverbs 19:23

The fear of the LORD leads to life,
And *he who has it* will abide in satisfaction;
He will not be visited with evil.

a. **The fear of the Lord leads to life**: Since the **fear of the Lord** is the beginning of wisdom, it wonderfully **leads to life**. If we want **life**, we should begin with this honor, reverent awe and submission to God.

b. **He who has it will abide in satisfaction**: When we have, and walk in, the **fear of the Lord**, it leads to a life of **satisfaction**. The world, the flesh, and the devil want to convince us that a life founded on **fear of the Lord** leads to misery, but the opposite is true. It brings **satisfaction** and keeps us from a future of **evil**.

i. **Will not be visited with evil**: "When one lives a life of piety, the Lord provides a quality of life that cannot be disrupted by such evil." (Ross)

Proverbs 19:24

A lazy *man* buries his hand in the bowl,
And will not so much as bring it to his mouth again.

a. **A lazy man buries his hand in the bowl**: Solomon pictured a **lazy man** sitting at his food, with **his hand** buried in his bowl of food.

i. "This humorous portrayal is certainly an exaggeration. It probably was meant more widely for anyone who starts a project but lacks the energy to complete it." (Ross)

ii. **In the bowl**: "The same word in 2 Kings 21:13 leaves no doubt of its meaning. The scene is thus a meal, and the example comically extreme." (Kidner)

b. **And will not so much as bring it to his mouth again**: In this humorous, exaggerated picture, the lazy man has so little energy and initiative that he won't even **bring** his hand from the **bowl** to **his mouth**. This exaggerated picture establishes a principle made elsewhere in proverbs: *the lazy man will go hungry.*

i. **Will not so much as bring it to his mouth again**: "To wit, to feed himself; he expects that the meat should drop into his mouth." (Poole)

ii. "Is it possible to find anywhere a more graphic or sarcastic description of absolute laziness?" (Morgan)

Proverbs 19:25

Strike a scoffer, and the simple will become wary;
Rebuke one who has understanding, *and* he will discern knowledge.

a. **Strike a scoffer, and the simple will become wary**: When a determined fool and opponent of wisdom (**a scoffer**) is punished, others will learn. The more innocent fool (**the simple**) may learn from this.

i. "Smite him never so much, there is no beating any wit into him. Pharaoh was not a button the better for all that he suffered; but Jethro, taking notice of God's heavy hand upon Pharaoh, and likewise upon the Amalekites, was thereby converted, and became a proselyte, as Rabbi Solomon noteth upon this text." (Trapp)

b. **Rebuke one who has understanding**: The rebuke of the **scoffer** seems to do the **scoffer** no good, though it may benefit the **simple**. Yet when someone who values wisdom (**one who has understanding**) is corrected, he learns. He grows in his ability to **discern knowledge**.

i. "Here are three varieties of mind: closed [**scoffer**]…empty (the *simple*—he must be startled into attention), and open [**understanding**] (…he accepts even a painful truth)." (Kidner)

Proverbs 19:26

He who mistreats *his* father *and* chases away *his* mother
Is a son who causes shame and brings reproach.

a. **He who mistreats his father and chases away his mother**: The Bible commands *honor your father and your mother* (Exodus 20:12). This proverb considers the person who does the opposite of Exodus 20:12.

i. "When the father and his household lies in ruin, the *mother* (see Proverbs 1:8) is left in a tragic situation without the provision and protection and of her husband. By ruining his father, the imbecile (cf. Proverbs 17:2) leaves his mother as good as a defenseless widow." (Waltke)

b. **Is a son who causes shame and brings reproach**: One cannot disobey God and the standards of human society without paying a price. One price to be paid from the mistreatment of parents is to bring **shame** and **reproach** upon one's self.

Proverbs 19:27

Cease listening to instruction, my son,
And you will stray from the words of knowledge.

a. **Cease listening to instruction, my son**: Solomon continued to give wisdom to his children, and here warned of the danger of *ceasing* to listen **to instruction**, to wisdom.

b. **And you will stray from the words of knowledge**: This shows us that attention and effort must be given to *remain* on the path of wisdom. If one does **cease listening to instruction**, then they will **stray from the words of knowledge**. One must set themselves on the path of wisdom and, with God's help, determine that they will stay upon in.

i. "The meaning here is that it is better not to learn than to learn to refuse to obey." (Morgan)

ii. "Without constant attention to wisdom depraved human beings unconsciously stray from it. Even Solomon, ancient Israel's paragon of wisdom, strayed when he ceased listening to his own proverbs." (Waltke)

Proverbs 19:28

A disreputable witness scorns justice,
And the mouth of the wicked devours iniquity.

a. **A disreputable witness scorns justice**: The **witness** who is not committed to truth doesn't care about the workings of **justice**. Great harm comes upon society and its legal system when there is not care and promotion of the truth and the **disreputable witness** is not punished.

i. "The perjurers in the lawsuit against Naboth are called *beliyyaal* (1 Kings. 21:10, 13), a story that illustrates the lying witnesses' lethal power." (Waltke)

b. **The mouth of the wicked devours iniquity**: The words of the **wicked** (coming from **the mouth**) love **iniquity** so much that they *devour* it, as a hungry man devours food. This is the kind of person who **scorns justice** and tears down society.

Proverbs 19:29

Judgments are prepared for scoffers,
And beatings for the backs of fools.

a. **Judgments are prepared for scoffers**: Those who reject wisdom with hostility (**scoffers**) will not escape penalty. **Judgments are prepared** for them.

i. **Are prepared for**: "For these scorners (that promise themselves impunity) are judgments, not one, but many, not appointed only, but prepared long since, and now ready to be executed." (Trapp)

b. **Beatings for the backs of fools**: Those who disregard wisdom, bound in their folly (**fools**) will also have their penalty. Correction will come to them in its appointed way, and sadly – the correction will do little good for them.

i. "*Profane* and *wicked* men expose themselves to the punishments denounced against such by just laws. Avoid, therefore, both their company and their end." (Clarke)

Proverbs 20 – Wisdom, Weights, and Wickedness

Proverbs 20:1

Wine *is* a mocker,
Strong drink *is* a brawler,
And whoever is led astray by it is not wise.

a. **Wine is a mocker, strong drink is a brawler**: This is true in at least two senses. First, alcohol *mocks* and *fights with* those who abuse it in any sense. Second, alcohol leads one to be a **mocker** and a **brawler**. Many men and women have had their lives dominated by the mockery and brawling of alcohol.

> i. "It mocks the drunkard, and makes a fool of him, promising him pleasure, but paying him with the stinging of an adder, and biting of a cockatrice, Proverbs 23:32." (Trapp)

> ii. **A mocker**: "It *deceives* by its *fragrance, intoxicates* by its *strength*, and renders the intoxicated *ridiculous*." (Clarke)

> iii. Trapp defined **strong drink**: "All kinds of drink that will alienate the understanding of a man and make him drunk, as ale, beer, cider."

b. **Whoever is led astray by it is not wise**: Wisdom is displayed by the ability to *not* be **led astray** by alcohol. For many, this means not drinking alcohol at all (especially pastors and church leaders). For others, this will mean the decided, evident moderation in their use of alcohol.

> i. **Led astray**: "So mighty is the spell that the overcome slave consents to be mocked again and again." (Bridges)

> ii. **Is not wise**: "For when the wine is in the wit is out. They have a practice of drinking the *Outs*, as they call it - all the wit out of the head, all the money out of the purse." (Trapp)

> iii. "Moreover, given the ease with which one may make a habit of this, it is wise to avoid alcohol entirely. In the Old Testament the use

239

of alcohol was not prohibited; in fact, it was regularly used at festivals and celebrations. But intoxication was considered out of bounds for a member of the covenant community (see Proverbs 23:20-21, 29-35; 31:4-7)." (Ross)

iv. "These two aspects of wine, its use and its abuse, its benefits and its curse, its acceptance in God's sight and its abhorrence, are interwoven into the fabric of the Old Testament so that it may gladden the heart of man (Psalm 104:15) or cause his mind to error (Isaiah 28:7), it can be associated with merriment (Ecclesiastes 10:19) or with anger (Isaiah 5:11), it can be used to uncover the shame of Noah (Genesis 9:21) or in the hands of Melchizedek to honor Abraham (Genesis 14:18)." (Fitzsimmonds, cited in Waltke)

Proverbs 20:2

The wrath of a king *is* like the roaring of a lion;
***Whoever* provokes him to anger sins *against* his own life.**

a. **The wrath of a king is like the roaring of a lion**: Using an image from a previous proverb (Proverbs 19:12), this proverb reminds us that those in power and leadership have potential for a great and fearful exercise of **wrath**.

b. **Whoever provokes him to anger sins against his own life**: Since in many ways the **king** held the power of life and death over his subjects, to provoke the king **to anger** was to endanger one's **own life**. Knowing this principle should make us more reverent to the King of Kings, and happy that our King of Kings is rich in mercy and slow to anger (Psalm 103:8, 145:8).

Proverbs 20:3

***It is* honorable for a man to stop striving,**
Since any fool can start a quarrel.

a. **It is honorable for a man to stop striving**: Many men feel that *honor* drives them to dispute and fight with others. This proverb reminds us that often times it is even more **honorable for a man to stop striving**.

i. "To stint it rather than to stir it; to be first in promoting peace and seeking reconciliation, as Abraham did in the controversy with Lot." (Trapp)

b. **Since any fool can start a quarrel**: In many circumstances, it takes a man of honor to **stop** the fight, but **any fool can start** the **quarrel** and continue it.

i. "The wise are more concerned to bring peace than a desire to be right, but the fool cannot restrain himself and at the first opportunity explodes and shows his teeth." (Waltke)

Proverbs 20:4

The lazy *man* will not plow because of winter;
He will beg during harvest and *have* nothing.

a. **The lazy man will not plow because of winter**: The **lazy man** always finds some excuse not to do his work. It is always too early or too late in the season to begin. It is always **winter**, and the ground is too hard for plowing. Any excuse will work when the heart is set on not working.

i. "*Winter* designates the Palestinian raining season from mid-October to April.... Since no sowing could have been done without plowing, the farmer waited for the first autumn rains to soften the ground. The sluggard, however, lacks the industry to plow from winter on, the only time that matters." (Waltke)

ii. "The right time for planting was the rainy season (see Genesis 8:22). It was cold, wet, and unpleasant. Perhaps such discomfort was his excuse." (Ross)

iii. "Suppose it were not cold; do' you know what he would say? 'Oh, it is so hot! I cannot plough; the perspiration runs down my cheeks. You wouldn't have me ploughing this hot weather, would you?' Supposing it were neither hot nor cold, why, then he would say, I believe, that it rained; and if it didn't rain, he would say the ground was too dry, for a bad excuse, he holds, is better than none; and therefore he will keep on making excuses to the end of the chapter; anything will he do rather than go and do the work he does not like – that is, ploughing." (Spurgeon)

b. **He will beg during harvest and have nothing**: The **lazy man** *will* work, after a fashion – he will do the work of begging. Having no reward from the work of his hands, he will even have to **beg during harvest**. Often his begging will go unrewarded (**have nothing**).

Proverbs 20:5

Counsel in the heart of man *is like* deep water,
But a man of understanding will draw it out.

a. **Counsel in the heart of man is like deep water**: Wisdom may lie **deep** within a man or woman, and not be immediately apparent. It may be a hidden reservoir, ready in the season of need.

i. "The metaphor is of a well whose waters are far beneath the surface of the ground so that one must use a bucket with a long rope to draw water to the surface. Thus a person's real motives are 'deep' in that they are difficult to extract; one must be wary of the pretenses of others." (Garrett)

b. **A man of understanding will draw it out**: Wisdom not only knows how to get and have wisdom; it also knows how to use it. The wise man – the **man of understanding** – knows how to **draw** wisdom **out** for practical and ready use.

i. **Will draw it out**: "By prudent questions and discourses, and a diligent observation of his words and actions." (Poole)

ii. "Those who are wise can discern the motives of the heart." (Ross)

Proverbs 20:6

Most men will proclaim each his own goodness,
But who can find a faithful man?

a. **Most men will proclaim each his own goodness**: It is true that **most** everyone feels they are good in their own eyes. Many are happy to **proclaim** it, wanting others to know all their supposed **goodness**.

b. **Who can find a faithful man?** True faithfulness in a man is different than self-advertised **goodness**. A **faithful man** doesn't want or need to **proclaim** his **own goodness**. The quiet satisfaction of faithfulness to God and man is enough.

i. "The paucity of pious persons makes them precious." (Trapp)

ii. "Look at yourself in the mirror of God's Word. Does your neighbor or your friend find that you are a faithful friend? Do you often speak what you know will be accepted rather than what is true? Never underrate the importance of moral integrity." (Bridges)

Proverbs 20:7

The righteous *man* walks in his integrity;
His children *are* blessed after him.

a. **The righteous man walks in his integrity**: For a **righteous man** or woman, their upright living and **integrity** will be actually lived out. They will walk in their **integrity**.

b. **His children are blessed after him**: The greatest gift a parent can give to a child is for that parent to be a **righteous**, upright person who **walks in his integrity**. That one will create a home and atmosphere that will be a blessing to the child.

i. "It answers the temptation to 'get on' at all costs 'for the children's sake'." (Kidner)

Proverbs 20:8

A king who sits on the throne of judgment
Scatters all evil with his eyes.

a. **A king who sits on the throne of judgment**: In the ancient world kings did not only govern, they were also the highest court and judge in their kingdom. A faithful king would carry out this responsibility and sit on his **throne of judgment**.

i. "That makes it his great care and business to execute judgment and justice among his people, especially if he do this in his own person, as was usual in ancient times, and sees things with his own eyes." (Poole)

ii. "Righteousness at the top was necessary to undergird the whole judicial system." (Waltke)

b. **Scatters all evil with his eyes**: The presence alone of a king in judgment over his realm is enough to scatter **all evil**. When a people know that evil will be punished by godly and just leadership, it makes **evil** scatter.

i. "Certainly the principle stands that a just government roots out the evils of society." (Ross)

ii. "The practised eye of a true ruler sifts the chaff from the wheat; still surer is the Spirit of the Lord: Isaiah 11:3; 1 Corinthians 2:15." (Kidner)

Proverbs 20:9

Who can say, "I have made my heart clean,
I am pure from my sin"?

a. **Who can say**: It is part of human nature to overestimate and boast over one's self. Many can say what this proverb says, but none with real humility and integrity.

i. "No man living upon earth can say this truly and sincerely. Compare 1 Kings 8:46; Job 14:4, 15:14; Ecclesiastes 7:20; 1 John 1:8. *I am pure from my sin*; I am perfectly free from all guilt and filth of sin in my heart and life." (Poole)

ii. "This is the eternal challenge which has but one answer. When a man recognizes this he begins to inquire for a Saviour." (Morgan)

b. **I have made my heart clean, I am pure from sin**: If meant in any ultimate sense, this is the boast or the claim of a fool. Sometimes there are claims to a **clean** heart or purity from **sin** by godly men in the Bible, but those are only true in a relative sense, such as the comparison between one's self and one's enemies.

i. "Only vain people can boast that they have pure hearts. But the boast, far from showing their goodness, demonstrates their blindness. Man is so depraved that he cannot understand his own depravity." (Bridges)

ii. "No man. But thousands can testify that the blood of Jesus Christ has cleansed them from all unrighteousness. And he is *pure from his sin*, who is justified freely through the redemption that is in Jesus." (Clarke)

Proverbs 20:10

Diverse weights *and* diverse measures,
They *are* both alike, an abomination to the LORD.

a. **Diverse weights and diverse measures**: God wants business and trading to be done fairly and justly. To have **diverse weights** and **measures** means that you will cheat both the buyer and the seller. God wants our **weights** and **measures** to be proper and consistent.

b. **They are both alike, an abomination to the LORD**: God feels so strongly about deceptive business practices that He used the strong word **abomination** to describe them. God Himself has fair **weights** and **measures**; He expects humanity made in His image to have them also.

i. "Traders used the scanty weights and measures for selling and the large ones for buying. Significantly, all the proverbs that denounce false scales and measures explicitly link the Lord's name in the abomination formula with them (Proverbs 11:1; 20:10, 23)." (Waltke)

Proverbs 20:11

Even a child is known by his deeds,
Whether what he does *is* pure and right.

a. **Even a child is known by his deeds**: Especially in the realm of religion and faith, it is easy for us to think of ourselves *only* by what we believe, instead of *also* by what we do. We are *more than* what we do, but **even a child is known by his deeds**. We shouldn't deny that others see and understand us by the measure of our **deeds**.

i. "We may easily learn from the *child* what the *man* will be. In general, they give indications of those *trades* and *callings* for which they are adapted by nature. And, on the whole, we cannot go by a surer guide in preparing our children for future life, than by observing their early propensities. The future *engineer* is seen in the little *handicraftsman* of two years old." (Clarke)

b. **Whether what he does is pure and right**: The outside world, our own community, and God in heaven look at our deeds to see if they are **pure and right**.

i. "Certainly no child who says, 'I am well behaved' will find his or her words taken at face value. People will evaluate the child by how he or she behaves. The implication is that appearances and words can be deceiving; behavior is a better criterion of judgment." (Garrett)

Proverbs 20:12

The hearing ear and the seeing eye,
The LORD has made them both.

a. **The hearing ear and the seeing eye**: God has given men and women remarkable capacity to see and understand the world around them. Our ability to hear and see should be for us gateways to wisdom.

i. "Listening and observing are important qualities of a good disciple and the sage regularly calls upon him to use them to read and hear his teaching." (Waltke)

b. **The LORD has made them both**: Since our hearing and our sight are gifts from God, we should determine to use them for His honor and glory. It also reminds us that we can hear and see because we are made in God's image; **the LORD** has a **hearing ear** and a **seeing eye**.

i. "Since God made the eyes and ears, he is the infallible judge. No one can deceive him with appearances." (Garrett)

Proverbs 20:13

Do not love sleep, lest you come to poverty;
Open your eyes, *and* you will be satisfied with bread.

a. **Do not love sleep, lest you come to poverty**: To **love sleep** and the laziness connected to it is to bring one's self to **poverty**.

i. "Immoderate sleep, or sloth, or idleness. Take sleep because necessity requires it, not from any love to it." (Poole)

ii. "The number of hours one sleeps per day is not the point here. Love of sleep refers to laziness, but one can be lazy although sleeping very little." (Garrett)

b. **Open your eyes, and you will be satisfied with bread**: It takes some initiative and energy to **open your eyes**, to get out of bed and get to work.

But the reward is worth it; you will avoid **poverty** and you **will be satisfied with bread**. In God's economic system, hard work is rewarded.

Proverbs 20:14

"*It is* good for nothing," cries the buyer;
But when he has gone his way, then he boasts.

a. **It is good for nothing**: This is what **the buyer** cries out. In the game and competition of bargaining, the **buyer** always wants to speak less of what he wants to buy, hoping to get a better price from the seller.

i. "This may simply reflect normal procedure in a world where haggling for prices was common, but it may also be a warning to the inexperienced on how things are done." (Ross)

b. **When he has gone his way, then he boasts**: The bargaining words of the **buyer** are empty. They are only a strategy for negotiation. This proverb reminds us that what people say isn't always what they believe, and people will speak falsehood for their own advantage.

i. "How apt are men to decry the goods they wish to purchase, in order that they may get them at a *cheaper rate*; and, when they have made their bargain and carried it *off*, *boast* to others at how much *less* than its *value* they have obtained it! Are such honest men?" (Clarke)

Proverbs 20:15

There is gold and a multitude of rubies,
But the lips of knowledge *are* a precious jewel.

a. **There is gold and a multitude of rubies**: Solomon presents the picture of a large pile of **gold** and precious stones. We think of this pile and are impressed at its value.

b. **But the lips of knowledge are a precious jewel**: Now Solomon presented another treasure, the **precious jewel** of wise words (**lips of knowledge**). We immediately see the value of the pile of **gold** and **rubies**, but we need to better appreciate the value of wise words.

Proverbs 20:16

Take the garment of one who is surety *for* a stranger,
And hold it as a pledge *when it* is for a seductress.

a. **Take the garment of one who is surety for a stranger**: Exodus 22:26-27 says an Israelite could take someone's outer **garment** as a deposit or a guarantee for a loan as long as they returned it each evening, so it could be used as a night covering or blanket. Solomon's advice here is that if you loan to someone who has already foolishly agreed to be **surety for a**

stranger, make sure you get the deposit or guarantee. If they were foolish enough to be **surety for a stranger**, they should be regarded as a credit risk.

i. "*Take his garment* means: 'Don't lend to him without security (Exodus 22:26); he is a bad risk!'" (Kidner)

ii. "People should be held to their obligations. Two synonymous lines teach that a person who foolishly becomes responsible for another person's debts should be made to keep his word. Taking the garment was the way of holding someone responsible to pay debts." (Ross)

b. **Hold it as a pledge when it is for a seductress**: Most translations favor *stranger* or *foreigner* instead of **seductress**. The idea seems to focus on someone outside the covenant community. One should demand more security for a loan to someone outside one's knowledge and reference.

i. "The parallelism suggests 'strangers' is the correct reading, although theories have been presented with regard to the idea of the wayward woman." (Ross)

ii. "Rather, the proverb emphasizes the stupidity of risking one's life to an unknown creditor by becoming security for stranger." (Waltke)

Proverbs 20:17

Bread gained by deceit *is* sweet to a man,
But afterward his mouth will be filled with gravel.

a. **Bread gained by deceit is sweet to a man**: Sin and transgression have their attraction. There is something in the nature of rebellion that can make **bread gained by deceit** even sweeter. It satisfied our desire to rebel, our desire for adventure, and our love of forbidden thrills. We might imagine that the forbidden fruit of Eden was delicious.

i. "Such a bitter-sweet was Adam's apple, Esau's mess, the Israelites' quails, Jonathan's honey, the Amalekites' cakes after the sack of Ziklag, [1 Samuel 30:16] Adonijah's dainties, [1 Kings 1:9] which ended in horror; ever after the meal is ended, comes the reckoning." (Trapp)

b. **Afterward his mouth will be filled with gravel**: The sweetness of forbidden bread (or fruit) is short-lived. There is nothing sweet or pleasant about a mouth **filled with gravel**. If we really desire pleasure in a lasting, ultimate sense, then obedience is the pathway to it (Psalm 16:11).

i. **Filled with gravel**: "It shall be bitter and pernicious at last, like gritty bread, which offends the teeth and stomach. It will certainly bring upon him the horrors of a guilty conscience, and the wrath and judgments of the Almighty God." (Poole)

Proverbs 20:18

Plans are established by counsel;
By wise counsel wage war.

a. **Plans are established by counsel**: There is help and wisdom in realizing our own limitations and seeking **counsel**. This often leads to our **plans** being **established** in the sense of coming to fulfillment.

b. **By wise counsel wage war**: This shows that **wise counsel** is even more important when great matters are involved – life and death matters, such as **war**. By spiritual analogy, we wage the spiritual warfare we must fight as believers with the **wise counsel** of God's word and other believers (Ephesians 6:10-18).

> i. **By wise counsel**: "This is necessary in every common undertaking, and much more in a thing of such high importance as war is." (Poole)

> ii. **By wise counsel wage war**: "Perhaps there is not a precept in this whole book so little regarded as this. Most of the *wars* that are undertaken are wars of injustice, ambition, aggrandizement, and caprice, which can have had no previous *good counsel*." (Clarke)

Proverbs 20:19

He who goes about *as* a talebearer reveals secrets;
Therefore do not associate with one who flatters with his lips.

a. **He who goes about as a talebearer reveals secrets**: The man or woman who is a **talebearer** or gossip loves to reveal things that should more properly be concealed. There are certainly some things that should be revealed (Ephesians 5:11), but many things should be concealed out of love (1 Peter 4:8). Wisdom will know which approach is appropriate in each situation.

b. **Therefore do not associate with one who flatters with his lips**: The person who **flatters with his lips** will often speak *against* you as quickly as they speak *for* you. It is better to stay clear of such people (**do not associate**).

> i. "The idea of 'opens his lips' is that such a one is always ready to talk; and if he is willing to talk to you about others, he will be willing to talk to others about you." (Ross)

Proverbs 20:20

Whoever curses his father or his mother,
His lamp will be put out in deep darkness.

a. **Whoever curses his father or his mother**: The Bible commands us to honor our **father** and **mother** (Exodus 20:12). To curse one's parents is to do the opposite of this command.

b. **His lamp will be put out in deep darkness**: God promised to bless those who keep the command to honor father and mother (Exodus 20:12, Ephesians 6:2). There is a corresponding principle that those who disobey and curse their father or mother will face the judgment of God.

Proverbs 20:21

An inheritance gained hastily at the beginning
Will not be blessed at the end.

a. **An inheritance gained hastily at the beginning**: When we get too much too soon, it is often isn't helpful for us. So, a large **inheritance** that comes **hastily** and towards the **beginning** of our life is a dangerous blessing.

i. "Gotten by *speculation*; by *lucky hits*; not in the fair *progressive* way of *traffic*, in which money has its *natural increase*. All such inheritances are short-lived; God's blessing is not in them, because they are not the produce of *industry*; and they lead to *idleness, pride, fraud,* and *knavery*." (Clarke)

ii. "The implication is that what is 'quickly gained' is either unlawful or unrighteous. The verb describes a hurried or hastened activity; perhaps a wayward son seizes the inheritance quickly (cf. Luke 15:12) or even drives out his parents (cf. Proverbs 19:26)." (Ross)

b. **Will not be blessed at the end**: This is often how it ends when someone gains too much, too soon, apart from their own work and initiative. When large amounts are freely received, it can work against blessing **at the end**.

i. "Easy money does not foster financial responsibility. The easily gained money is here not necessarily dishonestly gained, but even so, those who have amassed wealth slowly know better how to keep it." (Garrett)

ii. "But this, as well as many other proverbs, are to be understood of the common course, although it admit of some exceptions. For sometimes merchants or others get great estates speedily by one happy voyage, or by some other prosperous event." (Poole)

Proverbs 20:22

Do not say, "I will recompense evil";
Wait for the LORD, and He will save you.

a. **I will recompense evil**: This is what the wise man or woman should *not* say. Wisdom and obedience to God teach us that vengeance belongs to the Lord (Romans 12:19).

i. "Vengeance belongs to God. Nobody else is fit to wield this. God is omniscient; our knowledge is at most partial. God's judgment is perfect, while we are blinded by our prejudices and evil desires." (Bridges)

b. **Wait for the Lord, and He will save you**: Wisdom teaches us to rely on God and trust in Him to **recompense evil**. This does not mean that wisdom is indifferent to evil and will never oppose it; it means that wisdom recognizes that there are many times – more than we think – when we should let go of any kind of **recompense** towards **evil** and **wait for the Lord** to **save** us.

Proverbs 20:23

Diverse weights *are* an abomination to the Lord,
And dishonest scales *are* not good.

a. **Diverse weights are an abomination to the Lord**: God is righteous in all His measurements. When He measures something in the physical or moral realm, His measurement is always true. God tells us to imitate Him in this aspect and to understand that He regards dishonest, **diverse weights** as an **abomination**.

i. "According to Proverbs 16:11 the Lord created the weighing apparatus, every deceitful practice touches him…. Life in the marketplace and religion are inseparable." (Waltke)

b. **Dishonest scales are not good**: God cares that we do business honestly. The world often tells us that it doesn't matter how we make our money, but God warns us that **dishonest scales are not good**.

Proverbs 20:24

A man's steps *are* of the Lord;
How then can a man understand his own way?

a. **A man's steps are of the Lord**: Men and women rightly make their plans, but God guides **steps** according to His own will and wisdom. He certainly doesn't leave it all up the choices and plans of men and women.

b. **How then can a man understand his own way?** This proverb teaches us *humility* in regard to our life choices and path. We should not think or act as if it were all in our control or all according to our planned **steps**.

Proverbs 20:25

It is a snare for a man to devote rashly *something as* holy,
And afterward to reconsider *his* vows.

a. **It is a snare for a man to devote rashly something as holy**: This has in mind the practice of dedicating things to God for His use alone. When it comes to promises of dedication to God, we should avoid the **snare** of emotional, rash promises.

i. "To pronounce a thing sacred is to dedicate it. Here, then, is an impulsive man, pledging more than he seriously intends." (Kidner)

ii. Solomon also dealt with this matter in Ecclesiastes 5:4-7. These passages show us that a commonly overlooked and unappreciated sin among God's people is the sin of *broken vows* - promising things to God and failing to live up to the vow. Those who honor God:

- Will not be quick to make vows to God.
- Will be serious about fulfilling vows made.
- Will regard broken vows as sins to confessed and to be repented of.

b. **And afterward to reconsider his vows**: When a promise to God is made foolishly, it forces us to **reconsider** our **vows** – something wisdom would have protected us from to begin with.

i. "Leviticus 27 explains that Israelites could buy themselves out of rash vows—it was expensive." (Ross)

Proverbs 20:26

A wise king sifts out the wicked,
And brings the threshing wheel over them.

a. **A wise king sifts out the wicked**: An earthly ruler understands how important it is to administer justice, and part of that is to carefully examine (**sifts out**) **the wicked**. If it is wise for an earthly ruler to do this, we can expect that God also does it, and does it perfectly.

b. **And brings the threshing wheel over them**: A wise earthly ruler not only knows how to carefully examine the wicked, but then also to bring whatever punishment is appropriate, to use what is wise and necessary to separate the evil from the good (as a **threshing wheel** separates the chaff from the wheat grain).

i. **And brings**: "*He brings back* (literally, 'causes to return,' see Proverbs 1:23) represents the wheel of the cart going over the heads of grain many times to thresh it thoroughly." (Waltke)

Proverbs 20:27

The spirit of a man *is* the lamp of the LORD,
Searching all the inner depths of his heart.

a. **The spirit of a man is the lamp of the LORD**: There are mysteries and truths of the inner man (**the spirit of a man**) that only the **lamp of the LORD** can expose. In this respect, we can think of God's word as a lamp and a light (Psalm 119:105).

i. **Spirit**: "The *nesamah* is that inner spiritual part of human life that was inbreathed at the Creation (Genesis 2:7) and that constitutes humans as spiritual beings with moral, intellectual, and spiritual capacities." (Ross)

ii. "Within the mystery of the spirit-nature of every man there is light. It is the instrument of God. It illuminates life. It is that by which man is constantly kept face to face with truth. Let us make no mistake about it: the most evil men know that their works are evil." (Morgan)

b. **Searching all the inner depths of his heart**: The **lamp of the LORD** – God's word – can search the **depths** of a man's heart like nothing else. This is because God's word is living and active (Hebrews 4:12).

i. "Conscience has aptly been called 'God in man.' God brings the searching light of his lamp into the darkness." (Bridges)

ii. "God has given to every man a *mind*, which *he so enlightens by his own Spirit*, that the man knows how to distinguish good from evil; and *conscience*, which springs from this, searches the inmost recesses of the soul." (Clarke)

Proverbs 20:28

Mercy and truth preserve the king,
And by lovingkindness he upholds his throne.

a. **Mercy and truth preserve the king**: Any earthly **king** may be preserved by God's **mercy and truth** shown to the king, and by the **mercy and truth** the king shows to others.

i. "The principle of the proverb, which is the complement of verse 26, applies with equal force to lesser forms of authority." (Kidner)

i. "In the Davidic covenant (cf. 2 Samuel 7:11-16) God promised not to take his covenant love (*hesed*) from the king (cf. v. 15) but to make his house stable." (Ross)

b. **By lovingkindness he upholds his throne**: This is *hesed*, the great covenant love God shows to His people and they should show to others.

Men often assume that thrones are upheld by armies and raw power, but God has a better way to establish and uphold a king and his kingdom.

i. "When our queen, that stuck fast to her principles, was not more loved of her friends than feared of foes, being protected by God beyond expectation. Our King John thought to strengthen himself by gathering money, the sinews of war; but meanwhile he lost his people's affections, those joints of peace, and came, after endless turmoils, to an unhappy end." (Trapp)

ii. "The proverb finds its final fulfillment in Jesus Christ (see Psalm 72:1, 2, 4; Isaiah 16:4b-5)." (Waltke)

Proverbs 20:29

The glory of young men *is* their strength,
And the splendor of old men *is* their gray head.

a. **The glory of young men is their strength**: God has so designed human development that **young men** excel in physical strength, and this is a **glory** to them. It is wise and suitable for **young men** to take on tasks that fit this **glory**.

b. **The splendor of old men is their gray head**: What the **old men** lack in physical strength, they should make up for in wisdom that is appropriate for those who have a **gray head**.

i. "A proverb to lift the reader above the unfruitful attitudes of envy, impatience and contempt which the old and the young may adopt towards each other. Each age has its appointed excellence, to be respected and enjoyed in its time." (Kidner)

ii. "Let youth and old age both beware of defacing their glory. Each takes the precedence in some things and gives way in others. Let them not, therefore, envy or despise each other's prerogatives. The world, the state, and the church needs them both, the strength of youth for energy and the maturity of the old for wisdom." (Bridges)

Proverbs 20:30

Blows that hurt cleanse away evil,
As *do* stripes the inner depths of the heart.

a. **Blows that hurt cleanse away evil**: Pain is a burden, but it can bring a benefit. If we allow the unpleasant fire of pain to refine and **cleanse away evil**, then our sorrow and pain were not wasted. Something was gained.

i. "In context this is not parental discipline but beatings administered by the king's officers as punishment for crime. Yahweh can peer directly into a person's innermost being (v. 27), but the king can touch the criminal's soul by harsh retribution." (Garrett)

ii. "Some must be beaten black and blue ere they will be better; neither is wit anything worth with them till they have paid well for it." (Trapp)

b. **As do stripes the inner depths of the heart**: Solomon probably used **stripes** here in a symbolic sense for the chastening that comes in life. If we receive such discipline with wisdom, it will purify us in **the inner depths of the heart**.

i. "Physical punishment may prove spiritually valuable." (Ross)

ii. **As do stripes**: "The paradox of Isaiah 53:5 stands out sharply against this background: that with *his* stripes *we* are healed." (Kidner)

Proverbs 21 – Peace in the Home, Prosperity in Life, Preparation for Battle

Proverbs 21:1

The king's heart *is* in the hand of the LORD,
Like the rivers of water;
He turns it wherever He wishes.

> a. **The king's heart is in the hand of the LORD**: God holds and can guide the human heart. If God can do this with someone as powerful and noble as a king, He can do this with any man or woman He chooses.

> > i. "Thus he turned the heart of Pharaoh to Joseph; of Saul to David; of Nebuchadnezzar to Jeremiah; of Darius to Daniel; of Cyrus, and afterwards of Alexander the Great, to the Jews; of some of the Roman persecutors to the primitive Christians." (Trapp)

> > ii. "God's inscrutable mastery extends to the king, the most powerful of human beings, and to the heart, their most free member. The Lord rules even the most free and powerful of all human beings." (Waltke)

> > iii. This should build our faith that *God can guide and change hearts.* Sometimes we despair when we see the stubbornness and hardness of man's heart against God and His will, but **the king's heart is in the hand of the LORD** and He can guide it **wherever He wishes**.

> > iv. "He names *kings* not to exclude other men, but because they are more arbitrary and uncontrollable than other men." (Poole)

> b. **Like the rivers of water; He turns it wherever He wishes**: This analogy illustrates *how* God may guide the heart of man. In moving a river, one does not need to carry each drop of water to a place it where it is desired; if one can shape the banks and guide the direction of the river, the water will go where desired. So, God does not need to do violence to the human heart

to guide it; He may do it simply through arranging other circumstances like banks of a river to guide the flow where He wants it.

i. "Tiglath-pileser (Isaiah 10:6, 7), Cyrus (Isaiah 41:2-4) and Artaxerxes (Ezra 7:21) are all examples of autocrats who, in pursuing their chosen courses, flooded or fertilized God's field as he chose. The principle is still in force." (Kidner)

ii. "As a farmer channels the water where he wants and regulates its flow, so does the Lord with the king. No human ruler, then, is supreme; or, to put it another way, the Lord is truly the King of kings." (Ross)

Proverbs 21:2

Every way of a man *is* right in his own eyes,
But the Lord weighs the hearts.

a. **Every way of a man is right in his own eyes**: By nature, we justify ourselves. Sometimes we do this in sincerity, sometimes with deception, but stubborn pride makes us generally think **every way of a man is right in his own eyes**.

b. **But the Lord weighs the hearts**: Men and women are confident in their own **way**, but *God knows*. We justify things according to our **hearts** – "It was in my heart" or "I must follow my heart" or "In my heart, I know" – but God **weighs the hearts** of men and women, knowing that the heart itself doesn't justify anything.

i. "Yahweh's power of discernment goes beyond unmasking those who fool others; he even finds out those who have fooled themselves." (Garrett)

Proverbs 21:3

To do righteousness and justice
***Is* more acceptable to the Lord than sacrifice.**

a. **To do righteousness and justice**: The way we treat people – what might be called our *horizontal* relationship – is important to God. He wants us to **do righteousness and justice** in this world.

b. **Is more acceptable to the Lord than sacrifice**: Animal **sacrifice** was a way to walk in right relationship with *God* – what might be called our *vertical* relationship. God here says that how we treat others is more important than how we perform religious ceremonies such as **sacrifice**. This was the truth missed by the priest and the Levite in Jesus's story of the Good Samaritan (Luke 10:30-36).

Proverbs 21:4

A haughty look, a proud heart,
***And* the plowing of the wicked *are* sin.**

a. **A haughty look, a proud heart**: Often a **proud heart** is displayed through a **haughty look**. There is no shortage of either among humanity.

i. "This sin assumes so many different forms that until God's Spirit reveals a man to himself, he does not think it applies to him. Indeed, he manages to be proud of his pride!" (Bridges)

b. **And the plowing of the wicked are sin**: These three things – the **look**, the **heart**, and the **plowing of the wicked** are each called **sin**. Even the hard work (**plowing**) of the **wicked** can be regarded as **sin** before God because they often use the benefit of their hard work for an evil purpose.

i. **Plowing**: "The prosperity and posterity of the wicked; *is sin*-it is evil in the *seed*, and evil in the *root*, evil in the *branch*, and evil in the *fruit*. They are full of sin themselves, and what they do is sinful." (Clarke)

ii. "This figure indicates that the product of the wicked is sin." (Ross)

iii. Derek Kidner agreed with some other translations that have *lamp* here instead of **plowing**. "*Plowing*...should almost certainly be *lamp*."

Proverbs 21:5

The plans of the diligent *lead* surely to plenty,
But *those of* everyone *who is* hasty, surely to poverty.

a. **The plans of the diligent lead surely to plenty**: When good planning is combined with **diligent** work there will be a harvest of **plenty**.

b. **But those of everyone who is hasty, surely to poverty**: The one who wants to avoid work, find shortcuts, and cut corners will find failure instead of **plenty**. Their path leads **surely to poverty**.

i. **Everyone who is hasty**: "Elsewhere the diligent person stands over against the lethargic sluggard (Proverbs 10:4; 12:24, 27; 13:4), but here he stands opposed to the rash and imprudent. The lazy are defective in action; the hasty, in thought." (Waltke)

Proverbs 21:6

Getting treasures by a lying tongue
Is the fleeting fantasy of those who seek death.

a. **Getting treasures by a lying tongue**: There are some who hope to talk their way into money, and to do it with a **lying tongue**. They plan deals and make promises that aren't honest, hoping it can bring them **treasures**.

i. **Treasures by a lying tongue**: "As do seducers, sycophants, flatterers, corrupt judges, that say with shame, 'Give ye'; mercenary pleaders, that sell both their tongues and silence, and help their clients' causes." (Trapp)

b. **Is the fleeting fantasy of those who seek death**: The hope of great treasure through **lying** words is a dream of those who are on the path to destruction. They hope to find great **treasures** with little work and put their trust in **fleeting fantasy** instead of in God.

i. "The point of the verse, then, is that ill-gotten gain is a fleeting pleasure and a crime for which punishment is prepared." (Ross)

ii. **Those who seek death**: "Instead of procuring the fortune and life they hoped for, deceivers find that they were actually seeking death and so lose everything." (Waltke)

Proverbs 21:7

The violence of the wicked will destroy them,
Because they refuse to do justice.

a. **The violence of the wicked will destroy them**: The **wicked** often love **violence** and use it for their gain. This does not please God, and God allows such people to reap what they have sown.

i. "Judas was eager to rid himself of his ill-gotten treasure, as it became an intolerable curse. But he was unable to run away from his conscience, which tortured him." (Bridges)

b. **Because they refuse to do justice**: It isn't only what the **wicked** do; it is also what they *do not do*. What they do is **violence**; what they refuse to **do** is **justice**. God cares about both what they do and don't do, and will pass judgment over both.

Proverbs 21:8

The way of a guilty man *is* perverse;
But *as for* the pure, his work *is* right.

a. **The way of a guilty man is perverse**: Every life is on a **way**, and some people walk a **way** that is twisted and **perverse**. Those who walk this crooked way are **guilty** before God.

b. **As for the pure, his work is right**: The crooked way belongs to the **guilty** man, but right **work** belongs to the **pure** man. The path we walk will display who we are.

Proverbs 21:9

Better to dwell in a corner of a housetop,
Than in a house shared with a contentious woman.

a. **Better to dwell in the corner of a housetop**: The **corner of a housetop** is not a great place to live. It is small, confined, and exposed to the elements because it is on the roof. Yet in some circumstances, the **corner of a housetop** is a **better** place to live.

i. "The roof of the house, which in those countries was flat and plain, and habitable, but was exposed to all the injuries of the weather." (Poole)

ii. "A man had better abide abroad, *sub dio,* under the sun exposed to wind and weather, yea, to crowd into a corner, and to live in a little ease, than to cohabit in a convenient house with a contentious woman, that is ever brawling and brangling." (Trapp)

b. **Than in a house shared with a contentious woman**: To have the whole house but live in constant conflict with a **contentious woman** is misery. The same principle would be true of the **contentious** man. One would be **better** off in a more humble living situation and have peace in the home.

i. **A contentious woman**: "Also 'woman' is ambiguous for it could refer to other women in the household, mother, grandmother, mother-in-law, daughter (cf. Proverbs 11:16, 22), but the wife (Proverbs 12:4; 19:13-14) is more probably intended, as Proverbs 18:22 validates." (Waltke)

Proverbs 21:10

The soul of the wicked desires evil;
His neighbor finds no favor in his eyes.

a. **The soul of the wicked desires evil**: When a wicked man or woman does **evil**, it is because their **soul…desires** it. Their inward corruption is expressed through their **desires**.

i. "An important truth about depravity: men can sin not merely from weakness but eagerly and ruthlessly." (Kidner)

ii. "Here is a graphic picture of Satan himself! He not only does evil – he craves evil. Here we see that evil is natural to the wicked, for it is in their nature." (Bridges)

b. **His neighbor finds no favor in his eyes**: The **evil** that marks the **wicked** is expressed in their inability to get along with a **neighbor**. They look upon everyone else with **no favor** in their eyes. We should be careful of those who can't get along with other people.

Proverbs 21:11

When the scoffer is punished, the simple is made wise;
But when the wise is instructed, he receives knowledge.

a. **When the scoffer is punished, the simple is made wise**: There are degrees of fools and their foolishness. A **scoffer** is hardened in their rejection of wisdom, while the **simple** is more naïve and inexperienced. A **simple** man or woman can learn wisdom when they see **the scoffer is punished**.

b. **When the wise is instructed, he receives knowledge**: Wise men and women don't need to learn everything through their own misery or the misery of other people. The **wise** can learn as they are **instructed**.

i. "The simple learn wisdom, both from the punishment of wicked men, and from the prosperity of good men." (Poole)

Proverbs 21:12

The righteous *God* wisely considers the house of the wicked,
Overthrowing the wicked for *their* wickedness.

a. **The righteous God wisely considers the house of the wicked**: The LORD is a **righteous God**, and what happens in the **house of the wicked** does not escape His sight. He sees it and **wisely considers** it. God **considers** the **house of the wicked** with perfect wisdom and justice.

i. **Considers the house of the wicked**: "He foreseeth its fearful fall, and is not offended at their present prosperity; for God, he knows, will shortly overturn it. This consideration cures him of the fret, as it did David [Psalms 37:1-2].... The destruction of others should be an instruction to us." (Trapp)

b. **Overthrowing the wicked for their wickedness**: The **wicked** are judged for their **wickedness**. Whatever judgment they receive fits their actions.

Proverbs 21:13

Whoever shuts his ears to the cry of the poor
Will also cry himself and not be heard.

a. **Whoever shuts his ears to the cry of the poor**: Though many proverbs tell of poverty caused by bad conduct, other proverbs express God's compassion towards the **poor**. God cares about the **poor** and He commands us to have a compassionate heart towards them.

b. **Will also cry himself and not be heard**: We will reap what we have sown. It will be measured to us as we have measured to others. If we are silent to those in need, God may arrange it so we will **not be heard** in our time of need.

i. "See the conduct of the *priest* and *Levite* to the man who *fell among thieves*; and let every man learn from this, that he who shuts his ear against the cry of the poor, shall have the ear of God shut against his cry. The words are quite plain; there is no difficulty here." (Clarke)

Proverbs 21:14

A gift in secret pacifies anger,
And a bribe behind the back, strong wrath.

a. **A gift in secret pacifies anger**: This is among the proverbs that speak honestly about the *effectiveness* of a **gift** or a **bribe**. The **secret** nature of this **gift** shows that it isn't entirely proper, yet it may work to calm **anger** in an official or leader.

i. "I conceive the wise man's drift here is to show how prevalent gifts are, if closely conveyed especially - which takes away the shame of open receiving - and what a pave they have to an amicable reconciliation. Thus Jacob pacified Esau; Abigail, David; Hezekiah, the Assyrian that came up against him. [2 Kings 18:24-25]." (Trapp)

b. **A bribe behind the back, strong wrath**: Again, the *secret* nature of the **gift** or **bribe** is indicated. Though morally questionable, it may *work* with the corrupt leader or official.

i. "The verse does not condemn or condone; it merely observes the effectiveness of the practice." (Ross)

Proverbs 21:15

It is **a joy for the just to do justice,**
But destruction *will come* to the workers of iniquity.

a. **It is a joy for the just to do justice**: When a person is **just** (righteous, godly) in the inner man or woman, it gives them **joy** to **do justice**. Their good works flow out of who they are. For us to really walk in the way God wants us to walk, we need to be transformed on the inside.

b. **Destruction will come to the workers of iniquity**: Those who work **iniquity** also show what is in their heart, and it should make them tremble under the judgment of God. Instead of the **joy** of the **just**, they will experience **destruction**.

i. **Workers of iniquity**: "Wicked men are great workmen; they put themselves to no small pains in 'catering for the flesh to fulfil the lusts thereof'; yea, and this they do with singular delight." (Trapp)

Proverbs 21:16

A man who wanders from the way of understanding
Will rest in the assembly of the dead.

a. **A man who wanders from the way of understanding**: There are two paths or ways a man or woman can walk. It is dangerous to begin on **the way of understanding** but not to continue on it. To some extent, this became tragically true of Solomon, the author of Proverbs (1 Kings 11:1-11). The departure from the **way of understanding** doesn't have to be calculated and deliberate; it may feel like *wandering*.

i. "As every motion has an end, so every journey has a goal." (Waltke)

b. **Will rest in the assembly of the dead**: If one **wanders from the way of understanding**, they may well end up **in the assembly of the dead**. The path we walk on – *and remain on* – matters everything.

Proverbs 21:17

He who loves pleasure *will be* a poor man;
He who loves wine and oil will not be rich.

a. **He who loves pleasure will be a poor man**: To find success and prosperity, there must be a measure of discipline and self-denial. The person who **loves pleasure** lacks this discipline and self-denial and often ends up **a poor man**.

b. **He who loves wine and oil will not be rich**: In this proverb **wine and oil** represent the luxuries of life. There is an appropriate way to enjoy **wine and oil** without setting one's heart on them; but if these are *loved* beyond proper measure, it is a pathway to poverty (**will not be rich**).

i. "The 'love' that is here portrayed must be excessive or uncontrolled, because it brings one to poverty. Perhaps other responsibilities are being neglected or the people are trying to live above their means." (Ross)

Proverbs 21:18

The wicked *shall be* a ransom for the righteous,
And the unfaithful for the upright.

a. **The wicked shall be a ransom for the righteous**: This is a way of saying that the **righteous** will ultimately succeed and will triumph over the **wicked**.

i. **A ransom**: "The metaphor should not be pushed to walk on all fours by asking to whom the ransom is paid." (Waltke)

ii. "God often in his judgments cuts off the *wicked*, in order to prevent them from destroying the *righteous*. And in general, we find that the wicked fall into the traps and pits they have digged for the righteous." (Clarke)

b. **And the unfaithful for the upright**: God promises that in the end, all His **righteous** and **upright** will be lifted above the **wicked** and the **unfaithful**.

Proverbs 21:19

Better to dwell in the wilderness,
Than with a contentious and angry woman.

a. **Better to dwell in the wilderness**: In a previous proverb (Proverbs 21:9) it was thought **better** to live in the corner of a rooftop than with a contentious woman. This proverb removes the man from the house entirely and sets his **better** place in **the wilderness**.

b. **Than with a contentious and angry woman**: Proverbs 21:9 spoke of the **contentious** woman; this proverb adds the idea of *anger* to the picture and sets the unfortunate man even further from the house (**in the wilderness**). This shows the great value of peace and happiness in the home.

i. "Yet much prayer and forbearance are required to avoid being upset by every trifle. This will keep us from being irritated needlessly. We must also bear in mind that we have divine support for all our heavy crosses. We also look forward with intense longing for the home of everlasting peace." (Bridges)

Proverbs 21:20

There is **desirable treasure,**
And oil in the dwelling of the wise,
But a foolish man squanders it.

a. **There is a desirable treasure, and oil in the dwelling of the wise**: The **wise** man or woman lives a life blessed by God, and sometimes that blessing is shown in material things. They may have **desirable treasure** and good **oil** in their home.

b. **But a foolish man squanders it**: The **foolish man** would have trouble *gaining* what the wise man or woman has. He doesn't have the character of life or blessing of God that leads to prosperity. Yet even if he were to gain it, it would not last. His **foolish** nature dominates as he **squanders it**.

i. "The verse basically means that the wise gain wealth but the foolish squander it." (Ross)

Proverbs 21:21

He who follows righteousness and mercy
Finds life, righteousness, and honor.

a. **He who follows righteousness and mercy**: Each life is on a path, and here the path is **righteousness and mercy**. This is the path of wisdom, God's path for those who will listen and surrender to Him.

b. **Finds life, righteousness, and honor**: The path of **righteousness and mercy** isn't easy and is often opposed and mocked. Yet it is *rewarded*, and rewarded richly with **life, righteousness, and honor**. The wise path is worth it.

Proverbs 21:22

A wise *man* scales the city of the mighty,
And brings down the trusted stronghold.

a. **A wise man scales the city of the mighty**: The walls of a **city** are difficult obstacles, especially **the city of the mighty**. Yet with wisdom one can overcome such obstacles. The **wise man** can accomplish things impossible for others.

i. "It is more effective to use wisdom than to rely on strength." (Ross)

b. **Brings down the trusted stronghold**: Because the **wise man** enjoys the blessing and guidance of God, he can defeat obstacles as difficult as a **trusted stronghold**. This is true in military and practical life; wisdom and ingenuity have won many battles and destroyed many strongholds. It is also true in spiritual life. Cities and strongholds that stand against the progress of the believer can be broken down with the wisdom and power of God.

i. "The truth that wisdom may succeed where brute force fails (cf. Proverbs 24:5-6), has many applications, not least to spiritual warfare." (Kidner)

ii. "So spiritual wisdom, a direct gift from God, overcomes formidable difficulties. Let us be like soldiers who are strong in the Lord and put on all of God's armor (Ephesians 6:10). The victory is assured. The stronghold will be pulled down." (Bridges)

Proverbs 21:23

Whoever guards his mouth and tongue
Keeps his soul from troubles.

a. **Whoever guards his mouth and tongue**: What we say is important, and some of the instruments of speech are the **mouth and tongue**. It is good to guard what we say and not to speak everything that comes to mind.

b. **Keeps his soul from troubles**: Unguarded words can bring a lot of trouble. Having the wisdom to guard the **mouth and tongue** will keep us from many **troubles**.

Proverbs 21:24

A proud *and* haughty *man*—"Scoffer" *is* his name;
He acts with arrogant pride.

a. **A proud and haughty man**: Of the many types of fools, the **scoffer** is one of the worst. He is known to be **proud and haughty**, thinking himself better than others and even better than God.

b. **He acts with arrogant pride**: The **proud and haughty man** will be known by his actions. His life will be marked with great pride, **arrogant pride**.

i. "To say the proud act with pride is not tautology (a logical problem), but a rhetorical means of intensification, as in 'boys will be boys.' The proverb does not aim as much to define the mocker as to explain that his fury against God and humanity stems from his exaggerated opinion of his self-importance." (Waltke)

ii. "This is a vivid picture of Pharaoh, who in a proud and arrogant way asked who the Lord was that he should obey him (Exodus 5:2)." (Bridges)

Proverbs 21:25

The desire of the lazy *man* kills him,
For his hands refuse to labor.

a. **The desire of the lazy man kills him**: The **lazy man** has **desire**; he just doesn't have the initiative or the energy to fulfill it. His life of unfulfilled **desire** is unsatisfying and feels as if it **kills him**. This is a death to self, but not in the good and blessed way described by Jesus for His disciples (Matthew 10:38, Luke 9:23).

i. John Trapp explained that mere **desire** wasn't enough. "Balaam wished well to heaven; so did the young Pharisee in the gospel, that came to Christ hastily, but went away heavily. Herod for a long time desired to see Christ, but never stirred out of doors to see him. Pilate asked Christ, What is truth? but never stayed his answer."

b. **For his hands refuse to labor**: Having the **desire** for good and blessing and prosperity, but not the desire to work, the **lazy man** lives a life of constant frustration and disappointment. He does not know the satisfaction of earned achievement.

i. "Living in a world of wishful thinking and not working will bring ruin…the verse teaches that doing rather than desiring brings success." (Ross)

Proverbs 21:26

He covets greedily all day long,
But the righteous gives and does not spare.

a. **He covets greedily all day long**: The reference is likely to the lazy man of the previous proverb. With his desire, that lazy man **covets greedily**, and he does it **all day long** – yet the desire is unfulfilled because he does not *work* towards it.

b. **The righteous gives and does not spare**: The lazy man experiences constant disappointment, but the **righteous** man – who, by implication, works hard – he has so much that he **gives and does not spare**. He is so blessed that he has enough for himself and to give generously.

Proverbs 21:27

The sacrifice of the wicked *is* an abomination;
How much more *when* he brings it with wicked intent!

a. **The sacrifice of the wicked is an abomination**: God said, *to obey is better than sacrifice* (1 Samuel 15:22). Religious ceremonies do not cover over a **wicked** life, and God may regard those religious ceremonies as **an abomination**.

i. "I have read of one that would haunt the taverns, theatres, and whore houses at London all day; but he durst not go forth without private prayer in the morning, and then would say at his departure, Now devil do thy worst. The Circassians are said to divide their life between rapine and repentance." (Trapp)

b. **How much more when he brings it with wicked intent**: The religious ceremonies of the wicked are bad enough; they are even worse when made with **wicked intent**. When a **sacrifice** is offered, the priest or observers may not be able to see **wicked intent**, but God certainly can.

i. **With wicked intent**: "It is abominable for any man who is living wrongly to make an offering to God in the way of worship. That abomination becomes worse when the offering of the wicked comes from an ulterior motive. For a wicked man to give for his own pleasure is an evil thing; but if he hopes by his gift to win some spiritual favor while he continues in sin, that is a still deeper evil." (Morgan)

Proverbs 21:28

A false witness shall perish,
But the man who hears *him* will speak endlessly.

a. **A false witness shall perish**: God is against all liars, but a **false witness** is a special type of liar. The primary idea is of one who lies in court, such as those who gave **false witness** at the trial of Jesus (Matthew 26:60).

b. **The man who hears him will speak endlessly**: The second like of this proverb has in mind another kind of injustice in the court – the judge or lawyer in the court who **hears** the false witness and may **speak endlessly** about the matter without ever coming to a just and fair verdict.

Proverbs 21:29

A wicked man hardens his face,
But *as for* the upright, he establishes his way.

a. **A wicked man hardens his face**: One characteristic of the **wicked** is that they may be unsympathetic to others. Their face is hard and unfriendly to others, especially towards those in need.

i. **Hardens his face**: "He thinks to make good one lie by another; to outface the truth, to overbear it with a bold countenance. It seems to be a metaphor from a traveller that sets his face against the wind and weather, and holds on his journey, though he be taking long strides towards destruction." (Trapp)

ii. "Here a bold front, which has no shame and does not blush in the presence of sin, is a dreadful manifestation of a hardened heart. Cain stood boldly in God's presence while his hands dripped with his brother's blood. The traitor had the effrontery to kiss the sacred cheeks of our Lord. What a bold front these evil men had!" (Bridges)

b. **As for the upright, he establishes his way**: The **upright** man or woman does not face the same self-made obstacles the **wicked** man faces. **His way** is established and made sure.

i. "Kidner summarizes the verse to say that a bold front is no substitute for sound principles." (Ross)

Proverbs 21:30

***There is* no wisdom or understanding**
Or counsel against the LORD.

a. **There is no wisdom or understanding or counsel against the LORD**: To fight against God is to fight a losing battle. One can never succeed against the sovereign of the universe.

i. This means, *God wins and ultimately all His purposes will be accomplished.* "Oftentimes as we have watched, we have trembled; so subtle, so clever, so cunning are the ways of this underworld of antagonism to Jehovah. Yet look again. Just as persistent in human history, the futility, the feebleness, the failure of this antagonism has been manifested." (Morgan)

ii. "Therefore it is true, full and finally, that 'There is no wisdom nor understanding nor counsel against Jehovah.' And thus it becomes true that, 'To them that love God, all things work together for good.' Here, then, is the place of our rest; here is the secret of our confidence; here is the inspiration of songs in the darkest night." (Morgan)

b. **Wisdom or understanding or counsel**: These are three similar terms used to express wisdom and right knowledge. God is the God of all **wisdom** and **understanding** and **counsel**, so those things are always *for* Him and never **against the** LORD.

i. "The proverb drives home the vast and unbridgeable gulf between the best of human wisdom and the Lord's sovereignty." (Waltke)

Proverbs 21:31

The horse *is* prepared for the day of battle,
But deliverance *is* of the LORD.

a. **The horse is prepared for the day of battle**: In the days these proverbs were written, the effective use of the **horse** in the war could be overwhelming against the enemy. These horses had to be trained; it was wise to prepare the **horse** for the **day of battle**.

b. **But deliverance is of the** LORD: Though it is wise to make the best preparations for battle, ultimately one should not trust in horses or preparation, but in God Himself. **Deliverance is of the** LORD, not only of horses and preparation.

i. "We often give the credit of a victory to *man*, when they who consider the circumstances see that it came from *God*." (Clarke)

ii. "He gives it to which side he pleaseth, as he did to the Israelites in the conquest of Canaan, though they had no horses to help them, as their adversaries had, and chariots too, both Egyptians and Canaanites." (Trapp)

iii. "Use the means, but do not idolize them. Those who put their trust in them will fall. Those who remember that their safety is in the Lord will stand upright. When it comes to spiritual warfare, it is even more important to exercise active faith and dependence on God." (Bridges)

Proverbs 22 – Rich and Poor, Raising Children

Proverbs 22:1

A *good* name is to be chosen rather than great riches,
Loving favor rather than silver and gold.

> a. **A good name is to be chosen rather than great riches**: Wealth comes in many forms. The wealth of respect and recognized excellence in character – **a good name** – is valuable beyond **great riches**.

> > i. **A good name**: "This good name proceeding from a good conscience, this honour from virtue, [Isaiah 43:4] this perfume of faith and obedience, this splendour and sparkle of the 'white stone,' which only shines upon heavenly hearts - is far more desirable than great riches." (Trapp)

> > ii. "While it is true that reputation and the affection of others are more desirable than great riches, we must not forget that they may be in themselves vanity and a snare.... The only honor that is safe is that which comes from God." (Bridges)

> b. **Loving favor rather than silver and gold**: The man or woman who appreciates the value of **a good name**, of **favor** with God and man, recognizes that it is worth more than **silver and gold**.

> > i. "Riches are enjoyed but till death at utmost; but a good name outlives the man, and is left behind him for a blessing." (Trapp)

> > ii. **Loving favor**: "Our Lord carries this teaching a step further in Luke 10:20, to show that at a still higher level, not the power we wield, but the love in which we are held, is our proper joy." (Kidner)

Proverbs 22:2

The rich and the poor have this in common,
The LORD is the maker of them all.

a. **The rich and the poor have this in common**: The differences between **rich and poor** appear to be large in the present world. Jesus' story of the rich man and Lazarus (Luke 16:20-31) highlights these differences. Yet **rich** and **poor** do have some things **in common**.

b. **The LORD is maker of them all**: Those who are **rich** and those who are **poor** share the same Creator. Yahweh has made them all. Both **rich** and **poor** tend to see each other through stereotypes and should remember this towards each other.

i. "People often forget this and make value judgments; they would do well to treat all people with respect, for God can as easily reduce the rich as raise the poor." (Ross)

ii. "All are born into the world. All come into the world naked, helpless, unconscious beings. All stand before God. All are dependent on God for their birth. All are subject to the same sorrows, illnesses, and temptations. At the gate of the invisible world the distinction of riches and poverty is dropped." (Bridges)

Proverbs 22:3

A prudent *man* foresees evil and hides himself,
But the simple pass on and are punished.

a. **A prudent man foresees evil and hides himself**: Wisdom does not always engage in a fight; it knows there are times when the best response to **evil** is to hide and let the danger go past.

i. "Prevision is the best means of prevention." (Trapp)

b. **The simple pass on and are punished**: The foolish and **simple** man doesn't have the ability to perceive danger and respond correctly. They must endure more **evil** because of this, and it is something of a punishment.

Proverbs 22:4

By humility *and* the fear of the LORD
Are riches and honor and life.

a. **By humility and fear of the LORD**: These two qualities are connected. **Humility** is a proper view of self; **fear of the LORD** is a proper view of God. The person who has these two qualities is well on their way on the path the wisdom.

b. **Are riches and honor and life**: Blessing will come to the wise man or woman who has **humility and the fear of the LORD**. They can certainly expect *spiritual* **riches and honor and life**, and often those same things materially in *this* world.

i. "The most humble is the most triumphant Christian. He may be depressed, but he is highly exalted. He has the wealth of grace and of glory. Nobody can deprive him of these." (Bridges)

Proverbs 22:5

Thorns *and* snares *are* in the way of the perverse;
He who guards his soul will be far from them.

a. **Thorns and snares are in the way of the perverse**: Proverbs 13:15 told us that *the way of the unfaithful is hard*. **Thorns and snares** symbolically describe the hard **way of the perverse**.

i. "The metaphor refers to temptations such as easy sex and easy money that tempt youth. The morally degenerate tread a dangerous road infested with them." (Waltke) *If you want fewer temptations, change the road you're on.*

ii. "This is due to the love of God, shown in the constitution of the world. It would have been malignity indeed to have placed us in the world without the warning signal of pain to show us where we are wrong, and to sting us when we go astray." (Meyer)

b. **He who guards his soul will be far from them**: The wise man or woman, keeping watch over their life (**guards his soul**) will stay far from the **way of the perverse** and the **thorns and snares** associated with that way.

i. "Those who have the discipline of wisdom avoid life's dangers." (Ross)

Proverbs 22:6

Train up a child in the way he should go,
And when he is old he will not depart from it.

a. **Train up a child in the way he should go**: A child need training. The job of the parent is not to simply let him grow up in any particular way, but to **train** him, and that **in the way he should go**. The **way he should go** has at least two senses that complement each other.

• The sense of the Hebrew **the way he should go** speaks of the child's individual **way** and inclination. It speaks of discerning a child's strengths and weaknesses and parenting in a way that takes those into account.

• The Book of Proverbs often presents the concept of **the way** – being the path of wisdom and life in contrast to the way of folly and destruction (such as mentioned in Proverbs 22:5). Surely, this also is **the way** to train a child in.

i. **The way he should go**: "Here it would mean dedicate the child according to the physical and mental abilities of the developing youth" (Waltke). "The training prescribed is literally 'according to his (the child's) way', implying, it seems, respect for his individuality and vocation, though not for his selfwill" (Kidner).

ii. "What is the way in which a child should go? A more literal rendering of the Hebrew at once answers this question. Such translation would be: 'Train up a child *according to his way.*' In every child there are special and peculiar powers. The true business of training a child therefore, is that of discovering what those powers are, and developing them…. Herein is revealed the need for individual work. No two children are alike." (Morgan)

iii. **Train up**: "*Chanac*, which we translate *train up* or *initiate*, signifies also *dedicate*; and is often used for the *consecrating* any thing, house, or person, to the service of God. *Dedicate*, therefore, in the first instance, your *child* to *God*; and *nurse, teach*, and *discipline* him as God's child, whom he has intrusted to your care." (Clarke)

b. **When he is old he will not depart from it**: This is a wonderful principle that the Holy Spirit may quicken to a promise for parents troubled over their adult children. When a child is trained in the proper way, though they may depart for a season (and a long season), in principle they will return and **not depart from it**.

i. Solomon's own life displayed that this is a *principle* and not an absolute *promise*. "Other proverbs recognize that the youth's freedom to choose sin (cf. Ezekiel 18:20) and apostatize by taking up with villains (Proverbs 2:11-15) and whores (Proverbs 5:11-14)." (Waltke)

ii. "The book is addressed to youths, not parents. Were the parents ultimately responsible for his moral choice, there would be no point in addressing the book to youth (see Proverbs 1:4). Moreover, Solomon himself stopped listening to instruction and strayed from knowledge (Proverbs 19:27)." (Waltke)

Proverbs 22:7

The rich rules over the poor,
And the borrower *is* servant to the lender.

a. **The rich rules over the poor**: Proverbs 22:2 told us that there was one important respect in which **rich** and **poor** were the same; this proverb reminds us of a way they are very different. **Rich** people have more authority and voice in the community than the **poor** do.

i. "The point…is that one must regard indebtedness only as a last resort (wary of those who offer to lend money) and endeavor to get out of debt as rapidly as possible. Debt is debilitating and demoralizing." (Garrett)

ii. "Too often the rich rule over the poor in a harsh way. Indeed, without submitting to God's rule over us, we can hardly be trusted with power over our fellowmen." (Bridges)

b. **And the borrower is servant to the lender**: Those who borrow money are in a lower place than those who lend money. The obvious application of this proverb is that the wise man or woman will do all he or she can to walk in the path of godly prosperity; to be a **lender** and not a **borrower**.

i. "The verse may be referring to the apparently common practice of Israelites selling themselves into slavery to pay off debts (see Exodus 21:2-7). It is not appreciably different from the modern debtor who is working to pay off bills." (Ross)

Proverbs 22:8

He who sows iniquity will reap sorrow,
And the rod of his anger will fail.

a. **He who sows iniquity will reap sorrow**: A person's sins (**iniquity**) are like seeds that are sown. In time they will bring a harvest and the sinner **will reap sorrow**.

i. "The *crop* must be according to the *seed*. If a man sow *thistle seed*, is it likely he shall reap *wheat*? If he sow to the *flesh*, shall he not of the flesh reap *destruction*?" (Clarke)

b. **The rod of his anger will fail**: This mixing of metaphors (from the harvest to the shepherd's rod) probably has the idea that in the season when the sinner reaps his harvest from the seeds of **iniquity**, he will have no defense against it.

Proverbs 22:9

He who has a generous eye will be blessed,
For he gives of his bread to the poor.

a. **He who has a generous eye will be blessed**: According to this principle God will bless the one who is **generous** to others. When people are **generous** to God and His work, God will not allow them to be *more* generous than He is.

i. "Paradoxically the greedy loses his property and his power, and the liberal participates in a cycle of endless enrichment." (Waltke)

b. **For he gives of his bread to the poor**: One important way to express our generosity is to give to **the poor** and needy. His generosity is simply sharing, **for he gives of his bread**.

i. **Of his bread**: "He spares it out of his own belly to give to the hungry, as some have here gathered from the words 'his bread,' that which was appointed for his own eating - he voluntarily fasteth from a meal now and then that he may bestow it upon the needy, and he shall not lose his reward." (Trapp)

ii. "This person has a benevolent disposition, keen social conscience, and concern for the poor. The irony is that because he is not the prisoner of his selfish desires, he achieves the highest degree of self-fulfillment." (Ross)

Proverbs 22:10

Cast out the scoffer, and contention will leave;
Yes, strife and reproach will cease.

a. **Cast out the scoffer, and contention will leave**: The **scoffer** who spreads cynical discord causes **contention**. When that **scoffer** is **cast out**, then **contention** also leaves.

b. **Strife and reproach will cease**: The atmosphere of **strife** and shameful insults (**reproach**) stops when the divisive **scoffer** is gone. This reminds us that an atmosphere of **contention**, **strife**, and **reproach** is caused by *people*.

Proverbs 22:11

He who loves purity of heart
And has **grace on his lips,**
The king *will be* **his friend.**

a. **He who loves purity of heart and has grace on his lips**: Inner **purity** often shows itself through **grace**-filled words. These two are marks of godly, wise men and women.

b. **The king will be his friend**: This true godliness and wisdom – both on the inside and in spoken words – will make friends in high places. It will certainly contribute to ongoing fellowship with God, for such a person walks in the light as God is in the light (1 John 1:6-7).

i. **The king will be his friend**: "The greatest men will, or should, desire and highly prize the acquaintance and advice of such persons, rather than of dissemblers and flatterers, wherewith they are most commonly pestered." (Poole)

Proverbs 22:12

The eyes of the LORD preserve knowledge,
But He overthrows the words of the faithless.

a. **The eyes of the LORD preserve knowledge**: God sees, takes note of, and guards those with wisdom and **knowledge**. In this sense, it can be said that His **eyes…preserve knowledge**.

b. **He overthrows the words of the faithless**: For the **faithless** fool, they can expect that God would turn over their **words**. He will not stand with or support their **faithless** words.

i. "God causes their distortions of the truth to be shown for what they are." (Garrett)

Proverbs 22:13

The lazy *man* says, "*There is* a lion outside!
I shall be slain in the streets!"

a. **There is a lion outside**: This is the cry of the **lazy man**. In his imagination, the outside world and the work required to function in it are so frightening that it is best avoided. His excuse is crazy and absurd, but such is the refuge of the **lazy man**.

i. **The lazy man says**: Spurgeon spoke on Proverbs 22:13 and 26:13: "In both texts the slothful man is represented as having something to say, and I think that there are no people that have so much to say as those that have little to do. Where nothing is done much is talked about."

ii. "The sluggard is represented as finding fantastic and preposterous excuses to demonstrate that no idea is too odd or fantastic to him to keep him off welfare. His life and the community is not in danger from his phantom lion in the streets but from his lazy life-style." (Waltke)

iii. "Laziness is a great lion-maker. He who does little dreams much. His imagination could create not only a lion but a whole menagerie of wild beasts; and if some mighty hunter could hunt down all the lions that his imagination has let loose, he would soon distribute herds more of the terrible animals, with wolves and bears and tigers to match." (Spurgeon)

iv. John Trapp pointed out that this imaginary lion is not Satan nor is it the Messiah, Jesus. "Here is no talk of Satan, 'that roaring lion,' that lies couchant in the sluggard's bed with him, and prompts him to these senseless excuses. Nor yet of the 'lion of the tribe of Judah,' who will one day send out summons for sleepers, and tearing the very caul of their hearts in sunder, send them packing to their place in hell."

b. **I shall be slain in the streets**: The **lazy man** exaggerates the dangers and troubles **outside** his door, especially those connected with work.

i. **In the streets**: "Which is added to show the ridiculousness of his excuse; for lions abide in the woods or fields, not in the streets of towns or cities." (Poole)

ii. "But *why* does he say so? Because he is a *slothful* man. Remove his slothfulness, and these imaginary difficulties and dangers will be no more." (Clarke)

iii. The **lazy man** or woman should look to the Lord for victory over their sin. "Your lion is in the way. Shout, then, for a friend to come and help you; and within call there stands One who is a wonderful lion-killer. There is the Son of David." (Spurgeon)

Proverbs 22:14

The mouth of an immoral woman *is* a deep pit;
He who is abhorred by the LORD will fall there.

a. **The mouth of an immoral woman is a deep pit**: The **immoral woman** often sets her seductive trap by the words she speaks. Therefore, her **mouth** is a trap leading to death. Solomon knew something of this danger because he saw his father David fall into the **deep pit** of immorality.

i. **A deep pit**: "Into which it is easy to fall, but hard, if not impossible, to get out of it. It is a rare thing for any person, once entered into the course of whoredom, sincerely to repent of it, and turn from it." (Poole)

ii. "Unlike the sluggard's fantasy of a man-eating lion roaming the city streets, these harlots are very real deadly predators in the streets." (Waltke)

b. **He who is abhorred by the LORD will fall there**: God's wise ones are discerning enough to stay clear of this **deep pit**. But the fool – **he who is abhorred by the LORD** – is likely to **fall there**.

Proverbs 22:15

Foolishness *is* bound up in the heart of a child;
The rod of correction will drive it far from him.

a. **Foolishness is bound up in the heart of a child**: Children are not born as morally neutral beings. There is a moral problem (described here as **foolishness**) that is **bound up in the heart of a child**, evidenced by the fact that our children will naturally sin without be *taught* how to do it. This is our nature inherited from our ancient ancestors, Adam and Eve.

i. "The father must not underestimate the difficulty of his task, for he does battle with an innate recalcitrance and perversity. He must both tear down and build up; to eradicate and implant." (Waltke)

ii. "Note that what is being spoken about is foolishness, not childishness. 'A child is to be punished,' as Mr. Scott wisely observed, 'not for being a child, but for being a wicked child.'" (Bridges)

b. **The rod of correction will drive it far from him**: Physical discipline is one important way that a child can be morally trained. When wisely and properly applied, physical **correction** can help **drive** away a child's inborn **foolishness**.

i. Kidner titled Proverbs 22:15 as *knocking the nonsense out.*

ii. "Discipline will remove a child's bent to folly.... The child is morally immature; the training must suppress folly and develop potential." (Ross)

iii. The Bible gives some examples of men who did *not* follow the wisdom of this proverb. "Eli brought up his sons to bring down his house. David's sons were undone by their father's fondness. A fair hand, we say, makes a foul wound." (Trapp)

Proverbs 22:16

He who oppresses the poor to increase his *riches*,
***And* he who gives to the rich, *will* surely *come* to poverty.**

a. **He who oppresses the poor to increase his riches**: There are always those who prey upon their unfortunate fellow man and will oppress the **poor to increase his riches**.

b. **He who gives to the rich, will surely come to poverty**: The one who **gives to the rich** is like the one who **oppresses the poor** – he has no compassion for those in need. To such, the principle applies: he **will surely come to poverty**. God's blessing will not be on the life and wealth of such a man lacking in compassion.

i. **He who gives to the rich**: "The juxtaposition of one who takes money from the poor, who needs it, with the one who gives to the rich, who does not need it, points up the folly. For example, 'It happens when executives are paid exorbitant sums...and overwork their remaining employees.'" (Waltke)

ii. "Perhaps the verse is simply observing that it is easy to oppress the poor for gain, but it is a waste of money to try to buy a patron." (Ross)

A. Words of the wise.

Proverbs 22:17 begins a new section of the collection. We move from the long section (Proverbs 10:1 through 22:16) containing almost entirely two-phrase wisdom sayings with very little arrangement according to theme or context. Starting here, the structure of the wisdom sayings is often longer and they are more arranged according to some theme.

Most commentators believe this section begins here at 22:17 and ends at 24:22. Proverbs 22:20 uses the phrase, "I have written to you thirty [excellent] things," and it is likely that Solomon patterned this section after the Egyptian wisdom writing Amenemope, finding 30 wisdom sayings in the section. Waltke makes the point that Solomon used some of the structure of Amenemope to arrange this section, but not the content of the ancient Egyptian writing.

1. (17-21) The value of the words of the wise.

Incline your ear and hear the words of the wise,
And apply your heart to my knowledge;
For *it is* a pleasant thing if you keep them within you;
Let them all be fixed upon your lips,
So that your trust may be in the LORD;
I have instructed you today, even you.
Have I not written to you excellent things
Of counsels and knowledge,
That I may make you know the certainty of the words of truth,
That you may answer words of truth
To those who send to you?

> a. **Incline your ear and hear the words of the wise**: Another invitation to receive words of wisdom. Unless one's **heart** and mind are ready to receive wisdom, it does little good to present it. There should be a conscious readying of mind and heart to receive.

> > i. "The ear is the exterior organ that receives the information and the heart is the interior organ that directs the whole body (Proverbs 4:20-27)." (Waltke)

> b. **It is a pleasant thing if you keep them within you**: The value of gaining and keeping wisdom is **pleasant**. Sometimes we feel the way of wisdom is a difficult path to walk, but it is much more **pleasant** than the way of the fool.

> > i. **Keep them within you**: "Hebrew, *in thy belly.* i.e. in thine heart, which implies receiving them in love, and retaining them in mind and memory." (Poole)

ii. **Excellent things**: "The reference to 'thirty' [**excellent**] is significant, for Amenemope also had thirty sayings." (Ross)

c. **So that your trust may be in the LORD**: True wisdom makes us more dependent on God, not less. We grow in our **trust** in **the LORD**, realizing that the pursuit of wisdom begins and continues with a proper view of God.

i. **I have instructed you today**: "Even the most brilliant, moral sayings are powerless without personal application. *Today* refers to each day of the son's life, because he is to have all of them always ready on his tongue." (Waltke)

d. **That I may make you know the certainty of the words of truth**: The pursuit of wisdom makes us more confident in the truth, not less. Certainly, wisdom discovers that *some* things are more complicated and doubtful, but in *general* it sees God and His truth with more clarity and **certainty**.

2. (22-23) Treat the poor fairly

Do not rob the poor because he *is* poor,
Nor oppress the afflicted at the gate;
For the LORD will plead their cause,
And plunder the soul of those who plunder them.

a. **Do not rob the poor because he is poor**: The **poor** among us deserve more protection and compassion. Even if one is **poor** because of their moral failings or foolish behavior, they still should not be taken advantage of and robbed.

i. "If those that relieve not the poor shall be damned, surely they that rob them shall be double damned." (Trapp)

ii. **At the gate**: "Lacking financial resources to protect their legal rights they are a tempting target for the sharp practices and blatant injustices of their rich and powerful neighbors." (Waltke)

b. **For the LORD will plead their cause**: Even if the rich **rob** the poor, they still have a defender. God Himself **will plead their cause** and will **plunder the soul of those who plunder** the poor. Understanding God's concern for and protection of the poor, wisdom leads us to treat them honorably.

i. The poor can't defend themselves with great resources and influence. The rich man's treatment of the poor says a lot about the rich man's character. It shows how he treats those whom culture and the community may say are "beneath" him. This reveals one's heart in many ways.

ii. "Concern for the poor is common in both biblical and pagan wisdom literature. The distinctive Israelite perspective, however, is that Yahweh is viewed as protector of the oppressed." (Garrett)

iii. "Woe therefore to them that oppress them, for they will have *God*, not the *poor*, to deal with." (Clarke)

3. (24-25) Warning of the angry man.

Make no friendship with an angry man,
And with a furious man do not go,
Lest you learn his ways
And set a snare for your soul.

a. **Make no friendship with an angry man**: A person who often can't control their anger displays bad character and can be a dangerous companion. Wisdom chooses friends carefully and should **make no friendship with an angry man**.

i. "Anger is a short madness; it is a leprosy breaking out of a burning, [Leviticus 13:25] and renders a man unfit for civil society." (Trapp)

b. **Lest you learn his ways**: This is one of the important reasons why it is foolish to make a **friendship with an angry man**. His habits will influence yours, and as you become more of an **angry** person you will **set a snare for your soul**. *We are influenced by the habits of our friends*, so choose friends carefully.

i. "From those with whom we associate we acquire habits, and learn *their ways*, imbibe their *spirit*, show their *tempers* and walk in their *steps*. We cannot be too choice of our *company*, for we may soon *learn ways* that will *be a snare to our soul*." (Clarke)

ii. "Being friends of a hot-tempered man is like living in a house that is on fire. How quickly does a young person, living with a proud man, become like him and turn into an overbearing person." (Bridges)

4. (26-27) Stay away from the debts of others.

Do not be one of those who shakes hands in a pledge,
One of those who is surety for debts;
If you have nothing *with which* to pay,
Why should he take away your bed from under you?

a. **Do not be one of those who shakes hands in a pledge**: As mentioned in other proverbs, it is a dangerous thing to become responsible for the debts of other people. Personal debt is to be avoided (Proverbs 22:7), so how much more becoming **surety for debts** of another person.

b. **Why should he take away your bed from under you?** Under the laws and customs regarding the failure to pay debts in the world of the Bible, property could be easily seized and even people made forced servants for the repayment of debts. Don't take on the debts of other people.

i. "The risk is that if someone lacks the means to pay, his creditors may take his bed, i.e., his last possession (cf. our expressions 'the shirt off his back' or 'the kitchen sink')." (Ross)

5. (28) Respect ancient ways and wisdom.

Do not remove the ancient landmark
Which your fathers have set.

a. **Do not remove the ancient landmark:** From the days when Joshua divided the promised land for the people of Israel, there were **landmarks** showing the boundaries of property. It was a great crime and scandal to **remove** these landmarks.

i. **Landmark:** "Private land boundaries were marked out by stone pillars or cairns erected between property to mark legal ownership." (Waltke)

ii. "Do not take the advantage, in ploughing or breaking up a field contiguous to that of thy neighbour, to set the dividing stones *farther* into his *field* that thou mayest *enlarge thy own.* Take not what is not *thy own* in any case. Let all ancient *divisions,* and the *usages* connected with them, be held sacred." (Clarke)

iii. "The boundaries were sacred because God owned the land and had given it to the fathers as their inheritance; to extend one's land at another's expense was a major violation of covenant and oath." (Ross)

iv. **Do not remove:** "Unless ye covet a curse [Deuteronomy 27:17]…. know that property is God's ordinance; [Acts 5:4 Psalms 17:14]." (Trapp)

b. **Which your fathers have set:** We also understand this proverb in a spiritual sense. A **landmark** – a custom, a tradition, or a value – should not be removed lightly. We should never assume that our **fathers** set such landmarks for no reason or bad reason. We should not defend tradition for the sake of tradition, but neither should we destroy tradition just for the sake of destroying it.

i. "Unfortunately, the crime was easy to accomplish and difficult to prove. Probably the boundary stone was moved annually only about an inconspicuous half-inch, which in time could add up to a sizeable land grab." (Waltke)

6. (29) The reward of excellent work.

Do you see a man *who* excels in his work?
He will stand before kings;
He will not stand before unknown *men*.

a. **Do you see a man who excels in his work?** Wisdom pushes us toward excellence. God has given every **man** and woman **work** to do, and they should do that work with excellence as unto God and not only to men (Colossians 3:23).

i. **A man who excels**: "One who is improving his talents all the time and is making the most of his opportunities. He is like Henry Martyn, who was known in his college 'as the man who had not lost an hour.'" (Bridges)

ii. "Anyone who puts his workmanship before his prospects towers above the thrusters and climbers of the adjacent paragraphs." (Kidner)

b. **He will stand before kings**: The excellence of a man or woman's work can give them great standing in the world. More importantly, it gives them standing before the King of Kings, who promises to reward the one who works diligently unto Him (Colossians 3:23-24).

i. "How dear was Daniel to Darius, because, though sick, yet he despatched the king's business! What favourites to our Henry VIII were Wolsey, Cromwell, Cranmer, for like reason! A diligent man shall not sit long in a low place." (Trapp)

ii. "Jesus taught that the one who is trustworthy in the small matters of this world will be entrusted with ten cities in his coming kingdom (Matthew 25:14-30; Luke 19:11-27; cf. John 12:26)." (Waltke)

Proverbs 23 – Words of the Wise

A. Wisdom in the "do not" warnings.

1. (1-3) Do not be deceived at the ruler's table.

When you sit down to eat with a ruler,
Consider carefully what *is* before you;
And put a knife to your throat
If you *are* a man given to appetite.
Do not desire his delicacies,
For they *are* deceptive food.

a. **When you sit down to eat with a ruler**: The idea is of a generous invitation to eat with powerful people at a table loaded with delicious, well-prepared food. This was something like what Daniel and his companions later faced in Daniel 1.

i. "The rich do not give away their favors for free. They want something in return, and it is generally much more than what they have invested. One can lose one's own soul in the exchange." (Garrett)

b. **Consider carefully what is before you**: Don't be overwhelmed and seduced by the atmosphere of power and luxury. If you are vulnerable to these temptations, then beware (**put a knife to your throat**).

i. "The expression 'put a knife to your throat' (v. 2) means 'to curb your appetite' or 'to control yourself' (like 'bite your tongue')." (Ross)

ii. "It is a shame for a saint to be a slave to his palate. Isaac loved venison too, too well." (Trapp)

iii. **Given to appetite**: "Though referring here narrowly to food, can be interpreted broadly with reference to all appetites. Total prohibition is necessary for a person who cannot control his appetites; the disciple can give no place to lust (cf. Matthew 5:29-30)." (Waltke)

c. **They are deceptive food**: The ruler's table may be your ruin. You may be so seduced by the atmosphere of power and luxury that you surrender what should not be surrendered, you promise what should not be promised, and in effect you worship and serve what should not be worshipped and served.

i. "So the warning is not to indulge in his impressive feast—the ruler wants something from you or is observing you." (Ross)

ii. "Let every young man desirous of walking in the ways of wisdom, keep his eye illuminated by the fear of Jehovah, all who put before him their material dainties, lest they rob him of his spiritual excellencies." (Morgan)

2. (4-5) Do not make an idol of wealth.

Do not overwork to be rich;
Because of your own understanding, cease!
Will you set your eyes on that which is not?
For *riches* certainly make themselves wings;
They fly away like an eagle *toward* heaven.

a. **Do not overwork to be rich**: Many times, the Book of Proverbs rebukes and even mocks the lazy man. Yet this does not mean that work and the wealth that comes from work should be made an idol. One may begin to worship work; that one should **cease** and do so **because of your understanding**. You know better.

b. **Riches certainly make themselves wings**: Though working hard is a mark of wisdom, we don't live for the **riches** that may come from that work. Those **riches** are too vulnerable and temporary to be a worthy focus of our life.

i. **Like an eagle toward heaven**: "The addition adds to the metaphor of the swift and powerful eagle that he outstrips all attempts to capture him. Riches will certainly disappear, and once gone, they are gone forever." (Waltke)

3. (6-8) Do not eat at the table of a stingy man.

Do not eat the bread of a miser,
Nor desire his delicacies;
For as he thinks in his heart, so *is* he.
"Eat and drink!" he says to you,
But his heart is not with you.
The morsel you have eaten, you will vomit up,
And waste your pleasant words.

a. **Do not eat the bread of a miser**: The ruler's table was a dangerous place (Proverbs 23:1-3), but so is the table of the **miser**, the one with an evil or ungenerous eye.

i. **The miser**: "The envious or covetous man, who secretly grudgeth thee the meat which he sets before thee, as this phrase is used, Proverbs 28:22; Matthew 20:15; as, on the contrary, a liberal man is said to have a *good eye*, Proverbs 22:9." (Poole)

b. **"Eat and drink!" he says to you**: The stingy man *says* this to his guests, **but his heart is not with you**. He doesn't want you to really enjoy yourself at his table, because he wants to keep more food for himself. You will offend him if you are foolish enough to take him at his word.

i. "That is, of a miserly muckworm, that wisheth thee choked for so doing, even then when he maketh greatest show of hospitality and humanity." (Trapp)

ii. "But there are no such dangers linked to the invitations of the Gospel. The table is ready, and the invitations have been sent out. The only qualification is our own hunger to accept the invitation and eat the heavenly food. Then we discover that our appetite increases with every mouthful we consume." (Bridges)

c. **The morsel you have eaten, you will vomit up**: The table of the miser will be such an unpleasant experience that the food you enjoyed will come back to bother you. The **pleasant words** spoken at his table will seem wasted.

i. "These proverbs contradict the common notion that Proverbs regards the rich as righteous and thus favored by God. To the contrary, wealthy people often are viewed with a marked suspicion, and their company is not always valued." (Garrett)

4. (9) Do not waste your words on the fool.

Do not speak in the hearing of a fool,
For he will despise the wisdom of your words.

a. **Do not speak in the hearing of a fool**: This assumes that the one doing the speaking is not himself a **fool** and is a wise man.

i. **In the hearing**: "…rather, *in the ears* (King James Version); it is direct address, not something overheard." (Kidner)

b. **He will despise the wisdom of your words**: The **fool** will not receive or appreciate your wisdom. It will be as Jesus later described – like throwing pearls before pigs (Matthew 7:6).

5. (10-11) Do not steal from others.

Do not remove the ancient landmark,
Nor enter the fields of the fatherless;
For their Redeemer *is* mighty;
He will plead their cause against you.

a. **Do not remove the ancient landmark**: Literally, the **ancient landmark** was normally a stone marker for a property line. Moving the **landmark** was a way to make your field bigger and to steal from your neighbor. Symbolically, the **ancient landmark** was a tradition or custom from ancestors.

b. **Nor enter the fields of the fatherless**: The field of the orphan needed special care and protection. It was evil to **enter the fields of the fatherless** to take some of the harvest from those who had trouble protecting it.

c. **Their Redeemer is mighty**: The orphan and all who are vulnerable have a special protector, a **Redeemer**. He has vowed to **plead their cause against** all who would come to take what they have.

i. **Redeemer** is the meaningful Hebrew word *goel*. "The Redeemer/ Avenger (*goel*) was usually a powerful relative who would champion the rights of the defenseless; but if there was no human *goel* God would take up their cause (see Genesis 48:16; Exodus 6:6; Job 19:25; Isaiah 41-63)." (Ross)

6. (12) Do not neglect wisdom.

Apply your heart to instruction,
And your ears to words of knowledge.

a. **Apply your heart to instruction**: Wisdom can be given out, but it must be *received* to be of any lasting good. The reception of wisdom isn't passive; it is active, received with a heart that truly applies wisdom and **instruction**.

i. "The verse is in the imperative and suggests that education is vital to one's whole life." (Garrett)

b. **And your ears to words of knowledge**: We mostly receive wisdom by what we hear, especially in the guidance we receive from the wise. Our **ears** must be tuned to receive and apply God's wisdom. When the **heart** and the **ears** work together to receive wisdom, much is gained.

i. "When the heart is graciously opened and enlightened, the ears instantly become attentive." (Bridges)

7. (13-14) Do not fail to correct your children.

Do not withhold correction from a child,
For *if* you beat him with a rod, he will not die.
You shall beat him with a rod,
And deliver his soul from hell.

a. **Do not withhold correction from a child**: The concept here is not that **correction** is imposed on a child, but that it *properly belongs* to a child and to not bring needed **correction** is to **withhold** it.

b. **You shall beat him with a rod**: The figure of the **rod** in Proverbs is sometimes used literally and sometimes figuratively. There is place for both literal, physical correction of a child (such as spanking), and correction through the rod of an alternative punishment or word.

i. "However, the cleansing rod must be applied with the warmth, affection and respect for the youth. Warmth and affection, not steely discipline, characterize the father's lectures (cf. Proverbs 4:1-9). Parents who brutalize their children cannot hide behind the rod-doctrine of *Proverbs*." (Waltke)

ii. "This text does not justify brutalizing children. Parents who find it only too easy to apply the rod, and especially those who lose their tempers when doing so, should consider Ephesians 6:4." (Garrett)

iii. "An intemperate use of this scriptural ordinance brings discredit on its efficacy and sows the seed of much bitter fruit. Children become hardened under an iron rod. Sternness and severity close up their hearts. It is very dangerous to make our children afraid of us." (Bridges)

c. **And deliver his soul from hell**: The word translated **hell** here is actually *sheol*, which first has the idea of *the grave*. Sometimes it is used in the sense of physical death, and other times in the sense of eternal death. Either or both may be in view here.

8. (15-16) The joy of a father imparting wisdom.

My son, if your heart is wise,
My heart will rejoice—indeed, I myself;
Yes, my inmost being will rejoice
When your lips speak right things.

a. **If your heart is wise, my heart will rejoice**: The general context of the Book of Proverbs is of a father teaching wisdom to his children. Here Solomon reflected on the great happiness he would have if his children actually received and lived in this wisdom.

b. **When your lips speak right things**: Wisdom (or the lack of wisdom) is often seen in the words we speak. When the father hears his child's **lips**

speak right things, he has reason to believe that the lessons of wisdom have been learned.

i. **Inmost being**: "Of all human organs, the Old Testament associates the kidneys in particular with a variety of emotions. The range of usage is very wide; the kidneys are looked upon as the seat of emotions from joy to deepest agony." (Kellermann, cited in Waltke)

9. (17-18) Do not envy sinners.

Do not let your heart envy sinners,
But *be zealous* for the fear of the Lord all the day;
For surely there is a hereafter,
And your hope will not be cut off.

a. **Do not let your heart envy sinners**: This is an easy trap to fall into. On this side of eternity and the ultimate judgments of God it may seem that sin is unpunished and righteousness is unrewarded.

i. "Our hearts, instead of envying sinners, should be full of compassion for them, for they have nothing to look forward to but death." (Bridges)

b. **Be zealous for the fear of the Lord all the day**: Instead of being jealous of the wicked, determine to have an eternal perspective rooted in **the fear of the Lord**, an active recognition of the greatness and righteousness of God.

i. In a sermon on this verse, Charles Spurgeon gave a wonderful definition of **the fear of the Lord**: "The fear of the Lord is a brief description for true religion. It is an inward condition, betokening hearty submission to our heavenly Father. It consists very much in a holy reverence of God, and a sacred awe of him. This is accompanied by a child-like trust in him, which leads to loving obedience, tender submission, and lowly adoration."

ii. **All the day**: "Men must wake with God, walk with him, and lie down with him, be in continual communion with him and conformity unto him. This is to be in heaven beforehand." (Trapp)

c. **For surely there is a hereafter**: If this life was all there would be, then we would have much more reason to **envy sinners**. Yet, as the conclusion of the Book of Ecclesiastes demonstrates, **surely there is a hereafter**, and therefore wisdom means that we should live in the **fear of the Lord**.

B. A father warns his child about wine and women.

1. (19-21) The danger of drinking companions.

Hear, my son, and be wise;
And guide your heart in the way.

Do not mix with winebibbers,
Or with gluttonous eaters of meat;
For the drunkard and the glutton will come to poverty,
And drowsiness will clothe *a man* with rags.

a. **Hear, my son, and be wise**: This repeats the basic context of Proverbs, that it is the wise instruction and guidance of a father to his children.

i. **Hear**: "I have read that in the reign of Queen Elizabeth there was a law made that everybody should go to his parish church; but many sincere Romanists loathed to go and hear Protestant doctrine. Through fear of persecution, they attended the parish church; but they took care to fill their ears with wool, so that they should not hear what their priests condemned. It is wretched work preaching to a congregation whose ears are stopped with prejudices." (Spurgeon)

b. **Do not mix with winebibbers, or with gluttonous eaters of meat**: The wise counsel to a **son** or daughter is that they should not mix with those who overindulge in alcohol or food. The drunk and the glutton have a bad future (**poverty** and **rags**), and the wise man or woman will not share it with them.

i. "The 'drunkard' and the 'glutton' represent the epitome of the lack of discipline." (Ross)

ii. **Will come to poverty**: "Nay, to eternal misery in hell; [1 Corinthians 6:10] but few men fear that; beggary they hold worse than any hell.... But poverty to such is but a prelude to a worse matter." (Trapp)

iii. **Drowsiness**: "The self-indulgent are reduced to destitution (21a) due to the drowsiness that accompanies addiction to wine and over-eating (21b). Their full stomachs empty their minds." (Waltke)

2. (22) An exhortation to listen to parents.

Listen to your father who begot you,
And do not despise your mother when she is old.

a. **Listen to your father who begot you**: Wisdom can never be learned until the attention is won. There must be a deliberate effort to **listen**.

b. **Do not despise your mother when she is old**: This affirms the principle of *honor your father and mother* in Exodus 20:12 (and later in Ephesians 6:2). When parents become **old**, they should receive special attention and care.

3. (23) The attitude to have towards wisdom.

Buy the truth, and do not sell *it,*
Also wisdom and instruction and understanding.

a. **Buy the truth, and do not sell it**: We should have the mentality that we are willing to gain truth and wisdom and gain it at a cost instead of wanting to forsake it for profit.

> i. **Buy the truth**: "Purchase it upon any terms, spare no pains nor cost to get it." (Poole) "Buy the truth; that is, be willing at all risks to hold to the truth. Buy it as the martyrs did when they gave their bodies to be burned for it. Buy it as many have done when they have gone to prison for it." (Spurgeon)

> ii. **Do not sell it**: "Sell it not; sell it not; it cost Christ too dear. Sell it not; you made a good bargain when you bought it. Sell it not. Sell it not; it has not disappointed you; it has satisfied you, and made you blessed Sell it not; you want it. Sell it not, you will want it. The hour of death is coming on, and the day of judgment is close upon its heels. Sell it not; you cannot buy its like again; you can never find a better." (Spurgeon)

> iii. "The Savior says that we should buy from him (Revelation 3:18). This settles the matter. If we do not really want the goods, we will not pay much attention to the proverb. For we only buy what we eagerly desire." (Bridges)

b. **Also wisdom and instruction and understanding**: Proverbs often uses these terms to mean the same thing. **Truth**, **instruction**, and **understanding** in this context are all ways of describing **wisdom**.

4. (24-25) Wise children bring joy to their parents.

The father of the righteous will greatly rejoice,
And he who begets a wise *child* will delight in him.
Let your father and your mother be glad,
And let her who bore you rejoice.

a. **The father of the righteous will greatly rejoice**: It is a great blessing for parents to have **righteous** and wise children. That parent **will delight in him**.

b. **Let your father and your mother be glad**: One reason for a son or daughter to pursue and gain wisdom is that it will make one's parents **glad**. It will be an appropriate blessing and reward those who gave the son or daughter life and an upbringing.

5. (26-28) The danger of the immoral woman.

My son, give me your heart,
And let your eyes observe my ways.
For a harlot *is* a deep pit,

And a seductress *is* a narrow well.
She also lies in wait as *for* a victim,
And increases the unfaithful among men.

a. **Give me your heart**: Solomon understood that wisdom must be received with the **heart**. It can't only be a matter of facts or principles learned in the mind or even memorized. Wisdom must be received into a willing, given, **heart**.

b. **Let your eyes observe my ways**: At least at the time of writing this, Solomon could point to his *own life* as an example of wisdom when it came to the dangers of an immoral woman. He knew teaching is most effective when it comes from a life that knows and lives wisdom.

i. **Observe my ways**: "The Hebrew here hath it, Let thine eyes run through my ways. Get a full prospect of them, and diligently peruse them. Fix and feed thine eyes upon the best objects, and restrain them from gazing upon forbidden beauties, lest they prove to be windows of wickedness, and loopholes of lust." (Trapp)

c. **A harlot is a deep pit**: The **pit** in mind is the trap dug and concealed to capture a large animal. As an animal might fall into such a **deep pit**, so the danger of the **harlot** is real and concealed.

i. "This smooth talking beauty (see 5:1-6; 6:25; 7:10-21) engages in sexual intercourse for lust and/or money with no intention and/or capability of a binding and enduring relationship. Having trapped her victim, he cannot escape the pit because it is deep." (Waltke)

ii. "Samson broke the bonds of his enemies, but he could not break the bonds of his own lusts. He choked the lion, but he could not choke his own wanton love" (Ambrose, cited in Bridges).

d. **A seductress is a narrow well**: A well is a source of satisfying water, and the sexual relationship of a husband and wife is described as good water from a well (Proverbs 5:15). Here the idea is of a well that doesn't satisfy. The **seductress** offers great satisfaction but ultimately doesn't deliver, lacking the true intimacy and trust that build a satisfying sexual experience.

i. **Narrow well**: "Connotes that this sexual partner frustrates him. The fornicator came hoping to quench his sexual appetite, but…he finds her incapable of the intimacy necessary to satisfy that thirst." (Waltke)

e. **Increases the unfaithful among men**: This is not to lay all the blame upon the harlot or immoral woman, but her trap captures many. If there were fewer harlots and immoral women there would be fewer **unfaithful among men**.

i. "Unchastity may be romanticized, but the hard facts are faithfully given here: captivity (27: no unaided escape), ruthlessness (28a), social disruption (28b)." (Kidner)

ii. "She is the cause of innumerable sins against God, and against the marriage-bed, against the soul and body too, and by her wicked example and arts involveth many persons in the guilt of her sins." (Poole)

6. (29-35) The misery of abusing alcohol.

Who has woe?
Who has sorrow?
Who has contentions?
Who has complaints?
Who has wounds without cause?
Who has redness of eyes?
Those who linger long at the wine,
Those who go in search of mixed wine.
Do not look on the wine when it is red,
When it sparkles in the cup,
***When* it swirls around smoothly;**
At the last it bites like a serpent,
And stings like a viper.
Your eyes will see strange things,
And your heart will utter perverse things.
Yes, you will be like one who lies down in the midst of the sea,
Or like one who lies at the top of the mast, *saying:*
"They have struck me, *but* I was not hurt;
They have beaten me, but I did not feel *it*.
When shall I awake, that I may seek another *drink?*"

a. **Who has woe? Who has sorrow?** Solomon reminded us of many of the ill effects of alcohol and intoxicating drugs. They bring **woe** and **sorrow**. They bring **contentions** and **complaints**. They bring **wounds** and **redness of eyes**. Unrestrained, immoderate use of alcohol and abuse of drugs will bring these sorrows to one's life, and countless tragedies prove it.

i. "This poem is a small masterpiece; it is surely the most effective combination lampoon and lament over the sorry state of the drunkard." (Garrett)

b. **Those who linger long at the wine**: The picture is of those who abuse alcohol or other intoxicants, and who are always looking for a stronger drink (**go in search of mixed wine**).

i. "'Lingering over' alcohol describes those who derive comfort and security in knowing that a glass of wine is at hand, ready to deaden the senses." (Garrett)

c. **It sparkles in the cup**: Wine can be pleasing on many levels – in how it looks, smells, tastes, and makes one feel. These pleasing aspects of intoxicants never justify their unrestrained or immoderate use.

i. **When it swirls around smoothly**: "When it sparkleth and frisketh, and seems to smile upon a man." (Poole)

d. **At the last it bites like a serpent**: Eventually, the abuse of alcohol or drugs will bite and sting. As Solomon described, the **eyes will see strange things, and your heart will utter perverse things**.

i. Like several commentators, Waltke saw a deliberate purpose in setting the warning against the seductive woman (Proverbs 23:26-28) next to this warning against intoxication. "Both the vixen and wine are hidden and deadly traps. The preceding saying unmasks the unchaste wife as a triumphant huntress and this one uncovers wine as a poisonous snake."

e. **You will be like one who lies down in the midst of the sea**: The person who abuses alcohol or drugs will drown in their sin and misery. They will be like a person on a sinking ship who denies their danger. Living in denial, unable or unwilling to see their danger (**they have struck me, but I was not hurt**), their only thought is when they "**may seek another drink**."

i. "In a ship in the midst of the sea. This phrase notes the temper and condition of the drunkard, the giddiness of his brain, the unquietness of his mind, and especially his extreme danger joined with great security." (Poole)

ii. **One who lies at the top of the mast**: "Escalates his giddiness and danger by comparing him to one sleeping in the crow's nest on top of the rigging where the ship's rocking is greatest." (Waltke)

iii. "The passage describes more than a night's drinking and a morning's hangover. It describes the increasingly degenerative effects, physical and mental, of the habitual drinker and the alcoholic" (Aitken, cited in Waltke)

iv. "Wine (and in modern society, illicit drugs) brings physical pain and debilitation, exhausts one's resources, takes away mental acuity, and yet leaves one craving for more of the same." (Garrett)

v. Yet there is hope in Jesus for the drunkard and drug addict. "Is anything too hard for the Lord? May his name be praised for a full deliverance from the enslavement to sin—to all sins and to every individual sin—and even from the chains of this giant sin. The drunkard becomes sober, the unclean holy, the glutton temperate. The love of Christ overpowers the love of sin." (Bridges)

Proverbs 24 – Wisdom, Love, and Respect

A. The remaining of the 30 words of the wise.

1. (1-2) Don't envy or associate with evil men.

Do not be envious of evil men,
Nor desire to be with them;
For their heart devises violence,
And their lips talk of troublemaking.

a. **Do not be envious of evil men**: This is a common and sometimes difficult temptation for the righteous man or woman. There are times when **evil men** seem to prosper and we may become **envious** of them, and then **desire to be with them**.

i. Bridges on those **envious of evil men**: "This evil spirit, if it does not bring the scandal of open sin, curses our blessings, withers our virtues, destroys our peace, clouds our confidence, and stains our Christian profession."

b. **For their heart devises violence**: The kind of **evil** this proverb has in mind is the kind associated with **violence** and **troublemaking**. The seemingly quick and easy money and status gained through **violence** and **troublemaking** is a temptation to be resisted.

i. "The antidote to envy is the long view: the glory (Proverbs 23:18) or darkness (Proverbs 24:20) to come." (Kidner)

2. (3-4) Wisdom for the home.

Through wisdom a house is built,
And by understanding it is established;
By knowledge the rooms are filled
With all precious and pleasant riches.

a. **Through wisdom a house is built**: We think of the actual material building of a **house**, and how **wisdom**, proper engineering and construction are necessary. The same is true of the moral and spiritual values of a home. Those moral and spiritual values must be **built** through **wisdom** and **established** through **understanding**.

> i. The house of the wicked is not built on wisdom. "It is only the snow-palace built in the winter, and melting away under the power of the summer's sun." (Geier, cited in Bridges)

b. **By knowledge the rooms are filled with all precious and pleasant riches**: The blessing of building a home with God's **wisdom**, God's **understanding**, and God's **knowledge** will bring **precious and pleasant riches** in the spiritual sense and often in the material sense. God's blessing is on the home that seeks and honors His wisdom.

> i. "The precious jewels that fill the house are a harmonious, loving family and a sense of security and stability." (Garrett)

3. (5-6) The strength of wisdom.

A wise man *is* strong,
Yes, a man of knowledge increases strength;
For by wise counsel you will wage your own war,
And in a multitude of counselors *there is* safety.

a. **A wise man is strong**: Solomon understood the strength of wisdom, and how a **man of knowledge increases strength**. Folly makes a person weak and vulnerable.

> i. **A wise man is strong**: "Is courageous and resolute, and able by wisdom to do greater things than others can accomplish by their own strength." (Poole)

b. **By wise counsel you will wage your own war**: The strength of wisdom isn't solitary; it understands and relies upon the wisdom of others. It knows how to use the **wise counsel** of others and the **safety** of a **multitude of counselors**.

4. (7-9) The sin of folly.

Wisdom *is* too lofty for a fool;
He does not open his mouth in the gate.
He who plots to do evil
Will be called a schemer.
The devising of foolishness *is* sin,
And the scoffer *is* an abomination to men.

a. **Wisdom is too lofty for a fool**: The **fool** looks at wisdom and thinks it is above him or her in the sense of being **too lofty**. They think it is overly smart and superior and tend to glory in the lowness of their folly.

i. **Too lofty for a fool**: "In his opinion; he judgeth it too hard for him, he despairs of attaining it, he pretends the impossibility of it, because he will not put himself to the charge or trouble of getting it." (Poole)

ii. "The simple and diligent prove that the treasure is not really out of reach; but it is too high for a fool. His groveling mind can never rise to so lofty a matter. He has no understanding of it, no heart to desire it, no energy to hold it." (Bridges)

b. **He does not open his mouth in the gate**: Often, the fool will be denied influence and a platform of leadership. At the place where the elders gather and decisions are made (**the gate**), the fool will not **open his mouth**.

i. **Does not open his mouth in the gate**: "1. He can say nothing for himself when he is accused before the magistrate, for which he gives frequent occasion. Or, 2. He knows not how to speak acceptably and profitably in the public assembly among wise men." (Poole)

ii. "Noting the incompetence of fools to speak in the gate where public policy is formulated. This saying inferentially commends becoming competently wise by warning against being an incompetent fool." (Waltke)

c. **He who plots to do evil will be called a schemer**: The evil man who plots his **evil** will be recognized for the **schemer** he is – even though, **the devising of foolishness is sin**, and that evil person will be regarded as **an abomination to men**.

i. **Called a schemer**: "Hebrew, *a master of mischief*. The sense is, Though he cover his wicked devices with fair pretences, and would be better esteemed, yet he shall be noted and branded with that infamy which is due to him." (Poole)

ii. "Here the description 'schemer' portrays him as a cold, calculating, active person: 'the fool is capable of intense mental activity but it adds up to sin'…. This type of person flouts all morality, and sooner or later the public will have had enough of him." (Ross)

iii. **The scoffer is an abomination**: "The basest can mock, as the abjects did David, [Psalms 35:15] and Tobiah the servant did Nehemiah. [Nehemiah 2:19] Scorners are the most base spirits. The Septuagint call them pests, [Psalms 1:1] incorrigible, [Proverbs 21:11] proud persons, [Proverbs 3:34] naught, [Proverbs 9:12]." (Trapp)

5. (10) The measure of strength.

If you faint in the day of adversity,
Your strength *is* small.

a. **If you faint in the day of adversity**: The **day of adversity** comes to everyone. The godliest and the most evil will experience their own **adversity**, and that is a test to see whether or not they will **faint**.

> i. "In times of trial we should endeavour to be doubly courageous; when a man loses his courage, his strength avails him nothing." (Clarke)

b. **Your strength is small**: The **day of adversity** did not *make* your strength **small**; it *revealed* your **strength** to be **small**. There is a sense in which we should welcome **the day of adversity** as a revelation of our strength or weakness.

> i. Bridges had an encouraging word for the Christian who feels that their **strength is small**: "Commit yourself daily to him, for his supply of grace is sufficient for you. So go forward, weak and strong at the same time—weak in order to be strong, strong in your weakness."

6. (11-12) Help those on their way to destruction.

Deliver *those who* are drawn toward death,
And hold back *those* stumbling to the slaughter.
If you say, "Surely we did not know this,"
Does not He who weighs the hearts consider *it*?
He who keeps your soul, does He *not* know *it*?
And will He *not* render to *each* man according to his deeds?

a. **Deliver those who are drawn toward death**: The idea is of those who are on their way towards destruction, **those stumbling to the slaughter**. If we have the opportunity, we should **deliver** them, to **hold back** their progress to **slaughter**.

> i. **Those who are drawn toward death**: "These could be literal prisoners who have been (presumably wrongfully) condemned to die. The reader is to take extraordinary measures to secure their release (a dramatic modern example would be the extermination of the Jews in Europe during the Second World War). Alternatively, these are people stumbling toward death because of their moral and spiritual blindness." (Garrett)

> ii. The story of Esther is one wonderful example of someone who did **deliver those who are drawn towards death**. Esther's courage saved her people, even when it would have been easy for her to ignore her duty.

b. **Surely we did not know this**: We shouldn't be indifferent towards those headed **toward death**. Since they often reject God's wisdom and are hostile, it is easy to give up on them or ignore them. Yet God, **He who weighs the hearts**, does know and consider this.

i. "We cannot ignore the evil around us, and say we are not responsible for it. We cannot shut our eyes and avert our faces from wrongdoing, and tyranny, and oppression." (Meyer)

c. **Will He not render to each man according to his deeds?** God will make the fool to answer for his folly, but He will also cause the indifferent one to answer for their lack of care. God will **render to each man according to his deeds**.

i. **Render to each man according to his deeds**: "God will certainly deal with thee as thou hast dealt with him, either rewarding thy performance of this duty, or punishing thy neglect of it." (Poole)

ii. "The omniscient and omnipotent Sovereign will act justly, unlike the passive coward. If the son turns a blind eye to helping victims and does nothing to help them, the Protector of Life will turn a blind eye to him in his crisis. Count on it!" (Waltke)

7. (13-14) The sweetness of wisdom.

My son, eat honey because *it is* good,
And the honeycomb *which is* sweet to your taste;
So *shall* the knowledge of wisdom *be* to your soul;
If you have found *it*, there is a prospect,
And your hope will not be cut off.

a. **My son, eat honey because it is good**: Eating **honey** is rewarded by the sweetness of the taste. It is easy to understand the reward of **the honeycomb**.

i. "The proverb draws on the image of honey; its health-giving properties make a good analogy to wisdom." (Ross)

ii. "Right behavior is not recommended solely on the grounds of austere morality but also because it is the best route to sheer pleasure and the fulfillment of dreams." (Garrett)

b. **So shall the knowledge of wisdom be to your soul**: The gaining of **wisdom** rewards the life the way the sweetness of taste is the reward of honey. We should learn to discern and appreciate the sweetness of wisdom. Once we appreciate the reward of wisdom, our **hope will not be cut off**.

i. **If you have found it**: "Whereby he implies that there is indeed some difficulty and trouble in the pursuit of wisdom, but that it is abundantly compensated with the sweetness and advantage of it when a man arrives at it." (Poole)

8. (15-16) The resilience of the righteous.

Do not lie in wait, O wicked *man,* **against the dwelling of the righteous;**
Do not plunder his resting place;
For a righteous *man* **may fall seven times**
And rise again,
But the wicked shall fall by calamity.

a. **Do not plunder his resting place**: This proverb presents its wisdom in the form of a command to the **wicked man**, telling him to not rob or **plunder** the home of **the righteous** man.

b. **For a righteous man may fall seven times, and rise again**: The reason why the **wicked man** should not rob the righteous is that in the end, the **righteous man** will not be defeated. Even when he **may fall** – even **seven times**! – he shall **rise again**.

i. Many commentators insist that the **fall** that a **righteous man** may experience here is *trouble*, not *sin*. There is no adequate reason why it cannot include *both* ideas.

ii. "Though God permit the hand of *violence* sometimes to spoil his *tent, temptations* to assail his *mind,* and *afflictions* to press down his *body*, he constantly emerges; and every time he passes through the furnace, he comes out *brighter* and more refined." (Clarke)

c. **And rise again**: This should not only give warning to the **wicked** but also assurance to the **righteous**. The **righteous** can be *confident of this very thing, that He who has begun a good work in you will complete it until the day of Jesus Christ* (Philippians 1:6). They can use that confidence to strengthen their resolve to never give up, even though they **may fall seven times**.

i. "The real power to stand up against life, to profit by its buffetings, to make capital out of its disadvantages, to collect tribute from its tribulations, is that of the righteousness of conduct which results from walking in the ways of wisdom, by yielding to the inspiration and authority of the fear of Jehovah." (Morgan)

d. **But the wicked shall fall by calamity**: The wicked have a different destiny than the righteous. God will protect and preserve His righteous ones, but the **wicked shall fall** and stay fallen.

i. "Conversely, the wicked will not survive—without God they have no power to rise from misfortune. The point then is that ultimately the righteous will triumph and those who oppose them will stumble over their evil." (Ross)

9. (17-18) Don't rejoice in the tragic destiny of the wicked.

Do not rejoice when your enemy falls,
And do not let your heart be glad when he stumbles;
Lest the LORD see *it*, and it displease Him,
And He turn away His wrath from him.

a. **Do not rejoice when your enemy falls**: Knowing this, we should not **rejoice** when one falls. It should not make our **heart be glad**. David did not rejoice when Saul died in battle (2 Samuel 1:11-12).

i. "Caesar wept when Pompey's head was presented to him, and said, *Victoriam volui, non vindictam* [something like, 'I wanted victory, not revenge']." (Trapp)

b. **Lest the LORD see it, and it displease Him**: If God sees our rejoicing over the fall of the wicked, He may **turn away His wrath from** the wicked man just to rebuke our proud, unloving heart against the wicked man.

i. "So if we want God to continue his anger on the wicked, we better not gloat." (Ross)

10. (19-20) Don't let the wicked make you worry.

Do not fret because of evildoers,
Nor be envious of the wicked;
For there will be no prospect for the evil *man;*
The lamp of the wicked will be put out.

a. **Do not fret because of evildoers**: Proverbs 24:1 told us to not be *envious of evil men*; here we are told to also not *worry* (**fret**) because of them, as well as to not to **be envious of the wicked**.

i. "The translation 'Do not fret' is too mild. 'Do not get yourself infuriated over evildoers' is more accurate. Those who love the truth are naturally enraged by the effrontery of those who promote or practice godless behavior." (Garrett)

b. **The lamp of the wicked will be put out**: This speaks of death waiting for the **evil man** both in this life and the next. Any good or pleasure they experience in this life is the best they will ever have or experience. The wicked man has **no prospect** for the future.

i. **The lamp of the wicked will be put out**: "Keeping the extinction of their lamp in view will extinguish burning envy." (Waltke)

ii. "Sometimes people are bold enough to snuff out their own candle. 'I give,' said the godless Hobbes, 'my body to the dust, and my soul to the Great Perhaps. I am going to take a leap in the dark.' Alas, was it not a leap into darkness forever?" (Bridges)

iii. "Some have thought that this text intimates the *annihilation* of sinners; but it refers not to *being*, but to the *state* or *condition* of that being. The wicked shall *be*; but they shall not *be* HAPPY." (Clarke)

11. (21-22) Respect for God and king.

My son, fear the LORD and the king;
Do not associate with those given to change;
For their calamity will rise suddenly,
And who knows the ruin those two can bring?

a. **Fear the LORD and the king**: Wisdom tells us to **fear the LORD**, but it is also wisdom to **fear...the king**. Earthly rulers deserve our respect and honor (Romans 13:1-7).

i. "He puts God before the king, because God is to be served in the first place, and our obedience is to be giver, to kings only in subordination to God, and not in those things which are contrary to the will and command of God, as is manifest both from plain Scripture, as Acts 5:29, and from the judgment and practice of wise and sober heathens." (Poole)

b. **Do not associate with those given to change**: Those who want to overthrow or **change** the present system must take great care. The revolutionary often finds that **their calamity will rise suddenly**, and they can bring great **ruin** in their revolution.

i. "People should fear both God and the government, for both punish rebels." (Ross)

ii. **Those given to change**: "Such were Korah and his complices; Absalom; Sheba; the ten tribes that cried, *Alleys iugum,* Ease our yoke; and before them, those in Samuel's time that cried, 'Nay, but we will have a king.'" (Trapp)

B. Further sayings of the wise.

1. (23-25) The importance of true justice.

These *things* also *belong* to the wise:
***It is* not good to show partiality in judgment.**
He who says to the wicked, "You *are* righteous,"
Him the people will curse;
Nations will abhor him.
But those who rebuke *the wicked* will have delight,
And a good blessing will come upon them.

a. **These things also belong to the wise**: The series of 30 words of the wise ended at Proverbs 24:22. Here, until the end of Proverbs 24, is a set of additional sayings of **the wise**.

b. **It is not good to show partiality in judgment**: Whether it is in the formal court of law or in daily interactions, we should never make **judgment** simply on the basis of **partiality**. Those like us can be wrong, and those different from us can be right.

i. **To show partiality in judgment**: "Hebrew, To know faces; to regard not so much the matter as the man; to hear persons speak, and not causes; to judge not according to truth and equity, but according to opinion and appearance - to fear or favour." (Trapp)

c. **You are righteous**: This is what should *not* be said **to the wicked**. In a wise, moral society **the people will curse** someone with such confused moral judgment, and the **nations will abhor him**.

i. It is a mark of the folly of our present age that many monstrous examples of evil or wickedness today are told, **"You are righteous."** This proverb describes the working of a culture wiser than our present culture.

d. **Those who rebuke the wicked will have delight**: Evil should be addressed and rebuked. We should not romanticize or excuse **the wicked**.

2. (26) The beauty of a right response.

He who gives a right answer kisses the lips.

a. **He who gives a right answer**: The proper response to a question or a difficult problem is always welcome to the wise. We think of the many occasions when Jesus Christ was presented with difficult questions yet always gave **a right answer**.

i. "Note the paradox, that a proper forthrightness, costly though it may seem, wins gratitude, and has its special charm." (Kidner)

b. **Kisses the lips**: The **right answer** comes from the lips, just like a friendly and welcoming kiss.

i. "Shall treat him with affection and respect." (Clarke)

ii. "The symbol of specifically kissing on the lips is mentioned only here in the Bible. Herodotus (*History* 1.134) shows that among the Persians this was a sign of true friendship. The metaphor signifies that friendship is characterized by truth." (Ross)

3. (27) Order your work wisely.

Prepare your outside work,
Make it fit for yourself in the field;
And afterward build your house.

a. **Prepare your outside work**: The idea is that before a house is built, proper preparations must be made. The field and the ground must be readied. Wisdom tells us that work should be done with proper planning and in the proper order.

i. **Outside work**: "This would include plowing the land, planting gardens and orchards, so that it produces its fruit." (Waltke)

ii. "Do nothing without a *plan*. In *winter* prepare seed, implements, tackle, gears, etc., for *seed-time and harvest*." (Clarke)

b. **Afterward build your house**: Some want to skip right away to the building without preparing **the field**. This foolishness will not be blessed. Do the preparation work first, and then **afterward build your house**.

i. "It emphasizes the practical rule of producing before consuming, a rule the slothful do not accept." (Garrett)

ii. "Preparations for Solomon's magnificent temple were made before his house was built. The spiritual house is similarly made of materials that have been prepared and fitted and so grow into a holy temple in the Lord (Ephesians 2:21-22)." (Bridges)

iii. "As, in a rural economy, well-worked fields justify and nourish the farmhouse, so a well-ordered life (in things material and immaterial) should be established before marriage." (Kidner)

4. (28-29) The importance of speaking the truth about others.

Do not be a witness against your neighbor without cause,
For would you deceive with your lips?
Do not say, "I will do to him just as he has done to me;
I will render to the man according to his work."

a. **Do not be a witness against your neighbor without cause**: We should only speak **against** someone if there is good and righteous **cause** to do so. We often speak ill of others to entertain others, and ourselves – this is sin.

i. "Profit is the bait to the thief, lust to the adulterer, revenge to the murderer. But it is difficult to say what advantage the witness gains from testifying against his neighbor. The allurement of this sin is the same as Satan himself feels—that is, the love of sin for its own sake." (Bridges)

b. **Would you deceive with your lips?** When we speak against others **without cause**, we usually exaggerate or color the truth, making it a deception.

c. **I will do to him just as he has done to me**: This is what wisdom and grace tell us *not* to say. We should not return evil for evil (1 Thessalonians 5:15). Just because someone has spoken evil or lies against us does not mean that we should speak evil and lies against them.

i. "According to the Bible, an injured party must love his neighbor (Leviticus 19:18) and commit the injustice to the sublime God and his elect magistrate to adjudicate." (Waltke)

ii. "Nothing is more natural than revenge of wrongs, and the world approves it as right temper, true touch, as to put up wrongs is held cowardice and unmanliness. But we have not so learned Christ." (Trapp)

5. (30-34) The tragedy of the lazy man.

I went by the field of the lazy *man,*
And by the vineyard of the man devoid of understanding;
And there it was, all overgrown with thorns;
Its surface was covered with nettles;
Its stone wall was broken down.
When I saw *it,* I considered *it* well;
I looked on *it and* received instruction:
A little sleep, a little slumber,
A little folding of the hands to rest;
So shall your poverty come *like* a prowler,
And your need like an armed man.

a. **There it was, all overgrown with thorns**: This is what the wise man saw when he looked at **the field** or **the vineyard** of the **lazy man**. The lazy man did not plant the **thorns** or **nettles**, and he did not deliberately break down the **stone wall**. Yet his laziness made these things happen just as much as if he had deliberately done them.

i. "Isaiah 28:24-29 describes how careful, industrious field-work looks." (Waltke)

b. **When I saw it, I considered it well**: The wise man learned from the tragedy of the lazy man. He didn't have to suffer the same things the lazy man did to learn the lesson. This is one of the marks of wisdom.

i. "The anecdote invites the reader to recall similar observations of homes in disrepair and to draw the same conclusions even while participating in the poet's disgust over the shameful condition of the lackadaisical man's home." (Garrett)

c. **A little sleep, a little slumber**: This is how the lazy man rationalizes his neglect of duty. "A **little sleep** causes no harm; surely we all need a **little slumber**." The problem isn't the **sleep** of the lazy man; it is his neglect of duty.

> i. "Rest assured of that; the best will become the worse if we neglect it. Neglect is all that is needed to produce evil. If you want to know the way of salvation I must take some pains to tell you; but if you want to know the way to be lost, my reply is easy; for it is only a matter of negligence." (Spurgeon)

d. **So shall your poverty come like a prowler**: This is the destiny of the **lazy man** or woman. Because of their sinful neglect, **poverty** will come upon them as suddenly, as strongly, and as unwelcome as **an armed man**. In this case, the lazy man thinks himself innocent because he did not deliberately, actively sow the thorns or break the wall, but his neglect of duty did them – and he is without excuse.

> i. "But let us look at the spiritual sluggard. If a neglected field is a melancholy sight, what is a neglected soul! Such a soul, when it is left to its own barrenness, instead of being sown with the seeds of grace becomes overgrown with thorns and nettles." (Bridges)

Proverbs 25 – Hezekiah's Collection of Solomon's Proverbs

A. Wisdom before kings and judges.

1. (1) Hezekiah's collection of Solomon's proverbs.

These also *are* proverbs of Solomon which the men of Hezekiah king of Judah copied:

a. **These are the proverbs of Solomon**: This collection of proverbs is from 25:1 through 29:27, making up five chapters of the book of Proverbs. These also were written by **Solomon** yet collected under the supervision of **Hezekiah king of Judah** – some 270 years after Solomon's death.

i. 1 Kings 4:32 tells us that Solomon *spoke three thousand proverbs.* Even with Hezekiah's addition, not all of them are contained in the Book of Proverbs.

b. **Which the men of Hezekiah king of Judah copied**: King **Hezekiah** of **Judah** reigned over a time of national spiritual revival. He added these chapters to the previous collection of proverbs, having found these yet-to-be-published **proverbs of Solomon**.

i. **The men of Hezekiah**: "Certain persons appointed by Hezekiah for that work, whether prophets, as Isaiah, Hosea, or Micah, who lived in his days, or some others, it is neither evident nor material." (Poole)

2. (2-5) The wisdom of kings.

It is **the glory of God to conceal a matter,**
But the glory of kings *is* to search out a matter.
As **the heavens for height and the earth for depth,**
So the heart of kings *is* unsearchable.
Take away the dross from silver,
And it will go to the silversmith *for* jewelry.

Take away the wicked from before the king,
And his throne will be established in righteousness.

a. **It is the glory of God to conceal a matter**: There are many mysteries in the universe, both material and spiritual mysteries. There are many things God has concealed, and this is one expression of His **glory**. It is one of God's ways to say, "You are amazed by what you see; yet what you don't see, what I have concealed, is even greater."

i. "Those unsearchable secrets of his - such as are the union of the three persons into one nature, and of two natures into one person, his wonderful decrees, and the no less wonderful execution thereof, etc. – these make exceeding much to the glory of his infinite wisdom and surpassing greatness." (Trapp)

ii. "I know not, however, that there are not matters in the Book of God that will not be fully opened till mortality is swallowed up of life. For here we see through a glass darkly; but *there*, face to face: *here* we know in part; but *there* we shall know as we also are known." (Clarke)

b. **The glory of kings is to search out a matter**: It is the **glory** of great men (**kings**) to **search out** what God has concealed. This speaks to our pursuit of God's mysteries in the spiritual world, but perhaps even more so to God's mysteries in the material world. When men and women seek out scientific knowledge, trying to understand the mystery and brilliance of what God has concealed in His creation, they express an aspect of the **glory** of humanity, even **the glory of kings**. Therefore, we say to the scientist, *search on, and do so with all your strength.*

i. In all their searching, the scientist should still keep this humble remembrance: **It is the glory of God to conceal a matter**. "What I see amazes me, but God has concealed even greater treasures of knowledge and wisdom in His creation (Romans 1:19-20). I must not arrogantly think that I can figure it all out." As G. Campbell Morgan wrote, "That is the principle of all the triumphs of scientific investigations; and it is the deepest secret of all advance in spiritual strength."

ii. "It is suggestive that those scribes put this Proverb first…had not all this resulted from the fact that they had been under the rule of a king whose supreme glory had been that of searching out the secrets of wisdom in the fear of Jehovah?" (Morgan)

iii. "Verse 2 appears to be an intentional tribute to Solomon and Hezekiah as scholar-kings. This proverb comes from a time when academic inquiry and governmental power were closely linked; in the modern world they are more separated." (Garrett)

c. **So the heart of kings is unsearchable**: While it is part of the **glory of kings** to **search out a matter**, one thing every man has trouble searching is his own **heart**, and we have trouble searching the hearts of others. Such knowledge can be so far above us, like the **heavens** above the **earth**. Yet, God knows the heart (Romans 8:27, 1 Corinthians 2:10).

i. **As the heavens for height and the earth for depth**: "As the sky extends to apparently limitless heights above the surface of the earth, *with reference to depth* emphasizes the apparently limitless extent of the earth far below humankind's feet." (Waltke)

ii. **The heart of kings is unsearchable**: "The king's decisions are beyond the knowledge of the people…many things cannot be made known, being 'unsearchable' because, perhaps, of his superior wisdom, his caprice, or the necessity of maintaining confidentiality." (Ross)

d. **Take away the wicked man from before the king**: Like **dross** should be removed from **silver**, so **wicked** counselors and associates should be removed from the presence of kings and rulers. Then will their leadership (**throne**) be **established in righteousness**.

i. "You cannot have a *pure* silver vessel till you have purified the silver; and no nation can have a king a public blessing till the *wicked*-all bad counsellors, wicked and interested ministers, and sycophants-are banished from the court and cabinet." (Clarke)

3. (6-7) Conduct before kings.

Do not exalt yourself in the presence of the king,
And do not stand in the place of the great;
For *it is* better that he say to you,
"Come up here,"
Than that you should be put lower in the presence of the prince,
Whom your eyes have seen.

a. **Do not exalt yourself in the presence of the king**: We should always avoid self-exaltation. Even as we should humble ourselves in the sight of the Lord (James 4:10), we should also humble ourselves before others.

i. "Loving to be preeminent is the bane of godliness in the church. Let each of us set about the work of throwing down our high tower of conceit." (Bridges)

b. **Come up here**: When a man or a woman properly humbles themselves before God and kings, they may be invited to a higher place. This is much better than arrogantly setting ourselves high and then being **put lower in the presence of the prince**. Jesus gave much the same lesson in Luke

14:8-11, concluding with the thought: *For whoever exalts himself will be humbled, and he who humbles himself will be exalted* (Luke 14:11).

i. **In the presence of the prince**: "Now, if before an earthly prince men should carry themselves thus modestly and humbly, how much more before the King of heaven! And if among guests at a feast, how much more among the saints and angels in the holy assemblies!" (Trapp)

4. (8-10) Wisdom in avoiding court.

Do not go hastily to court;
For what will you do in the end,
When your neighbor has put you to shame?
Debate your case with your neighbor,
And do not disclose the secret to another;
Lest he who hears *it* expose your shame,
And your reputation be ruined.

a. **Do not go hastily to court**: Sometimes the **court** of law is necessary, but we should never **go hastily to court**. If it is possible to resolve a dispute any other way, we should do it that other way. This was Paul's later teaching to the Corinthian church (1 Corinthians 6:1-8).

i. "After squandering your money away upon lawyers, both *they* and the *judge* will at last leave it to be settled by *twelve* of your fellow citizens! O the folly of going to law! O the blindness of men, and the rapacity of unprincipled lawyers!" (Clarke)

ii. "Jesus gave a similar teaching in Luke 12:57-59." (Garrett)

b. **When your neighbor has put you to shame**: This is another strong reason why one should avoid court – *you might lose and be put* **to shame**. Many people who go to court have an unrealistic confidence that they will win.

c. **Debate your case with your neighbor**: Solomon's wise advice is to settle it out of court. If you can **debate your case** outside the court, do it there. The **debate** may expose a **secret** that would be to **your shame** in open court and from that **your reputation be ruined**.

i. "To run to the law or to the neighbours is usually to run away from the duty of personal relationship—see Christ's clinching comment in Matthew 18:15b." (Kidner)

ii. "One should not smear another's name to clear his own or a defendant's." (Waltke)

iii. Adam Clarke could not help but add this: "On this subject I cannot but give the following extract from Sir *John Hawkins's* Life of

Dr. Johnson, which he quotes from Mr. *Selwin*, of London: 'A man who deliberates about going to law should have, 1. A good cause; 2. A good purse; 3. A good skilful attorney; 4. Good evidence; 5. Good able counsel; 6. A good upright judge; 7. A good intelligent jury; and with all these on his side, if he have not, 8. *Good luck*, it is odds but he miscarries in his suit.'"

The remaining of Proverbs 25 contains one or two verse proverbs that will be considered individually.

Proverbs 25:11-12

**A word fitly spoken *is like* apples of gold
In settings of silver.
Like an earring of gold and an ornament of fine gold
Is a wise rebuker to an obedient ear.**

a. **A word fitly spoken is like apples of gold**: There is something special and powerful about **a word fitly spoken**. The right word at the right time has power to heal and strengthen, to guide and rescue. It is like an apple made of **gold** set on a beautiful **silver** platter.

i. **A word fitly spoken**: "Hebrew, Spoken upon his wheels - that is, rightly ordered and circumstantiated, spoken with a grace, and in due place. It is an excellent skill to be able to time a word, [Isaiah 50:4] to set it upon the wheels, as here. How 'good' are such words!" (Trapp)

b. **Is a wise rebuker to an obedient ear**: The **word fitly spoken** may also be a rebuke. When the one who is a **wise rebuker** meets an **obedient ear**, it is like beautiful jewelry (**an earring of gold and an ornament of fine gold**).

Proverbs 25:13

**Like the cold of snow in time of harvest
Is a faithful messenger to those who send him,
For he refreshes the soul of his masters.**

a. **Like the cold of snow in time of harvest**: This speaks of a cold drink, cooled by **the cold of snow**, given to a hardworking man in **time of harvest**. The refreshing, invigorating nature of that cold drink illustrates the blessing of **a faithful messenger to those who send him**. The **faithful messenger** is beloved by the one who sends the message. God wants His people to be faithful messengers of His gospel and work.

i. In the Apocrypha there is a description of a man who died from heat stroke during **time of harvest** (Judith 8:2-3).

ii. "Probably the reference is to drink cooled with snow. During the hot summers, laborers brought snow and ice from the high mountains and stored them in snow houses or snow caves; they were transported, for example, insulated by jute." (Waltke)

iii. "Verse 13 does not mean that it snows at harvest time—that would be an unmitigated disaster. It refers to bringing down snow from the mountains during the heat of harvest and the refreshment that gives to workers." (Garrett)

b. **He refreshes the soul of his masters**: The sender of the message is refreshed and comforted knowing that the message is being faithfully delivered. So, God is pleased with His faithful messengers today.

i. "The apostle Paul often acknowledged this refreshment to his anxious spirit when he was burdened with all the care of the churches (1 Corinthians 16:17-18; Philippians 2:25-30; 1 Thessalonians 3:1-7)." (Bridges)

Proverbs 25:14

Whoever falsely boasts of giving
***Is like* clouds and wind without rain.**

a. **Whoever falsely boasts of giving**: There are some who give nothing but want to be known as people who give; others give small gifts and want to be known as those who give great gifts (such as Ananias and Sapphira in Acts 5:1-11). They want the reputation of generosity without actually being generous.

i. "The lesson, of course, is not to make false promises." (Ross)

b. **Is like clouds and wind without rain**: When the **clouds and wind** of a storm come, we expect life-giving **rain**. When the **clouds and wind** are **without rain**, it is a disappointment – just like he who **falsely boasts of giving**.

i. The short New Testament letter of Jude used this figure to describe dangerous, unproductive people (Jude 12).

Proverbs 25:15

By long forbearance a ruler is persuaded,
And a gentle tongue breaks a bone.

a. **By long forbearance a ruler is persuaded**: Our self-control and patience can persuade great men to our cause, even **a ruler**. William Wilberforce persuaded the leaders of the British Empire to outlaw slavery through **long forbearance** and dedication to his righteous cause.

b. **A gentle tongue breaks a bone**: The patient, **gentle** words of a wise man or woman can have a great impact over a long period of time. Such words can have **bone**-breaking power.

i. "The gentle tongue breaking a bone might seem to be a paradox. But it is a fine illustration of the power of gentleness above hardness and irritation." (Bridges)

Proverbs 25:16

Have you found honey?
Eat only as much as you need,
Lest you be filled with it and vomit.

a. **Eat only as much as you need**: If someone has **found honey** – something good and wonderful to find – the honey should be enjoyed, but one should **eat only as much as you need**.

b. **Lest you be filled with it and vomit**: If something good (**honey**) is eaten beyond what one needs, if we fill ourselves with it, then it may cause an unpleasant reaction (**vomit**) and we lose the good thing we thought we gained. Overindulgence in good things is harmful and counterproductive.

i. "Since Eden, man has wanted the last ounce out of life, as though beyond God's 'enough' lay ecstasy, not nausea." (Kidner)

ii. "By *honey* he understands, not only all delicious meats, but all present and worldly delights, which we are here taught to use with moderation. Honey excessively taken disposeth a man to vomiting." (Poole)

Proverbs 25:17

Seldom set foot in your neighbor's house,
Lest he become weary of you and hate you.

a. **Seldom set foot in your neighbor's house**: It is expected that neighbors would visit neighbors, but such hospitality should not be abused.

i. "Blessed be God, there is no need of this caution and reserve in our approach to him. Once acquainted with the way of access, there is no wall of separation. Our earthly friend may be pressed too far; kindness may be worn out by frequent use. But never can we come to our heavenly Friend unseasonably." (Bridges)

b. **Lest he become weary of you and hate you**: The wise man or woman will be sensitive to the sense that a neighbor may **become weary** of their presence. Since good neighborly relationships make life much better, this is an important principle of wisdom.

i. "Friendship ripens through discreet sensitivity not to intrude on privacy and to allow space to be a person in his own right, not through self-enjoyment, impetuosity, or imposition. Without that discretion, instead of enriching life, friendship takes away from it." (Waltke)

ii. "At first thou mayest be *Oreach,* as the Hebrew proverb hath it, *i.e.,* welcome as a traveller that stays for a day. At length thou wilt be *Toveach,* a charge, a burden. And lastly, by long tarrying, thou shalt be *Boreach,* an outcast, hunted out of the house that thou hast so immodestly haunted." (Trapp)

Proverbs 25:18-19

A man who bears false witness against his neighbor
***Is like* a club, a sword, and a sharp arrow.**
Confidence in an unfaithful *man* in time of trouble
***Is like* a bad tooth and a foot out of joint.**

a. **A man who bears false witness against his neighbor**: Many proverbs speak against the **man who bears false witness**. This liar, whether in the court of law or common conversation, does great damage. He is **like a club, a sword, and a sharp arrow**. It is not a small sin to bear **false witness** against a **neighbor**.

i. The **man who bears false witness** "Is as cruel and pernicious to him as any instrument of death. The design of the proverb is to show the wickedness of slander, and that a false witness is in some respect as bad as a murderer." (Poole)

ii. "For in-close battle he used the *war club* (or mace), for less close but still hand to hand fighting the *sword* (or dagger or scimitar, see Proverbs 5:4) and for long distance fighting the bow and *arrow*." (Waltke)

iii. "Lo, here the mischief of an evil tongue, thin, broad, and long, like a sword to let out the life blood of the poor innocent – nay, to destroy his soul too, as seducers do that bear false witness." (Trapp)

iv. "The tongue wounds four people at one stroke. The person harms himself, the object of his attack, anyone who listens to his words, and the name of God. Flee from this deadly disease." (Bridges)

b. **Like a bad took and a foot out of joint**: These two proverbs are connected because the **man who bears false witness** is often also the **unfaithful man in time of trouble**. In one aspect he brings pain, in the other aspect he is a pain. The **unfaithful man** is useless and like a persistent, debilitating pain.

Proverbs 25:20

Like **one who takes away a garment in cold weather,**
And like **vinegar on soda,**
Is **one who sings songs to a heavy heart.**

a. **Like one who takes away a garment in cold weather**: Some people and their actions are especially troublesome. They bring discomfort (like leaving one without **a garment in cold weather**) and constant agitation (**like vinegar on soda**).

i. **Like vinegar on soda**: "To pour acid on this alkali is 'first of all to make it effervesce, and, secondly, to destroy its specific qualities'." (Martin, cited in Kidner)

b. **Is one who sings songs to a heavy heart**: The one who treats the **heavy heart** without sensitivity brings discomfort and the irritation of agitation. If **songs** are sung to a **heavy heart**, they should be sung in a minor key.

i. "The proverb indicates the impropriety of making merry in the presence of sorrow. It is wrong in method and serves to increase distress rather than to soothe it." (Morgan)

Proverbs 25:21-22

If your enemy is hungry, give him bread to eat;
And if he is thirsty, give him water to drink;
For *so* **you will heap coals of fire on his head,**
And the LORD **will reward you.**

a. **If your enemy is hungry, give him bread to eat**: The Bible commands us to have giving-love and care even to our **enemy**. Human nature would tell us to hate our enemy, but the Bible tells us to love our enemies and to do it practically (Matthew 5:44-47).

i. "The implication that one should refrain from extracting vengeance is obvious. Paul quoted this proverb in his discussion of 'love' in Romans 12:9-21." (Garrett)

b. **For so you will heap coals of fire on his head**: Commentators debate if this is a *good* thing or a *harsh* thing; if this is something good in the eyes of **your enemy** or not. Most likely it refers to a *burning conviction* that our kindness places on our enemy. Or, some think it refers to the practice of lending coals from a fire to help a neighbor start his or her own – an appreciated act of kindness. Either way, we can destroy our enemy by making him our friend, **and the L**ORD **will reward you.**

i. "Not to *consume*, but to melt him into kindness; a metaphor taken from smelting metallic ores." (Clarke)

ii. "Most commentators agree with Augustine and Jerome that the 'coals of fire' refers to 'burning pangs of shame' which a man will feel when good is returned for evil, his shame producing remorse and contrition." (Waltke)

iii. "By heaping courtesies upon him, thou shalt win him over to thyself.... In doing some good to our enemies, we do most to ourselves." (Trapp)

iv. "Do you think that others have wronged you? Pity them pray for them; seek them out; show them their fault, humbly and meekly; wash their feet; take the mote out of their eye; seek to restore them in a spirit of meekness, remembering that you may be tempted; heap coals of loving-kindness on their heads; bring them if possible into such a broken and tender frame of mind, that they may seek forgiveness at your hand and God's. If you cannot act thus with all the emotion you would feel, do it because it is right, and the emotion will inevitably follow." (Meyer)

Proverbs 25:23

The north wind brings forth rain,
And a backbiting tongue an angry countenance.

a. **The north wind brings forth rain**: Solomon mentioned this as an example of cause and effect. The **north wind** blows, and it **brings forth rain**.

b. **A backbiting tongue an angry countenance**: Those who speak ill of others with a **backbiting tongue** will provoke **an angry countenance** in others. This is a matter of cause and effect, just like the **north wind** bringing **forth rain**.

Proverbs 25:24

It is **better to dwell in a corner of a housetop,**
Than in a house shared with a contentious woman.

a. **Better to dwell in the corner of a housetop**: The **corner of a housetop** is not a great place to live. It is small, confined, and exposed to the elements because it is on the roof. Yet in some circumstances, the **corner of a housetop** is a **better** place to live.

i. "Hostile speech from the wife is as unexpected and unwelcome as the rain from the north wind and as from a sly tongue. Moreover, there may be a figurative connection between the north wind and exposure on the corner of the roof." (Waltke)

b. **Than in a house shared with a contentious woman**: To have the whole house but live in constant conflict with a **contentious woman** is misery. The same principle would be true of the **contentious** man. One would be **better** off in a humbler living situation and have peace in the home. For emphasis, this proverb is repeated from Proverbs 21:9.

> i. "Christian woman, do not think these proverbs are unworthy of your attention. Be sure you do not fit the description of this dreadful picture. And surely the repeated exhibition strongly inculcates the cultivation of the opposite graces, the absence of which clouds the female character in painful deformity." (Bridges)

Proverbs 25:25

As **cold water to a weary soul,**
So *is* **good news from a far country.**

a. **As cold water to a weary soul**: When a person is **weary**, a gift of **cold water** is greatly refreshing. **Soul** in this proverb is used in the same sense as most other proverbs, as a reference to the whole person and life, not only the inner spiritual aspect of a person.

> i. "Water could be cooled in porous containers made out of clay, for they were able to keep its content at a temperature at least five degrees below that of the storage place." (Meinhold, cited in Waltke)

b. **So is good news from a far country**: When we receive **good news**, especially **from a far country**, it brings great and life-giving refreshment. This applies to good news of many types, not the least is the gospel, that **good news** of what God has done in Jesus Christ to rescue all who put their trust in Him.

> i. The fact that someone travels **from a far country** to deliver **good** and important **news** makes the news all the more important. Many are willing to listen to the good news of Jesus Christ from someone who comes from a distance, just because the trouble they went to in bringing the message adds to its importance.

> ii. "In the Biblical world news traveled agonizingly slow and was delivered with great difficulty, so that extending the distance to a far off land heightens the refreshment." (Waltke)

Proverbs 25:26

A righteous *man* **who falters before the wicked**
Is like **a murky spring and a polluted well.**

a. **A righteous man who falters before the wicked**: Sometimes it is true that a **righteous man** stumbles and falters. This is always sad, but even more so when it happens **before the wicked**, in the view of those who reject God and His wisdom.

> i. "What a blemish was it for Abraham to fall under the reproof of Abimelech! for Samson to be taken by the Philistines in a whorehouse! for Josiah to be minded of his duty by Pharaoh Necho! for Peter to be drawn by a silly wench to deny his master!" (Trapp)

> ii. "The gross wickedness of the ungodly passes in silence. But Satan makes the neighborhood ring with the failings of those who profess to be Christians." (Bridges)

b. **Is like a murky spring and polluted well**: Instead of the clarity and life-giving property of clean, clear water, a compromised life is like a dirty pool. It gives no life, no clarity, no refreshment, and no help.

> i. "His despicable compromise disappoints, deprives and imperils the many who have learned to rely on him for their spiritual life." (Waltke)

> ii. "For a thirsty traveler expecting relief, the effect of coming upon a polluted well is disbelief and disappointment, and it serves as an apt metaphor for the profound disillusionment one feels when the righteous yield to evil." (Garrett)

Proverbs 25:27

It is **not good to eat much honey;**
So to seek one's own glory *is not* glory.

a. **It is not good to each much honey**: **Honey** is an example of one of God's great gifts. In the world of Solomon's day sweets were rare and nothing was sweeter than **honey**. Yet, overindulgence in even a good gift like **honey** is **not good**. Self-control must be practiced even with good things.

b. **So to seek one's own glory is not glory**: **Glory** can be a good thing, and it is part of God's promise to the believer (Romans 8:18). Yet to **seek one's own glory** is not good; it is **not glory** at all. We should seek God's glory and not worry about our **own glory**.

> i. "Much honey produces nausea. So eventually does self-glorification." (Morgan)

Proverbs 25:28

Whoever *has* no rule over his own spirit
Is like a city broken down, without walls.

a. **Whoever has no rule over his own spirit**: There are many who have so little self-control that it can be said that they have **no rule over** their **own spirit**. The world, the flesh, or the devil rule over such people, and not the spirit of self-control that is part of the fruit of the Spirit (Galatians 5:22-23).

b. **Is like a city broken down, without walls**: A **city broken down**, a city **without walls** has no defense and is vulnerable to every attack. It has no security, stability, and can protect nothing really valuable. This shows some of the terrible cost of having **no rule over** one's **own spirit**.

i. "Certainly the noblest conquests are gained or lost over ourselves. The first outbreak of anger resulted in murder. A king's lack of watchfulness about lust resulted in adultery." (Bridges)

Proverbs 26 – The Nature of the Fool and the Lazy Man

A. Fools and sluggards.

1. (1) Honor doesn't fit the fool.

As snow in summer and rain in harvest,
So honor is not fitting for a fool.

> a. **As snow in the summer and rain in the harvest**: These things are out of place and in an economy based on grain grown in the field, they are disasters of bad timing.

> > i. "A snow-fall in summer would signal the times are out of joint and would be catastrophic (cf. 1 Samuel 12:17). Snow or rain ruins the grain harvest by damaging and causing it to rot." (Waltke)

> b. **Honor is not fitting for a fool**: **Honor** for the **fool** is also out of place – and can lead to disaster.

> > i. "The 'fool' is the stupid person who is worthless and vain (just the kind of person popular culture seems to honor)." (Ross)

> > ii. "The present age, through the tricks of publicity, is especially prone to idolize 'vain and light persons', for whom the treatment of verse 3 might be better medicine." (Kidner)

> > iii. "Because he neither deserves it, nor knows how to use it, but his folly is both increased and publicly manifested by it." (Poole)

2. (2) The destiny of a curse without cause.

Like a flitting sparrow, like a flying swallow,
So a curse without cause shall not alight.

> a. **Like a flitting sparrow, like a flying swallow**: Solomon described birds that fly without taking rest on a branch or a surface.

b. **So a curse without cause shall not alight**: In the same way that a bird will fly without landing, so a **curse** that someone makes without proper **cause** before God will **not alight**. If someone pronounces a **curse** it does not have magical properties; there must be **cause** before God for it to have any power.

i. "Therefore, if the heart knows that a curse is unjust it may rest in the certainty that it cannot harm." (Morgan)

ii. "Since the Creator and Lord of history is the source of blessing and cursing through a fellow human being, the proverb infers that the undeserved/unfitting curse is ineffective because the Sovereign does not back it up." (Waltke)

iii. "What was David the worse for Shimei's rash railings? Or Jeremiah for all the people's cursings of him? [Jeremiah 15:10]." (Trapp)

iv. "Balaam is the reluctant witness against all superstition: 'How can I curse whom God has not cursed?' (Numbers 23:8)." (Kidner)

3. (3-6) Dealing with fools.

A whip for the horse,
A bridle for the donkey,
And a rod for the fool's back.
Do not answer a fool according to his folly,
Lest you also be like him.
Answer a fool according to his folly,
Lest he be wise in his own eyes.
He who sends a message by the hand of a fool
Cuts off *his own* **feet and drinks violence.**

a. **Whip for the horse, a bridle for the donkey**: There is an instrument appropriate for these animals. There is also an instrument that fits the fool: **a rod for the fool's back**. What they will not learn from the words of wisdom they must learn through the infliction of pain.

i. "Like brute animals, force is the only language they understand." (Garrett)

ii. "This proverb, with its fellows, is written for us in two capacities: as people dealing with fools, and as potential fools ourselves." (Kidner)

b. **Do not answer a fool according to his folly**: When a fool pours forth his foolishness, it is often right to **not answer** them. Sometimes contending with a fool can make one just like the fool.

i. **Do not answer a fool**: "When he is incorrigible, or when he is inflamed with passion or wine, etc., or when it is not necessary, nor likely to do him good." (Poole)

ii. "One should not descend to his level of thought. To get into an argument with a fool like that would only make one look like a fool as well." (Ross)

iii. "Hezekiah would not answer Rabshakeh, nor Jeremiah Hananiah; [Jeremiah 28:11] nor our Saviour his adversaries. [Matthew 26:62 John 19:9] He reviled not his revilers, he threatened not his open opposites. [1 Peter 2:23]." (Trapp)

c. **Answer a fool according to his folly**: Other times the right thing is to **answer a fool**. Sometimes a wise **answer** to a fool will expose his folly and prevent him from becoming **wise in his own eyes**.

i. **Answer a fool**: "When he is capable of receiving good by it, or when it is necessary for the glory of God, or for the discharge of a man's duty, or for the good of others." (Poole)

ii. "Answer that is in agreement with the Lord's wisdom puts the fool's topsy-turvy world right side up and so is fitting." (Waltke)

iii. Those who think Proverbs 26:4 contradicts Proverbs 26:5 are unfamiliar with the nature of practical wisdom in life. "They are put together to show that human problems are often complicated and cannot always be solved by appealing to a single rule." (Ross)

iv. "Oh, for wisdom to govern the tongue, to discover the right time to speak and the right time to stay silent. How instructive is the pattern of our great Master! His silence and his answers were equally worthy of himself. The former always conveyed a dignified rebuke. The latter responded to the confusion of his contentious enemies." (Bridges)

d. **He who sends a message by the hand of a fool**: One should never expect a good result from sending **a message by the hand of a fool**. It is like harming one's self. Curiously, God chose the foolish things of this world to be His messengers (1 Corinthians 1:27), but He wants them to be something better than fools in His work.

4. (7-12) The nature of the fool.

Like **the legs of the lame that hang limp**
Is **a proverb in the mouth of fools.**
Like one who binds a stone in a sling
Is **he who gives honor to a fool.**
Like **a thorn** *that* **goes into the hand of a drunkard**

Is a proverb in the mouth of fools.
The great *God* who formed everything
Gives the fool *his* hire and the transgressor *his* wages.
As a dog returns to his own vomit,
So a fool repeats his folly.
Do you see a man wise in his own eyes?
There is more hope for a fool than for him.

a. **Like the legs of the lame that hang limp is a proverb in the mouth of fools**: In a series of "**like the**" statements, Solomon colorfully explained the nature of the fool.

- The fool's possession of wisdom (such as **a proverb in the mouth**) is useless, **like the legs of the lame**.

- The fool's receiving of **honor** is stupid, **like the one who binds a stone in a sling** so that it can't be cast out.

- The fool's attempt to proclaim wisdom brings pain, **like a thorn that goes into the hand of a drunkard**.

i. These are absurd illustrations, but "no less absurd is he that giveth to a fool that honour and praise which he is not capable either of receiving, or retaining, or using aright, but it is quite wasted upon him, and doth him more hurt than good." (Poole)

ii. **Like the one who binds a stone in a sling**: "A sling was made of a leather or textile strip that had been broadened in the middle and into which the stone was placed, but never bound" (Waltke). "The stone tied in the sling may swing back around and hit the slinger" (Garrett).

iii. **Like a thorn that goes into the hand of a drunkard**: "He handleth it hard, as if it were another kind of wood, and it runs into his hand. So do profane persons pervert and pollute the Holy Scriptures, to their own and other men's destruction." (Trapp)

b. **Gives the fool his hire and the transgressor his wages**: God's guidance and governing over all things extends to the **fool** and the **transgressor**. He will make sure they get what is due, as both their **hire** and their **wages**.

i. "As he made all so he maintains all, even the evil and the unthankful… or he allows them a livelihood, gives them their portion in this life, fills their bellies with his good treasure, but by it sends leanness into their souls, or if he fattens them, it is to fit them for destruction, as fated ware is fitted for the meat market." (Trapp)

c. **As a dog returns to his own vomit, so a fool repeats his folly**: A fool will not change their ways apart from a dramatic transformation. Just as it is in the dog's nature to return **to his own vomit**, it is the fool's nature to repeat **his folly**. 2 Peter 2:22 used this verse to illustrate the repulsive nature of a sinner returning to their sin.

> i. "An intentionally repulsive simile. It juxtaposes a fool with the contemptible dog; his destructive folly with the dog's vomit; and the fool's incorrigibility with the dog's repulsive nature to return to its vomit, to sniff at it, to lick it, and finally to eat it." (Waltke)

> ii. "We naturally turn away from this sight. Would that we had the same disgust at the sin that it so graphically portrays." (Bridges)

d. **Do you see a man wise in his own eyes?** Despite the severe treatment of the fool, Solomon thought of a man in even worse danger – the proud man, the one **wise in his own eyes**. This is a special type of folly, one that will *never* learn the ways of wisdom.

> i. "The greatest fool is the fool who does not know he is a fool." (Morgan)

> ii. "The peril is a very subtle one. We are prone to be wise in our own conceits, without knowing that we are so. A simple test may be employed. When we fail to seek divine guidance in any undertaking it is because we do not feel our need of it; In other words, we are wise in our own conceit. There is no safer condition of soul, than that self-distrust, that knowledge of ignorance, which drives us persistently to seek for the wisdom which comes from above." (Morgan)

5. (13-16) The nature of the lazy man.

The lazy *man* says, "*There is* a lion in the road!
A fierce lion *is* in the streets!"
As **a door turns on its hinges,**
So *does* the lazy *man* on his bed.
The lazy *man* buries his hand in the bowl;
It wearies him to bring it back to his mouth.
The lazy *man is* wiser in his own eyes
Than seven men who can answer sensibly.

a. **There is a lion in the road**: The lazy man will create any excuse to avoid work. A **lion in the road** was a virtual impossibility in Biblical times. The **lazy man** shows creative talent (imagining not only a lion, but a **fierce lion**) and a form of work, but it is dedicated to the effort of *avoiding* work.

b. **As a door turns on its hinges**: The only way a door *can* turn is on its hinges. The only turning the **lazy man** does is **on his bed**.

i. **On his bed**: "But comes not off, unless lifted or knocked off. So neither comes the sluggard out of his feathered nest, where he lies soaking and stretching, unless hard hunger or other necessity rouse and raise him." (Trapp)

ii. **On its hinges**: "The humor in this verse is based on the analogy with a door—it moves but goes nowhere. Likewise, the sluggard is hinged to his bed." (Ross)

c. **It wearies him to bring it back to his mouth**: The lack of energy and initiative in the lazy man is so profound that he can't or won't properly care for his personal needs.

i. "The sluggard so dislikes any form of work that the very thought of exerting himself exhausts him." (Waltke)

ii. "Admiration for the wit of this portraiture has to be tempered with disquiet, on reflection that the sluggard will be the last to see his own features here (see 16), for he has no idea that he is lazy: he is not a shirker but a 'realist' (13); not self-indulgent but 'below his best in the morning' (14); his inertia is 'an objection to being hustled' (15); his mental indolence a fine 'sticking to his guns' (16)." (Kidner)

d. **The lazy man is wiser in his own eyes**: The lazy man may lack energy and initiative, but he doesn't lack a high opinion of himself. He considers himself smarter **than seven men who can answer sensibly**. The lazy man has great confidence in his own abilities but never seems to accomplish much.

i. **Seven men**: "*Seven* here only means *perfection, abundance,* or *multitude.* He is wiser in his own eyes than a *multitude* of the wisest men." (Clarke)

B. The wise person avoids sins of speech.

1. (17) The wisdom of not interfering in the disputes of others.

He who passes by *and* meddles in a quarrel not his own
***Is like* one who takes a dog by the ears.**

a. **He who passes by and meddles in a quarrel not his own**: Some find it irresistible to get involved in the disputes of other people. The **quarrel** doesn't really belong to them, but he makes it **his own**. Jesus knew when to not get involved in another's dispute (Luke 12:14).

i. **Meddles**: "The Hebrew verb literally means 'become excited'…the Hebrew could fit the line—someone who gets angry over the fight of another." (Ross)

b. **Is like one who takes a dog by the ears**: It is a foolish and dangerous thing to take **a dog by the ears**. Once one does, it's hard to let go without getting bit, and the dog never appreciates it.

i. "Exposeth himself to great and needless hazards, as a man that causelessly provoketh a mastiff dog against himself." (Poole)

ii. "Not even Samson grabbed the foxes by their ears (Judges 15:4)." (Waltke)

iii. "There is a world of difference between suffering as a Christian and suffering as a busybody. Even with Christian intentions, many of us are too fond of meddling in other peoples' affairs." (Bridges)

iv. "This proverb stands true *ninety-nine* times out of a *hundred*, where people meddle with *domestic broils*, or differences between *men* and their *wives*." (Clarke)

2. (18-19) The danger of the practical joker.

Like a madman who throws firebrands, arrows, and death,
Is the man *who* deceives his neighbor,
And says, "I was only joking!"

a. **Like a madman who throws firebrands, arrows, and death**: Solomon painted the picture of a fierce warrior with many weapons, spreading destruction everywhere.

b. **Is the man who deceives his neighbor**: The man who plays tricks on others, deceiving them, and covering it by saying, **"I was only joking!"** is a danger to others – and a very unwelcome companion.

i. "He bears no malice. He indulges only the pure love of mischief. He carries on a scheme of imposition as harmless play. His companions compliment him on his adroitness and join in the laugh of triumph over the victim of his cruel jest." (Bridges)

3. (20-22) The dangerous words of the talebearer.

Where *there is* no wood, the fire goes out;
And where *there is* no talebearer, strife ceases.
As charcoal *is* to burning coals, and wood to fire,
So *is* a contentious man to kindle strife.
The words of a talebearer *are* like tasty trifles,
And they go down into the inmost body.

a. **Where there is no talebearer, strife ceases**: Just as **wood** fuels a **fire**, so the **talebearer** or gossip fuels **strife**. The fire won't continue to burn without the wood, and the strife won't continue when the **talebearer** stops their work. James described the power of words to set a destructive fire (James 3:6).

> i. "As long as there is an ear to receive, and a tongue to pass on, some piece of malicious slander will continue to circulate. But directly it reaches a hearer who will not whisper it forward, in that direction at least its progress is arrested." (Meyer)

> ii. "The tale-*receiver* and the tale-*bearer* are the agents of discord. If none received the slander in the *first* instance, it could not be propagated. Hence our proverb, 'The receiver is as bad as the thief.' And our *laws* treat them equally; for the *receiver* of stolen goods, knowing them to be stolen, is *hanged*, as well as *he* who *stole them*." (Clarke)

b. **So is a contentious man to kindle strife**: **Strife** doesn't create itself. It has a maker, and it is the gossip, the **talebearer**, the **contentious man**.

> i. "In the absence of such a person, old hurts can be set aside, and discord can die a natural death. Even so, we often find a juicy tidbit of defamation irresistible." (Garrett)

c. **The words of a talebearer are like tasty trifles**: This proverb, repeated from 18:8, explains that the gossip and evil reports brought by the **talebearer** are almost impossible to resist. Those who should know better find it difficult to tell the **talebearer** to stop talking.

> i. "The words of a gossip [**talebearer**] in an unguarded moment may inflict irreparable injury. This evil may be welcomed in certain circles that thrive on scandal. But that does not alter the real character of a gossip, who is detested by both God and man." (Bridges)

d. **They go down into the inmost body**: When we receive the **words of a talebearer**, they normally have an effect on us. The words **go down into** us and often change the way we think and feel about people, even if what the **talebearer** says isn't true or isn't confirmed. God gave a strong word regarding the confirmation of testimony (Deuteronomy 19:15, 2 Corinthians 13:1, 1 Timothy 5:19).

> i. Once we start eating these **tasty trifles**, it is hard to stop. "When such tasty bits are taken into the innermost being, they stimulate the desire for more." (Ross)

> ii. "This was delivered before, Proverbs 18:8, and is here repeated, as being a point of great concernment to the peace and welfare of all societies, and fit to be oft and earnestly pressed upon the consciences of men, because of their great and general proneness to this sin." (Poole)

4. (23) Fair words covering a foul heart.

Fervent lips with a wicked heart
***Are like* earthenware covered with silver dross.**

a. **Fervent lips with a wicked heart**: There are people who are able to speak with power and persuasion, but they have a **wicked heart**. The ill effect of their **wicked heart** is made much more effective because of their **fervent** words.

i. "As Luther renders this text; - a bad mouth, and a worse heart. Wicked men are said to speak with a heart and a heart, [Psalms 12:2, *marg.*} as speaking one thing and thinking another, drawing a fair glove on a foul hand." (Trapp)

b. **Like earthenware covered with silver dross**: This is an example of something that looks superficially good with a **silver** veneer, but it is worthless **earthenware** on the inside. So, the man mentioned in the first line may attract people superficially, but inside he is worthless.

i. "Because of its silvery gloss, this slag was used as a glaze for ceramics." (Waltke)

ii. "Lips which make great professions of friendship are like a *vessel plated* over with *base metal* to make it resemble *silver*, but it is only a *vile pot*, and even the *outside* is not *pure*." (Clarke)

5. (24-26) The secret hater.

He who hates, disguises *it* with his lips,
And lays up deceit within himself;
When he speaks kindly, do not believe him,
For *there are* seven abominations in his heart;
***Though his* hatred is covered by deceit,**
His wickedness will be revealed before the assembly.

a. **He who hates, disguises it with his lips**: It is common for those who **hate** others – God or men – to disguise it with their words. They don't want to give up their **hate**, but they don't want to be known as a hater.

i. "Charming words might merely cover evil thoughts." (Ross)

b. **He lays up deceit within himself**: The secret hater deceives others, but he also deceives himself. He imagines himself to be a better man than he really is.

c. **When he speaks kindly, do not believe him**: This secret hater should not be trusted. Even if he **speaks kindly**, his words do not reflect the true thoughts of his heart – **his hatred is covered by deceit**.

i. **Seven abominations in his heart**: "Seven abominations is an abstraction for the full panoply of his wicked thoughts and deeds that utterly offend the moral sensibilities of the righteous." (Waltke)

d. **His wickedness will be revealed before the assembly**: Whether this **assembly** is in the world or the world to come, the **wickedness** and evil heart of the secret hater **will be revealed**.

i. "He shall be detected and detested of all, sooner or later. God will wash off his varnish with rivers of brimstone." (Trapp)

ii. **The assembly**: "refers to a legal assembly convoked to try the enemy's evil deeds and to mete out punishment. In *Proverbs* justice is meted out in an indefinite future that outlasts death." (Waltke)

6. (27-28) The self-appointed judgment on the lying tongue.

Whoever digs a pit will fall into it,
And he who rolls a stone will have it roll back on him.
A lying tongue hates *those who are* **crushed by it,**
And a flattering mouth works ruin.

a. **Whoever digs a pit will fall into it**: In His judgments, God often appoints that people reap what they sow; that He will treat them the same way they have treated others. They will **fall into** the **pit** they dug for others; the **stone** they rolled against someone else will **roll back on** them.

i. "For samples consider Haman (Esther 7:10) and Daniel's enemies (Daniel 6:24-28)." (Ross)

ii. "Cardinal Benno relates a memorable story of Pope Hildebrand, or Gregory VII, that he hired a base fellow to lay a great stone upon a beam in the church where Henry IV, the emperor, used to pray, and so to lay it that it might fall as from the top of the church upon the emperor's head, and kill him. But while this wretch was attempting to do it, the stone, with its weight, drew him down, and falling upon him, dashed him in pieces upon the pavement." (Trapp)

b. **A lying tongue hates those who are crushed by it**: The liar does his destruction without sympathy for others. He does not feel sorry for the ones he crushes; he actively hates them.

i. "Lying is an act of hatred. In one way or another, lies destroy those whom they deceive. Therefore the liar despises not only the truth but his victims as well." (Garrett)

ii. **Those who are crushed**: "Classifying himself among the oppressed Paul said: 'We are hard pressed on every side, but not crushed;

perplexed, but not in despair; persecuted, but not abandoned; struck down, but not destroyed' (2 Corinthians 4:8-9)." (Waltke)

c. **A flattering mouth works ruin**: Flattery is another way the **lying tongue** brings ruin. Their **flattering mouth** builds pride and manipulates others for deceptive goals.

i. "The heart of the matter is exposed in 28, with the fact that deceit, whether it hurts or soothes, is practical hatred, since truth is vital, and pride fatal, to right decisions." (Kidner)

ii. "False love proves to be true hatred." (Trapp)

iii. "Pray for wisdom to discover the snare, for gracious principles to raise us up above vain praises, for self-denial, for the capacity to be content and even thankful without such flatteries. This will be our security." (Bridges)

Proverbs 27 – Planning for the Future, Receiving Honor

Proverbs 27:1

Do not boast about tomorrow,
For you do not know what a day may bring forth.

a. **Do not boast about tomorrow**: It is human nature to be overly confident in what future days hold. It is easy to **boast about tomorrow**, especially with our modern arrogance of continual progress.

b. **For you do not know what a day may bring forth**: We don't know what tomorrow may hold, so we should have a humble attitude towards the future, as James 4:13-16 also speaks of.

i. "The verse is not ruling out wise planning for the future, only one's overconfident sense of ability to control the future—and no one can presume on God's future." (Ross)

ii. "Little doth any man know what is in the womb of tomorrow, till God hath signified his will by the event. David in his prosperity said, that he should 'never be moved'; but he soon after found a sore alteration: God confuted his confidence. [Psalms 30:6-7]." (Trapp)

iii. Spurgeon considered what a blessing it was that we **do not know what a day may bring forth**. "To know the good might lead us to presumption, to know the evil might tempt us to despair. Happy for us is it that our eyes cannot penetrate the thick veil which God hangs between us and to- morrow, that we cannot see beyond the spot where we now are, and that, in a certain sense, we are utterly ignorant as to the details of the future. We may, indeed, be thankful for our ignorance."

Proverbs 27:2

Let another man praise you, and not your own mouth;
A stranger, and not your own lips.

a. **Let another praise you, and not your own mouth**: We should stay away from self-promotion in its many forms. Modern technology gives us many more methods and opportunities to **praise** ourselves, but we should avoid such self-praise.

b. **A stranger, and not your own lips**: Honor means much more when it comes from an outside source, even a **stranger** than being the product of self-praise and self-promotion.

i. "A German proverb says: *'Eigen-Lob stinkt, Freundes Lob hinkt, Fremdes Lob klingt'*—'self-praise stinks, friend's praise limps, stranger's praise rings.'" (Waltke)

Proverbs 27:3

A stone *is* heavy and sand *is* weighty,
But a fool's wrath *is* heavier than both of them.

a. **A stone is heavy and sand is weighty**: Solomon appealed to self-evident truths. It is in the nature of a **stone** to be **heavy** and in the nature of **sand** to be **weighty**.

b. **But a fool's wrath is heavier than both of them**: When a **fool** – someone who rejects God's wisdom – expresses their anger and **wrath**, it is a weighty, dangerous thing. The wrath of any person may have great consequence; how much more a fool?

Proverbs 27:4

Wrath *is* cruel and anger a torrent,
But who *is* able to stand before jealousy?

a. **Wrath is cruel and anger a torrent**: In all its manifestations, **anger** is a dangerous and difficult to control expression – like a **torrent**.

i. "The metaphor depicts anger as a spiritual force that is destructive, irrational and violent." (Waltke)

b. **Who is able to stand before jealousy?** Solomon pointed out that there is a power and destructive capability in **jealousy** that can even go beyond **wrath** and **anger**. It can make a bigger torrent of evil. It was envy that motivated the religious leaders to arrange the death of Jesus (Matthew 27:18).

i. **Jealousy**: "Is a raging emotion that defies reason at times and takes the form of destructive violence, like a consuming fire." (Ross)

ii. Kidner notes that **jealousy** in the Scriptures is usually used in a positive sense; it is *jealousy for* – God's proper jealousy for our love. Yet passages like this also acknowledge that there is a dark side of jealousy, *jealousy of* and not *for*.

iii. Poole explained why **jealousy** is worse than **wrath** and **anger**: "Envy is worse than both of them, partly, because it is more unjust and unreasonable, as not caused by any provocation, as wrath and anger are, but only proceeding from a malignity of mind, whereby a man is grieved for another man's happiness…and partly, because it is more secret and undiscernible, and therefore the mischievous effects of it are hardly avoidable; whereas wrath and anger discover themselves, and so forewarn and forearm a man against the danger."

Proverbs 27:5

Open rebuke *is* better
Than love carefully concealed.

a. **Open rebuke is better**: Many are hesitant to **rebuke** others, especially others in God's family. But there is a time and place where **rebuke** is not only good it is **better** than the alternative.

i. "Rebuke—kindly, considerately, and prayerfully administered—cements friendship rather than weakens it." (Bridges)

ii. "We do not really like rebuke. We are inherently inclined to resent it. The fact that we really deserve it, or need it, does not make it pleasant…moreover, our dislike of rebuke leads us to think that those who love us serve us well when they are silent in the presence of our shortcomings." (Morgan)

iii. "Yet it is a *rough medicine*, and none can *desire* it. But the genuine open-hearted friend may be intended, who tells *you* your faults *freely* but conceals them from all *others*." (Clarke)

b. **Than love carefully concealed**: **Love** does little good when it is **concealed**. The honest love of an **open rebuke** can be much better than the **carefully concealed** love.

i. "Love that is hidden is not perfect love in either sense. The highest love must and does express itself. It does so in praise of the loved one…. Love that hides itself, professes not to see, perhaps does not see, and so remains silent, is love on a very low level." (Morgan)

Proverbs 27:6

Faithful *are* the wounds of a friend,
But the kisses of an enemy *are* deceitful.

a. **Faithful are the wounds of a friend**: A mark of a true **friend** is that they will be willing to wound us with loving correction. The correction may not feel good – as genuine **wounds** – but it will be an expression of the love and faithfulness **of a friend**.

i. "The 'wounds' are a metaphor for the painful and plain words that must be spoken in a true friendship in order to heal the beloved and/ or to restore a broken relationship." (Waltke)

b. **The kisses of an enemy are deceitful**: This cautions us that not all **kisses** are the greetings of friends. They may come from an **enemy** and be **deceitful**.

i. "Such as were the kisses of Joab, Judas, Absalom, and Ahithophel are not to be fancied, but deprecated and detested." (Trapp)

ii. "Who would not choose this faithful wound, however painful at the moment of infliction, rather than the multiple kisses of an enemy? The kiss of the apostate was a bitter ingredient in the Savior's cup of suffering." (Bridges)

Proverbs 27:7

A satisfied soul loathes the honeycomb,
But to a hungry soul every bitter thing *is* sweet.

a. **A satisfied soul loathes the honeycomb**: When our life is **satisfied** – either materially or physically – then we find it easy to hate and reject things that would otherwise be greatly desired, such as **the honeycomb**.

i. "Most agree that the proverb is capable of wider application than eating; it could apply to possessions, experiences, education, etc." (Ross)

ii. Spiritually, this can be understood in a *negative* sense: "May not satiety be as great a curse as famine? Is it not fearfully written on many a professing Christian, he who is full loathes honey?" (Bridges)

ii. Spiritually, this can be understood in a *positive* sense: "The best way of combating worldliness is by satisfying the heart with something better. The full soul loatheth even the honeycomb. When the prodigal gets the fatted calf, he has no further hankering after the husks which the swine eat…. Fill your heart with God and His sacred truth, and the things of the world will lose their charm." (Meyer)

b. **To a hungry soul every bitter thing is sweet**: When a life is truly hungry, they will eat almost everything and consider it **sweet**. This is true in the physical world, seen in those deprived of food for long periods. It is also seen in the spiritual world, when those who are awakened as truly **hungry** souls are ravenous for spiritual food.

i. Charles Spurgeon used this proverb as a basis to speak of the sweetness of Jesus and His work for us: "Sweet is liberty to the captive, and when the Son makes you free, you are free indeed; sweet is pardon to the condemned, and proclaims full forgiveness and salvation; sweet is health to the sick, and Jesus is the great physician of souls; sweet is light to those who are in darkness and to eyes that are dim, and Jesus is both sun to our darkness and eyes to our blindness."

Proverbs 27:8

Like a bird that wanders from its nest
***Is* a man who wanders from his place.**

a. **Like a bird that wanders from its nest**: With just a few words, Solomon painted a heart-touching picture of a **bird** away from its place of safety and security – the **nest** where it belongs.

i. This proverb made Charles Spurgeon think about those who seem to wander from church to church. "Too many in our London churches are a sort of flying camp, always flying from one place to another – a set of gipsy-Christians, who have no settled abode, and no local habitation."

b. **Is a man who wanders from his place**: We have a **place** appointed by God, and we can be as out of place as a bird without a nest if we wander from it. We need to take care that we perceive our **place** *not* as the one that culture or community may assign to us, but truly the **place** God has assigned us.

i. "Those who wander lack the security of their home and can no longer contribute to their community life." (Ross)

ii. "An honest man's heart is the place where his calling is: such a one, when he is abroad, is like a fish in the air, whereinto if it leap for recreation or necessity, yet it soon returns to its own element." (Trapp)

Proverbs 27:9

Ointment and perfume delight the heart,
And the sweetness of a man's friend *gives delight* by hearty counsel.

a. **Ointment and perfume delight the heart**: Solomon stated a self-evident truth. It is in the nature of an **ointment** or **perfume** to **delight the heart** through its pleasant smell.

b. **The sweetness of a man's friend gives delight by hearty counsel**: Strong, **hearty counsel** from a friend is sweet and can bring **delight** – just as it is natural for **ointment and perfume** to **delight the heart**. This proverb should make us ask, *Is there someone in my life who can give* **hearty counsel***? Can I give* **hearty counsel** *to someone else?*

i. "The gladdening oil and incense is a simile for the agreeable and delightful counsel of a friend that originates in his very being. Both the outward fragrances and the wholesome counsel produce a sense of wellbeing." (Waltke)

Proverbs 27:10

Do not forsake your own friend or your father's friend,
Nor go to your brother's house in the day of your calamity;
Better *is* **a neighbor nearby than a brother far away.**

a. **Do not forsake your own friend or your father's friend**: We should hold the bonds of friendship as dear and obligating, even beyond generations. Friends should not be forsaken.

i. "A well and long tried friend is invaluable. Him that has been a friend to thy *family* never *forget*, and never *neglect*." (Clarke)

ii. "Solomon exemplified his own rule by cultivating friendly links with Hiram, the friend of his father (1 Kings 5:1-10). The unprincipled contempt of this rule cost Solomon's foolish son his kingdom (1 Kings 12:6-19)." (Bridges)

iii. "Now, inasmuch as the Lord Jesus is 'thine own friend, and thy father's friend,' the injunction of the text comes to thee with peculiar force: 'Forsake him not.' Canst thou forsake him?" (Spurgeon)

b. **Nor go to your brother's house in the day of your calamity**: We should not assume that our birth **brother** is the best one to help in the **day** of **calamity**, especially if the **brother** is **far away**. Better is a lesser resource that is **nearby** than a better resource that is **far away**.

i. "The 'brother' in v. 10 is a close relative, one to whom people naturally turn in difficult times. Normally the close family identity of the Israelites would dictate that one go to a relative for help, and this verse is surprising for appearing to go against custom here." (Garrett)

Proverbs 27:11

My son, be wise, and make my heart glad,
That I may answer him who reproaches me.

a. **My son, be wise, and make my heart glad**: Solomon gave a simple encouragement to his **son** to **be wise** and therefore bring gladness to his father.

b. **That I may answer him who reproaches me**: A foolish son is a cause of insult and **reproach** to the parents. In some way, the son who rejects wisdom makes the parents look bad.

i. "In other words, his son will either publicly disgrace the father or enable him to stand proudly before even his enemies." (Garrett)

Proverbs 27:12

A prudent *man* foresees evil *and* hides himself;
The simple pass on *and* are punished.

a. **A prudent man foresees evil**: Wisdom will lead a man or woman to anticipate danger and to *take action*, such as to hide from the coming **evil**.

i. "This was delivered Proverbs 22:3, and is here repeated to enforce the foregoing exhortation, by representing the great advantage of wisdom." (Poole)

b. **The simple pass on and are punished**: Those who are naïve and untrained in wisdom are blind to the potential danger around them. They will eventually bear the bad consequence of their blindness and be **punished**.

i. "The verse is a motivation for the naive to be trained; for life would be far less painful for them if they knew how to avoid life's dangers." (Ross)

ii. **Pass on**: "The simple rush blindfolded into hell. The ox has to be driven to destruction, but the sinner plunges into it in spite of every effort to restrain him." (Bridges)

Proverbs 27:13

Take the garment of him who is surety for a stranger,
And hold it in pledge *when* he is surety for a seductress.

a. **Take the garment of him who is surety for a stranger**: If someone is a bad credit risk (foolish enough to be **surety for a stranger**), then we should hold a deposit as security against anything they owe to us (**take the garment**).

b. **When he is surety for a seductress**: The man is as immoral and foolish to be **surety for a seductress**, then we should especially regard them as a credit risk.

i. "Probably by her enticements and flatteries, she seduced some male to become indebted to her (see Proverbs 5 and 7). The proverb instructs the disciple to have nothing to do with these fools." (Waltke)

Proverbs 27:14

He who blesses his friend with a loud voice, rising early in the morning,
It will be counted a curse to him.

a. **He who blesses his friend with a loud voice**: The sense here is of an over-the-top greeting and blessing, meant to flatter and manipulate. It is **loud** and it starts **early in the morning**. Something is amiss in such excessive praise.

i. **Blesses his friend with a loud voice**: "That extols a man above measure, - as the false prophets did Ahab, and the people Herod, - that praiseth him to his face; which, when a court parasite did to Sigismund the emperor, he gave him a sound box on the ear." (Trapp)

ii. "His unnatural voice and timing betrays him as a hypocrite and no good will come of it." (Waltke)

iii. "Remember the Italian proverb elsewhere quoted: 'He who praises you more than he was wont to do, has either deceived you, or is about to do it.' Extravagant public professions are little to be regarded." (Clarke)

b. **It will be counted a curse to him**: Normally a friendly greeting is a blessing. Yet if that blessing is flattery or meant to manipulate it can be **counted a curse**.

i. "There is nothing more calculated to arouse suspicion than profuse protestations of friendship." (Morgan)

ii. "When a man exceeds all bounds of truth and decency, affecting pompous words and hyperbolical expressions, we cannot but suspect some sinister motive. Real friendship needs no such assurance." (Bridges)

Proverbs 27:15-16

A continual dripping on a very rainy day
And a contentious woman are alike;
Whoever restrains her restrains the wind,
And grasps oil with his right hand.

a. **A continual dripping on a very rainy day and a contentious woman are alike**: The scene is in a house with a bad roof, where a **rainy day** means **continual dripping**. That dripping shows there is a problem, it brings damage, and it greatly annoys. That is the same effect as a **contentious woman** in the house.

i. "The man takes shelter under the roof of his home expecting to find protection from the storm. Instead, he finds his leaky roof provides him no shelter from the torrential downpour. Likewise, he married with the expectation of finding good, but the wife from whom he expected protection from the rudeness of the world, harshly attacks him at home." (Waltke)

b. **Whoever restrains her restrains the wind**: To correct or reform a **contentious woman** can be a fool's errand. She can be as difficult to restrain as **the wind** or as hard to get a hold of as **oil** in the **hand**. Instead of trying to *change* a **contentious woman**, a wise and godly husband loves her as Jesus Christ loves His church (Ephesians 5:25-31) and leaves the changing up to God.

i. "The husband would be dealing with a woman who was as unpredictable and uncontrollable as a gust of wind or a hand grasping oil." (Ross)

ii. John Trapp saw in this a warning to men in how they chose their future spouse: "Let this be marked by those that venture upon shrews, if rich, fair, well descended, in hope to tame them and make them better."

Proverbs 27:17

As iron sharpens iron,
So a man sharpens the countenance of his friend.

a. **As iron sharpens iron**: A piece of **iron** can sharpen another piece of **iron**, but it happens through striking, friction, and with sparks. We think of the iron of a blacksmith's hammer working on a sword to make it sharp.

b. **So a man sharpens the countenance of his friend**: A **man** can be used to sharpen (improve and develop) **his friend**, but it may happen through a bit of friction and sparks. We shouldn't be afraid of such and expect that true sharpening can happen without the occasional use of friction.

i. "The analogy infers that the friend persists and does not shy away from critical, constructive criticism." (Waltke)

ii. "Gladly let us take up the bond of brotherhood. If a brother seems to walk alone, sharpen his **iron** by godly communication. Walk together in mutual concern for each other's infirmities, trials, and temptations." (Bridges)

iii. **Countenance**: "...almost equals 'personality' here. Like 'soul', it can stand for the man himself." (Kidner)

Proverbs 27:18

Whoever keeps the fig tree will eat its fruit;
So he who waits on his master will be honored.

a. **Whoever keeps the fig tree will eat its fruit**: The worker is worthy of his reward. If a man **keeps** a **fig tree**, it is appropriate for him to **eat its fruit**. It is cruel and unfair to keep the fruit of a man's labor from him.

i. "He mentions the fig tree, because they abounded in Canaan, and were more valued and regarded than other trees." (Poole)

ii. "The fig tree needed closer attention than other plants; so the point would include the diligent tending of it." (Ross)

b. **So he who waits on his master will be honored**: The appropriate fruit from properly serving one's **master** is to **be honored**. It isn't right to keep honor from the one who has faithfully waited **on his master**. God promised to reward those who wait upon Him. *Do your work diligently and leave promotion and reward up to God.*

i. In a sermon on this proverb Charles Spurgeon mentioned many ways that our Master may choose to honor His servants:

- We are honored in our Master's honor.
- We are honored with our Master's approval.
- We are honored by being given more to do.
- We are honored in the eyes of our fellow servants.
- We are honored by the Father, the Son, and the Holy Spirit.

Proverbs 27:19

As in water face *reflects* face,
So a man's heart *reveals* the man.

a. **As in water face reflects face**: Smooth and clear water can give a wonderful reflection of a man or woman's **face**.

i. "The Hebrew is very cryptic: literally, 'As the water the face to the face, so the man's heart to the man.'" (Kidner)

b. **So a man's heart reveals the man**: The feelings and thoughts that come from our heart reveal us as the reflection in smooth water reveals the face. Who we are will eventually be evident to others as our words and actions reveal our **heart**.

Proverbs 27:20

Hell and Destruction are never full;
So the eyes of man are never satisfied.

a. **Hell and Destruction are never full**: The grave and the world beyond will receive humanity and never become **full**. They are used here as figures of something that can never be satisfied.

i. "The grave devours all the bodies which are put into it, and is always ready to receive and devour more and more without end." (Poole)

b. **So the eyes of man are never satisfied**: Our longing to look upon things we desire will **never** be **satisfied**; it must be controlled and brought under God's dominion. A **man** will never see enough alluring images of women or enough beautiful machines. The answer is having the need channeled and satisfied in God and what He provides.

i. **The eyes of man**: "That is, their lusts, their carnal concupiscence. To seek to satisfy it is an endless piece of business." (Trapp)

ii. "The lust of the eye led Eve and Adam to transgress social boundaries in the first place. It is the bane of humanity, and this truism should drive the son to examine his own lusts." (Waltke)

iii. "As the *grave* can never be filled up with *bodies*, nor *perdition* with *souls*; so the restless desire, the lust of power, riches, and splendour, is never satisfied. Out of this ever unsatisfied desire spring all the changing fashions, the varied amusements, and the endless modes of getting money, prevalent in every age, and in every country." (Clarke)

Proverbs 27:21

The refining pot *is* for silver and the furnace for gold,
And a man *is valued* by what others say of him.

a. **The refining pot is for silver and the furnace for gold**: There is an appropriate place for **silver** and **gold** to be refined. It doesn't happen just anywhere, but in **the refining pot**.

b. **A man is valued by what others say of him**: We often know a man's value more **by what others say of him** than by what he thinks of himself. A man's self-estimation can be unreliable.

i. "There are three interpretations of this proverb. First, that you may know what a man is by the way he bears praise. Second, that you may know what a man is by the things he praises. Third, that a man who treats praise as the fining pot treats silver and gold purges it of unworthy substance." (Morgan)

ii. "Public praise formed a test for Saul and David (1 Samuel 18:7), David coming out the better for it." (Ross)

iii. "He who is praised is not only much *approved*, but much *proved*. The courting of the praise of our fellow creatures has to do with the world within. Praise is a sharper trial of the strength of principle than is reproach." (Bridges)

Proverbs 27:22

Though you grind a fool in a mortar with a pestle along with crushed grain,
***Yet* his foolishness will not depart from him.**

a. **Though you grind a fool in a mortar with a pestle**: Solomon used a striking and vivid image. Like **crushed grain** in a **mortar** and with a **pestle**, he pictured a **fool** being ground up.

b. **Yet his foolishness will not depart from him**: Despite the rough treatment mentioned in the previous line, **foolishness** does not **depart** from the **fool**. One of the sad marks of the fool is that *he will not learn.*

i. "Prisons were made into penitentiaries through the mistaken notion that confinement would bring repentance and effect a cure. Instead, many prisoners become hardened criminals. Divine grace that regenerates the fool is his only hope of being converted into a useful person." (Waltke)

Proverbs 27:23-27

Be diligent to know the state of your flocks,
***And* attend to your herds;**
For riches *are* not forever,
Nor does a crown *endure* to all generations.
***When* the hay is removed, and the tender grass shows itself,**
And the herbs of the mountains are gathered in,
The lambs *will provide* your clothing,
And the goats the price of a field;
***You shall have* enough goats' milk for your food,**
For the food of your household,
And the nourishment of your maidservants.

a. **Be diligent to know the state of your flocks**: Solomon wrote this with images from the world of agriculture (**flocks…herds…. hay…grass… lambs…goats**), but the principle applies in many other areas of life. We should work hard (**be diligent**) to **know the state** of whatever God has given us management over. If you don't know the condition of something, you can't effectively manage or lead it.

i. **Flocks** and **herds** "are here put for all riches and possessions, because anciently they were the chief part of a man's riches." (Poole)

ii. "This country scene is not designed to make farmers of everybody, but to show the proper interplay of man's labour and God's nurture, which a sophisticated society neglects at its peril." (Kidner)

iii. **Attend to your herds**: "Hebrew, Set thy heart to them - that is, be very inquisitive and solicitous of their welfare. Leave not all to servants, though never so faithful; but supervise and oversee business, as Boaz did." (Trapp)

b. **For riches are not forever**: We should give ourselves to **diligent** leadership and management because the future is uncertain. If we take good care of what God has given us now, it may provide for us in the future (**the lambs will provide your clothing** and so forth). If we don't take care of what we have, it won't be able to provide for us in an uncertain future.

i. "People should preserve what income they have because it does not long endure...the poem shows the proper interplay between human labor and divine provision." (Ross)

ii. **Goats the price of a field**: "Wherewith thou mayest pay thy rent, and besides hire tillage, or it may be purchase land, and have money in thy purse to do thy needs with." (Trapp)

iii. **Enough goats' milk**: "The milk is qualified by *goat's,* because goat's milk was by far the animal nutrient of choice in the ancient Near East. It is richer in protein and easier to digest than cow's milk." (Waltke)

iv. "Verse 27 need not be taken to imply that goat's milk will be the staple of everyone's diet; after v. 26b the intent is rather that one can sell surplus milk or barter it for other kinds of food...you will have more than enough to meet all of your family's needs." (Garrett)

Proverbs 28 – The Blessings and the Courage of Wisdom

Proverbs 28:1

The wicked flee when no one pursues,
But the righteous are bold as a lion.

a. **The wicked flee when no one pursues**: This speaks of a confusion and fear that properly belong to **the wicked**, not to the godly and wise. This is both because they are under God's displeasure and because they lack the strength and courage of the Holy Spirit.

i. "The proverb implies that the wicked, prompted by a guilty conscience or a fear of judgment, become fearful and suspicious of everyone." (Ross)

ii. "God sends a faintness into the hearts of the wicked, and the sound of a shaken leaf frightens them. In arithmetic, of nothing comes nothing, yet they fear where no fear is." (Trapp)

b. **The righteous are bold as a lion**: God's righteous ones stand even when one comes against them, and with God's strength they are **bold as a lion**.

i. **The righteous**: "The straightforward man, like the lion, has no need to look over his shoulder. What is at his heels is not his past (Numbers 32:23) but his rearguard: God's goodness and mercy (Psalm 23:6)." (Kidner)

ii. "Adam knew no fear until he became a guilty creature. But if guilt brings fear, the removal of guilt gives confidence." (Bridges)

iii. "Both psychologies are grounded in objective reality. God guarantees the safety of the righteous and dooms the wicked to punishment and disaster." (Waltke)

Proverbs 28:2

Because of the transgression of a land, many *are* its princes;
But by a man of understanding *and* knowledge
Right will be prolonged.

a. **Because of the transgression of a land, many are its princes**: To have **many princes** – rulers, officials – is not seen as a blessing. This speaks of how a large, complex, and multi-layered government can be a curse to a people, sent **because of the transgression of a land**.

i. "As a result of the land's total break with the Lord they need a large bureaucracy to keep an eye on one another and/or none survives.... An Arabic curse says, 'May God make your sheiks many.'" (Waltke)

b. **By a man of understanding and knowledge right will be prolonged**: Instead of **many…princes**, God blesses a land with **a man of understanding and knowledge**. Great and godly leaders can be a wonderful blessing to a nation.

Proverbs 28:3

A poor man who oppresses the poor
***Is like* a driving rain which leaves no food.**

a. **A poor man who oppresses the poor**: One might think that a **poor man** would have great sympathy for others who are **poor**, but this is not always the case. There are the poor who oppress the poor.

i. "Our Lord illustrates this proverb most beautifully, by the parable of the *two* debtors, Matthew 18:23, etc.... Here the *poor* oppressed the *poor*; and what was the consequence? The oppressing poor was delivered to the tormentors; and the forgiven debt charged to his amount, because *he showed no mercy*. The *comparatively poor* are often shockingly uncharitable and unfeeling towards the *real poor*." (Clarke)

b. **Like a driving rain which leaves no food**: This destructive **rain** leaves the people hungry and without hope. So is the effect of **a poor man who oppresses the poor**.

i. "Put an unprincipled spendthrift in power, and he will be like a destructive flood." (Bridges)

Proverbs 28:4

Those who forsake the law praise the wicked,
But such as keep the law contend with them.

a. **Those who forsake the law praise the wicked**: When the fundamental principles of justice are forsaken, it doesn't benefit the righteous. It gives benefit and **praise** to the **wicked**.

i. **Those who forsake the law**: "Without revelation, all is soon relative; and with moral relativity, nothing quite merits attack. So, e.g., the tyrant is accepted because he gets things done; and the pervert, because his condition is interesting." (Kidner)

ii. **Praise the wicked**: "Praising the wicked may mean calling them good, i.e., no longer able to discern good from evil" (Ross). "As Machiavel doth Caesar Borgia, that *bipedum nequissimum,* proposing him for a pattern to all Christian princes" (Trapp).

iii. "It is fearful to sin; more fearful to delight in sin; yet more to defend it." (Bishop Hall, cited in Bridges)

b. **Such as keep the law contend with them**: Those who do honor and promote the rule of **law** will resist and oppose **the wicked**. They understand the principle the Apostle Paul would later explain in Romans 13:1-7, that one reason God gives law and government to men is to restrain **the wicked**, to **contend** with them.

i. This proverb presents only two paths: **forsake the law** or **keep the law**. "The line dividing humanity is not racial, political or even religious, but spiritual. That line runs through every human heart." (Waltke)

ii. John Trapp used the phrase **contend with them** to remember the combative nature of Martin Luther: "It was the speech of blessed Luther, who though he was very earnest to have the communion administered in both kinds, contrary to the doctrine and custom of Rome, yet if the Pope, saith he, as pope, commanded me to receive it in both kinds, I would but receive it in one kind; since to obey what he commands as pope, is a receiving of the mark of the beast."

Proverbs 28:5

Evil men do not understand justice,
But those who seek the LORD understand all.

a. **Evil men do not understand justice**: There are those who are fundamentally **evil** or wicked, and simply do not **understand justice**. They do not understand the principles of justice and how they apply to themselves.

i. **Do not understand justice**: "Because their minds are naturally blind, and are further blinded by their own prejudices and passions, and by the god of this world, who rules in and over them." (Poole)

ii. "There are always those who believe justice is that which benefits them—otherwise it is not justice." (Ross)

b. **But those who seek the LORD understand all**: The godly understand justice and much more. They **seek the LORD**, fear the LORD, and have His wisdom.

i. "Many things, dark to human reason, are simplified by humility." (Bridges)

Proverbs 28:6

Better *is* the poor who walks in his integrity
Than one perverse *in his* ways, though he *be* rich.

a. **Better is the poor who walks in his integrity**: There are worse things than poverty, and to be a wicked man or woman who does not live in **integrity** is worse. This is an encouragement to the poor who often are despised.

i. "The verse only contrasts a poor man with integrity and a perverse rich man (see Proverbs 19:1)—there are rich people with integrity, and there are poor people who are perverse." (Ross)

b. **Than one perverse in his ways, though he be rich**: A **rich** man or woman who is twisted in their life before God or man is worse off than the godly poor person. We are defined more by our character than by our bank account or financial worth.

i. **Perverse in his ways**: "Hebrew, *in two ways*; halting between two ways, pretending to virtue, but practising vice; or covering his wicked designs with good pretences; or sometimes erring on one hand, and sometimes on the other, as wicked men commonly do." (Poole)

ii. "The double dealing rich person first defrauds the poor and the humble and then covers his wrongdoing over by making himself appear righteous." (Waltke)

iii. "Many will wish that they had lived and died in obscure poverty rather than having been entrusted with riches, which only made them boldly sin with a high hand against God and their own souls." (Bridges)

Proverbs 28:7

Whoever keeps the law *is* a discerning son,
But a companion of gluttons shames his father.

a. **Whoever keeps the law is a discerning son**: Obedience is a proof of wisdom. Those who claim to be **discerning** or wise yet live in fundamental disobedience show their folly.

b. **A companion of gluttons shames his father**: One does not have to be given over to ruinous appetites themselves to be a shame to their family; simply being **a companion** of such can embarrass the family.

i. "By identifying himself with those who squander all that is precious,—life, food and instruction—the foolish *puts to* public *shame* (see 25:8) *his father*." (Waltke)

Proverbs 28:8

One who increases his possessions by usury and extortion
Gathers it for him who will pity the poor.

a. **One who increases his possessions by usury and extortion**: There are some who become rich through economic violence. They charge high and unfair interest (**usury**) or they use their power to cheat and steal (**extortion**).

i. "In the Bible *nesek* [**usury**] occurs ten times and refers to the charge for borrowed money, which practice in Biblical times came to about 30% of the amount borrowed." (Waltke)

ii. **Usury**: "…the Mosaic law shows that the legitimacy of it depends on its context: what was quite proper in terms of economics (Deuteronomy 23:20) was pronounced improper in terms of family care (Deuteronomy 23:19)." (Kidner)

iii. Adam Clarke pronounced a sharp curse against those who took advantage of their brothers' need with **usury and extortion**: "O that the names of all those unfeeling, hard-hearted, consummate villains in the nation, who thus take advantage of their neighbour's necessities to enrich themselves, were published at every market cross; and then the delinquents all sent to their brother savages in New Zealand. It would be a happy riddance to the country."

b. **Gathers it for him who will pity the poor**: God will not allow these oppressive criminals to have the last word. In the resolution of God's judgment, the wealth of the wicked is simply gathered for those who have love and **pity** for the **poor**.

Proverbs 28:9

One who turns away his ear from hearing the law,
Even his prayer *is* an abomination.

a. **One who turns away his ear from hearing the law**: God wants us to always have an open and attentive **ear** towards His word (**the law**). To have no hunger for God's word or to give it no attention is a sign of spiritual sickness in the child of God.

i. "Many suppose, if they *do not know their duty, they shall not be accountable for their transgressions*; and therefore avoid every thing that is calculated to enlighten them…. But this pretense will avail them nothing; as he that *might have known his master's will*, but would not, shall be treated as he shall be who *did know* it, and disobeyed it." (Clarke)

b. **Even his prayer is an abomination**: God is not bound to hear or honor the one who neglects His word. Before we would speak to God in **prayer** we must humbly and attentively listen to His word, or our prayers may be an arrogant **abomination**.

i. "The prayer certainly will not be a proper prayer; someone who refuses to obey God will not pray according to God's will—he will pray for some physical thing, perhaps even making demands on God." (Ross)

Proverbs 28:10

Whoever causes the upright to go astray in an evil way,
He himself will fall into his own pit;
But the blameless will inherit good.

a. **Whoever causes the upright to go astray in an evil way**: There are those who take pleasure in causing the godly to **go astray**. It makes them feel better and perhaps superior to those who are **upright**.

i. **Causes the upright to go astray**: "This attracted some of Christ's strongest words: see Matthew 5:19; 18:6; 23:15." (Kidner)

b. **He himself will fall into his own pit**: God has a way of protecting His **upright**, even if they seem to, or actually do, **go astray** for a time. God knows how to put the wicked in their place (**his own pit**) and He knows how to make sure that **the blameless will inherit good**. God does not leave the final word to the wicked man with his evil plans.

i. "He who strives to pervert one really converted to God, in order that he may pour contempt on religion, shall fall into that hell to which he has endeavoured to lead the other." (Clarke)

ii. "The line shows that the wicked will be caught in their own devices; but it also shows that the righteous are corruptible—they can be led into morally bad conduct." (Ross)

Proverbs 28:11

The rich man *is* wise in his own eyes,
But the poor who has understanding searches him out.

a. **The rich man is wise in his own eyes**: It is not unusual for a **rich man** to be proud, and to think himself **wise**. Other proverbs explain that wisdom often leads to wealth, but not every **rich man** has gained his wealth through wisdom.

i. "Although riches do not always bring wisdom, the rich man often pretends to have it and ascribes his success to his own sagacity, though he may be manifestly simple and foolish." (Bridges)

b. **The poor man who has understanding searches him out**: The **poor man** with wisdom stands above the **rich man** with a fool's pride. That wise **poor man** may examine the rich man (**searches him out**), not the other way around.

i. **The poor who has understanding**: There are some lessons only poverty can teach, and one should never forget those lessons, even if they become wealthy.

ii. "Yet the universe does not possess a more dignified character than the poor man who has discernment. Did not the incarnate Lord honor this station supremely by taking it on himself? To walk in his footsteps, in his spirit, is wisdom, honor, and happiness infinitely beyond what this poor world of vanity can afford." (Bridges)

iii. **Searches him out**: "Knoweth him better than he knoweth himself; and, looking through all his pomp and vain show, he sees him to be what indeed he is, a foolish and miserable man, notwithstanding all his riches, and discovers the folly of his words and actions." (Poole)

Proverbs 28:12

When the righteous rejoice, *there is* great glory;
But when the wicked arise, men hide themselves.

a. **When the righteous rejoice, there is great glory**: When those who live with wisdom and righteousness **rejoice** because of the condition of their community, it is good for everyone. **There is great glory**.

b. **When the wicked arise, men hide themselves**: Even **wicked** men don't want to be ruled by other **wicked** men. A culture may live off the inheritance of a previous **righteous** generation, but when the **wicked arise** those benefits and the freedoms righteousness brings will slowly diminish.

i. "Thus the man Moses fled and hid himself from Pharaoh, David from Saul, Elijah from Ahab, Obadiah's clients from Jezebel, Jeremiah from Jehoiakim, Joseph and the child Jesus from Herod." (Trapp)

ii. **Men hide themselves**: "The state of that nation is so shameful and dangerous, that wise and good men, who only are worthy of the name of men, withdraw themselves, or run into corners and obscure places; partly out of grief and shame to behold the wickedness which is publicly and impudently committed; and partly to avoid the rage and injuries of wicked oppressors." (Poole)

iii. **The righteous rejoice...the wicked arise**: "The *first* was the case in this country, in the days of Edward VI; the *second* in the days of his successor, Mary I. Popery, cruelty, and knavery, under her, nearly destroyed the Church and the State in these islands." (Clarke)

Proverbs 28:13

He who covers his sins will not prosper,
But whoever confesses and forsakes *them* will have mercy.

a. **He who covers his sins will not prosper**: Since Adam and Eve, human instinct leads us to cover our **sins**. Our conscience makes us ashamed of our sin and we don't want others to see it. We even think we can hide it from God. Yet, this natural instinct to cover sin doesn't benefit us. It prevents us from being real about our condition before God.

i. In a sermon on this proverb, Charles Spurgeon described some of the many ways men attempt to cover their sin – all of them in vain.

- Excuses and justifications.
- Secrecy.
- Lies.
- Schemes to evade responsibility.
- Time.
- Tears.
- Ceremonies or sacraments.

ii. **He who covers his sins**: "Out of his sinful pride he pretends before God and people that he has no need to confess; instead, he seeks to deceive." (Waltke)

iii. "Sin and shifting came into the world together. Sin and Satan are alike in this, they cannot abide to appear in their own colour." (Trapp)

iv. "God and man each conceal sin—God in free unbounded grace, man in shame and hypocrisy." (Bridges)

b. **But whoever confesses and forsakes them will have mercy**: The path to receiving God's **mercy** is to confess and repent (forsake) our sin. This is the way to **prosper** spiritually and in life in general and receive God's mercy.

i. "Confession is to take God's side against sin. It is the lifting out of one thing after another from heart and life, and holding them for a moment before God, with the acknowledgment that it is our fault, our grievous fault." (Meyer)

ii. The Biblical practice of confessing sin can free us from the heavy burdens (spiritual and physical, as in James 5:16) of unresolved sin, and it can remove hindrances to the work of the Holy Spirit. It is a tragedy when the confession of sin is neglected or ignored among believers, and a cause of much spiritual weakness and hypocrisy.

iii. "Confess the debt, and God will cross the book; he will draw the red lines of Christ's blood over the black lines of our sins, and cancel the handwriting that was against us." (Trapp)

iv. In his commentary on James, Moffatt described how this was practiced in the early church: "Now, in the primitive church this was openly done as a rule, before the congregation. The earliest manual of the church practice prescribes: 'you must confess your sins in church, and not betake yourself to prayer with a bad conscience' (*Didache* iv.)." (Moffatt)

v. According to Moffatt, the English Prayer Book instructs that the minister is to give this invitation before the communion service: "Let him come to me or to some other discreet and learned minister of God's Word, and open his grief; that by the ministry of God's holy Word he may receive the benefit of absolution." There can be great value to *opening one's grief.*

vi. The great conviction of sin and the subsequent confession of sin are common during times of spiritual awakening. Charles Finney urged and described the confession of sin. In the North China revivals under Jonathan Goforth, confession was almost invariably the prelude to blessing; one writer describing the significant Korean revivals associated with Goforth wrote: *"We may have our theories of the desirability or undesirability of public confession of sin. I have had mine, but I know that when the Spirit of God falls upon guilty souls, there will be confession, and no power on earth can stop it."* (from *Calling to Remembrance* by William Newton Blair)

vii. Public confession of sin has the potential for great good or bad. Some guiding principles can help.

- *Confession should be made to the one sinned against.* "Most Christians display a preference for confession in secret before God, even concerning matters which involve other people. To confess to God seems to them to be the easiest way out. If offenders were really conscious of the presence of God, even secret confession of private sin would have a good effect. Alas, most offenders merely commune with themselves instead of making contact with God, who refuses their prayers under certain conditions. In the words of our Lord, it is clear that sin involving another person should be confessed to that person." (J. Edwin Orr)

- *Confession should often be public.* James 5:16 illustrates this principle. A.T. Robertson, the great Greek scholar, says that in James 5:16 the odd tense of the Greek verb "confess" in this verse implies group confession rather than private confession. It is confession "ones to others" not "one to one other."

- *Public confession must be discrete.* Often the confession needs to be no more than what is necessary to enlist prayer. It can be enough to say publicly, "Pray for me, I need victory over my besetting sin." It would be wrong to go into more detail, but saying this much is important. It keeps us from being "let's pretend Christians" who act as if everything is fine when it isn't. "Almost all sexual transgressions are either secret or private and should be so confessed. A burden too great to bear may be shared with a pastor or doctor or a friend of the same sex. Scripture discourages even the naming of immorality among believers, and declares that it is a shame even to speak of things done in secret by the immoral." (Orr)

- *Distinguish between secret sins and those which directly affect others.* Orr gives a good principle: "If you sin secretly, confess secretly, admitting publicly that you need the victory but keeping details to yourself. If you sin openly confess openly to remove stumbling blocks from those whom you have hindered. If you have sinned spiritually (prayerlessness, lovelessness, and unbelief as well as their offspring, criticism, etc.) then confess to the church that you have been a hindrance." (J. Edwin Orr)

- *Confession is often made to people, but before God.* At the same time, we notice that James 5:16 says "confess your trespasses to

one another." One of the interesting things about confession
of sin as noted in the writings of J. Edwin Orr is that the
confessions are almost always addressed to *people*, not to *God*.
It isn't that you confess your sin to God and others merely hear.
You confess your sin before others and ask them to pray for you
to get it right before God.

- *Confession should be appropriately specific.* When open confession
  of sin is appropriate – more than the public stating of spiritual
  need but confessing open sin or sin against the church – it must
  be *specific*. "*If* I made any mistakes, I'm sorry" is no confession of
  sin at all. You sinned specifically, so confess specifically. "It costs
  nothing for a church member to admit in a prayer meeting: 'I
  am not what I ought to be.' It costs no more to say: 'I ought to
  be a better Christian.' It costs something to say: 'I have been a
  trouble-maker in this church.' It costs something to say: 'I have
  had bitterness of heart towards certain leaders, to whom I shall
  definitely apologise.'" (Orr, *Full Surrender*)

- *Confession should be thorough.* "Some confessions are not
  thorough. They are too general. They are not made to the persons
  concerned. They neglect completely the necessary restitution.
  Or they make no provision for a different course of conduct in
  which the sin is forsaken. They are endeavours for psychological
  relief." (Orr)

- *Confession must have honesty and integrity.* If we confess with no
  real intention of battling the sin, our confession isn't thorough
  and it mocks God. The story is told of an Irishman who
  confessed to his priest that he had stolen two bags of potatoes.
  The priest had heard the gossip around town and said to the
  man, "Mike, I heard it was only one bag of potatoes stolen from
  the market." The Irishman replied, "That's true Father, but it was
  so easy that I plan on taking another tomorrow night." *By all
  means, avoid phony confession – confession without true brokenness
  or sorrow. If it isn't deeply real, it isn't any good.*

- *One need not fear that public confession of sin will inevitably get
  out of hand.* Orr tells of a time when a woman was overwrought
  by deep sorrow for sin and became hysterical. He saw the danger
  immediately and told her, "Quiet, sister. Turn your eyes on
  Jesus." She did and the danger of extreme emotion was avoided.

- *Those who hear a confession of sin also have a great responsibility.*
  Those who hear the confession should have the proper response:

loving, intercessory prayer, and not human wisdom, gossiping, or "sharing" the need with others.

viii. Real, deep, genuine confession of sin has been a feature of every genuine awakening or revival in the past 250 years. But it isn't anything new, as demonstrated by the revival in Ephesus recorded in Acts 19:17-20. It says, *many who believed came confessing and telling their deeds.* This was *Christians* getting right with God, and open confession was part of it.

ix. "Confession is the soul's vomit, and those that use it shall not only have ease of conscience, but God's best comforts and cordials to restore them again." (Trapp)

Proverbs 28:14

Happy *is* the man who is always reverent,
But he who hardens his heart will fall into calamity.

a. **Happy is the man who is always reverent**: Sadly, reverence and happiness are not commonly associated together. The **reverent** man is often thought to be sour and unpleasant. Nevertheless, to the degree that one can be **always reverent**, he can be genuinely **happy**.

i. **Always reverent**: "In all times, companies, and conditions; not only in the time of great trouble, when even hypocrites will in some sort be afraid of sinning, but in times of outward peace and prosperity." (Poole)

b. **He who hardens his heart will fall into calamity**: Here, reverence and hardness of heart are set as opposites. A man who **hardens his heart** will not be a truly reverent man, but he will **fall into calamity** either in this life or the life to come.

i. **Hardens his heart**: "When one hardens his heart his psyche can no longer feel, respond, and opt for a new direction. The hardened heart is fixed in unbelief and unbending defiance to God (Exodus 7:3; Psalm 95:8); insensible to admonition or reproof it cannot be moved to a new sphere of behavior." (Waltke)

ii. "When that fear [**reverent**] is absent, courage is mere hardening of the heart, recklessness, foolhardiness. The man who shuts his eyes to God, gathers himself up, and desperately plunges forward, is no hero; he is a fool, and without exception sooner or later lands himself in circumstances which break him; and brings those about him into suffering and catastrophe." (Morgan)

Proverbs 28:15-16

Like **a roaring lion and a charging bear**
Is **a wicked ruler over poor people.**
A ruler who lacks understanding *is* **a great oppressor,**
But **he who hates covetousness will prolong** *his* **days.**

a. **Like a roaring lion and a charging bear**: With these vivid images, Solomon described the effect of **a wicked ruler over poor people**. The **wicked ruler** treats those of low standing (**poor people**) with unpredictable, uncontrollable ferocity. He is dangerous toward them.

i. "Look how the lion frightens the poor beasts with his roaring, so that they have no power to stir, and then preys upon them with his teeth; and as the bear searches them out and tears them limb from limb: so deal tyrants with their poor subjects." (Trapp)

ii. "Because tyrants are like this, animal imagery (beast imagery?) is used in Daniel 7:1-8 for the series of ruthless world rulers. The poor crumple under such tyrants because they cannot meet their demands." (Ross)

b. **A ruler who lacks understanding is a great oppressor**: The foolish **ruler** (the one **who lacks understanding**) will oppress his people. His reign will be unhappy and insecure because of the foolish way he leads his people.

i. "The tyranny or oppression of a prince, though by some accounted wisdom, is in truth a manifest act and sign of great folly, because it alienateth from him the hearts of his people, in which his honour, and safety, and riches consist." (Poole)

ii. "No sentiment of pity softens his heart. No principle of justice regulates his conduct. Complaint only provokes further exactions. Resistance kindles his unfeeling heart into savage fury. Helpless and miserable indeed are the people whom divine anger has placed under his misrule." (Paxton, cited in Bridges)

c. **He who hates covetousness will prolong his days**: If a man is wise enough to hate **covetousness**, he will likely be wise in other responsibilities as a ruler. It is likely that **his days** as a ruler will be prolonged.

Proverbs 28:17

A man burdened with bloodshed will flee into a pit;
Let no one help him.

a. **A man burdened with bloodshed will flee into a pit**: We can suppose this may happen because the **man burdened with bloodshed** has a guilty, anxious mind that clouds and confuses his thinking, and he ends up in **a pit**. Or, it may happen because God's curse is on the **man burdened with bloodshed**.

> i. "The proverb states that the offender himself (like the smitten Azariah, 2 Chronicles 26:20) hastens to his punishment, once his conscience is awake." (Kidner)

> ii. **Flee into a pit**: "Shall speedily be destroyed, being pursued by Divine vengeance, and the horrors of a guilty conscience, and the avengers of blood." (Poole)

b. **Let no one help him**: As the man guilty of **bloodshed** falls into the consequences of his own actions, **let no one help him**. Often it is best to let people suffer the consequences of their sins.

> i. **Let no one help him**: "He who either *slays* the innocent, or procures his destruction, may flee to *hide* himself: but let none give him protection. The law demands his life, because he is a *murderer*; and let none deprive justice of its claim." (Clarke)

> ii. "Protests against all capital punishment is misnamed philanthropy. Shall man pretend to be more merciful than God? Pity is misplaced here. The murderer, therefore, of his brother is his own murderer. Let God's law take its course." (Bridges)

> iii. Charles Bridges was careful to add: "Yet we must not cast out his soul. Visiting the condemned cell is a special exercise of mercy. While we bow to the stern justice of the great Lawgiver, joyous indeed it is to bring to the sinner under the sentence of the law the free forgiveness of the Gospel; not as annulling his sin, but showing the over-abounding of grace beyond the abounding of sin."

Proverbs 28:18

Whoever walks blamelessly will be saved,
But *he who is* perverse *in his* ways will suddenly fall.

a. **Whoever walks blamelessly will be saved**: This proverb probably does not have *eternal* salvation in mind; instead, the idea is being **saved** or rescued from the calamities and troubles of life. Especially under the old covenant, God's blessing and protection was upon those who walk **blamelessly**.

b. **He who is perverse in his ways will suddenly fall**: The one who is twisted and crooked in his dealings can't expect God's blessing and protection. That crooked, twisted person should expect to **suddenly fall** one day.

Proverbs 28:19

He who tills his land will have plenty of bread,
But he who follows frivolity will have poverty enough!

a. **He who tills his land will have plenty of bread**: The reward of work is a harvest. The one who **tills his land** will enjoy the harvest that comes, and therefore have **plenty of bread**.

i. "If we are not to be lazy in business but fervent in spirit, in this world and in all its concerns, how much more we need to be like this in the momentous concerns of eternity!" (Bridges)

b. **But he who follows frivolity will have poverty enough**: The one who ignores his work to have a good time (following **frivolity**) will not enjoy the fruit of the harvest the way the hard-working man will. Instead of **plenty of bread**, the lazy, frivolous man will have plenty of **poverty**. The Prodigal Son was a fulfillment of this (Luke 15:13-17).

i. "There is a meaningful repetition here: the diligent person will have 'plenty [*yisba*] of bread,' but the lazy person will have 'plenty [*yisba*] of poverty'." (Ross)

Proverbs 28:20

A faithful man will abound with blessings,
But he who hastens to be rich will not go unpunished.

a. **A faithful man will abound with blessings**: This is true as a general principle; faithfulness and obedience to God's law brings **blessings**. It was especially true under the old covenant, where God promised blessings on the obedient and curses on the disobedient (Deuteronomy 27-28).

i. **The faithful man will abound**: "The man who makes fidelity the master principle will be rewarded. He who makes accumulation of wealth the master passion will be punished." (Morgan)

b. **He who hastens to be rich will not go unpunished**: The one who **hastens to be rich** is almost always willing to cheat or compromise to gain wealth. God promises that this one will be punished, either in this life or the next.

i. **He who hastens to be rich**: "While not condemning possessions in themselves, Proverbs always rejects greed. It contrasts financial prudence, diligence, and generosity with the desire for quick and easy money." (Garrett)

ii. "Even if no criminal means are resorted to, yet the immoderate desire, the perseverance in every track of Mammon, the laboring night and day for the grand object, and the delight and confidence in the acquisition all prove the idolatrous heart and will not go unpunished." (Bridges)

Proverbs 28:21

To show partiality *is* not good,
Because for a piece of bread a man will transgress.

a. **To show partiality is not good**: In the court of law and in our daily dealings with people, we should not **show partiality**. We should be those who do not favor or condemn others based on their race, class, nationality, or influence.

b. **Because for a piece of bread a man will transgress**: Because justice and the opinion of others can be easily bought, we should determine that we will not be bribed for partiality and we should be aware that others may be easily bought.

i. **For a piece of bread**: "For a trifle he will transgress, and sell his soul dog cheap for a groat, or less money." (Trapp)

ii. "The price can go still lower, to as little as the fancied approval of a stronger personality; and the preacher (Ezekiel 13:19) is as vulnerable as the judge." (Kidner)

Proverbs 28:22

A man with an evil eye hastens after riches,
And does not consider that poverty will come upon him.

a. **A man with an evil eye hastens after riches**: The stingy, ungenerous man will run after riches with the same energy that he will use to selfishly hold on to what he has.

b. **And does not consider that poverty will come upon him**: Because God's blessing does not rest on the stingy, ungenerous man, **poverty will come upon him** – and he will not **consider** or expect it.

i. "The Lord will see to it that only conscientious and compassionate people finally hold wealth in his kingdom." (Waltke)

Proverbs 28:23

He who rebukes a man will find more favor afterward
Than he who flatters with the tongue.

a. **He who rebukes a man will find more favor afterward**: It may be necessary to rebuke a man, but it is to invite his displeasure. Still, it should be done in confidence that when done well, the one who rebukes **will find more favor afterward**.

b. **Than he who flatters with the tongue**: The one who **rebukes** may not be as welcomed as **he who flatters**, but the sacrificial service of **he who rebukes** will bring him into **more favor** than the one who always praises.

Proverbs 28:24

Whoever robs his father or his mother,
And says, "*It is* no transgression,"
The same *is* companion to a destroyer.

a. **Whoever robs his father or his mother**: There are some who have little conscience about stealing from their parents. Out of some sense of entitlement, they rob them and then say, **"It is no transgression."**

   i. **Robs his father or mother**: "As that idolatrous Micah did his mother of her gold; [Judges 17:2] as Rachel did her father of his gods; as Absalom did David of his crown." (Trapp)

   ii. "He who robs his parents is worse than a common robber; to the act of dishonesty and rapine he adds ingratitude, cruelty, and disobedience." (Clarke)

   iii. "He may rationalize, 'eventually it all comes to me anyway'…or 'they can no longer manage their finances,' or 'as a family we own everything in common,' etc." (Waltke)

b. **The same is companion to a destroyer**: Despite whatever sense of entitlement the thief may have, they are right next to **a destroyer**, someone who spreads and even loves destruction.

   i. "The language is strong. The word for 'robs' could be rendered 'plunders.' 'Him who destroys' is someone who causes havoc in society." (Garrett)

Proverbs 28:25

He who is of a proud heart stirs up strife,
But he who trusts in the Lord will be prospered.

a. **He who is of a proud heart stirs up strife**: A **proud** man or woman is constantly causing **strife** because they want the attention and preeminence. That doesn't agree with most people, so there is **strife**.

   i. **Stirs up strife**: "Because he makes it his great business to advance and please himself, and hateth and opposeth all that stand in his way, and despiseth other men, and is very jealous of his honour, and impatient of the least slighting, or affront, or injury, and indulgeth his own passions." (Poole)

ii. "The greedy person's insatiable appetite brings him into conflict with others, for he transgresses social boundaries. Not content with his portion, he becomes disruptive and destructive, and whose person and property he violates fight back." (Waltke)

b. **He who trusts in the LORD shall be prospered**: To trust **in the LORD** is presented as a contrast to the **proud heart**. That one should expect to be **prospered**, as they humbly trust God and forsake pride.

i. "By contrast, those who trust in Yahweh can wait for their appetites to be satisfied, cause no discord, and in fact will be satisfied." (Garrett)

Proverbs 28:26

He who trusts in his own heart is a fool,
But whoever walks wisely will be delivered.

a. **He who trusts in his own heart is a fool**: There is a strong urge – promoted to us by the world, the flesh, and the devil – to trust our **own heart** and to "follow our heart" instead of humbly receiving our values, morals, and wisdom from God's word. This trusting in our **own heart** leads one to be **a fool**. For answers, values, and guidance we should not look within, but look to the Lord.

i. **He who trusts in his own heart**: "To trust an impostor who has deceived us a hundred times or a traitor who has proved himself false to our most important interests is surely to deserve the name of **fool**. This name, therefore, the Scriptures, using great plainness of speech, give to the person who trusts in himself." (Bridges)

ii. **A fool**: "For his heart, which is deceitful and desperately wicked, will infallibly deceive him." (Clarke)

b. **Whoever walks wisely will be delivered**: In contrast to trusting our **own heart**, we should instead give attention to walking **wisely**. Instead of operating on the basis of how we *feel*, we should direct ourselves to wise living in what we do.

i. **Walks wisely**: "Distrusting his own judgment, and seeking the advice of others, and especially of God, as all truly wise men do, he shall be delivered from those dangers and mischiefs which fools bring upon themselves; whereby he showeth himself to be a wise man." (Poole)

ii. "The teaching here recalls the wise and foolish builders of Matt 7:24-27." (Garrett)

Proverbs 28:27

He who gives to the poor will not lack,
But he who hides his eyes will have many curses.

a. **He who gives to the poor will not lack**: God promises to bless the generous heart, and one way that generosity should be expressed is to give **to the poor**.

i. **Will not lack**: "Not getting but giving is the way to wealth. God will bless the bountiful man's stock and store, his barn and his basket; [Deuteronomy 15:10] his righteousness and his riches together shall endure for ever. [Psalms 112:3]." (Trapp)

b. **He who hides his eyes will have many curses**: God will not bless the one who ignores the troubles of the poor and needy.

i. **He who hides his eyes**: "Describes an attitude which is very common, though popularly supposed not to be wrong. To hide the eyes means to refuse to see poverty. It is the sin of those who say they are too sensitive to visit the slums." (Morgan)

ii. **Many curses**: "Men shall curse him, and call him a *Pamphagus*, a churl, a hog in a trough, a fellow of no fashion, etc. God shall also curse him, and set off all hearts from him." (Trapp)

Proverbs 28:28

When the wicked arise, men hide themselves;
But when they perish, the righteous increase.

a. **When the wicked arise, men hide themselves**: When **wicked** men come to places of prominence and rule, it is bad for the community. Freedom and blessing to the community are much less present and in response, **men hide themselves**.

b. **When they perish, the righteous increase**: When the **wicked** and their influence pass, **the righteous increase**, along with their influence. This is a blessing for a community or a nation.

i. **The righteous increase**: "They who were righteous do now again appear in public, and being advanced to that power which the wicked rulers have lost, they use their authority to encourage and promote righteousness, and to punish unrighteousness, whereby the number of wicked men is diminished, and the righteous are multiplied." (Poole)

ii. "When the righteous increase in number and power, the people come out of their hiding…. This was the case during the reign of Hezekiah, whose men collected these proverbs (Proverbs 25:1; 2 Chronicles 29-30, esp. 30:13-27; cf. Esther 8:17; Acts 12:23, 24)." (Waltke)

iii. "In the early ages of the Christian church, after the death of the persecuting Herod, the Word of God grew and multiplied." (Bridges)

Proverbs 29 – Rulers, Servants, and the Fear of Man

Proverbs 29:1

He who is often rebuked, *and* hardens *his* neck,
Will suddenly be destroyed, and that without remedy.

a. **He who is often rebuked, and hardens his neck**: As in many places in the Bible, the *hard neck* is used as a figure of speech to speak of the stubborn attitude that resists and disobeys God. This proverb speaks about the man who **is often rebuked** but doesn't listen to the rebuke; instead he **hardens his neck**.

i. "The opposite of the stiff neck would be a bending neck, i.e., submission." (Ross)

b. **Will suddenly be destroyed**: This stubborn, rebellious man continues in his disobedience for a long time, until he is **suddenly...destroyed** – and there will be no hope for him (**that without remedy**). This describes the kind of person who thinks little of God's merciful patience and assumes judgment will never come for his continual rejection of wisdom and stubborn heart against God.

i. "When the door of opportunity to repent finally shuts, probably at death, the incorrigible fool is beyond all hope of a cure." (Waltke)

Proverbs 29:2

When the righteous are in authority, the people rejoice;
But when a wicked *man* rules, the people groan.

a. **When the righteous are in authority, the people rejoice**: It is to the benefit of the community or nation when **the righteous are in authority**. This shows that when **the righteous** govern, it should be for the benefit of the *entire* community, not only their own interests.

b. **When a wicked man rules, the people groan**: The community or the nation suffers when the **wicked** rule. Lawlessness increases and freedoms diminish. The rule of the **wicked** is bad for both the righteous and the wicked in the community or nation.

> i. **The people groan**: "Both for the oppressions and mischiefs which they feel, and for the dreadful judgments of God which they justly fear." (Poole)

> ii. "The sentiment of this proverb often recurs. On the surface it hardly appears to be true. To observe long issues is to be convinced of the absolute accuracy of the sentiment." (Morgan)

Proverbs 29:3

Whoever loves wisdom makes his father rejoice,
But a companion of harlots wastes *his* wealth.

a. **Whoever loves wisdom makes his father rejoice**: Children of any age bring happiness to their parents when they love and live **wisdom**. It gives the parents a justified pride in their children and gives peace about their children's future.

b. **A companion of harlots wastes his wealth**: This is one example of a foolish life, someone who chooses **harlots** and others of low character as their companions. This fool **wastes his wealth** on the **harlots** and other similar interests, showing they are the opposite of the one who **loves wisdom**.

> i. Comparing the first line of this proverb to the second line, Ross observed: "it would break a father's heart to see his son become a pauper through vice."

> ii. Adam Clarke asked a simple question in regard to Proverbs 29:3: "Has there ever been a single case to the *contrary*?"

Proverbs 29:4

The king establishes the land by justice,
But he who receives bribes overthrows it.

a. **The king establishes the land by justice**: A nation can only expect strength and progress when it is ruled with **justice**. When a community or nation sees evildoers punished and restrained, fairness in the legal system, and agreements honored, there will be **justice** and a foundation for growth and blessing.

b. **He who receives bribes overthrows it**: There are many ways that **justice** can be abused, but this is one of the worst ways. **Bribes** destroy the foundations of fairness and equality before the law. It means that the rich and devious prosper.

i. "The best laws are of little use when they are badly administered. Partiality and injustice make them null and void. And yet it requires great integrity and moral courage to withstand the temptations of worldly policy and self-interest." (Bridges)

ii. "This was notoriously the case in this kingdom, before the passing of the *Magna Charta*, or *great charter of liberties*.... I have met with cases in our ancient records where, in order to get his *right*, a man was obliged almost to ruin himself in *presents to the king, queen, and their favourites*, to get the case decided in his favour." (Clarke)

iii. The Puritan commentator John Trapp wrote of Proverbs 29:4: "This one piece of Solomon's politics hath much more good advice in it than all Lypsius's Beehive, or Machiavel's Spider web."

Proverbs 29:5

A man who flatters his neighbor
Spreads a net for his feet.

a. **A man who flatters his neighbor**: In this sense, to flatter is to excessively praise or give attention to a **neighbor** with the hope of gaining influence or status.

i. **A man who flatters his neighbor**: "A smooth boots, as the word signifies, a butterspoken man, {*see* Isaiah 55:21} or a divided man, for a flatterer's tongue is divided from his heart." (Trapp)

b. **Spreads a net for his feet**: Such flattery is a trap. It is a trap that the wise man knows how to avoid, and that catches the fool.

i. "Beware of a flatterer; he does not flatter merely to please you, but to *deceive you* and *profit himself*." (Clarke)

ii. "Oh, it is a cruel thing to flatter. The soul is often more exhausted and injured by disentangling itself from these nets than by the hottest contest with principalities and powers." (Bridges)

Proverbs 29:6

By transgression an evil man is snared,
But the righteous sings and rejoices.

a. **By transgression an evil man is snared**: A man may be **evil** in his character, yet it is his actual acts of **transgression** that ruin him. Most evil men think they are celebrating life and freedom through their **transgression**, but it will be a trap and a snare to them.

i. "The wicked man's jollity is but the hypocrisy of mirth; it may wet the mouth, but not warm the heart – smooth the brow, but not fill the breast. We may be sure, that as Jezebel had a cold heart under a painted complexion, so many a man's heart aches and quakes within him when his face counterfeits a smile." (Trapp)

b. **The righteous sings and rejoices**: If **transgression** belongs to the **evil man**, then singing and rejoicing belong to the **righteous**. The singing and rejoicing are an expression of what is inside them, just as much as the **transgression** is an expression of what is inside the **evil man**.

i. "Knox supplies the implicit comparison: 'innocence goes singing and rejoicing on its way.'" (Kidner)

Proverbs 29:7

The righteous considers the cause of the poor,
***But* the wicked does not understand *such* knowledge.**

a. **The righteous considers the cause of the poor**: One mark of the **righteous** man or woman is that they care for **the poor**. It is more than the response of feelings of pity; he **considers the cause of the poor**. It is thoughtful compassion in action.

b. **The wicked does not understand such knowledge**: Those who are **wicked**, rebellious against God and His wisdom, can't even **understand** such compassion. Since it doesn't directly serve their self-interest, they can't **understand** it.

i. "His ignorance and lack of understanding is not an intellectual defect but the expression of an evil perversion." (Waltke)

Proverbs 29:8

Scoffers set a city aflame,
But wise *men* turn away wrath.

a. **Scoffers set a city aflame**: In the family of fools, the **scoffers** are some of the worst offenders. They are so settled in their combative, cynical rejection of God and His wisdom that they may bring the judgment of God and fury of man against their own **city**.

i. "Mocking is catching [contagious], as the pestilence, and no less pernicious to the whole country." (Trapp)

ii. "Such scoffers make dangerous situations worse, whereas the wise calm things down and ensure peace in the community. See the account of the rebellion of Sheba the son of Bicri and how the wise woman averted disaster (2 Samuel 20)." (Ross)

b. **Wise men turn away wrath**: The opposite of the scoffer is the wise man. Collectively, **wise men** have the understanding, character, and righteousness that may **turn away** God's **wrath**.

i. G. Campbell Morgan said that Proverbs 29:8 was "A fine motto for engraving on the walls of the Foreign Office of any nation."

Proverbs 29:9

If **a wise man contends with a foolish man,**
Whether *the fool* **rages or laughs,** *there is* **no peace.**

a. **If a wise man contends with a foolish man**: Solomon considered some kind of argument or dispute between the **wise** and the **foolish**, likely set in a court of law. Since the two have different foundations and principles for living, it isn't a surprise that they would contend with each other.

i. "The setting of v. 9 is the court, in which the recklessness of the fool is given full vent." (Garrett)

b. **Whether the fool rages or laughs, there is no peace**: When two such different people contend, normally there will be **no peace**. The **fool** will respond with either anger or mocking, but neither will lead to **peace**. This should teach the **wise man** to be cautious about contending with the **foolish man**.

i. **There is no peace**: "No end or fruit of the debate, the fool will not be satisfied nor convinced." (Poole)

Proverbs 29:10

The bloodthirsty hate the blameless,
But the upright seek his well-being.

a. **The bloodthirsty hate the blameless**: There is a fundamental opposition between **the bloodthirsty** and **the blameless**. Those given to violence and brutality (**the bloodthirsty**) simply **hate the blameless**, both because the life and message of the **blameless** convicts the **bloodthirsty** and because the **bloodthirsty** hate all the **blameless** stand for.

i. John Trapp thought of some examples of **the bloodthirsty** in history: "Charles IX of France, author of the Parisian Massacre, looking upon the dead carcase of the admiral, that stank by being long kept unburied, uttered this most stinking speech: *Quam suaviter olet cadaver inimiei!* - How sweet is the smell of an enemy's carcase! And the queen mother of Scotland, beholding the dead bodies of her Protestant subjects, whom she had slain in battle, said that she never saw a finer piece of tapestry in all her life."

b. **The upright seek his well-being**: The **upright** men or women **seek** and care for the **well-being** of the **blameless**. This is a great contrast to the **bloodthirsty**.

Proverbs 29:11

A fool vents all his feelings,
But a wise *man* holds them back.

a. **A fool vents all his feelings**: It is the nature of **a fool** to think that everyone is interested in **all his feelings** and that he has some obligation to inflict **all his feelings** on others. This is a foolish offense to self-respect, self-restraint, and courtesy towards others.

b. **A wise man holds them back**: The **wise man** knows that there is a time and place to vent one's feelings, but one should never imitate the fool in exposing **all his feelings**.

i. **Holds them back**: "The verb (used in Psalm 89:9 of the stilling of a storm) speaks of anger overcome, not merely checked." (Kidner)

ii. "Or, In an inner room, in the bottom and bosom of his mind, till he see a fit season; as knowing well that all truths are not fit for all times, but discretion must be used." (Trapp)

Proverbs 29:12

If a ruler pays attention to lies,
All his servants *become* wicked.

a. **If a ruler pays attention to lies**: Anyone in authority will have many who want to use his or her power and position for their own advancement. Some of those may use **lies** to influence, frighten, manipulate, or simply deceive that **ruler**. The wise ruler **pays** no **attention to lies**.

i. "A king, a president, or any chief executive officer must set a high standard and rigorously maintain it or face the consequences of corruption running rampant in his administration." (Garrett)

b. **All his servants become wicked**: When the **servants** see that the **ruler** can be influenced by **lies**, it encourages them to lie. Deception is rewarded and telling the truth is discouraged. The atmosphere around that ruler and his **servants** becomes poisonous and incompetent.

i. **Become wicked**: "Partly because he chooseth only such for his service; and partly because they are either corrupted by his example, or engaged by their place and interest to please him, and comply with his base lusts." (Poole)

ii. "Courtiers adjust themselves to the prince—when they see that deception and court flattery win the day, they learn how the game is played." (Ross)

Proverbs 29:13

The poor *man* and the oppressor have this in common:
The LORD gives light to the eyes of both.

a. **The poor man and the oppressor have this in common**: It is difficult to think of two greater contrasts than the **poor man** and the **oppressor**. Despite their great differences, they have something **in common**.

b. **The LORD gives light to the eyes of both**: God gives some kind of **light**, some kind of revelation in creation and conscience, to every person (Romans 1:19-21). One may obey or reject God's message in that **light**, but God **gives light to the eyes of both**.

i. "That is to say, all intelligence is a divine gift, whether it be used in righteousness or in wickedness. Sin is always the prostitution of a God-given power to base purposes." (Morgan)

Proverbs 29:14

The king who judges the poor with truth,
His throne will be established forever.

a. **The king who judges the poor with truth**: Part of the responsibility of a **king** or any leader is to make judgments, and sometimes those regarding **the poor** and disadvantaged. That **king** or leader must be careful to not show partiality against (or for) **the poor**, but to make judgment according to **truth**.

b. **His throne will be established forever**: That king who refuses to show partiality and judges the **poor** according to **truth** can expect to have a long reign. Their reign will be blessed by God and received by the people.

i. "The poor are no less created in the image of God than the rich, and they have God as their avenger should the rich fail in their duty. For this reason the security of a king's reign depends on equitably dispensing justice." (Garrett)

ii. John Trapp thought of how this pointed to the throne of Jesus Messiah, **established forever**: "Lo, such a prince shall sit firm upon his throne; his kingdom shall be bound to him with chains of adamant, as Dionysius dreamt that his was; he shall have the hearts of his subjects, which is the best life-guard, and God for his protection; for he is professedly the poor man's patron, [Psalms 9:18-19] and makes heavy complaints of those that wrong them. [Isaiah 3:13-15; Isaiah 10:1-3; Amos 5:11-12; Amos 8:4-6; Zephaniah 3:12]."

Proverbs 29:15

The rod and rebuke give wisdom,
But a child left *to himself* brings shame to his mother.

a. **The rod and rebuke give wisdom**: We learn through correction. Jesus Himself learned through suffering (Hebrews 5:8) so we should not despise God's use of either **the rod** or the **rebuke**. No one is above learning through discipline.

i. "Discipline is the order of God's government. Parents are his dispensers of it to their children. Let correction be first tried, and if it succeeds, let the rod be spared. If not, let the rod do its work." (Bridges)

b. **A child left to himself brings shame to his mother**: The principle of the first line of this proverb is *especially* true regarding children. Children who are never trained with loving correction often bring **shame to** their parents.

i. "*His mother*, and father too; but he names only *the mother*, either because her indulgence oft spoils the child, or because children commonly stand in least awe of their mothers, and abuse the weakness of their sex, and tenderness of their natures." (Poole)

Proverbs 29:16

When the wicked are multiplied, transgression increases;
But the righteous will see their fall.

a. **When the wicked are multiplied, transgression increases**: There is something of a multiplication effect in the advance of wickedness. In some way, when the number of **wicked** people is doubled, then it seems **transgression increases** four or five times over.

b. **The righteous will see their fall**: This is welcome assurance when it seems that **transgression increases**. The righteous must not despair; God is still in control. Though the **wicked are multiplied**, God will not allow them to triumph in the end and they will **fall**.

i. "The faithful Christian minister, conscious of his inability to stem the ever-flowing torrent of iniquity, would sink in despair but for the assured confidence that he is on the conquering side, that his cause, being the cause of his Lord, must eventually prevail." (Bridges)

Proverbs 29:17

Correct your son, and he will give you rest;
Yes, he will give delight to your soul.

a. **Correct your son, and he will give you rest**: Many proverbs speak of the importance of correcting and training our children. If we leave them to themselves, to their peers, or to the culture, and fail to **correct** them, they will be an ongoing source of trouble and strife, giving us no **rest**.

b. **Yes, he will give delight to your soul**: Every parent wants this **delight** of **soul**. There is a sense in which God appeals to our own self-interest. If you won't **correct your son** because it is good for him, then do it because it is good for you!

Proverbs 29:18

Where *there is* no revelation, the people cast off restraint;
But happy *is* he who keeps the law.

a. **Where there is no revelation, the people cast off restraint**: The **revelation** in mind here is not the spontaneous word from a purported prophet. It is God's great **revelation**, His revealed word through the Hebrew prophets and later the apostles and prophets who gave us the New Testament. When God's word is unavailable or rejected, **the people cast off restraint**. They no longer have a standard greater than their own feelings or current opinions.

i. Other translations (such as the King James Version) express this in these words: *where there is no vision, the people perish*. This has often been taken to say, "Where there is no visionary leadership, people and enterprises fail." That is often a true principle, but *not* what Solomon wrote here. There is little doubt that the Hebrew word *hazon* means "God's revelation," and not "visionary leadership." "In sum, *hazon* refers here to the sage's inspired revelation of wisdom." (Waltke)

ii. "The word *hazon* refers to divine communication to prophets (as in 1 Samuel 3:1) and not to individual goals that are formed." (Ross)

iii. **Revelation**: "…is to be taken in its exact sense of the revelation a prophet receives." (Kidner)

iv. "Where Divine revelation, and the faithful preaching of the sacred testimonies, are neither reverenced nor attended, the ruin of that land is at no great distance." (Clarke)

v. "No greater calamity, therefore, can there be than the removal of the revelation…. Where revelation is withdrawn from a church, the people perish in ignorance and delusion." (Bridges)

b. **The people cast off restraint**: This principle was lived out in Israel's history. Judges 17:6, 21:25, and 1 Samuel 3:1 all describe such times when God's word was abandoned, and the people lived with no **restraint**.

i. **Cast off restraint**: "Or, *is made naked*; stripped of their best ornaments, God's favour and protection, as this word is taken, Exodus 32:25." (Poole)

c. **Happy is he who keeps the law**: In contrast, there is happiness and contentment for the one **who keeps the law**. In this sense, the Bible is something like a guide given to us by our owner and creator, telling us how to live a wise and blessed life. It is within **restraint**, but not in an oppressive sense. Only a fool thinks that all **restraint** is oppressive.

i. **He who keeps the law**: "Although the want of God's word be sufficient for men's destruction, yet the having, and hearing, or reading of it is not sufficient for their salvation, except they also keep or obey it." (Poole)

Proverbs 29:19

A servant will not be corrected by mere words;
For though he understands, he will not respond.

a. **A servant will not be corrected by mere words**: The idea is not of someone who has an honorable, **servant**-like heart. The idea is of someone of menial service who has a slave-like mentality that can't be lifted above his or her present misery. That person is unlikely to **be corrected by mere words**. Tough life experience and discipline will be more likely to teach them.

i. "In this democratic age the idea that one should have this kind of authority over someone is perhaps offensive, but in any age workers can become undisciplined and unreliable if some kind of authority and discipline procedure is not established." (Garrett)

ii. "The verse is probably a general observation on the times; doubtless there were slaves who did better (e.g., Joseph in Egypt; Daniel in Babylon)." (Ross)

b. **Though he understands, he will not respond**: This shows that the problem with such a one is not mental or intellectual. **He understands** well enough; the problem is that **he will not respond**. It will take more than words to get him or her to **respond** and learn wisdom.

i. **Will not respond**: "Either by words, expressing his readiness; or by deeds, speedily and cheerfully performing thy commands; but will neglect his duty, pretending that he did not hear or understand thee." (Poole)

Proverbs 29:20

Do you see a man hasty in his words?
There is **more hope for a fool than for him.**

a. **Do you see a man hasty in his words?** Proverbs often teaches us that a mark of a fool is that they don't have control over what they say. They are **hasty in** their **words**.

b. **There is more hope for a fool than for him**: To Solomon, the **man hasty in his words** was a special kind of a fool, a super-fool. Lacking wisdom, his impulsive speech sets him beyond the hope of even the normal **fool**.

Proverbs 29:21

He who pampers his servant from childhood
Will have him as a son in the end.

a. **He who pampers his servant from childhood**: The idea is of a man who is overly soft and generous towards his **servant**. He worries too much about making life easy and pleasant for his **servant**.

i. "A master that would be, as he ought, both loved and feared by his servants, must see to two things: - (1.) The well-choosing; and (2.) The well using of them." (Trapp)

b. **Will have him as a son in the end**: This isn't always in a good sense. The one who **pampers his servant** will make the servant so attached to him that he will end up with another obligation and another person who expects an inheritance.

i. "This is a simple statement of a fact. Whether it be one of blessing or of evil depends on the Christian's servant. An evil servant treated well assumes the position of a son in arrogance. A good servant treated well assumes the position of a son in devotion." (Morgan)

ii. "Such persons are generally forgetful of their obligations, assume the rights and privileges of children, and are seldom good for any thing." (Clarke)

iii. There is some dispute about the word here translated **a son**. Ross had an alternative idea: "The proverb says that if someone pampers his servant from youth, in the end (of this procedure) he will have 'grief' (*manon*)."

Proverbs 29:22

An angry man stirs up strife,
And a furious man abounds in transgression.

a. **An angry man stirs up strife**: It is in the nature of the **angry man** to spread his **strife** to others. With peace lacking in his own soul, it's easy to put his inner **strife** upon others.

i. "'Anger' describes his outward visage of snorting nostrils, and 'wrath' [**furious**], his inner heat of boiling emotions of resentment." (Waltke)

b. **A furious man abounds in transgression**: When the **angry** or **furious man** spreads his **strife**, it makes **transgression** abound. Sin **abounds** and the atmosphere is marked by a lack of self-control.

i. "His furious spirit is always carrying him into *extremes*, and each of these is a *transgression*." (Clarke)

Proverbs 29:23

A man's pride will bring him low,
But the humble in spirit will retain honor.

a. **A man's pride will bring him low**: Because God resists the proud (James 4:6 and 1 Peter 5:5), **pride** will naturally **bring** a man **low**. Like Satan, the one who hoped to rise higher through his pride will fall (Isaiah 14:13-15).

i. Waltke points out that the Hebrew word translated "'Pride' derives from a root meaning 'to be high' and so constitutes a precise antithetical parallel of 'lowly.'"

b. **The humble in spirit will retain honor**: Just as much as God resists the proud, He also gives grace to the humble (again, James 4:6 and 1 Peter 5:5). God's gracious blessing to the **humble in spirit** means they will gain and **retain honor**.

i. "Thus honour, like a shadow, flees from them that pursue it, and follows them who flee from it." (Poole)

Proverbs 29:24

Whoever is a partner with a thief hates his own life;
He swears to tell the truth, but reveals nothing.

a. **Whoever is a partner with a thief hates his own life**: To **partner with a thief** is to reject wisdom and embrace folly. The one who steals from others will steal from you, and perhaps with violence threatening your **own life**.

i. "The law makes no distinction between the thief and the accomplice. Consenting to sin, receiving the stolen goods, involves us in the guilt and punishment." (Bridges)

ii. "Paradoxically, the partner joined the thief to satisfy the greed of his swollen appetites, but instead he loses that very life with its drives and appetites." (Waltke)

b. **He swears to tell the truth, but reveals nothing**: The **partner** to the **thief** is the kind of man who will repeatedly vow **to tell the truth**, but **reveals nothing** about his partner's criminal activity. He places loyalty to his friend above his loyalty to God.

i. "The call to testify is actually a curse pronounced on anyone who will not testify. This proverb, using the same word for oath or curse, describes someone who has befriended a thief, becomes aware of his wrongdoing, but remains silent when he hears a call to come forward and give evidence. He has brought a curse down on his own head." (Garrett)

Proverbs 29:25-26

The fear of man brings a snare,
But whoever trusts in the LORD shall be safe.
Many seek the ruler's favor,
But justice for man *comes* from the LORD.

a. **The fear of man brings a snare**: Many people of good heart but not enough courage live in bondage to **the fear of man**. They worry far too much about what people think, instead of first being concerned about what God and wisdom say, and what integrity would lead them to do. This is a **snare** that traps many people.

i. "The 'fear of man' describes any situation in which one is anxious about not offending another person. For example, someone might be afraid to oppose the unethical actions of a superior out of fear of losing a job. This verse tells the reader to do what is right and trust the outcome to Yahweh." (Garrett)

ii. "And therefore they do not ask, 'What should I do?' but 'What will my friends think of me?' They cannot brave the finger of scorn.... Oh, for deliverance from this principle of bondage." (Bridges)

iii. **The fear of man**: Saul, Aaron, and Peter are examples of men who were stained by the fear of man. "How often has this led weak men, though *sincere* in their general character, to deny their God, and abjure his people!" (Clarke)

iv. "It was the fear of man that caused Pilate's name to become infamous in the history of the world and of the Church of God, and it will be infamous to all eternity. The fear of man led him to slay the Savior;

take care that it does not lead you to do something of the same kind." (Spurgeon)

v. "Why, I have known some who were afraid even to give away a tract; they were as much alarmed as though they had to put their hand into a tiger's mouth." (Spurgeon)

vi. "There is one sin which I believe I have never committed; I think that I have never been afraid of any of you, and I hope, by the grace of God, that I never shall be. If I dare not speak the truth upon all points, and dare not rebuke sin, what is the good of me to you? Yet I have heard sermons which seemed to me to have been made to the order of the congregation. But honest hearers want honest preaching; and if they find that the preachers message comes home to them, they thank God that it is so." (Spurgeon)

b. **But whoever trusts in the LORD shall be safe**: The contrast to the **fear of man** is he who **trusts in the LORD**. That person will be in the safest place imaginable – **safe** in the care of a loving, powerful God.

i. "Release from such bondage comes when people put their faith in the Lord alone. See Proverbs 10:27; 12:2; and the example of the apostles in Acts 5:29." (Ross)

ii. "It is not, 'He that trusteth in himself;' not, 'He that trusteth in a priest;' not, 'He that performs good works, and trusts in them,' but, 'whoso putteth his trust in the Lord shall be safe.' The man who is trusting in the blood and righteousness of Jesus may not always be happy, but he is safe; he may not always be singing, but he is safe; he may not always have the joy of full assurance, but he is safe. He may sometimes be distressed, but, he is always safe; he may sometimes question his interest in Christ, but he is always safe." (Spurgeon)

c. **Many seek the ruler's favor**: This is presented as a simple fact. There are many who long for the benefit that a ruler may give them. This relates to the **fear of man** mentioned in the previous verse; those who depend on the **ruler's favor** for their security and prosperity must fear and **seek the ruler's favor**.

d. **But justice for man comes from the LORD**: When we depend upon man for our **justice**, our security, or our prosperity, we will be disappointed. Such **justice** and its benefits come **from the LORD**, not primarily through even the mightiest ruler. If the ruler does give out **justice**, he does it as God's agent.

i. "Verse 26 does not forbid seeking relief from injustice through the legal system, but it does state that one should place more faith in Yahweh than in human institutions." (Garrett)

Proverbs 29:27

An unjust man *is* an abomination to the righteous,
And *he who is* upright in the way *is* an abomination to the wicked.

a. **An unjust man is an abomination to the righteous**: An **unjust man** does not please those among God's **righteous**. They share God's regard of the wicked, seeing them as an **abomination** for their sins against God and man.

i. "Who yet hates, *non virum sed vitium,* not the person of a wicked man, but his sin - as the physician hates the disease, but loves the patient, and strives to recover him - he abhors that which is evil, perfectly hates it." (Trapp)

b. **He who is upright in the way is an abomination to the wicked**: It works both ways. The **upright** man or woman is seen as **an abomination to the wicked**. Their righteous life is an unwelcome rebuke to the wicked.

i. "A statement of the necessary and abiding antipathy between righteousness and unrighteousness." (Morgan)

ii. "Here is the oldest, the most rooted, the most universal quarrel in the world. It was the first fruit of the Fall (Genesis 3:15). It has continued ever since and will last to the end of the world." (Bridges)

iii. "This proverb…serves as an apt summation of the whole Hezekiah text. Righteousness and immorality are mutually exclusive. One must follow one path or the other (Jeremiah 6:16)." (Garrett)

Proverbs 30 – The Wisdom of Agur

A. Agur the man.

1. (1) The words of Agur.

The words of Agur the son of Jakeh, *his* utterance. This man declared to Ithiel—to Ithiel and Ucal:

a. **The words of Agur the son of Jakeh**: Proverbs 30 is a collection of wisdom from a man known only to this chapter of the Bible. When the *men of Hezekiah* gathered additional material for Proverbs (Proverbs 25:1), they added these **words of Agur**. We have no other mention of **Agur the son of Jakeh**.

i. Solomon wasn't the *only* man of wisdom in his day or afterward. Other men of wisdom beside Solomon are described in 1 Kings 4:30-31.

ii. Some think that **Agur** is another name for Solomon (Ross says the Jewish Midrash asserts this) but this is unlikely. "From this introduction, from the names here used, and from the style of the book, it appears evident that Solomon was not the author of this chapter; and that it was designed to be distinguished from his work by this very preface, which specifically distinguishes it from the preceding work…I believe *Agur, Jakeh, Ithiel,* and *Ucal,* to be the *names of persons* who did exist, but of whom we know nothing but what is here mentioned. *Agur* seems to have been a public *teacher*, and *Ithiel* and *Ucal* to have been his *scholars*." (Clarke)

iii. "Nothing definite is known about the writers, and it is vain to speculate where God is silent. It is much better to give our full attention to the teaching than to indulge in unprofitable speculation about the writers." (Bridges)

b. **His utterance**: This has the sense of a prophetic word, inspired by God. Like Solomon earlier in the book (Proverbs 2:6), Agur understood that his words here came from God.

> i. The wisdom of Agur in Proverbs 30 is filled with observations on life and the natural world. Agur is one "inviting us to look again at our world with the eye of a man of faith who is an artist and an observer of character. Cf. the words of the Psalmist: 'I muse on the work of thy hands' (Psalm 143:5)." (Kidner)

c. **This man declared to Ithiel**: These proverbs are wisdom sayings that **Agur** spoke to two other men, **Ithiel** and **Ucal**. Again, we have no other mention of these men in the rest of the Bible.

> i. Some interpreters (such as Trapp) have thought that the names **Ithiel and Ucal** were symbolic, hidden references to the coming Messiah, Jesus Christ. This is unlikely. "Ithiel, which signifies *God with me*, and answers to *Immanuel*, which is *God with us*; and Ucal, which signifies *power* or *prevalency*. But if he had meant this of Christ, why should he design him such obscure and ambiguous names, as if he would not be understood?" (Poole)

2. (2-3) Agur's humble introduction.

Surely I *am* more stupid than *any* man,
And do not have the understanding of a man.
I neither learned wisdom
Nor have knowledge of the Holy One.

a. **Surely I am more stupid than any man**: Many previous proverbs teach that humility is an essential aspect of wisdom. Here, with poetic exaggeration, Agur declared his own limitations when it comes to **understanding** and **wisdom**. David said, *I was like a beast before you* (Psalm 73:22). Job spoke of *man, who is a worm* (Job 25:6).

> i. **I neither learned wisdom**: "I have not been taught in the schools of wisdom, as the sons of prophets were, but must own myself to be an unlearned man, as the prophet Amos was, Amos 7:14,15." (Poole)

> ii. "Philosophy had failed him, and revelation was his sole confidence." (Spurgeon)

b. **Nor have knowledge of the Holy One**: Agur was also careful not to boast of his spiritual **knowledge**. He brings his lesson to us with great humility, not from a position of superiority.

i. "Earthbound mortals cannot find transcendent wisdom apart from the transcendent Lord. Real wisdom must find its starting point in God's revelation; in his light, we see light." (Waltke)

B. Agur's wisdom

1. (4) Man's humble place before God.

Who has ascended into heaven, or descended?
Who has gathered the wind in His fists?
Who has bound the waters in a garment?
Who has established all the ends of the earth?
What *is* His name, and what *is* His Son's name,
If you know?

a. **Who has ascended into heaven**: In a section that sounds much like Job 38-39, Agur called men and women to understand their limitations in understanding God and His creation. The wise and humble answer to each of these questions is, *God, and not man.*

i. "Where is there a man that can do this? And none but he who made and governs all the creatures can know and teach these things." (Poole)

b. **What is His name, and what is His Son's name**: After challenging his readers regarding the natural world, Agur finished with a challenge regarding man's limitations in spiritual knowledge. One can only know **what is His name** (God's nature, character) **and His Son's name** by God's own revelation. In all these things, we humbly depend on God's revelation for our knowledge.

c. **His Son's name**: Agur knew there was something special about the Son of God. We don't know to what extent he prophetically anticipated the Messiah, God the Son, Jesus Christ – but Agur knew that God had a Son, and the Son had a **name**.

i. "The Christian interpreter, however, cannot but think of the Son of God here and recall that he came down from above to reveal the truth to his people (John 3:31-33). Also, since 'God' is the only possible answer to the questions here, it is striking that the text speaks of his 'son.'" (Garrett)

2. (5-6) The purity, strength, and integrity of God's word.

Every word of God *is* pure;
He *is* a shield to those who put their trust in Him.
Do not add to His words,
Lest He rebuke you, and you be found a liar.

a. **Every word of God is pure**: Agur valued and explained the *purity* of God's word. It is all good and all helpful, being completely **pure**. Because it is **pure** it can and should be trusted.

> i. **Every word of God is pure**: "A metaphor taken from the *purifying of metals*. Every thing that God has pronounced, every inspiration which the prophets have received, is pure, without mixture of error, without dross. Whatever trials it may be exposed to, it is always like *gold*: it *bears the fire*, and comes out with the same *lustre*, the same *purity*, and the same *weight*." (Clarke)

> ii. "Nothing is learned solidly by abstract speculation. Go to the Book. Here all is light and purity. While the secret things belong to the Lord our God, yet the things that are revealed are our holy directory." (Bridges)

b. **He is a shield to those who put their trust in Him**: In the context of writing about God's word, Agur explained that God is **a shield**. The sense is that God gives His **pure** word to protect His people if they will use the wisdom and encouragement of His word to **put their trust in Him**. Additionally, a **shield** is something we **trust**, and if we wisely trust God and His revelation of Himself in His word, He will protect us.

> i. It isn't enough to know **every word of God is pure** if you don't take the next step and **trust** Him as your **shield**. "Notice (5b) that the aim of revelation is to promote trust, not bare knowledge, and trust that goes behind the words to the Speaker." (Kidner)

c. **Do not add to His words**: God's word needs no addition or improvement from us. We don't need to take away from His words or **add to His words** (as in Revelation 22:18-19). If we do, we are targets of God's **rebuke** and will be exposed as liars. If we say something different than God's word, then He is right and we are wrong. He tells the truth and we will **be found a liar**.

> i. "The temptation is to improve on the text if not by actually adding new material then by interpreting it in ways that make more of a passage's teaching than is really there. It is what Paul called 'going beyond what is written' (1 Corinthians 4:6)." (Garrett)

> ii. "Such add to God's word as wrest it and rack it; making it speak that which it never thought; causing it to go two miles where it would go but one; gnawing and tawing it to their own purposes, as the shoemaker taws upper leather with his teeth." (Trapp)

> iii. "Such a practice is apt to make one a popular Bible teacher since people think that the teacher has profound insight into the text and

can find hidden truths. Sooner or later, however, such superinterpreters will be shown to be wrong." (Garrett)

iv. "How amply has this been fulfilled in the case of the *Romish Church*! It has *added* all the *gross stuff* in the *Apocrypha*, besides innumerable *legends* and *traditions*, to the word of God! They have been tried by the *refiner's fire*. And this Church has been *reproved*, and *found to be a liar*, in attempting to filiate on the most holy God *spurious writings* discreditable to his nature." (Clarke)

3. (7-9) A prayer for integrity.

Two *things* I request of You
(Deprive me not before I die):
Remove falsehood and lies far from me;
Give me neither poverty nor riches—
Feed me with the food allotted to me;
Lest I be full and deny *You*,
And say, "Who *is* the Lord?"
Or lest I be poor and steal,
And profane the name of my God.

a. **Two things I request of You**: These verses contain a wise and humble prayer from Agur. He earnestly asked God for **two things**, and he wanted to receive them on *this* side of eternity (**Deprive me not before I die**).

i. "The author recognizes his weaknesses, both in his tendency to forget God when life is too easy and to turn in desperation away from God when life is too hard." (Garrett)

b. **Remove falsehood and lies far from me**: Agur first asked for personal integrity. He wanted to be a man marked by truth, and not by **falsehood and lies**. Knowing God is a God of truth (Proverbs 30:5-6), he didn't want such deception anywhere near him.

i. "The 'falsehood and lies' of v. 8 are the deceptiveness of both wealth and poverty. The former convinces one that God is not necessary; and the latter, that either he is of no help or that his laws are impossible to keep." (Garrett)

c. **Give me neither poverty nor riches**: Agur's second request was to have neither great **poverty** nor great **riches**. He wanted to be satisfied with God's provision in his life (**feed me with the food allotted to me**).

i. **Feed me with the food allotted to me**: "But there is other food which is needful. The daily bread of love, of hope, of holy thought, and fellowship. There is other hunger than that of the body. But this also will be provided, according as each day requires." (Meyer)

d. **Profane the name of my God**: Agur wanted **neither poverty nor riches** out of concern that either extreme might lead him to **profane the name** of God. He did not want to arrogantly **deny** God because he felt he was so rich he didn't need God. He did not want to be so **poor** that he would use poverty as an excuse to sin (**lest I be poor and steal**). Either path would **profane the name** of God.

i. If a wise man like Agur was tempted to allow riches to **profane the name of my God**, we must also be on guard. "Even an Agur full fed may grow wanton, and be dipping his fingers in the devil's sauce; yea, so far may he forget himself, as to deny the Lord." (Trapp)

ii. **And profane the name of my God**: We instinctively want to honor and even protect the name of our God, even if our god is an idol. This statement of Agur showed that "In sum, the glory of God, not his personal need, motivates Agur's requests." (Waltke)

4. (10) Speaking ill of others.

Do not malign a servant to his master,
Lest he curse you, and you be found guilty.

a. **Do not malign a servant to his master**: This proverb has to do with harsh, unfair criticism (**malign**) spoken to another about a third party not present. It shouldn't be done, and doing it without the knowledge of the one spoken against makes it even worse. If it is wrong to do this in regard to a **servant**, it is even worse to do it against someone else.

i. "Do not bring a *false* accusation against a *servant*, lest *thou be found guilty* of the falsehood, and he *curse thee* for having traduced his character, and in his turn traduce thine. In general, do not meddle with other people's servants." (Clarke)

ii. "Behind this injunction is a demand that one respect the person of the menial worker. His work relationship with his master is between the two of them; one should no more interfere here than one would interfere in a matter involving a superior or an equal." (Garrett)

b. **Lest he curse you**: The one spoken against may rightfully speak a **curse** against the one who secretly maligns others. The **curse** may in fact come to pass if the one who maligns is **found guilty** of the offense.

i. "If the servant is innocent, his curse will count (cf. Proverbs 26:2), for there is a Judge." (Kidner)

5. (11-15a) Foolish, sinful generations.

***There is* a generation *that* curses its father,**
And does not bless its mother.

There is a generation *that is* pure in its own eyes,
Yet is not washed from its filthiness.
There is a generation—oh, how lofty are their eyes!
And their eyelids are lifted up.
There is a generation whose teeth *are like* swords,
And whose fangs *are like* knives,
To devour the poor from off the earth,
And the needy from *among* men.
The leech has two daughters—
Give *and* Give!

a. **There is a generation that curses its father**: The generation that disobeys God's command to honor father and mother (Exodus 20:12, Ephesians 6:2) puts its folly on full display. That **generation** sows seeds of conflict that will grow into a bitter harvest of personal and community strife.

i. "Many are the forms in which this proud abomination shows itself: resistance to a parent's authority, contempt of his reproof, shamelessly defiling his name, needlessly exposing his sin, coveting his substance, denying his obligation." (Bridges)

b. **There is a generation that is pure in its own eyes**: The generation that is blind to their own stain of sin will never be **washed from its filthiness**. When we ignore or cover our sin, it never gets resolved.

i. "Anyone who thinks he is pure apart from God's divine cleansing conceals an unsuspected depth of depravity (Proverbs 3:7; 12:15). Jesus condemned the self-righteous Pharisees of murder and of belonging to this generation." (Waltke)

ii. "There is a generation, a group of people, who may observe all outer ritual but pay no attention to inner cleansing (see Isa 1:16; Matt 23:27). Such hypocrisy is harmful in every walk of life." (Ross)

c. **There is a generation—oh, how lofty are their eyes**: The generation that walks in pride and arrogance will experience God's resistance, because God resists the proud but gives grace to the humble (James 4:6, 1 Peter 5:5).

i. "Who are proud and insolent, advancing themselves, and despising all others in comparison of themselves, and showing the pride of their hearts in their countenances and carriages." (Poole)

d. **There is a generation whose teeth are like swords**: The generation filled with greed devours everything as if their **teeth** were **swords** and their **fangs** like **knives**. They **devour the poor from off the earth** and, like the **leech**, can never be satisfied (**give and give**).

i. **Devour the poor**: "These cruel oppressors are marked by pitiful cowardice. They vent their wantonness only where there is little or no power of resistance as they devour the poor." (Garrett)

ii. **The leech has two daughters**: "Personifies the blood-sucking *horseleech,* which had two sucking organs at each end (one to suck blood, the other to attach itself to its host), as a mother of *two* (see v. 7) *daughters.* This leech could be found in all stale waters of Palestine and attached itself above all in nostrils and palate of drinking horses." (Waltke)

iii. "Implicitly, just as the parasitical, loathsome leech must be quickly eliminated from doing more damage, so also the wise must either exercise precaution to avoid the greedy or take quick and decisive action to get rid of them and so preserve his life and health." (Waltke)

6. (15b-16) Never satisfied.

There are three *things that* are never satisfied,
Four never say, "Enough!":
The grave,
The barren womb,
The earth *that* is not satisfied with water—
And the fire never says, "Enough!"

a. **Three things that are never satisfied, four never say "Enough!"**: The thought of the generation that greedily devours everything made Agur consider that there were **four** things that could never be satisfied.

i. As was with the pattern back at Proverbs 6:16, the formula *three and then four* implies that the list is specific but not exhaustive.

b. **The grave, the barren womb**: The dead never seem to stop dying and the **grave** of humanity never seems to be filled. The **barren womb** feels the ache of its emptiness and what is often felt like an unfulfilled purpose.

i. "Barren women are most desirous of children, which yet are certain cares, but uncertain comforts. How impatient was Rachel! how importunate was Hannah!" (Trapp)

c. **The earth that is not satisfied with water—and the fire**: The earth seems to continually drink and absorb the water poured out upon it, and **fire** will burn as long as there is fuel to burn. These all are examples of things that never seem to say, **"Enough!"**

7. (17) The mocking eye.

The eye *that* mocks *his* father,
And scorns obedience to *his* mother,

The ravens of the valley will pick it out,
And the young eagles will eat it.

a. **The eye that mocks his father**: This **eye** belongs to the fool, the one who **mocks** and disobeys **father** and **mother**. This upsets the social order and sets the generations in conflict.

i. "His *eye* reveals his inner cast of mind." (Waltke)

b. **The ravens of the valley will pick it out**: Agur used a vivid poetic description to tell of the ruin waiting for the child who **mocks** and **scorns** their parents. The poetic image is doubled, sending multiple **ravens** and **young eagles** to do the terrible but fitting work. This fool was blind in his mocking and disobedience; this poetic image tells of a fit penalty for someone so morally and spiritually blind.

i. "The ravens of the valleys or brooks are said to be most ravenous; and the young eagles or vultures smell out carcases, and the first thing they do to them is to pick out their eyes." (Trapp)

ii. **The young eagles**: "The mother eagle shall scoop out such an eye, and carry it to the nest to feed her young. Many of the *disobedient to parents* have come to an *untimely end*, and, in the *field of battle*, where many a profligate has fallen, and upon *gibbets*, have actually become the prey of ravenous birds." (Clarke)

8. (18-19) Four amazing things.

There are three *things which* are too wonderful for me,
Yes, four *which* I do not understand:
The way of an eagle in the air,
The way of a serpent on a rock,
The way of a ship in the midst of the sea,
And the way of a man with a virgin.

a. **Three things which are too wonderful for me, yes, four**: Agur gave no advice in the proverb, but reminded us all that there are things that **are too wonderful** for our complete understanding, things we should simply be amazed at and a bit humbled in the presence of. Agur gave his list of **four** amazing things.

i. It isn't entirely clear what these four things have in common. There are many suggestions, and they can collectively be true.

- All four things are visible for a while, then hidden.

- All four things progress without leaving a trace.

- All four things have a mysterious means of progress or motivation.

- All four things move in the domain of something else.

ii. "The way of all four wonders move in and cleave to their appropriate and difficult environments according to an invisible course in an easy, intriguing, gracious, undulating manner, without leaving a trace and without being taught, and yet reaching their goals." (Waltke)

iii. "It would be better sought in that of the easy mastery, by the appropriate agent, of elements as difficult to negotiate as air, rock, sea—and young woman." (Kidner)

b. **The way of an eagle in the air**: The flight of a majestic **eagle** amazes us with its power, height, and grace.

c. **The way of a serpent on a rock**: The **serpent** suns itself on the rock, yet is ready to flee at the slightest disturbance – and can slither itself over hard and sharp rock without injury!

d. **The way of a ship in the midst of the sea**: A **ship** is so small **in the midst of the sea**, yet it virtually conquers the sea by using it as a road for travel and trade.

e. **The way of a man with a virgin**: The power of young love and its desire seems that it would overwhelm both **a man** and **a virgin**, but they marry and make a productive life together.

i. "This mystery might begin with the manner of obtaining the love of the woman but focuses on the most intimate part of human relationships. So the most intimate moments of love are at the heart of what the sage considers to be wonderful." (Ross)

ii. "Using delicate imagery for love…his small poem sings implicit praise to God for the glories of creation, especially for sexual love." (Van Leeuwen, cited in Waltke)

iii. "His awe of human 'eros' with a virgin stands in contrast to the adulteress's who sees nothing wrong with demeaning her sexuality with another sexual partner to nothing more than eating a meal (v. 20)." (Waltke)

9. (20) The wickedness of the adulterous woman.

This *is* the way of an adulterous woman:
She eats and wipes her mouth,
And says, "I have done no wickedness."

a. **This is the way of the adulterous woman**: Like Solomon, Agur presented his wisdom in proverbs to his son or a young man. Surely this proverb also applies to the **adulterous** man, but because of his audience he has first in view **the way of the adulterous woman**.

i. "The fifth, and unnatural, marvel (20) is that of a person utterly at ease and in her element in sin; an act of adultery is as unremarkable to her as a meal." (Kidner)

b. **She eats and wipes her mouth**: Since this woman is characterized by her adultery, her eating here is a tasteful reference to her sin of adultery. She satisfies her hunger for adultery, then (according to this poetic picture) casually **wipes her mouth** and considers herself blameless (**I have done no wickedness**). This **adulterous woman** represents many who sin against God, their marriage, their family, their community, their partner in adultery, and their own bodies yet consider it no **wickedness** at all.

i. **She eats**: Once before in Proverbs, eating was used as a symbol of sexual activity (Proverbs 9:17).

ii. "The adulteress lacks any conscience against smashing the very foundations of an ordered society, because, for her, gratifying her sexual appetite is no different from gratifying her gastronomical appetite." (Waltke)

iii. "Wiping her mouth after eating means that the adulteress treats sexual liaisons the same way she does eating: she just finishes up and goes home without a care and certainly without a sense of guilt." (Garrett)

10. (21-23) Four unbearable things.

For three *things* the earth is perturbed,
Yes, for four it cannot bear up:
For a servant when he reigns,
A fool when he is filled with food,
A hateful *woman* when she is married,
And a maidservant who succeeds her mistress.

a. **For three things the earth is perturbed**: Using the three-and-four phrasing once again (previously in Proverbs 30:15 and 18), Agur spoke of four things that trouble **the earth**: things that are fundamentally not right. Agur gave his list of four unbearable things.

b. **A servant when he reigns**: Agur did not mean a man with a servant's heart like Jesus would later perfectly display. He meant a man with a servile, debased mind, who thought and lived as a slave instead of a free man. It is unbearable when such a man **reigns**.

i. "A servant who gains authority over others has neither the training nor disposition to rule well." (Garrett)

ii. "The proverb does not have in view a slave like Joseph who rose to power through wisdom (Genesis 41:41)." (Waltke)

c. **A fool when he is filled with food**: When **a fool** is satisfied, it only rewards his folly and gives him the energy and the resources to be even more foolish. This, Agur tells us, is unbearable.

i. "Can we wonder that he causes trouble and is a curse, since he gives full rein to his appetite and becomes even more devoid of understanding than before?" (Bridges)

d. **A hateful woman when she is married**: This is unbearable because the **hateful woman** should never be able to find a husband, and there seems to be a fundamental injustice when she does. It is also unbearable for her husband and her family, to live with a **hateful woman**.

i. **A hateful woman**: "Points to an odious, quarrelsome, unlovable woman whom society rejects, the opposite of a prudent wife." (Waltke)

ii. "The implication may be that she is naturally unpleasant…or that she is merely old-maidish, and her success has gone to her head." (Kidner)

e. **A maidservant who succeeds her mistress**: This case is similar to the previously described **servant when he reigns**. When the social order is upset and unworthy ones dominate the culture, it becomes unbearable.

i. "The tension from the threat of Hagar in Genesis 16:5 and 21:10 shows how unbearable this could be." (Ross)

11. (24-28) Four small yet wise creatures.

There are four *things which* are little on the earth,
But they *are* exceedingly wise:
The ants *are* a people not strong,
Yet they prepare their food in the summer;
The rock badgers are a feeble folk,
Yet they make their homes in the crags;
The locusts have no king,
Yet they all advance in ranks;
The spider skillfully grasps with its hands,
And it is in kings' palaces.

a. **There are four things which are little on the earth**: Agur looked to the world of animals and noted **four** small animals (**little on the earth**), yet they are **exceedingly wise**. No human trained them in their wisdom; they are truly taught of God – and so we may also be.

b. **They are exceeding wise**: Size doesn't determine wisdom. There are big fools and those who are small and not just **wise**, but **exceedingly** so. Agur listed these four examples which each teach a principle of wisdom.

i. "*But they are wise* uniquely uses 'wise' for animals to denote their skill to cope and their masterful cunning to survive in spite of their severe limitations that expose them to threats that endanger their very existence." (Waltke)

c. **The ants are a people not strong**: Ants are small and don't have much strength compared to a person or a large animal. Their wisdom is shown in that **they prepare their food in the summer**. They work in the time when work can be done, and aren't lazy or procrastinators. *Hard work can overcome individual weakness.*

i. "A quickening sermon do these little insects preach to us as they prepare for the coming winter. What must be the thoughtlessness of men who make no provision for the coming eternity!" (Bridges)

d. **The rock badgers are a feeble folk**: The conies or **rock badgers** (also known as marmots) don't have the speed or strength to stand against a large predator, especially one with sharp teeth. But they wisely **make their homes in the crags** and make the strength of the rock their own strength. *Find refuge among the strong.*

i. "It shall be our wisdom to work ourselves into the rock Christ Jesus, where we shall be safe from hellish hunters." (Trapp)

e. **The locusts have no king**: The **locusts** don't seem to have any kind of appointed leadership or structure. Yet they have the wisdom to **advance in ranks**, overwhelming anything that is in their way. If the locusts fought against themselves, they would get nowhere. They fight against the vegetation that they consume. *Teamwork can win the day.*

i. "They are well known for their amazing ability to form gigantic swarms that can wreak devastation of a scale almost beyond imagination. Highly reliable eyewitness accounts of modern locust plagues border on the incredible." (Waltke)

f. **The spider skillfully grasps with its hands**: The **spider** isn't loved, but it wisely uses its skill and unique abilities to go anywhere it wants to, even in **king's palaces**. *Using your gifts and unique skills can take you anywhere.*

i. Waltke (along with Ross and Kidner) suggests that **spider** may actually be *gecko* here, a "wall-lizard."

ii. "If we take it for the spider, she doth her work painfully and curiously, spins a finer thread than any woman can do, builds a finer house than any man can do, in manner and form like to the tent of an emperor. This base creature may teach us this wisdom, saith one, not to be bunglers or slubberers in our works, but to be exact in our trades, and labour so to excel therein, that our doings may be commendable and admirable." (Trapp)

12. (29-31) Four examples of majesty.

There are three *things which* are majestic in pace,
Yes, four *which* are stately in walk:
A lion, *which is* mighty among beasts
And does not turn away from any;
A greyhound,
A male goat also,
And a king *whose* troops *are* with him.

a. **There are three things which are majestic in pace**: For the fourth time in his brief collection of proverbs, Agur used the three-and-four structure to explain four wonderful things, **four** examples of majesty.

b. **A lion, which is mighty among beasts**: The first example is given a brief explanation. A **lion** has respect from all other animals, moves swiftly, and never retreats (**does not turn away from any**). *Courage displays majesty.*

c. **A greyhound, a male goat also, and a king whose troops are with him**: The last three examples are given without explanation. Yet when we consider the speed and grace of **a greyhound**, we see majesty. When we think of the stubborn persistence of the **male goat**, we see majesty. When we think of the power and determination of **a king whose troops are with him**, we see majesty. Each of these moves with majestic **pace**: swiftly, stubbornly, or powerfully.

i. Waltke (along with Kidner) has *strutting rooster* instead of **greyhound**.

ii. "It is *most likely* that this was the *greyhound*, which in the *East* are remarkably fine, and very *fleet*. Scarcely any thing can be conceived to *go* with greater fleetness, in full chase, than a greyhound with its prey in view: it seems to *swim* over the earth." (Clarke)

iii. **Male goat**: "How he walks, and what *state* he assumes, in the presence of his part of the flock, every one knows, who has at all noticed this animal." (Clarke)

13. (32-33) The foolishness of self-exaltation.

If you have been foolish in exalting yourself,
Or if you have devised evil, *put your* hand on *your* mouth.
For *as* the churning of milk produces butter,

And wringing the nose produces blood,
So the forcing of wrath produces strife.

a. **If you have been foolish in exalting yourself**: Agur personally expressed his own humility in the beginning of this chapter (Proverbs 30:1-4). Here he advises his readers to not be **foolish in exalting yourself**. Instead, follow what James wisely told us to do: *Humble yourselves in the sight of the Lord, and He will lift you up* (James 4:10). If you start to exalt yourself, **put your hand on your mouth**.

i. "A humble heart will repress the sparks of this unholy fire." (Bridges)

b. **If you have devised evil**: If you use the power and resources of your mind to devise **evil**, then *stop*. It is better to **put your hand on your mouth** and not say another word.

c. **The forcing of wrath produces strife**: This is the result of self-exaltation and the plotting of evil. As surely as **the churning of milk produces butter** and as surely as **wringing the nose produces blood**, so the expressions of **wrath** will make for conflict and **strife**. The wise man or woman knows a better way.

i. "*Churning…wringing…forcing* all translate one recurring word, *pressing…*or squeezing." (Kidner)

ii. "Those who make trouble get into trouble…. Hidden in the second simile, however, is the warning that those who make trouble are liable to get punched in the nose!" (Garrett)

iii. "So the intent of this concluding advice is to strive for peace and harmony through humility and righteousness." (Ross)

iv. "Too much stirring in an offensive matter bringeth forth brawling, lawing, warring, fighting." (Trapp)

Proverbs 31 – The Wisdom of King Lemuel

A. Wisdom from King Lemuel.

1. (1) The wisdom of King Lemuel – and his mother.

The words of King Lemuel, the utterance which his mother taught him:

a. **The words of King Lemuel**: As with Agur in Proverbs 30, we don't know anything about **King Lemuel**. He is not in any recorded list of the kings of Judah or Israel, so he was probably a pagan king who put his trust in Yahweh, the covenant God of Israel, and through the fear of the Lord learned wisdom.

> i. The name **Lemuel** means, *belonging to God*. There was no king of Israel (or Judah) with this name, so either he was a foreign king, or it is a pen name for the author. Several older commentators and Jewish legends often say **Lemuel**, the one *belonging to God*, was Solomon himself and his mother was Bathsheba.

> ii. "Jewish legend identifies Lemuel as Solomon and the advice as from Bathsheba from a time when Solomon indulged in magic with his Egyptian wife and delayed the morning sacrifices…. But there is no evidence for this." (Ross)

> iii. "There have been many conjectures as to who King Lemuel was, but nothing certainly can be said." (Morgan)

> iv. "There is no evidence whatever that *Muel* or *Lemuel* means *Solomon*; the chapter seems, to be much later than his time, and the several *Chaldaisms* which occur in the very opening of it are no mean proof of this. If *Agur* was not the author of it, it may be considered as another *supplement* to the book of Proverbs. Most certainly Solomon did not write it." (Clarke)

> v. "With a minor punctuation change, however, one may translate v. 1a as, 'The sayings of Lemuel, king of Massa,' instead of 'The sayings

of King Lemuel—an oracle.' McKane notes that Massa may have been a north Arabian tribe (Genesis 25:14; 1 Chronicles 1:30) and that several Aramaisms appear in the text." (Garrett)

b. **The utterance**: Like Solomon (Proverbs 2:6) and Agur (Proverbs 30:1), Lemuel understood that his words were an **utterance**, a prophecy or revelation, from God.

c. **Which his mother taught him**: Perhaps like Timothy (2 Timothy 1:5) Lemuel had a Jewish mother who taught him the fear of the LORD and God's wisdom.

2. (2-3) Warning a son of the danger of sexual immorality.

What, my son?
And what, son of my womb?
And what, son of my vows?
Do not give your strength to women,
Nor your ways to that which destroys kings.

a. **My son…. son of my womb…. son of my vows**: King Lemuel's mother spoke to him with great tenderness, describing her connection with him in three ways. He was her **son**; but then also the son of her **womb**, having given birth to him, and finally, he was the son of her **vows**; her promises and commitments.

i. "There is an ocean of love in a parent's heart, a fathomless depth of desire after the child's welfare, in the mother especially." (Trapp)

ii. **Son of my vows**: "A child born after vows made for offsprings is called the *child* of a person's *vows*." (Clarke)

iii. "She traces his close connection to her backward from the present, to his gestation in her womb and to her vows before pregnancy. The latter epithet probably refers to a vow she made that, that if God gave her a son she would dedicate him to live according to God's wisdom (cf. 1 Samuel 1:11)." (Waltke)

b. **Do not give your strength to women**: The sense is that an excessive sexual interest in women wastes a man's **strength**. This speaks of an unhealthy obsession with romance or sex, which have a proper place in life, but should not be made into a reason for living. The practice of sexual immorality and sex obsession gives away a man's **strength**, in the sense of his spiritual strength, his self-respect, his self-control, his example and standing in the community.

i. Of course, it could also be rightly said that in sexual immorality and sex obsession a woman gives away her strength as well, but King

Lemuel's mother spoke this to her son, not directly to her daughter. Both men and women need to remain faithful to God in regard to sex and romance, or they will give away their **strength**.

ii. "The point of the verse is that while it would be easy for a king to spend his time and energy enjoying women, that would be unwise." (Ross)

c. **Nor your ways to that which destroys kings**: Connected with the previous line, it seems that Lemuel's mother warned him, and us all, against sexual and romantic obsession, something so powerful it **destroys kings** – even the greatest kings. King Solomon himself was destroyed as he gave his **strength to women** (1 Kings 11:1-10). Solomon's father, King David, suffered tragically when he gave his **strength to women** (2 Samuel 11-12).

i. "Obsession with such women corrupts the king's sovereign power.... David's lust for Bathsheba made him callous toward justice and cost Uriah his life, and Solomon's many sexual partners made him callous toward pure and undefiled religion and incapable of real love. In other words, obsession with women has the effect as obsession with liquor." (Waltke)

3. (4-7) Warning a son of the danger of alcohol.

It is **not for kings, O Lemuel,**
It is **not for kings to drink wine,**
Nor for princes intoxicating drink;
Lest they drink and forget the law,
And pervert the justice of all the afflicted.
Give strong drink to him who is perishing,
And wine to those who are bitter of heart.
Let him drink and forget his poverty,
And remember his misery no more.

a. **It is not for kings to drink wine**: Kings and those who lead should avoid alcohol (**intoxicating drink**). This idea is repeated three times for emphasis. Though the Bible does see a potential blessing in wine (Psalm 104:15, Proverbs 3:10), it is a dangerous blessing that must be carefully regarded and for many (such as **kings** and leaders), voluntarily set aside.

i. "The Carthagenians made a law that no magistrate of theirs should drink wine. The Persians permitted their kings to be drunk one day in a year only. Solon made a law at Athens that drunkenness in a prince should be punished with death. See Ecclesiastes 10:16-17." (Trapp)

b. **Lest they drink and forget the law**: The responsibilities of a king are so great that it is essential that he not be impaired in his judgment or abilities in any way. This principle is true not only for **kings**, but for leaders of many types, including and especially those who consider themselves leaders among God's people today.

> i. **Pervert the justice of all the afflicted**: "Which may easily be done by a drunken judge, because drunkenness deprives a man of the use of reason; by which alone men can distinguish between right and wrong." (Poole)

c. **Give strong drink to him who is perishing**: King Lemuel's mother thought of two more appropriate drinkers rather than the king. First, she thought of the condemned criminal who needs to be numbed by **strong drink** on his way to execution. Second, she thought of **those who are bitter of heart**, who could **drink and forget his poverty and remember his misery no more**. It isn't that there are no consequences for drinking in these two cases, but that the consequences have little impact in comparison to the king or leader.

> i. "We have already seen, that inebriating drinks were mercifully given to condemned criminals, to render them less sensible of the torture they endured in dying. This is what was offered to our Lord; but he refused it." (Clarke)

> ii. "The queen-mother does not recommend a free beer program for the poor or justify its use as an opiate for the masses; her point is simply that the king must avoid drunkenness in order to reign properly." (Garrett)

d. **And remember his misery no more**: King Lemuel's mother understood that **strong drink**, **wine**, and other intoxicants *take away* from a person's performance and excellence. For this and other reasons, many people – especially those in leadership – should avoid alcohol altogether.

> i. "If any man should be wicked enough to draw from it the inference that he would be able to forget his misery and poverty by drinking, he would soon find himself woefully mistaken; for if he had one misery before, he would have ten miseries afterwards; and if he was previously poor, he would be in still greater poverty afterwards. Those who fly to the bottle for consolation might as soon fly to hell to find a heaven; and, instead of helping them to forget their poverty, drunkenness would only sink them still more deeply in the mire." (Spurgeon)

4. (8-9) Defending the defenseless.

Open your mouth for the speechless,
In the cause of all *who are* appointed to die.

Open your mouth, judge righteously,
And plead the cause of the poor and needy.

a. **Open your mouth for the speechless**: The idea is that there are those who can't speak for themselves, to defend themselves in a court of law or in less formal circumstances. The wise and godly man or woman will speak **for the speechless**, and take up the cause of the defenseless (**those appointed to die**).

i. As a unit, Proverbs 31:1-9 raises an important question. Being a leader means some level of position and power. Will you use it indulge yourself (here the indulgence is women and wine, Proverbs 31:3-7), or will you use your position and power to protect and benefit those you lead (as in Proverbs 31:8-9)?

b. **Open your mouth, judge righteously**: This was especially important for a king like Lemuel, but applies to everyone. If we have the opportunity to right a wrong or see that a wrong is punished, we should speak up (**open your mouth**) and **judge righteously**. We should **plead the cause of the poor and needy** who have trouble properly defending themselves.

i. "It is noteworthy that this is her sole political concern; she does not say anything about building up the treasury, creating monuments to his reign, or establishing a dominant military power. For her the king's throne is truly founded on righteousness." (Garrett)

B. Searching for the woman of character and virtue.

The 22 verses (Proverbs 31:10-31) each begin with a successive letter of the Hebrew alphabet. This acrostic construction was used in several psalms (such as Psalms 9-10, 25, 34, 37, 111, 112, 119, and 145 and Lamentations 4). The purpose was to make the passage memorable (easier to memorize), and to express poetic skill. This is, "An Alphabet of Wifely Excellence" (Kidner)

"This and the following verses are *acrostic*, each beginning with a consecutive letter of the *Hebrew alphabet*: Proverbs 31:10, *aleph*; Proverbs 31:11, *beth*; Proverbs 31:12, *gimel*; and so on to the end of the chapter, the last verse of which has the letter *tau*." (Clarke)

"The arrangement made memorization easier and perhaps also served to organize the thoughts. We may say, then, that the poem is an organized arrangement of the virtues of the wise wife—the ABC's of wisdom." (Ross)

The author of the commentary wishes to thank his wife Inga-Lill for her valuable collaboration on this portion of the commentary.

1. (10) Searching for and finding a virtuous woman and wife.

Who can find a virtuous wife?
For her worth *is* far above rubies.

a. **Who can find a virtuous wife?** In this last section of Proverbs 31, Lemuel's mother spoke to him about the qualities of **a virtuous wife**. The following verses speak of her character and activity, giving Lemuel an idea of the woman to search for and to prize. This passage is traditionally understood as being addressed to women but is more accurately spoken *by* a woman *to* a man so he could know the character and potential character of a good wife before marriage, and value and praise his wife for her **virtuous** character once married. It is primarily a *search-list* for a man, and only secondarily a *check-list* for a woman.

- This passage describes the kind of wife the Christian man should pray for and seek after.

- This passage gives a guide, a goal for the Christian woman, showing the kind of character she can have as she fears and follows the Lord.

- This passage reminds the Christian man that he must walk in the fear and wisdom of God so that he will be worthy of and compatible with such a virtuous woman.

b. **A virtuous wife**: She is called **a virtuous wife**, not because only married women can have these qualities, but because this is marriage guidance from a mother to a son. The **virtuous** woman can be single or married, but each will have particular ways the virtue is expressed, either in their singleness or as family.

i. Waltke calls this woman *the valiant wife*, and notes that *eseth hayil* [**virtuous wife**] is translated as the *excellent wife* of Proverbs 12:4. The term is also applied to men and translated *mighty men of valor* in 2 Kings 24:14, *competent men* in Genesis 47:6, *able men* in Exodus 18:21.

ii. "She is a *virtuous woman* – a woman of power and strength. *Esheth chayil*, a strong or virtuous wife, full of mental energy." (Clarke)

iii. "The vocabulary and the expressions in general have the ring of an ode to a champion." (Ross) What this woman has did not simply fall to her; it is her victory through wisdom, her hard-won reward. The battle or military allusions are many, including:

- **Virtuous wife** is the same expression translated *mighty man of valor* in Judges (as in Judges 6:12).

- The word *strength* in Proverbs 31:17 is used in other places for great and heroic victories (as in Exodus 15:2 and 1 Samuel 2:10).

- The word *gain* in Proverbs 31:11 is actually the word for *plunder* (as in Isaiah 8:1 and 8:3).

- The expression *excel them all* in Proverbs 31:29 "is an expression that signifies victory." (Ross)

iv. The qualities of this **virtuous wife** as described in Proverbs 31:11-31 are often mentioned in previous proverbs. As a whole, the proverbs have much to say about wisdom, a diligent work ethic, wise business practices, honorable speech, compassion for the poor, and integrity. Here those same qualities are explained in connection to a **virtuous wife**. Coming at the end of the collection of proverbs, one might say that this is a *strong woman* – and her greatest strength is her wisdom, rooted in the fear of the Lord.

c. **Her worth is far above rubies**: Precious gems like **rubies** are both valued and rare. In a sense, the complete profile of the "Proverbs 31 Woman" is an ideal goal, much as the listing of the character of the godly man for leadership in both 1 Timothy 3 and Titus 1. It would be *rare* to find a woman who excels in *every* aspect of the list, so it should not be used to compare or condemn, either one's self or another woman. Rather, this character should reflect the values and aspirations of the woman who walks in the fear of the Lord and godly wisdom.

i. **Rubies**: "The precise meaning of the word translated 'rubies' is unknown; other suggested translations are 'pearls' and 'corals.' The reference is to some kind of precious stone." (Garrett)

d. **Her worth is far above rubies**: The woman described in the rest of the chapter is rare and valuable, but her *value* (**worth**) is *greater* than what she *does*, as explained in the following verses. Her value or **worth** should not be reduced to the performance of these qualities; she will *be* virtuous before she *acts* in a virtuous manner.

i. **Her worth is far above rubies**: Wisdom itself is also described as being more valuable than rubies (as in Proverbs 3:15 and 8:11). This is one reason why some think this description of the virtuous wife in Proverbs is more a poetic description of wisdom as woman (as in Proverbs 1:20-33 and 7:4-5). "Since it is essentially about wisdom, its lessons are for both men and women to develop. The passage teaches that the fear of the Lord will inspire people to be faithful stewards of the time and talents that God has given; that wisdom is productive and beneficial for others, requiring great industry in life's endeavors; that wisdom is best taught and lived in the home." (Ross)

2. (11-12) Her relationship with her husband.

The heart of her husband safely trusts her;
So he will have no lack of gain.
She does him good and not evil
All the days of her life.

a. **The heart of her husband safely trusts her**: The virtuous wife not only has the trust of her husband, but it is **safely** given to her. Her character is *trustworthy*, filled with integrity. She will speak, act, and live with wisdom – and therefore God's blessing will be on their home (**he will have no lack of gain**). A foolish woman, who can't be trusted, takes some measure of blessing away from the home, and this is often seen financially or materially.

i. "But in the whole delineation there is hardly any trait more beautiful than this—absolute trustworthiness…he seeks her confidence and advice. He has no fear of her betraying his secrets. He can safely trust her." (Meyer)

ii. "He is confident of her love, care, and fidelity. He dare trust her with his soulsecrets, etc.; he doubteth not of her chastity, secrecy, or care to keep his family." (Trapp)

iii. "Outside of this text and Judges 20:36, Scripture condemns trust in anyone or anything apart from…the Lord…. This present exception elevates the valiant wife, who herself fears the Lord, to the highest level of spiritual and physical competence." (Waltke)

iv. "The greatest gift of God is a pious amiable spouse who fears God and loves his house, and with whom one can live in perfect confidence." (Martin Luther's description of his wife, cited in Bridges)

b. **He will have no lack of gain**: Some think a wife is a burden or hindrance to **gain** and a better life. This is not so in God's plan and with the presence and influence of a virtuous wife. She brings **gain** to her husband on many levels, and in great measure (**no lack**).

i. **Gain** "usually means 'plunder'; the point may be that the gain will be as rich and bountiful as the spoils of war." (Ross)

c. **She does him good and not evil**: Several previous proverbs explained the bad effect of a bad wife. The opposite is also true; a virtuous wife **does** her husband **good and not evil**, and she continues being a blessing **all the days of her life**. The sense is that her goodness and faithful character becomes deeper and greater through the passing years.

i. **All the days of her life**: "*Her good* is not *capricious,* it is *constant* and *permanent*, while she and her husband live." (Clarke)

given to sudden +
unaccountable changes of mood or behavior

ii. "Her commitment to her husband's well being is true, not false; constant, not temperamental; reliable, not fickle." (Waltke)

3. (13-16) Her work and ingenuity.

She seeks wool and flax,
And willingly works with her hands.
She is like the merchant ships,
She brings her food from afar.
She also rises while it is yet night,
And provides food for her household,
And a portion for her maidservants.
She considers a field and buys it;
From her profits she plants a vineyard.

a. **She seeks wool and flax**: Using wonderful poetic images, King Lemuel's mother described not the résumé of a godly woman, but life-like examples of the busy, hard-working, and creative character of the virtuous wife. A woman who felt burdened to complete each of these tasks in a day, week, or even month would be exhausted and probably discouraged. Yet the character poetically described can be evident in a wise and godly woman's life in its own way.

i. The flurry of activity described in these verses doesn't mean that she does all these things in a day or even a week, but it does point to how much work and how many different kinds of work are involved in wisely and properly managing a home. Women today can take comfort and confidence in God's recognition here of just how big their job is.

b. **She seeks wool and flax**: The virtuous woman knows how to seek and find things that are necessary resources for her family and home.

c. **Willingly works with her hands**: The virtuous wife is not proud or haughty and does not think that working **with her hands** is beneath her. She **works** in simple and practical ways for her family and home.

i. "In an age long before the industrial revolution, women had to work at spinning wool and making clothes in every spare moment; fidelity in this labor was a mark of feminine virtue." (Garrett)

ii. Yet, what sets this virtuous wife apart is that she **willingly works**. "And all her labour is a *cheerful service*; her *will*, her *heart*, is in it." (Clarke)

d. **She is like the merchant ships, she brings her food from afar**: The virtuous wife provides **food** for her family and home after the pattern of a **merchant ship**, which operates with regularity and effort. If required, she even **rises while it is yet night** to either get or prepare **food for her household**.

> i. "The simile with the merchant ships suggests that she brings a continual supply of abundance." (Ross)

e. **And a portion for her maidservants**: It wasn't uncommon for many families in Biblical times to have servants or hired workers. The virtuous wife wisely manages and cares for such **maidservants**, showing her compassion and care even beyond her immediate family.

> i. "This implies first that she cares even for the serving girls and second that she is diligent about overseeing them." (Garrett)

f. **She considers a field and buys it**: The virtuous wife is forward thinking, combining her creativity with hard work. She thoughtfully (**considers**) invests and uses the **profits** to better her family and their future, in this case by planting a **vineyard**.

> i. Isaiah 5:2 describes all that was involved in planting a vineyard in ancient Israel and making it productive. It was a lot of work.

> ii. "She does not restrict herself to the bare *necessaries* of life; she is able to procure some of its *comforts*. She plants a *vineyard*, that she may have wine for a *beverage*, for *medicine*, and for *sacrifice*. This also is procured of her own labour." (Clarke)

4. (17-20) Her strength and compassion.

She girds herself with strength,
And strengthens her arms.
She perceives that her merchandise *is* good,
And her lamp does not go out by night.
She stretches out her hands to the distaff,
And her hand holds the spindle.
She extends her hand to the poor,
Yes, she reaches out her hands to the needy.

a. **She girds herself with strength**: The virtuous wife is noted for her **strength**, and it is strength in action (**her arms**). She uses her **strength** for productive purpose.

> i. The idea of "girding" one's self – setting a strengthening belt around the midsection – "means to get ready for some 'kind of heroic or difficult action,' such as hard running (1 Kings 18:46; 2 Kings 4:29), escape from Egypt (Exodus 12:11), or physical labor (Proverbs 31:17)." (Waltke)

ii. "She takes care of her own health and strength, not only by means of useful labour, but by healthy exercise. She avoids what might enervate her body, or soften her mind-she is ever active, and *girt* ready for every necessary exercise. Her *loins* are *firm*, and her *arms strong*." (Clarke)

b. **She perceives that her merchandise is good**: She is wise and experienced enough to get **good** materials and **merchandise** for her home. Her wisdom teaches her to buy oil for **her lamp**, of such quality that it burns through the night and **does not go out**.

i. "She takes care to manufacture the *best articles* of the kind, and to lay on a *reasonable price* that she may secure a *ready sale*. Her *goods* are in high repute, and she knows she can *sell* as much as she can *make*. And she finds that while she pleases her customers, she *increases her own profits*." (Clarke)

c. **She stretches out her hands to the distaff**: The virtuous wife knows how to use the tools and technology available to manage the home well. The **distaff** is a stick or spindle onto which wool or flax is wound for spinning, and she uses both **hands** to do the work well.

i. "The 'distaff' is the straight rod, and the 'spindle' is the round or circular part." (Ross)

ii. "The *spindle* and *distaff* are the most *ancient* of all the instruments used for *spinning*, or making *thread*. The *spinning-wheel* superseded them in these countries; but still they were in considerable use till *spinning machinery* superseded both them and the *spinning-wheels* in general." (Clarke)

iii. "Sarah (Genesis 18:6-8), Rebekah (Genesis 24:18-20) and Rachel (Genesis 29:9, 10) show that women of high social rank and wealth were not above manual, even menial, labor." (Waltke)

d. **She extends her hand to the poor**: The virtuous wife is much more than a skillful manager or homemaker; she is also a woman of great compassion. She cares for and helps both **the poor** and **the needy**, doing more than throwing money to them, but she actually draws near to them and **extends her hand** and **reaches out** to those in need.

i. Her hard work was not only for her own needs and the needs of her family; she also worked to help **the poor** and **the needy**. "This was the hand that was diligently at work in the previous verse with an acquired skill; it is not the hand of a lazy, wealthy woman. She uses her industry in charitable ways." (Ross)

5. (21-23) God's blessing on the virtuous wife.

She is not afraid of snow for her household,
For all her household *is* clothed with scarlet.
She makes tapestry for herself;
Her clothing *is* fine linen and purple.
Her husband is known in the gates,
When he sits among the elders of the land.

a. **She is not afraid of snow for her household**: The virtuous wife has the wisdom, diligence, and preparation to ready **her household** for all kinds of challenges and adversity. Her fear of the Lord, and the wisdom that flows from it, invites God's blessing, even being able to clothe **all her household** in prestigious **scarlet**.

i. "She hath provided enough, not only for their necessity and defence against cold and other inconveniences, which is here supposed, but also for their delight and ornament." (Poole)

b. **Her household is clothed in scarlet**: Some wonder why **scarlet** clothing would be connected to the fact that **she is not afraid of snow for her household**. It has been suggested that the **scarlet** color of the clothing makes her children easy to find in heavy **snow**, but given the relatively light snowfall in that part of the world, this is unlikely. It is possible that this does not describe a color, but doubly thick garments.

i. "The word has a plural ending, which is abnormal for 'scarlet'; so that both form and sense arouse suspicion. The consonants allow the reading *double*…i.e. double thickness, which is supported by Vulgate and Septuagint." (Kidner)

ii. "But *shanim*, from *shanah*, to *iterate*, to *double*, signifies not only *scarlet*, so called from being twice or doubly dyed, but also *double garments*, not only the *ordinary coat* but the *surtout* or *great-coat* also, or a *cloak* to cover all. But most probably *double garments*, or *twofold* to what they were accustomed to wear, are here intended." (Clarke)

c. **She makes a tapestry for herself**: With God's blessing on her wisdom and diligence, the virtuous wife **makes** good things **for herself** and enjoys personal marks of God's material blessing on her family (**her clothing is fine linen and purple**).

i. **Purple**: "To produce this red dye was costly because it comes from a seashell off the Phoenician coast and so connotes wealth and luxury." (Waltke)

ii. "Clothe yourselves with the silk of piety, with the satin of sanctity, with the purple of modesty, etc. See 1 Peter 3:3-4." (Trapp)

d. **Her husband is known in the gates**: The virtuous wife sees such a blessing on her family and household that her **husband** is also esteemed and honored **among the elders of the land**. All this is the blessing of God that often comes to the wife who walks in virtue, wisdom, and the fear of the LORD.

> i. "She is a loving wife, and feels for the *respectability* and *honour* of her husband…. He is respected not only on account of the *neatness* and *cleanliness* of his *person* and *dress*, but because he is the husband of a woman who is justly held in universal esteem. And her complete management of household affairs gives him full leisure to devote himself to the civil interests of the community." (Clarke)

6. (24-25) The clothing she sells and the clothing she has.

She makes linen garments and sells *them*,
And supplies sashes for the merchants.
Strength and honor *are* her clothing;
She shall rejoice in time to come.

a. **She makes linen garments and sells them**: The wisdom and diligence of the virtuous wife leads her to not only provide the necessities for her family, but she makes enough and of such great quality that she **sells** those necessities to the sellers (**the merchants**). She cares deeply for her family, but her mind and vision go beyond them to the outside world where she does good for herself and her family.

> i. "The poet did not think it strange or unworthy for a woman to engage in honest trade. In fact, weaving of fine linens was a common trade for women in Palestine from antiquity." (Ross)

b. **Strength and honor are her clothing**: The fact that she is willing to distribute and sell **linen garments** she makes, and has, shows that her first priority isn't in what is in her closet or what she wears. She cares even more about the display of her *character* than the outward display of her clothing. When it comes to character, she is one of the best dressed, clothed with **strength and honor**, so that **she shall rejoice** not only in the present day, but also **in time to come**.

> i. **Strength and honor**: "The praise of the woman can hardly be higher: it attributes to her the advantages of both youth and old age (i.e., 'power and splendor,' Proverbs 20:29)." (Waltke)

7. (26-27) Her inner life.

She opens her mouth with wisdom,
And on her tongue *is* the law of kindness.

She watches over the ways of her household,
And does not eat the bread of idleness.

a. **She opens her mouth with wisdom**: The description of her inner life continues from the previous verse. The virtuous wife has what is often described and valued in the Book of Proverbs – wise speech and words that show **the law of kindness**. Both her deliberate speech (**she opens her mouth**) and her spontaneous words (**on her tongue**) are marked by **wisdom** and **kindness**.

i. "She is neither sullenly silent, nor full of vain and impertinent talk, as many women are, but speaks directly and piously, as occasion offereth itself." (Poole)

ii. "Tatianus tells us that in the primitive Church every age and sex among the Christians were Christian philosophers; yea, that the very virgins and maids, as they sat at their work in wool, were wont to speak of God's word." (Trapp)

iii. **In her tongue is the law of kindness**: "This is the most distinguishing excellence of this woman. There are very few of those who are called managing women who are not *lords* over their *husbands*, *tyrants* over their *servants*, and *insolent* among their *neighbours*. But this woman, with all her eminence and excellence, was of a *meek* and *quiet spirit*. Blessed woman!" (Clarke)

iv. "Specifically *loving teaching* (*torat hesed*) *is on her tongue* (*al lesonah*, see Proverbs 21:23) probably signifies that her teaching is informed by her own loving kindness." (Waltke)

b. **She watches over the ways of her household**: As a faithful guardian, the virtuous wife is observant of her family and their **ways**. The choice to watch so carefully means that she does not choose to **eat the bread of idleness**.

i. "She hath an oar in every boat, an eye in every business; she spies and pries into her children's and servants' carriages, and exacts of them strict conversation and growth in godliness: she overlooks the whole family no otherwise than if she were in a watch tower." (Trapp)

ii. "Here the text explicitly states that she avoids laziness; eating the 'bread of idleness' is idiomatic for indulging in laziness." (Garrett)

8. (28-29) Her family's public praise.

Her children rise up and call her blessed;
Her husband *also*, and he praises her:

"Many daughters have done well,
But you excel them all."

a. **Her children rise up and call her blessed**: A woman of such character and wisdom rightfully receives the blessings and **praises** of her family. *Both* **her children** and **her husband** not only see, but also speak of the blessedness of the woman who brings such blessing to their household. This is not only a description of the virtuous wife, but also an exhortation to **children** and a **husband** to bless and praise the mother and wife of godly character.

i. "Her children are *well bred* [polite]; they *rise up* and pay *due respect.*" (Clarke)

b. **Many daughters have done well, but you excel them all**: These are the words of the **husband** as he praises his wife, with words that encourage, reward, and nourish her. In a completely literal sense, this could only be true of *one* woman in any given community at any given time. Yet, we perfectly understand the sense of this. *Every* home can have a wife and mother that does **excel them all**; every husband can legitimately feel "I've got the best wife" and children feel, "We have the best mom."

i. In his remarks on this verse, Adam Clarke thought of a woman who perhaps truly did **excel them all** – Susanna Wesley. "But high as the character of this Jewish matron stands in the preceding description, I can say that I have met at least *her equal*, in a *daughter* of the Rev. Dr. *Samuel Annesly*, the *wife* of *Samuel Wesley*, rector of Epworth in Lincolnshire, and *mother* of the late extraordinary brothers, *John* and *Charles Wesley*. I am constrained to add this testimony, after having traced her from her *birth* to her *death*, through all the relations that a woman can bear upon earth. Her Christianity gave to her virtues and excellences a heightening, which the Jewish matron could not possess. Besides, she was a woman of great *learning* and information, and of a depth of mind, and reach of thought, seldom to be found among the daughters of Eve, and not often among the sons of Adam."

9. (30-31) The praise and the reward of the wise woman.

Charm *is* deceitful and beauty *is* passing,
But a woman *who* fears the LORD, she shall be praised.
Give her of the fruit of her hands,
And let her own works praise her in the gates.

a. **Charm is deceitful and beauty is passing**: King Lemuel's mother noted the **passing** nature of outer **beauty** and the **deceitful** nature of manipulative

charm. In contrast, **a woman who fears the** L ord has **beauty** that does not pass and **charm** that does not deceive.

> i. **Charm is deceitful:** "Because it gives a false representation of the person, being ofttimes a cover to a most deformed soul, and to many evil and hateful qualities." (Poole)

> ii. "Physical appearance is not necessarily dismissed—it simply does not endure as do those qualities that the fear of the Lord produces... one who pursues beauty may very well be disappointed by the character of the 'beautiful' person." (Ross)

> iii. "Charm and beauty are not bad; they simply are inadequate reasons to marry a girl. The young man should first seek a woman who fears the Lord. And whoever finds such a woman should make sure that her gifts and accomplishments do not go unappreciated." (Garrett)

b. **A woman who fears the** L ord, **she shall be praised**: Proverbs begins with a strong connection between wisdom and the fear of the L ord (Proverbs 1:7). Here the collection ends describing the virtuous wife as filled with the wisdom, beauty, and charm that marks **a woman who fears the** L ord.

> i. The fact that she truly **fears the** L ord shows that she had a real relationship with Him. She was not only a Martha, busy with service; she was also Mary, walking in fear and reverence toward the L ord.

> ii. *She* – the **woman who fears the** L ord – has the character of the virtuous wife. The way the character is expressed will differ according to time and culture, but the character itself is universal. God honors the virtuous wife, the woman of wisdom and diligence, and makes her one of the greatest blessings given to humanity.

> iii. "By definition, the fear of the Lord means in part living according to the wisdom revealed in this book. This woman's itemized, self-sacrificing activities for others exemplify the fear of the Lord." (Waltke)

> iv. "Coming at the end of the poem, and of the book, this pinpoints the organizing factor in this brilliant woman's universe. It is her fear of Yahweh that enables her to see that real greatness will come to her, not through self-centered aggressiveness, and not through merely external beauty, but through godly devotion and the wholehearted commitment to God's creational intention for her." (Philips)

c. **Give her the fruit of her hands**: This virtuous woman *will* be rewarded by the God she fears and rewarded by what she has accomplished for her family and herself, as they publicly speak of her godliness and wisdom (**let her own works praise her in the gates**). For the woman (and man) of wisdom, this reward is not their primary motivation, but the fitting result of their life lived in fear of the LORD.

i. **The fruit of her hands**: "She is no less than Woman Wisdom made real. The riches Woman Wisdom offers (Proverbs 8:18) are brought home by the hard work of the good wife (Proverbs 31:11)." (Garrett)

ii. "It is but just and fit that she should enjoy those benefits and praises which her excellent labours deserve.... If men be silent, the lasting effects of her prudence and diligence will loudly trumpet forth her praises." (Poole)

Proverbs – Bibliography

Bridges, Charles *Proverbs* (Wheaton, Illinois: Crossway Books, 2001 edition of 1846 original)

Clarke, Adam *The Holy Bible, Containing the Old and New Testaments, with A Commentary and Critical Notes, Volume III – Job to Song of Solomon* (New York: Eaton and Mains, 1827?)

Garrett, Duane A. *Proverbs, Ecclesiastes, Song of Songs* (Nashville, Tennessee: Broadman and Holman, 1993)

Kidner, Derek *Proverbs – An Introduction and Commentary* (Nottingham, England: InterVarsity Press, 1964)

Meyer, F.B. *Our Daily Homily* (Westwood, New Jersey: Revell, 1966)

Morgan, G. Campbell *Searchlights from the Word* (New York: Revell, 1926)

Morgan, G. Campbell *An Exposition of the Whole Bible* (Old Tappan, New Jersey: Revell, 1959)

Orr, J, Edwin *Full Surrender* (Santa Barbara, California: Enduring Word, 2017)

Philipps, Dan *God's Wisdom in Proverbs* (The Woodlands, Texas: Kress Biblical Resources, 2011)

Poole, Matthew *A Commentary on the Holy Bible, Volume 2* (London: The Banner of Truth Trust, 1968)

Ross, Allen P. "Proverbs," *The Expositor's Bible Commentary, Volume 5* (Grand Rapids, Michigan: Zondervan, 1992)

Spurgeon, Charles Haddon *The New Park Street Pulpit, Volumes 1-6* and *The Metropolitan Tabernacle Pulpit, Volumes 7-63* (Pasadena, Texas: Pilgrim Publications, 1990)

Trapp, John *A Commentary on the Old and New Testaments, Volume 3 – Proverbs to Daniel* (Eureka, California: Tanski Publications, 1997)

Waltke, Bruce K. *The Book of Proverbs, Chapters 1:1-15:29* (Grand Rapids, Michigan: Eerdmans, 2004)

Waltke, Bruce K. *The Book of Proverbs, Chapters 15:30-31:31* (Grand Rapids, Michigan: Eerdmans, 2005)

Wiersbe, Warren W. *Be Skillful* (Wheaton, Illinois: Victor Books, 1995)

As the years pass I love the work of studying, learning, and teaching the Bible more than ever. I'm so grateful that God is faithful to meet me in His Word.

Much thanks to Alison Turner, for her wonderful work in proofreading the manuscript and her manu helpful suggestions.

Thanks to Brian Procedo for the cover design and the graphics work.

Most especially, thanks to my wife Inga-Lill. She is my loved and valued partner in life and in service to God and His people. She is a true "Proverbs 31" woman.

David Guzik

David Guzik's Bible commentary is regularly used and trusted by many thousands who want to know the Bible better. Pastors, teachers, class leaders, and everyday Christians find his commentary helpful for their own understanding and explanation of the Bible. David and his wife Inga-Lill live in Santa Barbara, California.

You can email David at
david@enduringword.com

For more resources by David Guzik,
go to www.enduringword.com

9 781939 466563